P9-DEH-651

WITHDRAWN

WITHDRAWN

AAX-5365
VCLib

WITHDRAWN

Clashing Views on Controversial Issues in Childhood and Society

Second Edition

Edited, Selected, and with Introductions by

Diana S. DelCampo
New Mexico State University

and

Robert L. DelCampo
New Mexico State University

Dushkin/McGraw-Hill
A Division of The McGraw-Hill Companies

Cover Art Acknowledgment

Charles Vitelli

Copyright © 1998 by Dushkin/McGraw-Hill,
A Division of The McGraw-Hill Companies, Inc., Guilford, Connecticut 06437

Copyright law prohibits the reproduction, storage, or transmission in any form by any means of any portion of this publication without the express written permission of Dushkin/McGraw-Hill and of the copyright holder (if different) of the part of the publication to be reproduced. The Guidelines for Classroom Copying endorsed by Congress explicitly state that unauthorized copying may not be used to create, to replace, or to substitute for anthologies, compilations, or collective works.

Taking Sides ® is a registered trademark of Dushkin/McGraw-Hill

Manufactured in the United States of America

Second Edition

10 9 8 7 6 5 4 3 2

Library of Congress Cataloging-in-Publication Data

Main entry under title:
   Taking sides: clashing views on controversial issues in childhood and society/edited, selected, and with introductions by Diana S. DelCampo and Robert L. DelCampo.—2nd ed.
   Includes bibliographical references and index.
   1. Children—United States. 2. Child Welfare—United States. I. DelCampo, Diana S., comp. II. DelCampo, Robert L., comp.
                                                           305.23
   0-697-39104-3   ISSN: 1094-7558

 Printed on Recycled Paper

PREFACE

Children are society's most valuable resource, and however clichéd that idea may be, there can be no doubt about the urgency of the issues confronting children today and the people who care for them and care about them. Each day we are bombarded with media reports on issues affecting children—complex issues related to child care, schooling, violence, sexuality, gangs, divorce; the list goes on. In this book we look at 17 of those controversial issues and ask you to think about them, perhaps for the first time, or perhaps in ways you may not have previously considered.

For the student who likes to memorize facts and learn *the* right answer, the controversies in this book could be most unsettling! However, a good education should include the nurturing of your ability to think critically and to be an active learner. This book endeavors to put you on the path toward further developing these skills. As you read each side of an issue and grapple with the points made by the authors, you will be moved to consider the merits of each position. In the process, you may adopt the point of view of one side, or the other, or formulate an opinion completely your own on the issue. And when you attend class, you will be exposed to your classmates' and instructor's ideas on the issue as well. This may further challenge you to reconsider and defend your position, which is the essence of critical thinking and a primary purpose of this book.

Plan of the book   *Taking Sides: Clashing Views on Controversial Issues in Childhood and Society*, Second Edition, is designed to be used for courses in child development, human development, or parenting. The issues can be studied consecutively or in any order, as each is designed to be independent of the other. We have included 17 issues encompassing 34 selections from a wide variety of sources and authors. Each part of the book deals with one of four developmental phases of childhood: infancy, early childhood, middle childhood, and adolescence. Within each part are issues related to aspects of child development at that stage. Each issue has an *introduction*, which provides some background about the controversy, briefly describes the authors, and gives a brief summary of the positions reflected in the issue. Each issue concludes with a *postscript*, which contains some final thoughts on the issue and offers a bibliography of related readings should you want to explore the topic further.

A listing of all the *contributors* to this volume is included at the back of the book to give you additional information on the scholars, practitioners, educators, policymakers, and social critics whose views are debated here.

Changes to this edition   The second edition of *Taking Sides: Clashing Views on Controversial Issues in Childhood and Society* includes some important changes from the first edition. Five completely new issues have been added: *Should Hospitals Continue Early Discharge Policies for Newborns?* (Issue 3); *Is the Welfare of Our Disadvantaged Children Improving?* (Issue 4); *Will Stricter Dress Codes Improve the Educational Environment?* (Issue 13); *Should Children Who Are at Risk for Abuse Remain With Their Families?* (Issue 14); and *Can Memories of Childhood Sexual Abuse Be Recovered?* (Issue 17). For three of the issues, we have retained the topic from the first edition but have replaced one or both of the selections in order to bring the debate up-to-date or to focus more clearly on the controversy: Issue 1 on maternal employment; Issue 5 on spanking; and Issue 7 on divorce, and Issue 16 on abstinence education as the best sex education. As a result, there is a total of 16 new readings. The issue introductions and postscripts have also been revised and updated.

In addition to changes in topics and selections, a new feature, *On the Internet*, has been added to each part opener. Several relevant sites on the World Wide Web have been identified and annotated.

A word to the instructor   An *Instructor's Manual With Test Questions* (multiple-choice and essay) is available through the publisher for the instructor using this volume of *Taking Sides*. A general guidebook, *Using Taking Sides in the Classroom*, which discusses methods and techniques for integrating the pro-con approach into any classroom setting, is also available. An online version of *Using Taking Sides in the Classroom* and a correspondence service for Taking Sides adopters can be found at www.dushkin.com/usingtakingsides/. For students, we offer a field guide to analyzing argumentative essays, *Analyzing Controversy: An Introductory Guide*, with exercises and techniques to help them to decipher genuine controversies.

Taking Sides: Clashing Views on Controversial Issues in Childhood and Society is only one title in the Taking Sides series. If you are interested in seeing the table of contents for any of the other titles, please visit the Taking Sides Web site at http://www.dushkin.com/takingsides/.

Acknowledgments   We are most grateful to our son, Robert G. DelCampo, and graduate students A. Elaine Crnkovic and Joellyn M. Johnson for their enthusiasm and perseverance in helping us to undertake the research for this volume. The process of searching for and identifying appropriate selections, and preparing background information for the issues, was difficult and trying at times. Sharing this challenge with these three competent individuals was instrumental in our completing this project.

We would like to thank those professors who adopted the first edition of this book and took the time to make suggestions for this edition:

Jeanette Bemis
San Francisco State
  University

Laura M. Bennett-Murphy
Otterbein College

Brenda Boyd
Washington State University

Cindy Decourse
Le Moyne College

Maribeth Downing
Harding University

James M. Jingles
University of Wisconsin

Cathy LaSalle
Rivier College

Frank Manis
University of Southern
  California

Jane L. Mathews
Chaffey College

Judy Nixon
Fort Hays State University

Vicki Pappas
Indiana University at
  Bloomington

Eileen Parsons
Lenoir Rhyne College

Tracy Spinrad
Pennsylvania State
  University–University Park
  Campus

Doug Trimble
Northwestern College

We also want to extend warm thanks to David Dean, list manager of the Taking Sides series, and David Brackley, developmental editor, at Dushkin/ McGraw-Hill.

We will look forward to receiving feedback and comments on this second edition of *Taking Sides: Clashing Views on Controversial Issues in Childhood and Society* from both faculty and students who experience the book. We can be reached via the Internet (ddelcamp@nmsu.edu or rdelcamp@nmsu.edu), or you can write us in care of the Taking Sides series at Dushkin/McGraw-Hill.

Diana S. DelCampo
New Mexico State University

Robert L. DelCampo
New Mexico State University

CONTENTS IN BRIEF

CONTENTS

Jay Belsky and David Eggebeen conclude that maternal employment during
a child's infancy has detrimental effects on its social and behavioral development. K. Alison Clarke-Stewart finds that children who attend child care
centers are more socially and intellectually advanced than children who are
cared for in the home by their mother or another caregiver.

Doreen Kimura believes that biological differences in the male and female
brain explain behavioral differences between the genders. Carol Tavris concludes that there is no scientific evidence that the brains of males and females
are different

John B. Britton, Helen L. Britton, and Susan A. Beebe summarize some of the studies that promote early discharge. Elizabeth H. Thilo and Susan F. Townsend are concerned that the recently recommended 48-hour hospital stay for newborns may still not be long enough to catch some of the medical problems that infants could develop.

Lisbeth B. Schorr contends that organized intervention programs are working to circumvent social problems such as teen pregnancy, juvenile crime, and school dropout rates. William J. Bennett argues that children have many problems that will probably not be solved in the near future.

Murray A. Straus believes that frequent spanking teaches children aggressiveness. John K. Rosemond contends that spankings, not beatings, should be administered at the discretion of loving parents and should not be considered child abuse.

Barbara Byrd, Arnold DeRosa, and Stephen Craig assert that only children are less autonomous than firstborn children. Steven Mellor reports that only children are similar to firstborns in terms of their developmental path.

Karl Zinsmeister presents a case for parents staying together for the sake of the children. David Gately and Andrew I. Schwebel contend that children of divorce are not doomed to failure; they often display positive characteristics such as enhanced levels of maturity, self-esteem, empathy, and adaptability.

Brandon S. Centerwall argues that children act out the violence they see on television shows and carry the violent behaviors into adulthood. Brian Siano argues that variables other than TV violence are to blame for aggression in children.

Carol Mills, Karen Ablard, and Heinrich Stumpf report that boys perform better than girls on tests for math reasoning ability. A report developed by the Center for Research on Women at Wellesley College, for the American

Association of University Women, concludes that the differences in math achievement between boys and girls are not significant.

Sherryll Kraizer and her colleagues found that children in self-care did not respond to dangerous situations safely. John Woodard and Mark Fine conclude that self-care can be a positive learning experience for children.

David Guterson argues that home schooling is more effective than public schooling. Jennie F. Rakestraw and Donald A. Rakestraw argue that interaction with a school peer group, which is usually missing in home schools, is imperative for the healthy social development of children.

Diane Ravitch, who has written widely on educational issues, suggests that bilingual education programs are ineffective and that they have become simply a means to attain certain political ends. Donaldo Macedo maintains that bilingual education programs are effective for educating children who cannot speak or read English and that they improve the academic performance of non-English-speaking children.

Jessica Portner reports that uniforms are good for schools. Karon L. Jahn contends that strict dress code policies interfere with students' First Amendment right of freedom of speech.

Lisa Kolb believes that the family preservation model is more successful than taking the children to foster homes or other out-of-home placements because parents and children are more receptive to treatment in their own homes. Mary-Lou Weisman argues that orphanages and out-of-home placements are necessary for children whose parents abuse or neglect them.

William J. O'Malley posits that children lack the ability to understand the implications of adulthood and its responsibilities because parents shield them from any real decision making and encounters with adversity. Kathleen Kennedy Townsend contends that expecting parents to instill values is not realistic and that teaching values in the schools instead can yield excellent results for children and for society.

Thomas Lickona states that Americans need to promote a higher standard
of sexual morality in our society through "directive" sex education, which
promotes abstinence before marriage. Peggy Brick and Deborah M. Roffman
refute the directive approach to sex education by suggesting that a comprehensive approach to sex education is more effective.

May Benatar argues that the mass media and contemporary culture question
the accuracy and truthfulness of survivors of sexual abuse. Susan P. Robbins contends that the reason some professionals are skeptical of recovered
memories is that there is no research that supports the accuracy of recovered
memory.

INTRODUCTION
Children in Society

Diana S. DelCampo
Robert L. DelCampo

Childhood can be a wondrous time when days are filled with play and new discoveries, nights provide rest and security, and dedicated, loving parents nurture their children and meet their needs. Some children do indeed experience the full joy of childhood; however, regretfully, there are other, more sobering scenarios: There are children who do not have nurturing adults to guide them, who go to bed hungry, and some who do not even have homes. Most typically, childhood experiences fall between these two extremes. So there is a wide variety of experiences that can impact the developing child, and larger social forces are at work as well. Ask yourself as you debate these issues the extent to which society must collectively address and resolve them. This a vital function of society because children are society's future.

In order to understand and appreciate children in contemporary society, it may be useful to briefly review how society's views of children have changed over time. In their book *Looking at Children: An Introduction to Child Development* (Brooks-Cole, 1992), David and Barbara Bjorklund discuss the history of adult perceptions of children in western European society. Would it surprise you to know that in ancient times children were sometimes killed as religious sacrifices and buried in the walls of buildings? People believed that this practice would strengthen a building's structure. Up until the fourth century, parents were legally allowed to kill their newborns if the children were not in good health at birth. They were also permitted to do away with a child if they already had too many children, if the child was female, or if the child was illegitimate. In 374 A.D., the Romans outlawed infanticide, hoping that this would end the killing. Since parents could no longer legally kill their children, unwanted infants began to be abandoned. This practice endured for over 1,000 years. It was not until the 1600s that child abandonment was outlawed throughout most of Europe.

During the seventeenth century, foundling homes were established to provide for the needs of unwanted children. In their text *Middle Childhood: Behavior and Development*, 2d ed. (Macmillan, 1980), Joyce W. Williams and Marjorie Smith describe how during this period children were considered to be miniature adults. They were dressed like adults and were expected to act as adults would act. By our contemporary standards, parents took a rather casual attitude toward their children. This was probably due to the high child mortality rate at the time. Since parents thought it likely that their children would die in infancy or childhood, they did not get as emotionally close to their young children as parents typically do today. It was not until the end of the century that society began to look upon children as different from adults.

Early in the 1700s, European societal attitudes about children underwent further change. Children were no longer considered to be miniature adults, and literature written specifically for children began to emerge. By the end of the century, children who went to school were grouped by age, reflecting an awareness of stages of growth. The eighteenth century also marked the rise of the systematic study of children, which centered around the moral development of children and child-rearing problems.

According to Williams and Smith, it was not until the beginning of the twentieth century that three distinct age groupings emerged in the study of human development: infancy through age four or five; childhood to late puberty or early adulthood; and adulthood. This time period also marked the beginnings of the distinct field of child study. Early child study emphasized descriptive accounts of individual children and was mainly concerned with aspects of physical growth. As the century progressed, the term *child study* was changed to *research in child development*. Mothering became an important concept in the study of early child development, and the psychological aspects of development began to be examined more rigorously. Today, in the latter part of the twentieth century, research in child development focuses on issues related to family systems and the larger social issues that affect child development.

NATURE-NURTURE CONTROVERSY

There are many things that impact individuals as they progress through the human life cycle. People, places, events, illnesses, education, success, failure —have you ever thought about the number of experiences each of us encounters in our lives? If one were to place all of the variables that influence human development into two general categories, those categories would be heredity and environment. As you may know, your genetic blueprint was determined at the moment of conception with chromosomes contributed by your father and mother. In a sense, for many of us, environment is also determined at the moment of conception. A good portion of the major elements of what makes up one's environment is often determined before a person is born. The society in which one will live, one's cultural and ethnic heritage, and one's family and subsequent socioeconomic status, for example, are usually predetermined for a child.

In *Taking Sides: Clashing Views on Controversial Issues in Childhood and Society*, Second Edition, we have selected articles that look at children in general and how they affect or are affected by the issues raised, rather than give you, the reader, clinical case examples of issues related to a certain child or children. For the purposes of this book, we make three assumptions: (1) When we discuss a child's environment, we are usually describing elements of the society in which a child is growing, developing, and otherwise being socialized. (2) All child development occurs within this social context. (3)

Children cannot help but affect and be affected by the societal forces that surround them. In most university classes, students derive a certain sense of security in receiving definitions of terms that are used frequently in a given class. We offer the following one for *society*, which we have adapted from Gelles's 1995 textbook *Contemporary Families*:

> Society is a collection of people who interact within socially structured relationships. The only way that societies can survive their original members is by replacing them. These "replacements" are the children about whom the issues in this book are concerned.

Determining an appropriate group of societal issues and fitting them into the confines of only one work on children and society is a challenging task. Consider, for example, the diversity of our contemporary society. We live in a sea of divergent and unique subcultures and ethnicities. Categorizing and describing the myriad values, customs, and belief systems of these groups could fill many volumes. In America and Canada, for example, there are many ethnic subgroups of citizens, such as English, Irish, Italians, Polish, Germans, Greeks, Russians, Scots, who are considered to be of Anglo descent. There are people of native descent, sometimes referred to as Indians, who are affiliated with scores of different tribes and subtribes. Some Canadian and American citizens trace their heritages to a variety of Asian countries, including China, Japan, Vietnam, Cambodia, Thailand, and the Philippines. Even among blacks, there are those who trace their roots to the Caribbean region and those that identify with different regions of Africa.

In light of the above, it may be reasoned that there are really no "typical" children in society! Although there are strong arguments supporting similarities within each of these general groups, there is a wide array of subgroupings and differences in customs and beliefs. As a consequence, when reading a book such as this one, it is important to be mindful of the extent to which differences might exist for those who may be of another race, ethnicity, religion, or socioeconomic status than the target group of children about which a selection focuses. It would also be prudent to consider geographic locale —rural, urban, northeastern, southwestern—considering the relevance of a given argument to a specific subgroup of children.

CHILDREN IN CONTEMPORARY SOCIETY

It is worth understanding children's points of view as they are molded by society. It can be astonishing to take a step back and observe children as they undergo the socialization process in contemporary society. They come into the world totally helpless, unable to feed, care for, or protect themselves. As they grow and develop, children undertake the process of acquiring a sense of identity and learning the rules of the society in which they live. This process of socialization is fostered by many of the subsystems of society that provide prescriptions for behavior in particular areas of life. These subsystems include the family, the peer group, the school system, religion, and the media.

One important consideration is that up to about age five, children are oblivious to most racial, ethnic, religious, or socioeconomic differences. Typically, children can only realize differences in external appearance. One implication of this fact is that children can be much more amenable to learning and embracing a variety of cultural behaviors, attitudes, and even languages when they are young. Only as children move into middle childhood do they begin to recognize and understand other, more subtle differences. It is important to note that although young children may be oblivious to these differences, they are nonetheless impacted by them in the way they are socialized by their parents, families, and the significant others in their lives. This is done through family rituals, traditions, and outings, religious ceremonies, types of food prepared in the home, location where children live, and things such as books, magazines, music, and so on, which are found in the home.

Societal influences on children do not stop within the family system. As children grow, other institutions in society, such as schools, the economy, politics, and religion, expand their life experiences. Controversy arises as to how children react to these experiences. Consider, for example, what happens to children when both parents are employed outside the home. There are factions in our society who adamantly ascribe many of the problems associated with children to the fact that many parents are overly involved with work at the expense of time with their children. They contend that one parent (usually the mother) should stay home with the children, especially when they are young. Children who care for themselves after school and the quality of after-school child care are also hotly contested, related issues.

Few readers of this book will be unfamiliar with the attacks on the mass media for its portrayal of violence in movies, television programming, and video games targeted at children. Again, researchers, clinicians, teachers, policymakers, and others fall on both sides of what should be done to address this.

As children move toward adolescence and become more independent, concerns regarding identity, values, morals, and sexual behavior become issues of controversy. Homosexuality, for example, which often is first evidenced by a person in adolescence, is considered by many to be a learned and abhorrent form of sexual expression. Others believe that there are people who are predisposed to homosexuality for reasons that are as yet unclear.

Events in contemporary society have a direct or indirect impact on children, despite attempts to protect them. Violence, inflation, war, poverty, AIDS, racism, and new technology are just a few of the phenomena that shape the society in which our children are socialized.

RESEARCHING CHILDREN

In finding answers to controversial topics, policymakers and the public alike often look to research literature for clues. The typical college student might think of researching a topic as going to the library and looking up information on a subject, reading that information, formulating a conclusion or opinion about the topic, and writing a paper that conveys the student's findings. This is not the type of research about which we are referring! The type of research that we refer to here is called empirical research. This means that there is some question or group of interrelated questions to be answered about a topic. Data are then collected relative to the topic, which typically sheds light on how one goes about answering the question.

Data collection in research on children is undertaken from a variety of approaches. It could entail things like observing children at play in preschool or interacting with their parents at home. This is called observing children in a natural setting. With this method, observers must code behavior in the same way each and every time it is seen. Most of the information we have today on physical growth and developmental stages was acquired through observation by child development pioneers such as Arnold Gessell and Louise Bates Ames. You can imagine how time-consuming this form of study must be.

Another type of data collection is called an experiment. Experimental researchers systematically control how certain things happen in a situation and then observe the results. In this type of research, an experimental group and a control group are chosen. Both groups are examined to determine that they are the same before the experiment begins. The experimental group then receives some kind of treatment, while the control group receives no treatment. Then tests are conducted to see what kind of change, if any, has occurred between the two groups.

Interviewing children with a structured set of questions or giving children a structured questionnaire on a given research topic are other ways of collecting data. Projective techniques, where children might reveal their first thoughts about a picture or word, is also a form of the interview method.

The study of children can be organized in a variety of ways. One is by stages. The parts of this book (infancy, early childhood, middle childhood, and adolescence) are one type of stage organization. Another way to organize research endeavors is by topics. Topics are usually organized within the context of social, emotional, intellectual, physical, creative, and even spiritual aspects of development.

The time frames used to gather data on children also varies. In longitudinal data collection, information is collected from the same subjects over a long period of time. For example, one could examine the effects of preschool education on performance in elementary school by following and testing the same children during the preschool years and all the way through the elementary years. Because this type of research can take years to complete, a shorter method, cross-sectional research, could be used. In the previous example, one group of preschoolers would be compared to a similar group of elementary school children in order to answer the research question.

There are ethical considerations in studying children that some other disciplines may not face. Children should never be manipulated or put in danger in designing an experiment to answer research questions. Similarly, experiments that would not be in a child's best interests should not be conducted. Studies of abuse and neglect, for example, rely on retrospective techniques in which children who have already been abused report what has previously happened to them. No ethical researcher would ever put children at risk in order to observe the effects of abuse on children. Because of these ethical constraints, it can be frustrating for a researcher to fully answer questions raised in a research project. Additionally, it may take years to demonstrate the effectiveness of intervention for a particular social problem. Consequently, research on children and resultant intervention initiatives rarely offer "quick fixes" to the problems of children and society.

PROFESSIONAL ORGANIZATIONS

There are several major national and international professional organizations that promote research and policy making on issues related to children. It would behoove the beginning student of child development to become familiar with one or more of these organizations. Ask the instructor of this and similar classes for the names of the professional organizations to which they belong and for additional ones that they believe are important. Also ask them why they believe these particular organizations are important. Most of these organizations publish professional journals and host annual conferences where the latest information about issues related to children is presented. They can also provide students with contacts in the professional communities that share similar interests. Members of these organizations possess the expertise for undertaking research, education, and clinical practice related to issues of interest. There are numerous intangible benefits in affiliating with professional organizations as well. Typically, student members enjoy significant reductions in fees for membership dues and subscriptions to professional journals published by the organizations. Some of the major organizations that examine issues and promote policies related to children include

- The American Association for Marriage and Family Therapy
  1100 17th Street, NW, 10th Floor
  Washington, DC 20036
  (202) 452-0109
  http://www.aamft.org

- The American Association of Family and Consumer Sciences
  1555 King Street
  Alexandria, VA 22314
  (703) 706-4600
  http://www.aafcs.org

- The Association for Childhood Education International
  11141 Georgia Avenue, Suite 200
  Wheaton, MD 20902
  (800) 423-3563
  http://www.udel.edu
- The Children's Defense Fund
  122 C Street, NW, Suite 400
  Washington, DC 20001
  (202) 628-8787
  http://childrensdefense.org
- Le Conseil de la Famille
  1245, chemin Sainte-Foy
  Bureau 342
  Quebec, Quebec G1S 4P2 Canada
  (418) 646-7678
- The Family Service of Canada
  #600, 220 Laurier Avenue W
  Ottawa, Ontario K1Y 4G1 Canada
  (613) 230-9960
- The National Association for the Education of Young Children
  1509 16th Street, NW
  Washington, DC 20036-1426
  (800) 424-2460
  http://www.naeyc.org
- The National Council on Family Relations
  3989 Central Avenue, NE, Suite 550
  Minneapolis, MN 55421
  (612) 781-9331
  http://www.ncfr.com
- The Sex Information and Education Council of the United States
  130 W. 42nd Street, Suite 2500
  New York, NY 10036
  (212) 819-9770
  http://www.siecus.org
- The Society for Research in Child Development
  5720 S. Woodlawn Avenue
  Chicago, IL 60637
  (312) 702-7470
  http://www.journals.uchicago.edu/SRCD

FUTURE DIRECTIONS

The study of children in society can begin to offer solutions to many of the more pressing societal problems. Quality child care, parenting skills education, stress reduction, affordable housing, job training, and humane political policies are a few ideas for solutions to some of the controversies that will be raised in this book.

The imbalance between work and family in the United States has created problems in the economy as well as in the family system. Workers are expected to produce quality goods and services but they receive little social support in raising their families. When it comes to caring for children, each family is on its own, piecing together supervised child care with self-care and hoping for the best until the children graduate from high school, only to enter the same workforce with the same problems. Employers must acknowledge the strain that workers feel as they are pulled between work and family responsibilities. Health insurance, family-friendly work policies, flexible work schedules, parental and dependent care leave, exercise facilities, quality child care and sick child care, on-site or nearby one-stop service centers with post offices, grocery stores, and dry cleaners would be ways of providing support for families in the workplace.

Schools contribute to the problems of child care arrangements by keeping to an antiquated schedule that was first developed to meet the needs of the farm family. Years ago, schools were let out in the early afternoon and all summer so that children could help with the crops, livestock, and other farm-related chores before sunset. However, ours has been a predominantly industrial society for a large part of the twentieth century. As a result, a different type of schedule is required. Many concerned families advocate activities for children after school and schools that are open all year long to match the schedules of workers. The economy has changed and families have changed; why have educational institutions remained static?

The majority of children somehow manage to grow and develop successfully in a variety of family forms, but, the stressors on all families are constantly increasing, which may, in turn, decrease the likelihood of continued success. Parents worry that the cost of a college education will be more than they can afford; parents worry about their children and AIDS, violence, and drugs. Parents are concerned that in adulthood their children will not be able to live as well as they have lived. Families need emotional support, and parents need opportunities to learn stress management and parenting skills.

Society can promote the optimal growth and development of its children by taking responsibility for them. There is an old saying, "It takes a village to raise a child." Our society can raise its children by establishing policies in schools, workplaces, and other institutions that reflect the importance of nurturing children.

On the Internet...

http://www.dushkin.com

Families and Work Institute
This Web site provides resources from the Families and Work Institute, which conducts policy research on issues related to the changing workforce and operates a national clearinghouse on work and family life.
http://www.familiesandworkinst.org

Babyworld
This Web site provides extensive information on caring for infants. There are links to numerous other related sites.
http://www.babyworld.com

NPIN: The National Parent Information Network
The National Parent Information Network contains resources related to many of the controversial issues faced by parents raising children in contemporary society. In addition to articles and resources, discussion groups are also available.
http://www.ericps.ed.uiuc.edu/npin/pnews.html

Zero to Three: National Center for Infants, Toddlers, and Families
This national organization is dedicated solely to infants, toddlers, and their families. It is headed by recognized experts in the field and provides technical assistance to communities, states, and the federal government. This site provides information that the organization gathers and disseminates through its publications.
http://www.zerotothree.org

National Center for Health Statistics (NCHS)
This Web site provides access to NCHS information, including what's new, products, data warehouse, news releases, and fact sheets.
http://www.cdc.gov/nchswww/nchshome.htm

PART 1

Infancy

Infancy and toddlerhood encompass the time period between birth and ages two or three. During this time, the most dramatic growth of a child's life takes place. Traditionally, much of the literature on infancy has dealt with the physical aspects of development; more recently, however, researchers, practitioners, and policymakers have begun to be concerned with the interaction of brain development on later learning and the social and emotional aspects of the infant's development. The issues examined in this section focus on how the family, social institutions, and heredity influence children's development from the time they are born.

■ Does Maternal Employment Have a Negative Effect on Infant Development?

■ Are Gender Differences Rooted in the Brain?

■ Should Hospitals Continue Early Discharge Policies for Newborns?

■ Is the Welfare of Our Disadvantaged Children Improving?

ISSUE 1

Does Maternal Employment Have a Negative Effect on Infant Development?

YES: Jay Belsky and David Eggebeen, from "Early and Extensive Maternal Employment and Young Children's Socioemotional Development: Children of the National Longitudinal Survey of Youth," *Journal of Marriage and the Family* (November 1991)

NO: K. Alison Clarke-Stewart, from "A Home Is Not a School: The Effects of Child Care on Children's Development," *Journal of Social Issues* (vol. 47, no. 2, 1991)

ISSUE SUMMARY

YES: Jay Belsky, a long-time researcher on infant development from Pennsylvania State University, and David Eggebeen, from the College of Health and Human Development at Pennsylvania State University, conclude that maternal employment during a child's infancy has detrimental effects on its social and behavioral development.

NO: K. Alison Clarke-Stewart, from the program in social ecology at the University of California–Irvine, finds that children who attend child care centers are more socially and intellectually advanced than children who are cared for in the home by their mother or another caregiver.

As more women moved into the workforce in the 1960s, research on maternal employment and its effect on children became a popular topic of study. In the past several decades maternal employment has evolved from being studied as one factor that affects children to a more complex issue. It was once thought to have a direct influence on development; now researchers agree that maternal employment is more than a question of just whether or not the mother works. The issue must be studied within the context of the family system and must simultaneously answer questions such as What quality of care does the child receive? How does the mother feel about her work? What societal and family support do the mother and child receive?

Researchers are divided on what variables to study, as well as what methods to use in studying maternal employment effects. For example, some combine several social classes to study the interactive effect of working mothers with type of child care arrangements, whereas others examine only one social class and its interaction with the mother's personality traits and family environment type.

The effects of maternal employment are determined by many factors, such as a mother's work satisfaction and morale, amount of work, and a mother's perception of quality verses quantity time with children. Depending on which study one reads, how the data were collected, and which combination of variables was studied, different conclusions are reported. For example, some research states that employed mothers spend more quality time with their children whereas others show exactly the opposite, that nonemployed mothers spend more quality time with their children.

Research on maternal employment has become more sophisticated in recent years, yet the question still remains: Should mothers stay home with their babies? Often women will drop out of the workforce, for at least the first few years, to stay home and care for their children. The concept that an attachment to the mother in the first few years is critical to a child's later development may indeed have validity, according to some researchers. Conversely, other research suggests that quality child care providers may be able to meet the same needs that mothers previously met.

In the following selections, Jay Belsky and David Eggebeen use the database from the National Longitudinal Survey of Youth to examine maternal employment in children's infancy and its effect on children's later development at four to six years of age. K. Alison Clarke-Stewart studies alternate forms of child care and their effects on child development, but her conclusions relate directly to the effects of maternal employment.

YES

Jay Belsky and David Eggebeen

EARLY AND EXTENSIVE MATERNAL EMPLOYMENT AND YOUNG CHILDREN'S SOCIOEMOTIONAL DEVELOPMENT

Dramatic changes took place in the United States in the 1980s in the timing of mothers' return to work, with increasing numbers of women returning to paid employment within a year of their infant's birth. The implications of this change for the care and development of children have been hotly debated in recent years. The purpose of the present investigation is to address some, though by no means all, features of what became known as the infant day care controversy (Fox and Fein, 1990).

Upon reviewing studies of maternal employment and of nonparental care involving infants, Belsky (1988, 1990a) concluded that children who experienced 20 or more hours per week of nonparental care in their first year of life of the kind routinely available in the United States (often proxied by extensive maternal employment) are at elevated risk of developing insecure attachments to their mothers (e.g., Belsky and Rovine, 1988; Jacobson and Wille, 1984; Vaughn, Gore, and Egeland, 1980) and of being more disobedient toward adults and aggressive toward peers as three- to eight-year-olds (e.g., Haskins, 1985; Rubenstein and Howes, 1983; Schwarz, Strickland, and Krolick, 1974) than other children. Vandell and Corasaniti (1990) sought to evaluate empirically Belsky's conclusion and extend research by focusing not simply upon the first year of life but on child-care experience *across* the preschool years. They discovered, in the course of analyses designed specifically to address the controversy stimulated by Belsky's (1988) review, that children who had initiated care for 30 or more hours per week in their first year and whose care at this level continued through their preschool years evinced poorer academic and social functioning than did children whose full-time care began sometime later—and that this was true whether one looked at teacher reports, parent reports, peer reports, or the children's own self-reports. Particularly interesting from the standpoint of the current inquiry

From Jay Belsky and David Eggebeen, "Early and Extensive Maternal Employment and Young Children's Socioemotional Development: Children of the National Longitudinal Survey of Youth," *Journal of Marriage and the Family*, vol. 53 (November 1991). Copyright © 1991 by The National Council on Family Relations, 3989 Central Ave. NE, Suite 550, Minneapolis, MN 55421. Reprinted by permission.

were their related findings that in the case of many dependent measures of child functioning, children whose full-time care (30 hours per week) began in their second year often functioned just as poorly as those whose care was initiated in their first year.

Critics of such findings have highlighted many limitations of the studies reviewed by Belsky (1988, 1990a) and thus of conclusions drawn by him. Especially important for the current investigation is the observation that effects attributed to early and extensive maternal employment and/or child care may be the result of selection factors. Because subjects are not randomly assigned to family and rearing conditions, it may be that certain families that rely upon particular rearing arrangements would, for example, raise insecure, aggressive, and disobedient offspring irrespective of their maternal employment or child-care situation. As a result of this cogent criticism, it is widely recognized that background differences between families need to be examined and, if necessary, controlled before comparisons are made of the development of children with varying child-care and maternal employment histories.

Many studies—and the conclusions that Belsky (1988, 1990a) drew on the basis of them—also have been criticized because they involve small samples of convenience. Thus, it remains unclear how representative the data base is and how generalizable are the findings derived from it. In light of this state of affairs, and the need for extensive background controls, it was judged that the National Longitudinal Survey of Youth represented a unique opportunity to examine the developmental correlates of early and extensive maternal employment/child care. This national sample is larger, more diverse, and more representative than any ever studied with a concern for socio-emotional development and early and extensive maternal employment and child care. Moreover, the data base includes a wealth of background information on the child, the mother, and the family.

On the basis of the work summarized and the issues raised, we set out to create three discrete groups of four-, five-, and six-year-olds from the survey data base pertaining to the Children of the National Longitudinal Survey of Youth (Baker and Mott, 1989) so that they could be compared on the available indices of social and emotional functioning once confounding background factors were identified and statistically controlled. One group was to be of children whose mothers were employed, on average, for 30 or more hours per week in their first year and who continued paid employment in their second and third year; a second of children whose mothers did not begin employment on such a full-time basis until their second year and who continued such work through their third year; and the third of children whose mothers were not employed or employed on only a minimal basis (less than 10 hours per week) throughout their child's first three years of life. Thus, we chose to follow Vandell and Corasaniti's (1990) innovative lead by constructing multiyear patterns of maternal employment and child care, rather than focusing upon a single year. Further, we selected 30 hours per week as the marker of full-time maternal employment, not only because this was the cutoff that Vandell and Corasaniti used, but also because Belsky and Rovine (1988) found, in the only study of first-year maternal employment and child care to distinguish between extensive and full-time employment and care, that the rate of insecure infant-mother attachments was greater in households in which mothers worked 35 or more hours per week than in those in which they were employed between 20 and 35 hours per week. Finally, we chose to include a group of children whose mothers began full-time employment in their second year so we could test Vandell and Corasaniti's (1990) findings regarding full-time care initiated in the second year of life. It was anticipated that group differences in measures of adjustment would be most likely to emerge when the two early and extensive employment and care groups (full-time initiated in first or second year) were contrasted with the third group (no employment and minimal employment), though differences between the early and extensive care groups also were examined.

Like much research on maternal employment and child care, the current investigation is not without limitations. Perhaps most noteworthy is the absence of information pertaining to the quality of child care that children experience when the mother is employed. The fact that quality of nonmaternal care influences children's development makes this lacuna all the more serious (for reviews, see Belsky, 1984, 1990b; Phillips et al., 1987). Moreover, in the only study to date to examine *simultaneously* age of entry into full-time care and quality of care, Howes (1990) discovered that the effects of care of limited quality are most pronounced when care is initiated in the first year. This finding suggests that power to discern effects in the present investigation may be limited by the inability to examine timing of entry into care in the context of quality of care.

Although the NLSY data set does not permit examination of interactions between quality of care and timing of mother's return to work, the sample size and its racial and economic diversity do make possible evaluations of other notable interactions. In this inquiry we sought to determine whether the effects of early and extensive maternal employment and child care were moderated either by indices of family socioeconomic status or by child temperament. The focus upon socioeconomic moderators is based upon speculation that developmental costs may be associated with extensive maternal employment and child care in the case of children from economically advantaged families who "lose" time with their well-educated and highly skilled mothers, whereas developmental benefits may accrue to children from economically disadvantaged and/or single-parent families because of the much-needed financial resources that maternal employment brings to the family or to the enriched experiences that nonmaternal care might provide (Bronfenbrenner and Crouter, 1983; Lande, Scarr, and Gunzenhauser, 1989). The focus upon child temperament is based upon Kagan and colleagues' (1978) proposition that temperamentally shy, inhibited, and/or fearful children may find early child care particularly stressful and may be least able to cope with and thus benefit from early maternal employment.

DATA AND METHOD

The NLSY Sample
The data for this study are drawn from the National Longitudinal Survey of Labor Market Experience of Youth (NLSY). This survey is a national probability sample of 12,686 men and women who were aged 14 to 21 in 1979, and who have been

nterviewed annually since. Included in his sample is an oversample of black, Hispanic, and economically disadvantaged nonblack, non-Hispanic youths. The annual interviews have generated a wealth of information on employment, educational, and family-related experiences. The retention rate for this panel has been extremely good, with nearly 92% of the original respondents retained as of the 1986 interview and with little variation across subgroups (Baker and Mott, 1989).

As part of the 1986 interview, the 2,918 women in the sample who had become mothers were given supplemental questionnaires to gather information on maternal and child health, the home environment, family relationships, child's behavior and activities, and child-care histories. In addition, 4,971 children of these women (nearly 95% of the eligible children) were assessed. Trained interviewers gathered information on children's cognitive, social, emotional, and physiological development through maternal report, direct observation, and the use of standardized tests administered in the child's home. These data were then integrated with selected information from the eight years of data collected on their mothers to form a child-mother data set (Baker and Mott, 1989).

We have selected to sample from all white and black children from four to six years old ($n = 1,248$)....

Child Outcome Measures

Available for investigation of four-to-six-year-olds in the NLSY were five measures of socioemotional functioning: compliance, inhibition, attachment insecurity, sociability, and behavior problems (see Baker and Mott, 1989, for extensive dis-

cussion of scale origins, construction, and psychometric properties)....

... Maternal Employment and Child Care Groups

Two sets of information pertinent to the timing and extent of maternal employment were available in the longitudinal data set that we planned to use to create discrete maternal employment/child care groups. One involved detailed information on the number of hours and weeks of employment mothers reported for each quarter of each year and the other involved a simple yes-no answer for each year of the child's life to the question of whether the child was "cared for in any regular arrangement such as a babysitter, relative, daycare center, nursery school, play group or some other *regular* arrangement" (emphasis in original).

... [E]mployment patterns... were reduced to three types (and a residual group) to reflect distinct family ecologies that might differ, according to the literature reviewed in the introduction, with respect to their impact on the developing child: (*a*) children whose mothers were classified as not working in each of their first three years of life (and who were presumed not to have received routine nonparental care); (*b*) children whose mothers were not classified as employed full-time in their first year, but who were so classified in their second and third year (and presumed not to have received routine nonmaternal care on a full-time basis in their first year but to have done so thereafter); (*c*) children whose mothers were classified as employed full-time in their first year and extensively thereafter (i.e., at minimum, part-time) (and presumed to have experienced routine nonmaternal care across their first three years); and (*d*) all other children. . . .

Background Factors
Three sets of background factors, reflecting child, mother, and household characteristics, were selected for consideration.

Child characteristics. . . . A child's weight at birth was reported by the mother in the first interview after the birth. . . .

Mother characteristics. Mother's age at the child's birth was coded into four categories (less than 20; 20–21, 22–23, and 24–26). Years of completed education by the first interview after the child's birth was represented by a three-level variable (less than high school, high school diploma, some college) for the descriptive analysis but was kept as a continuous measure in the multivariate models. Finally, marital status at the first interview after the birth of the child was coded to distinguish mothers who were never married, currently married with spouse present, or "other" (separated, divorced, widowed, spouse absent).

Mother's self-esteem was measured by a summary variable created from Rosenberg's (1965) 10-item self-esteem scale, which was administered to all the mothers in the 1980 NLSY main survey. . . . Mother's attitudes toward appropriate family roles were measured by responses to the question "Are traditional husband/wife roles best?" Answers were scored on a 4-point scale ranging from "strongly disagree" to "strongly agree." Mother's intellectual ability was measured by her score on the Armed Forces Qualification Test (AFQT), which was taken by all NLSY participants in 1980. . . . Mother's contribution to the family income was measured by taking mother's total income as a percentage of the total family income. . . . This was obtained two interview rounds before the birth of the child in order to avoid any confounds caused by reduced employment due to pregnancy and birth.

Household and family characteristics. The various indicators of household and family size (presence of grandparents, number of working adults, household size, urban or rural residence) were all obtained from the first interview after the child was born. . . .

The two measures of economic resources (total family income and whether the family was below the poverty line) were obtained from the last interview before the child was born. . . .

RESULTS

Before examining the relation between maternal employment and children's socioemotional development, it was necessary to determine which of the background maternal and family household factors as well as newborn characteristics varied across employment groups. Thus, in a series of preliminary analyses, the three groups were compared. In a subsequent series of regression analyses, we examined the relation between maternal employment during the first three years of the child's life and child functioning at four, five, or six years of age, after controlling for differences between maternal employment groups that emerged from the preceding analysis of the ecology of maternal employment.

The Ecology of Early and Extended Maternal Employment
. . . With respect to child characteristics, no relation was discerned between mater-

nal employment and infant gender, birth weight, and gestational age. Black children, however, were disproportionately likely to have mothers who did not work during their entire first three years of life; and firstborn children were more likely to have mothers who worked full-time in their first or second year of life than were later-born children. In both cases, though, the major differences were between children whose mothers were not employed at all and children whose mothers entered full-time employment in either their first or second year.

... Mothers who were not employed across the first three years of the child's life were most likely to have given birth to the child while teenagers, to have the fewest years of education, to have never been married at the child's birth, to have contributed the least to the family's income, to attend church more frequently, to have low self-esteem, to have scored the lowest on the measure of intelligence, and to have held the most traditional attitudes toward gender roles.

In light of these findings and others reported in the literature (e.g., Eggebeen, 1988), it should not be surprising to discover that the maternal employment groups also differed with respect to household composition and economic resources. As expected, mothers were less likely to be employed across the child's first three years when there were more people living in the household and when more working adults were present in the household. Maternal employment, however, was unrelated to the presence of a grandparent in the household. Finally, children living in rural areas were more likely to have a nonemployed mother.

With respect to economic factors,... children whose mothers were not employed in their first three years of life were disproportionately concentrated in the lowest income groups and significantly more likely to be in poverty, while children of mothers who initiated employment in the first year were more likely to be in the highest income brackets and the least likely to be in poverty.

Maternal Employment and Socioemotional Development

The preceding analyses, consistent with other research, clearly indicate that maternal employment is not randomly assigned. As a result, selection effects plague virtually all efforts to illuminate the effects of maternal employment and child care upon child development. In order to address this problem, we sought to identify factors that covaried significantly with both maternal employment and the indices of socioemotional development (ADJUST, SHY), so that these could be statistically controlled in subsequent regression analyses. This would permit an assessment of the relation between maternal employment and child development that was relatively unconfounded with ecological and demographic factors.

Four variables were identified that covaried significantly with maternal employment and with at least one of the two socioemotional composite measures: child birth order (firstborn vs. later-born), maternal education (in years at time of child's birth), family poverty status (at time of birth), and maternal intelligence as indexed by the Air Force Qualifying Test (AFQT).[1] In addition to these factors, child gender, age, and race were also added to the list of control variables so that interactions between these factors and maternal employment could be examined once the main effects of these factors were controlled.[2] ...

DISCUSSION

Research during the past decade on early and extensive maternal employment and infant day care led Belsky (1988, 1990a) to call attention to developmental risks associated with more than 20 hours per week of nonparental care (as routinely available in the U.S.) initiated in the first year. This analysis of NLSY data was designed to address two specific criticisms of much previous work and to build upon Vandell and Corasaniti's (1990) empirical test of Belsky's conclusions.

By relying upon the NLSY data base, we sought to study a larger and more representative sample of young children than has been studied to date. Because the sample we subjected to empirical analysis consists of higher percentage of black, uneducated, young, and unmarried women than exists in the national population, however, we must exercise caution against generalizing the results of the study too broadly. Nevertheless, the fact that none of the discerned effects of early and extensive maternal employment were moderated by a host of demographic factors suggests, in this sample at least, that those effects are not restricted to some subset of subjects studied.

The NLSY data set also enabled us to control for a host of background factors that differed across maternal employment groups in an effort to control for selection effects. The fact that the variables we controlled reflect only a subset of all that could be controlled means, of course, that not every conceivable selection effect has been taken into account. This should caution us from concluding that truly causal effects have been discerned in regression analyses of the kind employed in this inquiry. However, when the analyses reported were rerun with control for every single background variable... the effects of early and extensive maternal employment remained statistically significant.

The design of the study built directly upon Vandell and Corasaniti's (1990) discovery that developmental outcomes that Belsky (1988, 1990a) found to be associated with more than 20 hours per week of nonparental care in the first year of life were often associated with full-time nonparental care that began in the second year. It was because the data reviewed by Belsky did not permit consideration of this timing-of-entry distinction, and because Vandell and Corasaniti (1990) discerned relations between child-care experience *across* the preschool years and the behavioral development of children in elementary school, that we chose to create a quasi-experimental design that identified children whose mothers began working full-time in their first year of life and in their second year of life. Throughout this work it has been our presumption that within the very first years of life full-time maternal employment and reliance upon extensive nonmaternal care typically co-occur. While it is certainly the case that many four-year-olds in child care programs for even 20 hours per week have mothers who are not employed, it is just as certainly the exception to find a mother working more than 30 hours per week in the first and second year of life and not relying upon some form of routine nonmaternal care during this time.

The findings of this inquiry provide only mixed support for Belsky's (1988, 1990a) conclusion that more than 20 hours per week of nonparental care in the first year of life is a risk factor for the development of aggression and noncompliance. As suggested by the findings of Vandell and Corasaniti (1990), analyses of the NLSY data indicate that full-time employment initiated in the first or second year is associated with lower levels of adjustment than more limited maternal employment across the child's first three years of life. This broad conclusion is warranted because the results presented remained unchanged when the analyses reported were modified so that the comparison group comprised not simply children whose mothers were not employed or only minimally employed across their first three years ($n = 398$), but all children whose mothers did not work full-time in the first or second year ($n = 661$).

The absence of any effects uniquely attributable to full-time employment in the first year may be the direct result of the absence of any information on the quality of nonparental care. This suggestion is based upon Howes's (1990) recent discovery that the effects of full-time nonparental care in the first year are consistently moderated by quality of care, whereas this is far less the case of care initiated thereafter.

Despite this study's failure to reveal any effects specifically attributable to full-time maternal employment initiated in the first year of life, it is noteworthy that, as anticipated—and consistent with Belsky's analysis of the literature—it was the composite dependent measure ADJUST rather than SHY that turned out to be associated with early and extensive maternal employment, once confounding background factors were controlled. Thus, statistical effects of maternal employment emerged not simply on one of the two composite variables subject to analysis, but on the very measure that was hypothesized to be most likely asso-

ciated with early and extensive maternal employment.

When the composite ADJUST measure was decomposed into its three constituent elements, it was discovered that only for the index of compliance did a reliable association between early and extensive maternal employment and child functioning obtain. The absence of a relation between employment and either the index of behavior problems or of attachment security may reflect the fact that no such associations exist or, alternatively, that the methods used to study these constructs in the NLSY were limited. Certainly, most attachment researchers would question the validity of using a few maternal-report items to measure this developmentally dynamic construct. Questions can be raised also about the maternal-report index of behavior problems, especially since research linking aggression with early and extensive maternal employment and child care has focused upon aggression *toward peers*, with measures based upon actual observations of children's behavior in group settings (e.g., Haskins, 1985) or teacher reports (e.g., Vandell and Corasaniti, 1990). Before embracing the null hypothesis—that is, that early and extensive maternal employment is not related to attachment security and aggression—we must keep issues of measurement in mind.

It is noteworthy that the component analysis of the adjustment composite variable revealed that it was not simply the case that children whose mothers did not work (or who worked only minimally) during their first three years of life were simply excessively compliant in comparison with agemates whose mothers were employed on a full-time basis beginning in their first or second year of life. Recall that it was the latter children who were significantly more likely to score in excess of one standard deviation below the mean on the compliance measure. These findings are consistent with Belsky's (1988) original conclusion that early and extensive child care/maternal employment is a risk factor for the development of noncompliance.

An alternative interpretation is also possible. Rather than providing evidence of noncompliance, which carries with it developmentally negative overtones, the effects discerned may merely reflect the fact that children whose mothers initiate full-time employment during their first or second year of life are more assertive than the children to whom they were compared. Unlike noncompliance, the notion of increased assertiveness does not carry with it such negative overtones. Perhaps consistent with this alternative interpretation of the compliance data is the fact that the evidence ... reveals that as children get older they tend to become less compliant (i.e., more assertive?). Thus, it may be argued that early and extensive maternal employment speeds up the developmental process, perhaps making children "precociously independent."

While this is certainly a tenable argument—and one that cannot be resolved with the data at hand—it is worth noting that the noncompliance-equals-assertiveness line of reasoning presumes that psychological and behavioral developments that typically occur later in children's lives are developmentally beneficial when they transpire earlier. Thus, if children tend to become less compliant and more assertive as they grow up, becoming this way at an earlier age is evidence of precocity and thereby, developmental advantage.

The problem with such reasoning becomes apparent when behaviors other than compliance are considered. Just because children are more likely to drink, drive, stay out late, and commit petty acts of delinquency as they get older does not mean that doing these things earlier in life reflects maturity. We know, in fact, that such behavioral precocity is often a harbinger of more serious problems to come. The point here is not to equate the kind of noncompliance measured with the few items available to this study with much more serious risk-taking behavior, but rather to raise questions about the interpretation that earlier is better, that noncompliance reflects assertiveness, and that early and extensive maternal employment fosters precocious independence. Needless to say, this is an issue that should be addressed in future research.

Despite the fact that early and extensive maternal employment was found to predict less adjustment and, more specifically, greater noncompliance, it must be noted that, however statistically significant this effect was, it accounted for very little variance in the dependent measures. In fact, in the final regression model, the main effect of employment and the interaction between employment and shyness explained only 1.56% of the variance in the composite measure ADJUST. ...

Our work with the NLSY data set—and particularly our analysis of the one-item child-care variable—convinces us that measurement error in survey data such as we analyzed is probably not minimal. While this does not lead us to dismiss the utility of the NLSY data base, it does lead us to be cautious about dismissing statistically significant findings that are consistent with other research and with our predictions. Indeed, from our standpoint, the results of the present inquiry do not indicate that early and extensive maternal employment, as it is routinely experienced in the United States, has a dramatic and devastating effect upon the socioemotional development of young children, but rather that Belsky's (1988, 1990a) risk-factor conclusion remains valid. Still to be determined are the processes by which such early experience becomes related to the developmental outcomes with which we have found them to be associated. After all, the study reveals that an anticipated, statistically significant association of only modest magnitude exists between early and extensive maternal employment and a composite index of adjustment in the NLSY data set. What remains to be explained, now that this predicted relation has been chronicled, are the mechanisms that account for it. There is no shortage of possibilities that merit empirical consideration. Unfortunately, those that concern the quality of nonmaternal care that children experience when their mothers work are beyond the purview of the NLSY.

NOTES

1. Age of mother at birth of the child was related to the pattern of employment over the first three years of a child's life. However, no relationship between age and any of the outcome measures was discerned in these data.

2. Results of these analyses, and other analyses discussed in the text, are available from the authors.

REFERENCES

Baker, Paula, and Frank Mott. 1989. NLSY Child Handbook 1989. Columbus: Center for Human Resources Research, Ohio State University.

Belsky, Jay. 1984. "Two waves of day care research: Development effects and conditions of quality."

Pp. 1–34 in Ricardo Ainslie (ed.), The Child and the Day Care Setting. New York: Praeger.

Belsky, Jay. 1988. "The 'effects' of infant day care reconsidered." Early Childhood Research Quarterly 3: 235–272.

Belsky, Jay. 1990a. "Developmental risks associated with infant day care: Insecurity, aggression, and noncompliance?" In S. Chehrazi (ed.), Balancing Work and Parenting: Psychological and Developmental Implications of Day Care. New York: American Psychiatric Press.

Belsky, Jay. 1990b. "Parental and nonparental care and children's socioemotional development: A decade in review." Journal of Marriage and the Family 52: 885–903.

Belsky, Jay, and M. Rovine. 1988. "Nonmaternal care in the first year of life and infant-parent attachment security." Child Development 59: 157–176.

Bronfenbrenner, Urie, and Anne Crouter. 1983. "The evolution of environmental models in developmental psychology." Pp. 358–414 in P. Mussen (ed.), Handbook of Child Psychology (Vol. 1). New York: Wiley.

Eggebeen, David J. 1988. "Determinants of maternal employment for white preschool children: 1960–1980. Journal of Marriage and the Family 50: 149–159.

Fox, N., and G. Fein (eds.). 1990. "Infant day care: The current debate." Norwood, NJ: Ablex.

Haskins, Ronald. 1985. "Public school aggression among children with varying day-care experience." Child Development 56: 689–703.

Howes, Carollee, 1990. "Can the age of entry into child care and the quality of child care predict adjustment in kindergarten?" Developmental Psychology 26: 292–303.

Jacobson, Joseph L., and Diane E. Wille. 1984. "Influence of attachment and separation experience on separation distress at 18 months." Child Development 20: 477–484.

Kagan, Jerome, Richard Kearsley, and Phillip Zelazo. 1978. Infancy. Cambridge, MA: Harvard University Press.

Lande, Jeff, Sandra Scarr, and Nina Gunzenhauser (eds.). 1989. Caring for Children. Hillsdale, NJ: Erlbaum.

Phillips, Deborah, K. McCartney, S. Scarr, and C. Howes. 1987. "Selective review of infant day care research: A cause for concern!" Zero to Three 7(2): 18–21.

Rosenberg, Morris. 1965. Society and the Adolescent Self-image. Princeton, NJ: Princeton University Press.

Rubenstein, Judy, and Carollee Howes. 1983. "Adaptation to toddler day care." In S. Kilmer (ed.), Advances in Early Education and Day Care. Greenwich, CT: JAI Press.

Schwarz, J. Conrad, R. C. Strickland, and G. Krolick. 1974. "Infant day care: Behavioral effects at preschool age." Developmental Psychology 10: 502–506.

Vandell, Deborah, and Mary Corasaniti. 1990. "Child care and the family: Complex contributors to child development." In K. McCartney (ed.), Child Care and Maternal Employment: A Social Ecology Approach. San Francisco: Jossey-Bass.

Vaughn, Brian, Fred Gore, and Byron Egeland. 1980. "The relationship between out-of-home care and the quality of infant-mother attachment in an economically disadvantaged population." Child Development 51: 1203–1214.

NO

K. Alison Clarke-Stewart

A HOME IS NOT A SCHOOL

Assessments of 150 2–4-year-olds in six different child care arrangements revealed that the social and intellectual development of children in centers (part time or full time) was advanced over that of
the children in home care (with mother, sitter, or day care home
provider). Previous research was reviewed to account for this finding. It was concluded that the most likely causes of the difference
in children's development were educational lessons, opportunities
to practice skills and follow rules with a variety of peers and nonparental adults, and encouragement of independence by nonauthoritarian teachers—experiences that are qualitatively different from
the experiences most children have in home care environments.

There has been a dramatic shift over the past 15 years in the environments
in which young American children spend their time. Whereas 15 years ago
fewer than one-third of the preschool-aged children in this country were
in any kind of preschool program, now over half attend a nursery school,
kindergarten, or day care center (U.S. Bureau of the Census, 1987). An even
more striking rise has occurred for infants and toddlers; their participation in
such programs has more than doubled in the same period. In addition, over 5
million young children now spend a significant portion of their time in other
kinds of nonparental care—with a babysitter, a neighbor, an aunt, or a paid
day care home provider. Every year the number of young children in some
form of "nontraditional" child care environment increases markedly.

A question that concerns parents, politicians, and psychologists is what
effects these alternative forms of child care have on children's development.
Until quite recently, however, data about the effects of different kinds of
child care were lacking Although day care had existed in this country since
at least 1838, when the first day nursery was opened in Boston (Steinfels,
1973), and for longer than that if informal arrangements between neighbors
or with live-in housekeepers are included, the first systematic studies of child
care environments and effects did not appear until 1970 (Caldwell, Wright,
Honig, & Tannenbaum, 1970; Keister, 1970). Since that time, a sizable number
of studies of child care have been undertaken, and now important evidence is

From K. Alison Clarke-Stewart, "A Home Is Not a School: The Effects of Child Care on Children's
Development," *Journal of Social Issues*, vol. 47, no. 2 (1991), pp. 105–121. Copyright © 1991 by
The Society for the Psychological Study of Social Issues. Reprinted by permission of Blackwell
Publishers. References omitted.

beginning to accumulate. The evidence concerning the effects of child care on *infants* has been spotlighted lately (e.g., Clarke-Stewart, 1989; Howes, 1990). But there are still unanswered questions about the effects of child care on toddlers and preschoolers. For these children, the major issue is not whether daily separations from mother impair development —the burning question for infants—but rather, what are the relative advantages and disadvantages of different types of child care for children's social and cognitive development? The present paper offers one answer to this question, based upon the results of available research.

DIFFERENCES BETWEEN CHILDREN IN DIFFERENT CHILD CARE ENVIRONMENTS

In research conducted in Chicago (Clarke-Stewart, 1984; Clarke-Stewart & Gruber, 1984), 150 children, 2 and 3 years old, were selected for a study of child care. They were in six different child care arrangements: (1) care at home by parents, (2) care by a sitter in the child's home, (3) care in a day care home, (4) care in a center or nursery school part time; (5) care in a center full time, and (6) care in a center part time and with a sitter at home part time. To ensure a wide and representative sampling of the kinds of child care environments available, the study included no more than 4 children from any single child care setting. The children were in their first nonparental child care environments and had been there for less than a year. They were followed over a year-long period, observed six times in their family and child care settings, and their moment-to-moment experiences were recorded. Children also were brought into a labo-

ratory playroom on two occasions for extensive assessments of their social skills, and on one occasion were given standard assessments of social, emotional, and cognitive development at home (see Clarke-Stewart, 1984, for details). The researchers assessing the children's development were not the same ones who had observed them at home or in their day care settings; they were blind to the care arrangements of the children they were assessing. From the data collected in the assessments of the children's development, a set of complex, empirically intercorrelated, and conceptually meaningful variables was created. . . .

Differences between children in the six child care arrangements were estimated by analyzing differences in mean scores on these seven child development variables, covarying out the child's age and family SES. The results of these analyses . . . were clear and consistent. On all these variables reflecting advanced social and intellectual skills—verbal ability, nonverbal cognition, social cognition, creativity with materials, cooperation with the examiner, cooperation with an unfamiliar peer, and overall social competence—there were no significant differences among the children in different home care environments (with mother, sitter, or day care home provider), nor were there differences among the children in different center environments (part time or full time); but the children in center care (child care arrangements, 4–6) performed at higher levels than the children in home care (child care arrangements 1–3). Only 2 of the 15 analyses did not reveal a significant difference between children in home care and center care, and these two analyses (for creative play with materials and cooperation with the examiner during the first assess-

nent) were in the same direction and approached significance.

The difference between children in
home and center environments did not
occur, however, for another set of variables that assessed children's social relationships rather than their social or intellectual competence. No differences were
found between these settings for children's security of attachment to mother,
hostility toward mother, help or comfort-
ing of mother, compliance with mother's
requests, or positive interaction with a
familiar playmate. Marked variability
among individual children was observed
for these variables, but it was not related
to type of child care. This suggests that
the observed difference between children
in home and center care is specific to the
development of social competence and
intellectual knowledge rather than occur-
ing for all kinds of behavior or development.

The findings from this study are consistent with the results of other research (reviewed by Clarke-Stewart & Fein, 1983;
and more recent studies by Andersson,
1989; Burchinal, Lee, & Ramey, 1989;
Robinson & Corley, 1989; Tietze, 1987;
Wadsworth, 1986). These studies all suggest that children in day care centers and
preschool programs tend to be more socially skilled and intellectually advanced
than children at home with their parents, sitters, or in day care homes. Significant differences favoring center atten-
dees have not been found in all studies,
in all samples, or on all indices of social or cognitive competence, of course
(e.g., Ackerman-Ross & Khanna, 1989;
Lamb, Hwang, Broberg, & Bookstein,
1988; Scarr, Lande, & McCartney, 1988).
But when differences have been found,
they consistently favor children in center
care.

In the realm of social competence, there
is evidence that children in center care
are more self-confident, self-assured and
outgoing, less timid and fearful, more assertive, self-sufficient, and independent
of parents and teachers, yet more helpful
and cooperative with peers, mother, or
examiner when the situation requires it.
They are more verbally expressive, more
knowledgeable about the social world
(e.g., they know their own name, address, and birthday earlier), more comfortable in a new or stressful situation,
and more competent to manage on their
own (Cochran, 1977; Fowler, 1978; Kagan,
Kearsley, & Zelazo, 1978; Lally & Honig,
1977; Rubenstein, Howes, & Boyle, 1981;
Schwarz, Krolick, & Strickland, 1973).
When they get to school, they are better adjusted, more task oriented and
goal directed, and show more leadership and persistence (Fowler & Khan,
1974; Howes, 1990; Lally & Honig, 1977).
in Sjolund's (1971) international review,
only 3 of the available 56 studies failed to
find a significant difference favoring the
social skills of children in nursery school
compared to children without this experience.

In the domain of intellectual ability, of
the more than 20 studies of child care
that have included some measure of children's intelligence or intellectual development, only 2 have reported significantly higher scores for children reared
at home than for children of comparable family backgrounds who were in day
care centers (Melhuish, 1990, for vocabulary only; Peaslee, 1976, for language
and IQ). Other studies consistently show
that children in day care centers do at
least as well as those at home with
their parents and often they do better,
at least for a time (e.g., Cochran, 1977;
Fowler, 1978; Golden et al., 1978; Kagan et

al., 1978; Ramey, Dorval, & Baker-Ward, 1983; Robinson & Robinson, 1971; Rubenstein & Howes, 1983; Winnett, Fuchs, Moffatt, & Nerviano, 1977). In Sjolund's (1971) review, 21 of 36 studies assessing children's intellectual development showed advanced development in children attending nursery school compared to those who were not in nursery school; the other 15 showed no significant difference. Comparisons of children in day care homes and day care centers, similarly, have often revealed significant differences between children in these two kinds of day care, favoring the children in centers (e.g., Bruner, 1980; Robinson & Corley, 1989; Winnett et al., 1977).

In the assessments of particular kinds of intellectual abilities, differences favoring center care children have been found in eye–hand coordination (Cochran, 1977; Kagan et al., 1978), creative use of materials (Provost, 1980), memory (Ramey et al., 1983), problem solving and reasoning (Fowler, 1978; Garber & Heber, 1980; Moss, Blicharski, & Strayer, 1987), and knowledge about the physical world (Stukat, 1969). Advanced language abilities have also been observed in children who are in center care (Fowler, 1978; Garber & Heber, 1980; Ramey et al., 1983; Rubenstein & Howes, 1983; Rubenstein et al., 1981; Scarr et al., 1988; Stukat, 1969).

In brief, then, differences favoring children in center care appear across a range of intellectual abilities including both verbal and nonverbal skills. These differences are not permanent, but they have been observed to last for a year or two after "graduation" into elementary school (Haskins, 1989; Larsen & Robinson, 1989; Lee et al., 1989; Tietze, 1987; Wadsworth, 1986). There is some evidence to suggest that they are more likely for children who have been in center care from infancy (Andersson, 1989). There is also evidence to suggest that they are more likely for children from low-income families who are in model child care programs (see Clarke-Stewart & Fein, 1983). But differences also appear for middle-class children in community child care. In our Chicago study, no effort was made to select child care of high quality. The child care settings observed were just the ones that parents had come up with; they were not model programs. They were, however, generally of decent quality (the average adult–child ratio in the centers was 1 to 5, standard deviation = 4).

CAUSES OF THE DIFFERENCE BETWEEN CHILDREN IN DIFFERENT CHILD CARE ENVIRONMENTS

More than simply documenting the differences between children in different child care environments, research offers some tentative suggestions about what causes these differences. Here, four possible reasons for the differences between children are examined: (1) differences in the *amount* of attention and stimulation in centers and homes, (2) differences in the *kind* of attention and stimulation in centers and homes, (3) differences in the *quality* of attention and stimulation in centers and homes, and (4) preexisting differences in the children themselves and their families.

Differences in Amount of Attention and Stimulation

One reason that the development of children in center care is advanced might be that center programs simply provide *more* of the same kind of stimulation that predicts advanced development in other care environments. Perhaps centers are just like homes, but more so.

One piece of evidence that could be used to support this hypothesis would be a finding that centers offer children more physical stimulation—more space and materials—of the same kind as found in homes, and that this stimulation predicts advanced child development. The available evidence, however, offers no support for this idea. Although extreme differences in the amount of space per child have indeed been related to children's behavior and development in child care environments (Prescott, 1973; Rohe & Patterson, 1974; Ruopp, Travers, Glantz, & Coelen, 1979; Smith & Connolly, 1980), because homes generally offer more space per child than centers, this relation cannot explain the advanced development of children in centers. There may be more play materials in centers than in homes (e.g., Golden et al., 1978), but probably this is not important in accounting for the difference in children's development either, because studies of the effects of the number of toys in children's environments suggest that toys alone are not a direct promoter of development (Golden et al., 1978; Rubenstein & Howes, 1979).

Another kind of evidence that could support the hypothesis that centers offer children more stimulation would be a finding that care givers in centers interact more with children than do care givers at home. The social and intellectual development of individual children in day care centers has indeed been positively related to the amount of adult attention they receive (Carew, 1980; Clarke-Stewart, 1984; Phillips, McCartney, & Scarr, 1987; Phillips, Scarr, & McCartney, 1987; Ruopp et al., 1979; Whitebook, Howes, & Phillips, 1990). But of the

studies comparing the amount of caregiver attention in homes and in centers, the majority show that children at home receive more attention from the care giver than do children in centers (Clarke-Stewart, 1984; Cochran, 1977; Golden et al., 1978; Hayes et al., 1983; Melhuish, 1990; Prescott, 1973; Tizard et al., 1980; Tyler & Dittman, 1980). Once again, the available data do not support the hypothesis that the important difference between center and home environments is simply the amount of stimulation that children receive.

Differences in Kind of Attention and Stimulation

Perhaps, then, the important difference between homes and centers is not the amount of stimulation the child receives, but the kind. Center environments differ qualitatively from home environments in a number of ways.

Peers. Most obviously, perhaps, centers offer children the opportunity to interact with other children their age. It has been observed that playing with a peer raises the complexity and creativity of children's activities with materials (Rubenstein & Howes, 1983; Sylva, Roy, & Painter, 1980), that social play is more advanced with a familiar playmate (Doyle, Connolly, & Rivest, 1980; Rubenstein & Howes, 1979), and that this more complex level of play then generalizes to interaction with unfamiliar peers (Lieberman, 1977). However, interaction with agemates is less likely to have a direct effect on the child's language acquisition. Language development is facilitated by hearing a more advanced language model, not by listening to peer chatter (McCartney, 1984; Sjolund, 1971). It seems unlikely, therefore, that the presence of other children alone would account for the observed difference in intellectual development typically found for children in different child care environments—although it may affect their social development.

Results of studies comparing different types of child care support this suggestion. First, if peers were the critical factor, then all group programs, not just programs in centers should show the effect. But as has already been noted, children in day care homes do not generally show the same level of competence as children in centers—despite the fact that they spend as much time interacting with peers (Clarke-Stewart, 1984; Howes & Rubenstein, 1981). Second, more peer interaction occurs in more "open" or unstructured preschool programs—programs with fewer teacher-directed activities like lessons—but gains in cognitive development and achievement are typically lower in these programs than in more structured programs (Miller & Dyer, 1975). Third, measures of social and intellectual competence in our research in Chicago (Clarke-Stewart, 1984) and in research in Bermuda (McCartney, 1984) were not significantly positively correlated with the amount of peer interaction experienced by individual children.

Children's competence in the Chicago study was, however, correlated with the number of different children interacted with in the care setting. Thus, children may gain from exposure to a wider *variety* of other children. Dunn and Kontos's (1989) observation that when there were more children in day care homes children engaged in higher levels of play would support this suggestion. But the advantage of diversity exists only up to a certain point. When the number of children becomes too large (larger than 11 toddlers or 18 preschoolers in a group), a lower level of play and intellectual development is observed (Ruopp et al., 1979; Smith & Connolly, 1980; Sylva et al., 1980). Altogether, then, there seems to be little evidence to support the hypothesis that the important difference between center care and home care is simply the presence of any other children or the amount of interaction with other children. Contact in centers with a greater diversity of peers, who vary in age, sex, race, and individual qualities, may, however, be a significant contributor. In the Chicago study, children who had the opportunity to interact with older peers in their classes were developmentally advanced (Clarke-Stewart, 1984).

Care Givers. The variety of different adults with whom the child has an opportunity to interact also may contribute to development. In the study in Chicago, the number of adults that children encountered in centers was, on the average, greater than in homes (see also Howes, 1983), and the number of adults so encountered was positively related to children's competence (Clarke-Stewart, 1984).

The adults encountered in homes and centers are also different in another way that is likely to affect children's development: Center care givers are more likely to have been trained in child development (Clarke-Stewart, 1984; Goelman & Pence, 1987). Care givers with more training are more interactive, helpful, talkative, and didactic Fosburg et al., 1980; Kinney, 1989; Lazar et al., 1977; Tyler & Dittman, 1980), and the children in their care make more cognitive gains (Clarke-Stewart, 1984; Ruopp et al., 1979). When preschool teachers are trained to use more cognitively demanding strategies in talking to the children, the children's achievement is advanced (Sigel, 1986).

Perhaps because of their training, center care givers compared to home care givers (whether mothers or sitters) are less directive and authoritarian, more likely to help, to explain, to make tasks into games, and to respond to children's initiation of play (Bryant, Harris, & Newton, 1980; Cochran, 1977; Hess, Price, Dickson, & Conroy, 1981; Howes & Rubenstein, 1981; Prescott, 1973; Rubenstein & Howes, 1979; Tyler & Dittman, 1980). Because authoritarian discipline is related to children's lower intellectual and social competence (see Clarke-Stewart & Apfel, 1979), this difference between homes and centers may be another part of the explanation for the observed difference between settings in children's development.

Physical Equipment and Materials. Another possibility is that different kinds of physical equipment and materials are provided in day care centers and homes, and that this contributes to the observed differences in children's development. Within center settings, high-level, cognitively challenging, and constructive activity with materials is more likely with building materials or during teacher-directed art or music activities (Pellegrini, 1984; Sylva et al., 1980)—and these kinds of opportunities are likely to be more frequent in centers than in homes. In homes, the opportunities are greater for tactile exploration with sand, water, dough, and soft objects, for cooking and "messing around" (Cochran, 1977; Prescott, 1973; Rubenstein & Howes, 1979), but academic and construction materials are less common. The physical materials and

equipment in centers, then, may encourage more frequent intellectual activities.

But the physical environment alone is unlikely to account for all the differences observed. Simply adding novel materials to preschool classrooms or having more varied materials accessible does not lead to cognitive gains; it is only in combination with teacher behavior that materials are related to children's advanced development (Busse, Ree, Gatride, & Alexander, 1972; Ruopp et al., 1979). Moreover, toys and materials are not likely to account for observed differences in social competence; advanced social behavior involving cooperation, conversation, and complex interaction with peers is more common with dolls, dress-ups, dramatic props, and social toys like checkers and pickup sticks than with puzzles, art, books, or intellectual exercises (e.g., Howes & Rubenstein, 1981; Smith & Connolly, 1980; Quilitch & Risley, 1973; Sylva et al., 1980), and the former materials are more common in homes than in centers (Rubenstein & Howes, 1979). Although physical materials may contribute to children's development, in themselves they cannot account for the differences in competence observed in different child care environments.

Program and Curriculum. Other qualitative differences between home and center care involve the kind of activities the programs offer. In centers, rules, lessons, and schedules are more likely to be fixed and based on the needs of the group rather than those of the individual child. Thus, children in centers must learn to recognize and adapt to "abstract," arbitrary, general rules and to take in information presented formally, whereas children at home operate in a concrete "hands-on" context, where rules and lessons, as such, are limited. Children who have been in day care center programs for some time have been found to display a more advanced understanding of social rules than newly enrolled children (Siegal & Storey, 1985). It has been suggested (Cole, Gay, Glick, & Sharp, 1971) that "schooling" in this institutional sense facilitates the development of advanced intellectual skills. It is also plausible to expect that it would foster the social, language, and test-taking skills and knowledge in which center children are advanced.

Another difference in program activities is the extent of educational instruction. Most home care providers, whether parents or paid professionals, do not have education as their primary goal. Nor do they follow a set curriculum. There are several hints that this may be an important distinction between home and center care. Children in more educationally oriented programs—ones with more prescribed educational activities such as lessons, guided play sessions, teaching of specific content, and more direct teacher instruction—perform better than those in less educationally oriented programs, for example. They do more constructive and complex play with materials and with peers, and score higher on intelligence and achievement tests (Clarke-Stewart, 1984; Ferri, 1980; Fowler, 1978; Johnson, Ershler, & Bell, 1980; Lazar et al., 1977; McCartney, 1984; Miller & Dyer, 1975; Sylva et al., 1980; Tizard, Philips, & Plewis, 1976; Winnett, Fuchs, Moffatt, & Nerviano, 1977). In correlational analyses, the more direct teaching children receive, the greater is their competence (Clarke-Stewart, 1984; McCartney, 1984). There may even be a match between the particular content taught and the outcomes exhibited (Fowler, 1978; Miller & Dyer, 1975). Most telling, when care in

day care homes was enriched by the experimental addition of a structured educational curriculum, the intellectual competence of the children was observed to improve to the level of children in day care centers (Goodman & Andrews, 1981). An educational curriculum, then, seems a likely candidate for contributing to the advanced cognitive development of children in centers.

Qualitative differences between the kinds of teaching that occur in center environments and in home environments may also be involved. In homes, "teaching" is likely to be casual and informal; children have more free time and time alone, and they learn from exploring household objects, helping the care giver, performing real-life tasks, and seeing real live role models—not from explicit lessons (Cochran, 1977; Prescott, 1973; Tyler & Dittman, 1980). Conversations are longer, include more complex utterances, offer children more opportunities to ask questions and express opinions, and are more "inductive" (Cochran, 1977; Fiene, 1973; Prescott, 1973; Tizard et al., 1980; Tyler & Dittman, 1980)—e.g., "What would you like for lunch?" might lead to a long discussion about individuals' food preferences, the time it takes to prepare food, what foods are nutritious, and so on. In centers, conversations are more likely to be "deductive" and convergent, taking the form of teacher questions and child answers (Cochran, 1977; Fiene, 1973; Prescott, 1973; Tyler & Dittman, 1980; Wittmer & Honig, 1989). The parallel question in a center would be "What are we having for lunch today?" and it might lead to a discussion of peas as vegetables, other vegetables the child can name, what colors and sizes they are, and so on. It seems reasonable that the kinds of conversations occurring in ceners are the kind that would prepare children to do well on standardized tests of intelligence. They may not be designed to enhance practical problem solving or sensitivity to human needs, but they are directed toward the kinds of school skills that are assessed in tests of intellectual development.

In sum, it appears that differences in the kinds of attention and stimulation in home and center environments account for many of the differences observed in children's competence. In particular, it seems likely that the educational emphasis and nonauthoritarian style of center care givers, combined with the availability of stimulating educational materials, the presence of a variety of adults and other children, and the influence of institutional regulations, create a school-like environment that facilitates the development of social skills and intellectual competence as measured by standardized tests.

Differences in Quality of Stimulation

It has been suggested recently (e.g., Lamb et al., 1988), however, that observed differences in children's development in centers and homes are the result of differences in the quality of child care rather than the type of child care environment. Lamb and his associates found that the social skills of preschool children in Sweden were related to the observed quality of their experiences in child care rather than to whether the children were in home care or centers. In that study, the day care centers they observed were of lower quality than the homes (more negative events occurred). Similarly, in another study, conducted in England, in which children in centers did not show advanced intellectual development, the centers

observed were of generally poor quality (Melhuish, 1990). It makes sense that children would do better in a high-quality home than in a poor quality center. But in the real world of child care in America, or at least in the centers and homes that have been the targets of study, it seems likely that centers, on the average, offer care and stimulation of higher quality than do homes, on the average. Thus, perhaps quality and type of care are confounded. Differences between children in different child care environments are most marked when the centers are of high quality and/or the children come from disadvantaged families (Andersson, 1989; Fowler & Khan, 1974; Robinson & Robinson, 1971; Scarr et al., 1988). Differences are least when the homes are of high quality. For example, in research by Goelman and Pence (1987), although the competence of children in *unregulated* day care homes in Canada was inferior to that of children in centers, the competence of children in *regulated* homes was equivalent.

We do not have a clear answer to the question of whether the differences observed between children in homes and in centers are due to differences in overall quality or to differences in the specific kinds of stimulation each offers. Center environments may confer unique benefits. Certain things may be easier to accomplish in centers. There may be subtle differences between environments that are glossed over by an emphasis on global quality. Or it may be that, although typical practice in centers is often more educational than typical practice in homes, this is not a *necessary* difference between the two environments. Untangling these possibilities remains a task for future research.

Preexisting Differences in Children and Families

Before concluding that children's competence is solely the result of differences in their child care experiences, however, the contributions of the family and of the child to the advanced competence of children in center care must be examined. Although socioeconomic differences had been statistically controlled in the reported analyses of the Chicago study, there is always the possibility that family variables contribute to the observed pattern of advanced development in center children.

Parents of children in centers may provide more stimulation and education for their children than do parents of children in home care. In well-controlled studies in which center and home care families have been matched (e.g., on SES), there are generally large areas of overlap where no differences between the groups of parents are observed. But when differences are observed, they are in the direction of greater verbal stimulation and play, and less authoritarian discipline for mothers using center care than for mothers using only home care (Garber & Heber, 1980; Clarke-Stewart, 1984; Ramey et al., 1979; Rubenstein et al., 1981)....

The difference is less likely to be the result of changes in the parents' behavior as a result of learning about child development from center staff. Although one study did show that parents whose children were attending a model day care center program, in which they were encouraged to visit and participate, became more child centered and more like the teachers in the program (less likely to ignore, scold, refuse, or coax the child) than a matched sample of parents whose children were not in the program (Edwards, Logue, Loehr, & Roth, 1985), in most centers little communication between parents and teachers occurs spontaneously, and when it does, it does not lead to more agreement (Powell, 1978). Moreover, even when a formal parent education component is part of the day care program, this does not ensure that parents' behavior will change (e.g., Fowler, 1978; Lally & Honig, 1977). It is unlikely, therefore, that parent education at the center is a strong contributor to the difference observed between parents using center care and home care.

There is, however, always the possibility that something in the children themselves who are placed in centers accounts for their advanced development. Perhaps they are selected for center care (by staff or by parents) because they are already more competent. This possibility cannot be ruled out. It is a fact that many centers accept only children who are toilet trained. This would force mothers who must work to use day care homes or babysitters for care of less mature toddlers. But, once the child is toilet trained, center staff would be unlikely to be able to select on the basis of maturity or competence without more screening than is commonly done. Moreover, advanced development in center children has also been observed in studies where children were matched on IQ at the beginning of their child care experience (Fowler, 1978) or in which self-selection was eliminated by randomly assigning children to center or home care (Garber & Heber, 1980; Ramey et al., 1983). While self-selection may magnify the differences in children's development, then, it is unlikely to be the most significant contributor.

CONCLUSIONS AND IMPLICATIONS FOR FUTURE RESEARCH

In sum, preschool children who have spent some time in center child care are, on the average, socially and intellectually advanced over their peers who have only been at home. This advanced development is likely to arise from a combination of factors, not a single critical cause. Experiences at home, including those initiated or evoked by the child, may contribute to the advanced development of children whose parents have chosen to put them in centers. Even more important, the advanced development of children in centers is likely to be the result of lessons to foster social and intellectual skills, instructions in recognizing and following rules, opportunities to practice skills and follow rules with a variety of peers and nonparental adults, and encouragement of independence and self-direction by trained and nonauthoritarian teachers. The experiences of children in centers are substantially different from those children are likely to have at home —with parents, babysitters, or day care home providers. Home is where the heart is, but the head is influenced by more than home experiences. A home is not a school. Center environments differ qualitatively from home environments, and the differences in the kinds of experience they offer are likely to have significant effects on the development of children growing up in them.

The test of just how significant these effects are remains for future researchers.

In the past, researchers took an overly simple approach to defining and assessing child care, as if "child care" were a single uniform condition rather than an enormous variety of environments, programs, and settings (see Clarke-Stewart & Fein, 1983). They did not study the full range of home and center care for the whole range of children. They did not observe and compare children's experiences in home and center environments. They did not analyze the relations between child care and family factors. They sidestepped the issues of causal direction and extent. They did not allow for the further complicating factor that children often move from one type of child care setting to a different type.

In order to investigate more fully the effects of child care on children's development, researchers must overcome these limitations. They must examine in detail the nature of children's experiences in different kinds of child care environments, paying particular attention to the educational content of those experiences, and attempting to identify intellectually and socially valuable components. They then should probe the implications of their descriptive observations experimentally, by controlling the components of programs in centers and by supplementing the components of experiences in homes. Only by systematically enriching home care with the educationally focused opportunities more typically found in centers, only by unconfounding quality and type of care, will we find out with any degree of certainty whether a home cannot be a school.

POSTSCRIPT

Does Maternal Employment Have a Negative Effect on Infant Development?

Belsky and Eggebeen found that children who were four to six years old scored more poorly on a composite measure of adjustment if their mothers worked during the first three years of their lives. Children with early and extensive maternal employment were more noncompliant than their counterparts whose mothers did not work during their infancy. In this study, mothers who were not working were more likely to be in a low-income group, whereas mothers who worked were likely to be from a middle-income group. The authors concluded that the quality and type of nonparental care that children received (which was not addressed in this study) could account for the effects that maternal employment had on the children.

Clarke-Stewart studied two- to four-year-olds who were in six different types of child care settings. She concluded that children who spend some amount of time in child care settings are usually more advanced socially and intellectually than children who stay at home with their mother or some other caregiver. Children in centers have a double advantage of learning from the home as well as from another setting. Children who stay at home for care, regardless of who the caregiver is, have only one setting from which to learn.

Although Belsky and Eggebeen's research promotes mothers staying home with infants and Clarke-Stewart supports the idea that children can flourish in nonmaternal settings, both selections point to the need to study the quality of early child care and its effects on child development. The National Institute of Child Health and Human Development recently released its first results from an extensive study on the quality of early child care on children. The report concluded that more hours of child care made for less sensitive and engaged mother-child interactions for the first three years, but the amount of child care was not related to children's cognitive and language development. Positive caregiving, especially language stimulation, was related to higher scores on cognitive and language tests for young children. Whether or not the mother worked was not a predictor of children's intellectual development, but the quality of the caregiver's verbal interaction and stimulation was predictive of a more favorable outcome.

Although researchers agree that maternal employment studies need to examine the interaction of several variables, such as the quality of child care, they do not agree on which sets of variables combine to give an accurate picture of how a mother's employment affects children. A balanced perspective on maternal employment effects can be found in *Working Women and Their Families* by Jacqueline Lerner (Sage Publications, 1994).

Attitudes toward maternal employment effects have been altered by societal changes such as time-saving appliances (for example, the dishwasher, automatic washer and dryer, self-cleaning oven, and microwave), drive-through food eateries, the women's liberation movement, the election of more women to political office, and the economic necessity for single as well as both parents to work.

With the current political discussions regarding welfare reform, it is more important than ever to examine maternal employment and its effects in a critical, realistic light. If single welfare mothers are required to work, how will their children fare? Does the research tell us enough about the need for mothers to be with their children in their first three years of life? Are child care centers an appropriate option for the working mother? Or should mothers stay home with their young children and delay entrance to the workforce?

SUGGESTED READINGS

Bogenschneider, K., & Steinberg, L. (1994, January). Maternal employment and adolescents' academic achievement: A developmental analysis. *Sociology of Education, 67*, 60–77.

Goldman, K. W. (1993). *My mother worked and I turned out ok.* New York: Garnet Press.

Greenberger, E., & O'Neil, R. (1992). Maternal employment and perceptions of young children: Bronfenbrenner et al. revisited. *Child Development, 63*, 431–448.

Greenstein, T. N. (1993, September). Maternal employment and child behavioral outcomes: A household economics analysis. *Journal of Family Issues, 14*, 323–354.

ISSUE 2

Are Gender Differences Rooted in the Brain?

YES: Doreen Kimura, from "Sex Differences in the Brain," *Scientific American* (September 1992)

NO: Carol Tavris, from *The Mismeasure of Woman* (Simon and Schuster, 1992)

ISSUE SUMMARY

YES: Doreen Kimura, a neuropsychologist, believes that biological differences at birth in the male and female brain explain the subsequent differences in behavior between boys and girls.

NO: Carol Tavris, a social psychologist, concludes that there is no scientific evidence that the brains of males and females are different.

Nature versus nurture? Heredity or environment? Biology or behavior? The debate over how to explain human behavior has been going on for years. Generally speaking, researchers have concluded that the question is *not* whether environment or heredity explain behavior. Instead, the question has become To what extent is each responsible for behavior? In the recent past, it was thought that environment had more to do with human behavior than genetics. Currently, many studies are concluding that heredity plays a larger role in development than environment.

Classic studies conducted to get answers to the nature versus nurture debate have used identical twins and adopted children for the research. If identical twins, who have the same genetic makeup, are reared apart, will they have similar behavior or personality traits? If so, researchers say, then heredity must account for behavior. Conversely, if identical twins are reared together but still have different personalities or cognitive abilities, then the implication is that environment accounts for behavior. Adoption studies operate on a similar premise. Children from impoverished biological parents who were adopted by middle-class families have been studied to determine the effects that environment had on their development.

Researchers have studied a number of personality traits, diseases, and abilities in their attempts to determine the role that genetics plays in shaping human behavior. For example, there is evidence that shyness or being inhibited has a biological basis. And there have been some reports suggesting that alcoholism may be heritable. But researchers caution that biology is not destiny. Shy children brought up in supportive homes could well overcome their predisposition to shyness. And there may be social, psychological, and economic influences that shape a person's drinking to a greater extent than any genetic predisposition.

In the following debate, researcher Doreen Kimura argues that sex hormones affect the brain prenatally and cause it to become organized differently for each gender. But Carol Tavris, a well-known social psychologist, attacks the studies that conclude that the brain is different for males and females. She argues that some scientists ignore the facts about brain research in their eagerness to prove that men are intellectually superior to women.

YES

Doreen Kimura

SEX DIFFERENCES IN THE BRAIN

Women and men differ not only in physical attributes and reproductive function but also in the way in which they solve intellectual problems. It has been fashionable to insist that these differences are minimal, the consequence of variations in experience during development. The bulk of the evidence suggests, however, that the effects of sex hormones on brain organization occur so early in life that from the start the environment is acting on differently wired brains in girls and boys. Such differences make it almost impossible to evaluate the effects of experience independent of physiological predisposition.

Behavioral, neurological and endocrinologic studies have elucidated the processes giving rise to sex differences in the brain. As a result, aspects of the physiological basis for these variations have in recent years become clearer. In addition, studies of the effects of hormones on brain function throughout life suggest that the evolutionary pressures directing differences nevertheless allow for a degree of flexibility in cognitive ability between the sexes.

* * *

Major sex differences in intellectual function seem to lie in patterns of ability rather than in overall level of intelligence (IQ). We are all aware that people have different intellectual strengths. Some are especially good with words, others at using objects—for instance, at constructing or fixing things. In the same fashion, two individuals may have the same overall intelligence but have varying patterns of ability.

Men, on average, perform better than women on certain spatial tasks. In particular, men have an advantage in tests that require the subject to imagine rotating an object or manipulating it in some other way. They outperform women in mathematical reasoning tests and in navigating their way through a route. Further, men are more accurate in tests of target-directed motor skills —that is, in guiding or intercepting projectiles.

Women tend to be better than men at rapidly identifying matching items, a skill called perceptual speed. They have greater verbal fluency, including the ability to find words that begin with a specific letter or fulfill some other constraint. Women also outperform men in arithmetic calculation and in

From Doreen Kimura, "Sex Differences in the Brain," *Scientific American* (September 1992). Copyright © 1992 by Scientific American, Inc. All rights reserved. Reprinted by permission.

ecalling landmarks from a route. Moreover, women are faster at certain precision manual tasks, such as placing pegs in designated holes on a board.

Although some investigators have reported that sex differences in problem solving do not appear until after puberty, Diane Lunn, working in my laboratory at the University of Western Ontario, and have found three-year-old boys to be better at targeting than girls of the same age. Moreover, Neil V. Watson, when in my laboratory, showed that the extent of experience playing sports does not account for the sex difference in targeting found in young adults. Kimberly A. Kerns, working with Sheri A. Berenbaum of the University of Chicago, has found that sex differences in spatial rotation performance are present before puberty.

Differences in route learning have been systematically studied in adults in laboratory situations. For instance, Liisa Galea in my department studied undergraduates who followed a route on a tabletop map. Men learned the route in fewer trials and made fewer errors than did women. But once learning was complete, women remembered more of the landmarks than did men. These results, and those of other researchers, raise the possibility that women tend to use landmarks as a strategy to orient themselves in everyday life. The prevailing strategies used by males have not yet been clearly established, although they must relate to spatial ability.

Marion Eals and Irwin Silverman of York University studied another function that may be related to landmark memory. The researchers tested the ability of individuals to recall objects and their locations within a confined space—such as in a room or on a tabletop. Women were better able to remember whether an item had been displaced or not. In addition, in my laboratory, we measured the accuracy of object location: subjects were shown an array of objects and were later asked to replace them in their exact positions. Women did so more accurately than did men.

It is important to place the differences described above in context: some are slight, some are quite large. Because men and women overlap enormously on many cognitive tests that show average sex differences, researchers use variations within each group as a tool to gauge the differences between groups. Imagine, for instance, that on one test the average score is 105 for women and 100 for men. If the scores for women ranged from 100 to 110 and for men from 95 to 105, the difference would be more impressive than if the women's scores ranged from 50 to 150 and the men's from 45 to 145. In the latter case, the overlap in scores would be much greater.

One measure of the variation of scores within a group is the standard deviation. To compare the magnitude of a sex difference across several distinct tasks, the difference between groups is divided by the standard deviation. The resulting number is called the effect size. Effect sizes below 0.5 are generally considered small. Based on my data, for instance, there are typically no differences between the sexes on tests of vocabulary (effect size 0.02), nonverbal reasoning (0.03) and verbal reasoning (0.17).

On tests in which subjects match pictures, find words that begin with similar letters or show ideational fluency—such as naming objects that are white or red—the effect sizes are somewhat larger: 0.25, 0.22 and 0.38, respectively. As discussed above, women tend to outperform men on these tasks. Researchers have reported the largest effect sizes for certain tests measuring spatial rotation (effect size 0.7) and targeting accuracy (0.75). The large effect size in these tests means there are many more men at the high end of the score distribution.

*　*　*

Since, with the exception of the sex chromosomes, men and women share genetic material, how do such differences come about? Differing patterns of ability between men and women most probably reflect different hormonal influences on their developing brains. Early in life the action of estrogens and androgens (male hormones chief of which is testosterone) establishes sexual differentiation. In mammals, including humans, the organism has the potential to be male or female. If a Y chromosome is present, testes or male gonads form. This development is the critical first step toward becoming a male. If the gonads do not produce male hormones or if for some reason the hormones cannot act on the tissue, the default form of the organism is female.

Once testes are formed, they produce two substances that bring about the development of a male. Testosterone causes masculinization by promoting the male, or Wolffian, set of ducts and, indirectly through conversion to dihydrotestosterone, the external appearance of scrotum and penis. The Müllerian regression factor causes the female, or Müllerian, set of ducts to regress. If anything goes wrong at any stage of the process, the individual may be incompletely masculinized.

Not only do sex hormones achieve the transformation of the genitals into male organs, but they also organize corresponding male behaviors early in life. Since we cannot manipulate the hormonal environment in humans, we owe much of what we know about the details of behavioral determination to studies in other animals. Again, the intrinsic tendency, according to studies by Robert W. Goy of the University of Wisconsin, is to develop the female pattern that occurs in the absence of masculinizing hormonal influence.

If a rodent with functional male genitals is deprived of androgens immediately after birth (either by castration or by the administration of a compound that blocks androgens), male sexual behavior, such as mounting, will be reduced. Instead female sexual behavior, such as lordosis (arching of the back), will be enhanced in adulthood. Similarly, if androgens are administered to a female directly after birth, she displays more male sexual behavior and less female behavior in adulthood.

Bruce S. McEwen and his co-workers at the Rockefeller University have shown that, in the rat, the two processes of defeminization and masculinization require somewhat different biochemical changes. These events also occur at somewhat different times. Testosterone can be converted to either estrogen (usually considered a female hormone) or dihydrotestosterone. Defeminization takes place primarily after birth in rats and is mediated by estrogen, whereas masculinization involves both dihydrotestosterone and estrogen and occurs for the most part before birth rather than after, according to studies by McEwen. A substance called alpha-fetoprotein may protect female brains from the masculinizing effects of their estrogen.

The area in the brain that organizes female and male reproductive behavior is the hypothalamus. This tiny structure at the base of the brain connects to the pituitary, the master endocrine gland. Roger A. Gorski and his colleagues at the University of California at Los Angeles have shown that a region of the pre-optic area of the hypothalamus is visibly larger in male rats than in females. The size increment in males is promoted by the presence of androgens in the immediate postnatal, and to some extent prenatal, period. Laura S. Allen in Gorski's laboratory has found a similar sex difference in the human brain.

Other preliminary but intriguing studies suggest that sexual behavior may reflect further anatomic differences. In 1991 Simon LeVay of the Salk Institute for Biological Studies in San Diego reported that one of the brain regions that is usually larger in human males than in females—an interstitial nucleus of the anterior hypothalamus—is smaller in homosexual than in heterosexual men. LeVay points out that this finding supports suggestions that sexual preference has a biological substrate.

Homosexual and heterosexual men may also perform differently on cognitive tests. Brian A. Gladue of North Dakota State University and Geoff D. Sanders of City of London Polytechnic report that homosexual men perform less well on several spatial tasks than do heterosexual men. In a recent study in my laboratory, Jeff Hall found that homosexual men had lower scores on targeting tasks than did heterosexual men; however, they were superior in ideational fluency—listing things that were a particular color.

This exciting field of research is just starting, and it is crucial that investigators consider the degree to which differences in life-style contribute to group differences. One should also keep in mind that results concerning group differences constitute a general statistical statement; they establish a mean from which any individual may differ. Such studies are potentially a rich source of information on the physiological basis for cognitive patterns.

* * *

The lifelong effects of early exposure to sex hormones are characterized as organizational, because they appear to alter brain function permanently during a critical period. Administering the same hormones at later stages has no such effect. The hormonal effects are not limited to sexual or reproductive behaviors: they appear to extend to all known behaviors in which males and females differ. They seem to govern problem solving, aggression and the tendency to engage in rough-and-tumble play—the boisterous body contact that young males of some mammalian species display. For example, Michael J. Meaney of McGill University finds that dihydrotestosterone, working through a structure called the amygdala rather than through the hypothalamus, gives rise to the play-fighting behavior of juvenile male rodents.

Male and female rats have also been found to solve problems differently. Christina L. Williams of Barnard College has shown that female rats have a greater tendency to use landmarks in spatial learning tasks—as it appears women do. In Williams's experiment, female rats used landmark cues, such as pictures on the wall, in preference to geometric cues, such as angles and the shape of the room. If no landmarks were available, however, females used geometric cues. In contrast, males did not use landmarks at all, preferring geometric cues almost exclusively.

Interestingly, hormonal manipulation during the critical period can alter these behaviors. Depriving newborn males of testosterone by castrating them or administering estrogen to newborn females results in a complete reversal of sex-typed behaviors in the adult animals. (As mentioned above, estrogen can have a masculinizing effect during brain development.) Treated females behave like males, and treated males behave like females.

Natural selection for reproductive advantage could account for the evolution of such navigational differences. Steven J. C. Gaulin and Randall W. FitzGerald of the University of Pittsburgh have suggested that in species of voles in which a male mates with several females rather than with just one, the range he must traverse is greater. Therefore, navigational ability seems critical to reproductive success. Indeed, Gaulin and FitzGerald found sex differences in laboratory maze learning only in voles that were polygynous, such as the meadow vole, not in monogamous species, such as the prairie vole.

Again, behavioral differences may parallel structural ones. Lucia F. Jacobs in Gaulin's laboratory has discovered that the hippocampus—a region thought to be involved in spatial learning in both birds and mammals—is larger in male polygynous voles than in females. At present, there are no data on possible sex differences in hippocampal size in human subjects.

Evidence of the influence of sex hormones on adult behavior is less direct in humans than in other animals. Researchers are instead guided by what may be parallels in other species and by spontaneously occurring exceptions to the norm in humans.

One of the most compelling areas of evidence comes from studies of girls exposed to excess androgens in the prenatal or neonatal stage. The production of abnormally large quantities of adrenal androgens can occur because of a genetic defect called congenital adrenal hyperplasia (CAH). Before the 1970s, a similar condition also unexpectedly appeared when pregnant women took various synthetic steroids. Although the consequent masculinization of the genitals can be corrected early in life and drug therapy can stop the overproduction of androgens, effects of prenatal exposure on the brain cannot be reversed.

Studies by researchers such as Anke A. Ehrhardt of Columbia University and June M. Reinisch of the Kinsey Institute have found that girls with excess exposure to androgens grow up to be more tomboyish and aggressive than their unaffected sisters. This conclusion was based sometimes on interviews with subjects and mothers, on teachers' ratings and on questionnaires administered to the girls themselves. When ratings are used in such studies, it can be difficult to rule out the influence of expectation either on the part of an adult who knows the girls' history or on the part of the girls themselves.

Therefore, the objective observations of Berenbaum are important and convincing. She and Melissa Hines of the University of California at Los Angeles observed the play behavior of CAH-affected girls and compared it with that of their male and female siblings. Given a choice of transportation and construction toys, dolls and kitchen supplies or books and board games, the CAH girls preferred the more typically masculine toys—for example, they played with cars for the same amount of time that normal boys did. Both the CAH girls and the boys differed from unaffected girls in their patterns of choice. Because there is every reason to think that parents would be at least as likely to encourage feminine preferences in their CAH daughters as in their unaffected daughters, these findings suggest that the toy preferences were actually altered in some way by the early hormonal environment.

Spatial abilities that are typically better in males are also enhanced in CAH girls. Susan M. Resnick, now at the National Institute on Aging, and Berenbaum and their colleagues reported that affected girls were superior to their unaffected sisters in a spatial manipulation test, two spatial rotation tests and a disembedding test—that is, the discovery of a simple figure hidden within a more complex one. All these tasks are usually done better by males. No differences existed between the two groups on other perceptual or verbal tasks or on a reasoning task.

* * *

Studies such as these suggest that the higher the androgen levels, the better the spatial performance. But this does not seem to be the case. In 1983 Valerie J. Shute, when at the University of California at Santa Barbara, suggested that the relation between levels of androgens and some spatial capabilities might be nonlinear. In other words, spatial ability might not increase as the amount of androgen increases. Shute measured androgens in blood taken from male and female students and divided each into high- and low-androgen groups. All fell within the normal range for each sex (androgens are present in females but in very low levels). She found that in women, the high-androgen subjects were better at the spatial tests. In men the reverse was true: low-androgen men performed better.

Catherine Couchie and I recently conducted a study along similar lines by measuring testosterone in saliva. We added tests for two other kinds of abilities: mathematical reasoning and perceptual speed. Our results on the spatial tests were very similar to Shute's: low-testosterone men were superior to high-testosterone men, but high-testosterone women surpassed low-testosterone women. Such findings suggest some optimum level of androgen for maximal spatial ability. This level may fall in the low male range.

No correlation was found between testosterone levels and performance on perceptual speed tests. On mathematical reasoning, however, the results were similar to those of spatial ability tests for men: low-androgen men tested higher, but there was no obvious relation in women.

Such findings are consistent with the suggestion by Camilla P. Benbow of Iowa State University that high mathematical ability has a significant biological determinant. Benbow and her colleagues have reported consistent sex differences in mathematical reasoning ability favoring males. These differences are especially sharp at the upper end of the distribution, where males outnumber females 13 to one. Benbow argues that these differences are not readily explained by socialization.

It is important to keep in mind that the relation between natural hormonal levels and problem solving is based on correlational data. Some form of connection between the two measures exists, but how this association is determined or what its causal basis may be is unknown. Little is currently understood about the relation between adult levels of hormones and those in early life, when abilities appear to be organized in the nervous system. We have a lot to learn about the precise mechanisms underlying cognitive patterns in people.

Another approach to probing differences between male and female brains is to examine and compare the functions of particular brain systems. One noninvasive way to accomplish this goal is to study people who have experienced damage to a specific brain region. Such studies indicate that the left half of the brain in most people is critical for speech, the right for certain perceptual and spatial functions.

It is widely assumed by many researchers studying sex differences that the two hemispheres are more asymmetrically organized for speech and spatial functions in men than in women. This idea comes from several sources. Parts of the corpus callosum, a major neural system connecting the two hemispheres, may be more extensive in women; perceptual techniques that probe brain asymmetry in normal-functioning people sometimes show smaller asymmetries in women than in men, and damage to one brain hemisphere sometimes has a lesser effect in women than the comparable injury has in men.

In 1982 Marie-Christine de Lacoste, now at the Yale University School of Medicine, and Ralph L. Holloway of Columbia University reported that the back part of the corpus callosum, an area called the splenium, was larger in women than in men. This finding has subsequently been both refuted and confirmed. Variations in the shape of the corpus callosum that may occur as an individual ages as well as different methods of measurement may produce some of the disagreements. Most recently,

Allen and Gorski found the same sex-related size difference in the splenium.

The interest in the corpus callosum arises from the assumption that its size may indicate the number of fibers connecting the two hemispheres. If more connecting fibers existed in one sex, the implication would be that in that sex the hemispheres communicate more fully. Although sex hormones can alter callosal size in rats, as Victor H. Denenberg and his associates at the University of Connecticut have demonstrated, it is unclear whether the actual number of fibers differs between the sexes. Moreover, sex differences in cognitive function have yet to be related to a difference in callosal size. New ways of imaging the brain in living humans will undoubtedly increase knowledge in this respect.

The view that a male brain is functionally more asymmetric than a female brain is long-standing. Albert M. Galaburda of Beth Israel Hospital in Boston and the late Norman Geschwind of Harvard Medical School proposed that androgens increased the functional potency of the right hemisphere. In 1981 Marian C. Diamond of the University of California at Berkeley found that the right cortex is thicker than the left in male rats but not in females. Jane Stewart of Concordia University in Montreal, working with Bryan E. Kolb of the University of Lethbridge in Alberta, recently pinpointed early hormonal influences on this asymmetry: androgens appear to suppress left cortex growth.

Last year de Lacoste and her colleagues reported a similar pattern in human fetuses. They found the right cortex was thicker than the left in males. Thus, there appear to be some anatomic reasons for believing that the two hemispheres might not be equally asymmetric in men and women.

Despite this expectation, the evidence in favor of it is meager and conflicting, which suggests that the most striking sex differences in brain organization may not be related to asymmetry. For example, if overall differences between men and women in spatial ability were related to differing right hemispheric dependence for such functions, then damage to the right hemisphere would perhaps have a more devastating effect on spatial performance in men.

My laboratory has recently studied the ability of patients with damage to one hemisphere of the brain to rotate certain objects mentally. In one test, a series of line drawings of either a left or a right gloved hand is presented in various orientations. The patient indicates the hand being depicted by simply pointing to one of two stuffed gloves that are constantly present.

The second test uses two three-dimensional blocklike figures that are mirror images of one another. Both figures are present throughout the test. The patient is given a series of photographs of these objects in various orientations, and he or she must place each picture in front of the object it depicts (These nonverbal procedures are employed so that patients with speech disorders can be tested.)

As expected, damage to the right hemisphere resulted in lower scores for both sexes on these tests than did damage to the left hemisphere. Also as anticipated, women did less well than men on the block spatial rotation test. Surprisingly, however, damage to the right hemisphere had no greater effect in men than in women. Women were at least as affected as men by damage to the right hemisphere. This result suggests that the normal differences between men and women on such rotational tests are not the result of differential dependence on the right hemisphere. Some other brain systems must be mediating the higher performance by men.

Parallel suggestions of greater asymmetry in men regarding speech have rested on the fact that the incidence of aphasias, or speech disorders, are higher in men than in women after damage to the left hemisphere. Therefore, some researchers have found it reasonable to conclude that speech must be more bilaterally organized in women. There is, however, a problem with this conclusion. During my 20 years of experience with patients, aphasia has not been disproportionately present in women with right hemispheric damage.

* * *

In searching for an explanation, I discovered another striking difference between men and women in brain organization for speech and related motor function. Women are more likely than men to suffer aphasia when the front part of the brain is damaged. Because restricted damage within a hemisphere more frequently affects the posterior than the anterior area in both men and women, this differential dependence may explain why women incur aphasia less often than do men. Speech functions are thus less likely to be affected in women not because speech is more bilaterally organized in women but because the critical area is less often affected.

A similar pattern emerges in studies of the control of hand movements, which are programmed by the left hemisphere. Apraxia, or difficulty in selecting appropriate hand movements, is very common after left hemispheric damage. It is also strongly associated with difficulty in organizing speech. In fact, the critical functions that depend on the left hemisphere may relate not to language per se but to organization of the complex oral and manual movements on which human communication systems depend. Studies of patients with left hemispheric damage have revealed that such motor selection relies on anterior systems in women but on posterior systems in men.

The synaptic proximity of women's anterior motor selection system (or "praxis system") to the motor cortex directly behind it may enhance fine-motor skills. In contrast, men's motor skills appear to emphasize targeting or directing movements toward external space—some distance away from the self. There may be advantages to such motor skills when they are closely meshed with visual input to the brain, which lies in the posterior region.

Women's dependence on the anterior region is detectable even when tests involve using visual guidance—for instance, when subjects must build patterns with blocks by following a visual model. In studying such a complex task, it is possible to compare the effects of damage to the anterior and posterior regions of both hemispheres because performance is affected by damage to either hemisphere. Again, women prove more affected by damage to the anterior region of the right hemisphere than by posterior damage. Men tend to display the reverse pattern.

Although I have not found evidence of sex differences in functional brain asymmetry with regard to basic speech, motor selection or spatial rotation ability, I have found slight differences in more abstract verbal tasks. Scores on a vocabulary test, for instance, were affected by damage to either hemisphere in women, but such scores were affected only by left-sided injury in men. This finding suggests that in reviewing the meanings of words, women use the hemispheres more equally than do men.

In contrast, the incidence of non-right-handedness, which is presumably related to lesser left hemispheric dependence, is higher in men than in women. Even among the right-handers, Marion Annett, now at the University of Leicester in the U.K., has reported that women are more right-handed than men—that is, they favor their right hand even more than do right-handed men. It may well be, then, that sex differences in asymmetry vary with the particular function being studied and that it is not always the same sex that is more asymmetric.

Taken altogether, the evidence suggests that men's and women's brains are organized along different lines from very early in life. During development, sex hormones direct such differentiation. Similar mechanisms probably operate to produce variation within sexes, since there is a relation between levels of certain hormones and cognitive makeup in adulthood.

* * *

One of the most intriguing findings is that cognitive patterns may remain sensitive to hormonal fluctuations throughout life. Elizabeth Hampson of the University of Western Ontario showed that the performance of women on certain tasks changed throughout the menstrual cycle as levels of estrogen went up or down. High levels of the hormone were associated not only with relatively depressed spatial ability but also with enhanced articulatory and motor capability.

In addition, I have observed seasonal fluctuations in spatial ability in men. Their performance is improved in the spring when testosterone levels are lower. Whether these intellectual fluctuations are of any adaptive significance or merely represent ripples on a stable baseline remains to be determined.

To understand human intellectual functions, including how groups may differ in such functions, we need to look beyond the demands of modern life. We did not undergo natural selection for reading or for operating computers. It seems clear that the sex differences in cognitive patterns arose because they proved evolutionarily advantageous. And their adaptive significance probably rests in the distant past. The organization of the human brain was determined over many generations by natural selection. As studies of fossil skulls have shown, our brains are essentially like those of our ancestors of 50,000 or more years ago.

For the thousands of years during which our brain characteristics evolved, humans lived in relatively small groups of hunter-gatherers. The division of labor between the sexes in such a society probably was quite marked, as it is in existing hunter-gatherer societies. Men were responsible for hunting large game, which often required long-distance travel. They were also responsible for defending the group against predators and enemies and for the shaping and use of weapons. Women most probably gathered food near the camp, tended the home, prepared food and clothing and cared for children.

Such specializations would put different selection pressures on men and women. Men would require long-distance route-finding ability so they could recognize a geographic array from varying orientations. They would also need targeting skills. Women would require short-range navigation, perhaps using landmarks, fine-motor capabilities carried on within a circumscribed space, and perceptual discrimination sensitive to small changes in the environment or in children's appearance or behavior.

The finding of consistent and, in some cases, quite substantial sex differences suggests that men and women may have different occupational interests and capabilities, independent of societal influences. I would not expect, for example, that men and women would necessarily be equally represented in activities or professions that emphasize spatial or math skills, such as engineering or physics. But I might expect more women in medical diagnostic fields where perceptual skills are important. So that even though any one individual might have the capacity to be in a "nontypical" field, the sex proportions as a whole may vary.

NO

Carol Tavris

MEASURING UP

BRAIN: DISSECTING THE DIFFERENCES

In recent years the sexiest body part, far and away, has become the brain. Magazines with cover stories on the brain fly off the newsstands, and countless seminars, tapes, books, and classes teach people how to use "all" of their brains. New technologies, such as PET scans, produce gorgeous photographs of the brain at work and play. Weekly we hear new discoveries about this miraculous organ, and it seems that scientists will soon be able to pinpoint the very neuron, the very neurotransmitter, responsible for joy, sadness, rage, and suffering. At last we will know the reasons for all the differences between women and men that fascinate and infuriate, such as why men won't stop to ask directions and why women won't stop asking men what they are feeling.

In all this excitement, it seems curmudgeonly to sound words of caution, but the history of brain research does not exactly reveal a noble and impartial quest for truth, particularly on sensitive matters such as sex and race differences. Typically, when scientists haven't found the differences they were seeking, they haven't abandoned the goal or their belief that such differences exist; they just moved to another part of the anatomy or a different corner of the brain.

A century ago, for example, scientists tried to prove that women had smaller brains than men did, which accounted for women's alleged intellectual failings and emotional weaknesses. Dozens of studies purported to show that men had larger brains, making them smarter than women. When scientists realized that men's greater height and weight offset their brain-size advantage, however, they dropped this line of research like a shot. The scientists next tried to argue that women had smaller frontal lobes and larger parietal lobes than men did, another brain pattern thought to account for women's intellectual inferiority. Then it was reported that the parietal lobes might be associated with intellect. Panic in the labs—until anatomists suddenly found that women's parietal lobes were *smaller* than they had originally believed. Wherever they looked, scientists conveniently found evidence of

From Carol Tavris, *The Mismeasure of Woman* (Simon & Schuster, 1992). Copyright © 1992 by Carol Tavris. Reprinted by permission of Simon & Schuster, Inc. Notes omitted.

female inferiority, as Gustave Le Bon, a Parisian, wrote in 1879:

> In the most intelligent races, as among the Parisians, there are a large number of women whose brains are closer in size to those of gorillas than to the most developed male brains. This inferiority is so obvious that no one can contest it for a moment; only its degree is worth discussion.

We look back with amusement at the obvious biases of research a century ago, research designed to prove the obvious inferiority of women and minorities (and non-Parisians). Today, many researchers are splitting brains instead of weighing them, but they are no less determined to find sex differences. Nevertheless, skeptical neuroscientists are showing that biases and values are just as embedded in current research—old prejudices in new technologies.

The brain, like a walnut, consists of two hemispheres of equal size, connected by a bundle of fibers called the corpus callosum. The left hemisphere has been associated with verbal and reasoning ability, whereas the right hemisphere is associated with spatial reasoning and artistic ability. Yet by the time these findings reached the public, they had been vastly oversimplified and diluted. Even the great neuroscientist Roger Sperry, the grandfather of hemispheric research, felt obliged to warn that the "left-right dichotomy... is an idea with which it is very easy to run wild." And many people have run wild with it: Stores are filled with manuals, cassettes, and handbooks that promise to help people become fluent in "whole-brain thinking," to beef up the unused part of their right brain, and to learn to use the intuitive right brain for business, painting, and inventing.

The fact that the brain consists of two hemispheres, each characterized by different specialties, provides a neat analogy to the fact that human beings consist of two genders, each characterized by different specialties. The analogy is so tempting that scientists keep trying to show that it is grounded in physical reality. Modern theories of gender and the brain are based on the idea that the left and right hemispheres develop differently in boys and girls, as does the corpus callosum that links the halves of the brain.

According to one major theory, the male brain is more "lateralized," that is, its hemispheres are specialized in their abilities, whereas females use both hemispheres more symmetrically because their corpus callosum is allegedly larger and contains more fibers. Two eminent scientists, Norman Geschwind and Peter Behan, maintained that this sex difference begins in the womb, when the male fetus begins to secrete testosterone —the hormone that will further its physical development as a male. Geschwind and Behan argued that testosterone in male fetuses washes over the brain, selectively attacking parts of the left hemisphere, briefly slowing its development, and producing right-hemisphere dominance in men. Geschwind speculated that the effects of testosterone on the prenatal brain produce "superior right hemisphere talents, such as artistic, musical, or mathematical talent."

Right-hemisphere dominance is also thought to explain men's excellence in some tests of "visual-spatial ability"— the ability to imagine objects in three-dimensional space (the skill you need for mastering geometry, concocting football formations, and reading maps). This is apparently the reason that some men won't stop and ask directions when they are lost; they prefer to rely on their right brains, whereas women prefer to rely on a local informant. It is also supposed to be the reason that men can't talk about their feelings and would rather watch television or wax the car. Women have interconnected hemispheres, which explains why they excel in talk, feelings, intuition, and quick judgments. Geschwind and Behan's theory had tremendous scientific appeal, and it is cited frequently in research papers and textbooks. *Science* hailed it with the headline "Math Genius May Have Hormonal Basis."

The theory also has had enormous popular appeal. It fits snugly, for example, with the Christian fundamentalist belief that men and women are innately different and thus innately designed for different roles. For his radio show "Focus on the Family," James Dobson interviewed Donald Joy, a professor of "human development in Christian education" at Asbury Theological Seminary, who explained Geschwind and Behan's theory this way:

> JOY: ... this marvelous female brain, is a brain that's not damaged during fetal development as the male brain is, but the damage gives a specialization to the male brain which we don't get in the female.
>
> DOBSON: I want to pick up on that concept of us brain-damaged males. [laughter, chuckling]
>
> JOY: ... It's giving a chemical bath to the left hemisphere and this connecting link between the two hemispheres that reduced the size and number of transmission passages that exist here ... So males simply can't talk to themselves across the hemispheres in a way that a woman does.

> DOBSON: So some of the sex differences that we see in personality can be tracked back to that moment.
>
> JOY: Oh, absolutely. And when we're talking about this now, we're talking about a glorious phenomenon because these are intrinsic sex differences ... this is glorious because we are fearfully and wonderfully differentiated from each other.
>
> DOBSON: Let's look at 'em, name 'em.
>
> JOY: We're, we're mutually interdependent. Every household needs both a male brain and a female brain, for example. The woman's brain works much like a computer ... lateral transmission in her brain allows her to consult all of her past experience and give you an instant response. She can make a judgment more quickly than a male can.... [but how she arrives at it is] hidden even from her, because it is like a computer, all it gives is the answer, it doesn't give you the process.

The male brain, Joy added, is more like an "adding machine," in which facts are totaled and a logical solution presents itself. So males are good at logical reasoning, and females at intuitive judgment because of the prenatal "chemical bath" that affects the male brain....

Now it may be true that men and women, on the average, differ in the physiology of their brains. It may even be true that this difference explains why James Dobson's wife Shirley can sum up a person's character right away, while he, with his slower, adding machine brain, takes weeks or months to come to the same impressions. But given the disgraceful history of bias and sloppy research designed more to confirm prejudices than to enlighten humanity, I think we would all do well to be suspicious and to evaluate the evidence for these assertions closely.

This is difficult for those of us who are not expert in physiology, neuroanatomy, or medicine. We are easily dazzled by words like "lateralization" and "corpus callosum." Besides, physiology seems so *solid*; if one study finds a difference between three male brains and three female brains, that must apply to all men and women. How do I know what my corpus callosum looks like? Is it bigger than a man's? Should I care?

For some answers, I turned to researchers in biology and neuroscience who have critically examined the research and the assumptions underlying theories of sex differences in the brain. The first discovery of note was that, just like the nineteenth-century researchers who kept changing their minds about which *lobe* of the brain accounted for male superiority, twentieth-century researchers keep changing their minds about which *hemisphere* of the brain accounts for male superiority. Originally, the left hemisphere was considered the repository of intellect and reason. The right hemisphere was the sick, bad, crazy side, the side of passion, instincts, criminality, and irrationality. Guess which sex was thought to have left-brain intellectual superiority? (Answer: males.) In the 1960s and 1970s, however, the right brain was resuscitated and brought into the limelight. Scientists began to suspect that it was the source of genius and inspiration, creativity and imagination, mysticism and mathematical brilliance. Guess which sex was now thought to have right-brain specialization? (Answer: males.)

It's all very confusing. Today we hear arguments that men have greater left-brain specialization (which explains their intellectual advantage) *and* that they have greater right-brain specialization (which explains their mathematical and artistic advantage). *Newsweek* recently asserted as fact, for instance, that "Women's language and other skills are more evenly divided between left and right hemisphere; in men, such functions are concentrated in the left brain." But [in their book *The Language of Love,* Christian fundamentalists Gary Smalley and John Trent] asserted that

> most women spend the majority of their days and nights camped out on the right side of the brain [which] harbors the center for feelings, as well as the primary relational, language, and communication skills... and makes an afternoon devoted to art and fine music actually enjoyable.

You can hear the chuckling from men who regard art museums and concert halls as something akin to medieval torture chambers, but I'm sure that the many men who enjoy art and fine music, indeed who create art and fine music, would not find that last remark so funny. Geschwind and Behan, of course, had argued that male specialization of the right hemisphere explained why men *excel* in art and fine music. But since Smalley and Trent apparently do not share these prissy female interests, they relegate them to women—to women's brains.

The two hemispheres of the brain do have different specialties, but it is far too simple-minded (so to speak) to assume that human abilities clump up in opposing bunches. Most brain researchers today believe that the two hemispheres complement one another, to the extent that one side can sometimes take over the functions of a side that has been damaged. Moreover, specific skills often involve components from both hemispheres: one side has the ability to tell a joke, and the other has the ability to laugh at one. Math abilities include both visual-spatial skills and reasoning skills. The right hemisphere is involved in creating art, but the left hemisphere is involved in appreciating and analyzing art. As neuropsychologist Jerre Levy once said, "Could the eons of human evolution have left half of the brain witless? Could a bird whose existence is dependent on flying have evolved only a single wing?"

These qualifications about the interdependence of brain hemispheres have not, however, deterred those who believe that there are basic psychological differences between the sexes that can be accounted for in the brain. So let's consider their argument more closely.

The neuroscientist Ruth Bleier . . . carefully examined Geschwind and Behan's data, going back to many of their original references. In one such study of 507 fetal brains of 10 to 44 weeks gestation, the researchers had actually stated that they found *no significant sex differences* in these brains. If testosterone had an effect on the developing brain, it would surely have been apparent in this large sample. Yet Geschwind and Behan cited this study for other purposes and utterly ignored its findings of no sex differences.

Instead, Geschwind and Behan cited as evidence for their hypothesis a study of *rats'* brains. The authors of the rat study reported that in male rats, two areas of the cortex that are believed to be involved in processing visual information were 3 percent thicker on the right side than on the left. In one of the better examples of academic gobbledygook yet to reach the printed page, the researchers interpreted their findings to mean that "in the male rat it is necessary to have greater spatial orientation to interact with a female rat during estrus and to integrate that input

into a meaningful output." Translation: When having sex with a female, the male needs to be able to look around in case a dangerous predator, such as her husband, walks in on them.

Bleier found more holes in this argument than in a screen door. No one knows, she said, what the slightly greater thickness in the male rat's cortex means for the rat, let alone what it means for human beings. There is at present no evidence that spatial orientation is related to asymmetry of the cortex, or that female rats have a lesser or deficient ability in this regard. And although Geschwind and Behan unabashedly used their limited findings to account for male "superiority" in math and art, they did not specifically study the incidence of genius, talent, or even modest giftedness in their sample, nor did they demonstrate a difference between the brains of geniuses and the brains of average people.

Bleier wrote to *Science*, offering a scholarly paper detailing these criticisms. *Science* did not publish it, on the grounds, as one reviewer put it, that Bleier "tends to err in the opposite direction from the researchers whose results and conclusions she criticizes" and because "she argues very strongly for the predominant role of environmental influences." Apparently, said Bleier, one is allowed to err in only one direction if one wants to be published in *Science*. The journal did not even publish her critical Letter to the Editor.

At about the same time, however, *Science* saw fit to publish a study by two researchers who claimed to have found solid evidence of gender differences in the splenium (posterior end) of the corpus callosum. In particular, they said, the splenium was larger and more bulbous in the five female brains than in the nine male brains they examined, which had been obtained at autopsy. The researchers speculated that "the female brain is less well lateralized—that is, manifests less hemispheric specialization—than the male brain for visuospatial functions." Notice the language: The female brain is *less specialized* than, and by implication inferior to, the male brain. They did not say, as they might have, that the female brain was *more integrated* than the male's. The male brain is the norm, and specialization, in the brain as in academia, is considered a good thing. Generalists in any business are out of favor these days.

This article, which also met professional acclaim, had a number of major flaws that, had they been part of any other research paper, would have been fatal to its publication. The study was based on a small sample of only fourteen brains. The researchers did not describe their methods of selecting the brains in that sample, so it is possible that some of the brains were diseased or otherwise abnormal. The article contained numerous unsupported assumptions and leaps of faith. For example, there is at present absolutely no evidence that the number of fibers in the corpus callosum is even related to hemispheric specialization. Indeed, no one knows what role, if any, the callosum plays in determining a person's mental abilities. Most damaging of all, the sex differences that the researchers claimed to have found in the size of the corpus callosum were not statistically significant, according to the scientific conventions for accepting an article for publication.

Bleier again wrote to *Science*, delineating these criticisms and also citing four subsequent studies, by her and by others, that independently failed to find gender differences of any kind in the corpus callosum. *Science* failed to publish this criticism, as it has failed to publish all studies that find no gender differences in the brain.

Ultimately, the most damning blow to all of these brain-hemisphere theories is that the formerly significant sex differences that brain theories are attempting to account for—in verbal, spatial, and math abilities—are fading rapidly. Let's start with the famed female superiority in verbal ability. Janet Hyde, a professor of psychology at the University of Wisconsin, and her colleague Marcia Linn reviewed 165 studies of verbal ability (including skills in vocabulary, writing, anagrams, and reading comprehension), which represented tests of 1,418,899 people. Hyde and Linn reported that at present in America, there simply are no gender differences in these verbal skills. They noted: "Thus our research pulls out one of the two wobbly legs on which the brain lateralization theories have rested."

Hyde recently went on to kick the other leg, the assumption of overall male superiority in mathematics and spatial ability. No one disputes that males do surpass females at the highly gifted end of the math spectrum. But when Hyde and her colleagues analyzed 100 studies of mathematics performance, representing the testing of 3,985,682 students, they found that gender differences were smallest and favored *females* in samples of the general population, and grew larger, favoring males, only in selected samples of precocious individuals.

What about spatial abilities, another area thought to reveal a continuing male superiority? When psychologists put the dozens of existing studies on spatial ability into a giant hopper and looked at the overall results, this was what they reported: Many studies show no sex differences. Of the studies that do report sex differences, the magnitude of the difference is often small. And finally, there is greater variation *within* each sex than *between* them. As one psychologist who reviewed these studies summarized: "The observed differences are very small, the overlap [between men and women] large, and abundant biological theories are supported with very slender or no evidence."

Sometimes scientists and science writers put themselves through contortions in order to reconcile the slim evidence with their belief in sex differences in the brain. The authors of a popular textbook on sexuality, published in 1990, acknowledge that "sex differences in cognitive skills have declined significantly in recent years." Then they add: "Notwithstanding this finding, theories continue to debate why these differences exist." Pardon? Notwithstanding the fact that there are few differences of any magnitude, let's discuss why there are differences? Even more mysteriously, they conclude: "If Geschwind's theory is ultimately supported by further research, we will have hard evidence of a biological basis for alleged sex differences in verbal and spatial skills." "Hard evidence" for *alleged* sex differences—the ones that don't exist!

It is sobering to read, over and over and over again in scholarly papers, the conclusions of eminent scientists who have cautioned their colleagues against generalizing about sex differences from poor data. One leader in brain-hemisphere research, Marcel Kinsbourne, observing that the evidence for sex differences "fails to convince on logical, methodological, and empirical grounds," then asked:

Why then do reputable investigators persist in ignoring [this evidence]? Because the study of sex differences is

not like the rest of psychology. Under pressure from the gathering momentum of feminism, and perhaps in backlash to it, many investigators seem determined to discover that men and women "really" are different. It seems that if sex differences (e.g., in lateralization) do not exist, then they have to be invented.

These warnings have, for the most part, gone unheeded. Poor research continues to be published in reputable journals, and from there it is disseminated to the public. Many scientists and science writers continue to rely on weak data to support their speculations, like using pebbles as foundation for a castle. Because these speculations fit the dominant beliefs about gender, however, they receive far more attention and credibility than they warrant. Worse, the far better evidence that fails to conform to the dominant beliefs about gender is overlooked, disparaged, or, as in Bleier's experience, remains unpublished.

As a result, ideas enter the common vocabulary as proven facts when they should be encumbered with "maybes," "sometimes," and "we-don't-know-yets." Scientist Hugh Fairweather, reviewing the history of sex differences research in cognition, concluded: "What had before been a possibility at best slenderly evidenced, was widely taken for a fact; and 'fact' hardened into a 'biological' dogma."

Now, it is possible that reliable sex differences in the brain will eventually be discovered. Will it then be all right for Dobson to go on the air to celebrate how delightfully but innately different men and women are? Should we then all make sure we have a male brain and a female brain in every household? Should we then worry about the abnormality of households like mine, in which the male is better at intuitive judgments and the female has the adding-machine mentality?

The answers are no, for three reasons. First, theories of sex differences in the brain cannot account for the complexities of people's everyday behavior. They cannot explain, for instance, why, if women are better than men in verbal ability, so few women are auctioneers or diplomats, or why, if women have the advantage in making rapid judgments, so few women are air-traffic controllers or umpires. Nor can brain theories explain why abilities and ambitions change when people are given opportunities previously denied to them. Two decades ago, theorists postulated biological limitations that were keeping women out of men's work like medicine and bartending. When the external barriers to these professions fell, the speed with which women entered them was dizzying. Did everybody's brain change? Today we would be amused to think that women have a brain-lateralization deficiency that is keeping them out of law school. But we continue to hear about the biological reasons that keep women out of science, math, and politics. For sex differences in cognitive abilities to wax and wane so rapidly, they must be largely a result of education, motivation, and opportunity, not of innate differences between male and female brains.

Second, the meanings of terms like "verbal ability" and "spatial reasoning" keep changing too, depending on who is using them and for what purpose. For example, when conservatives like Dobson speak of women's verbal abilities, they usually mean women's interest in and willingness to talk about relationships and feelings. But in studies of total talking time in the workplace, men far exceed women in the talk department. In everyday life, men interrupt women more than vice versa, dominate the conversation, and are more successful at introducing new topics and having their comments remembered in group discussions. What does this mean for judgments of which sex has the better "verbal ability"?

Third, the major key problem with biological theories of sex differences is that they deflect attention from the far more substantial evidence for sex similarity. The finding that men and women are more alike in their abilities and brains than different almost never makes the news. Researchers and the public commit the error of focusing on the small differences—usually of the magnitude of a few percentage points—rather than on the fact that the majority of women and men overlap. For example, this is what the author of a scientific paper that has been widely quoted as *supporting* sex differences in brain hemispheres actually concluded:

> Thus, one must not overlook perhaps the most obvious conclusion, which is that basic patterns of male and female brain asymmetry seem to be more similar than they are different.

Everyone, nevertheless, promptly overlooked it.

The habit of seeing women and men as two opposite categories also leads us to avoid the practical question: How much ability does it take to do well in a particular career? When people hear that men are better than women in spatial ability, many are quick to conclude that perhaps women, with their deficient brains, should not try to become architects or engineers. This reaction is not merely unfortunate; it is cruel to the women who *do* excel in architectural or engineering ability. The fields of math and science are losing countless capable women because girls keep hearing that women aren't as good as men in these fields.

None of this means that biology is irrelevant to human behavior. But whenever the news trumpets some version of "biology affects behavior," it obscures the fact that biology and behavior form a two-way street. Hormones affect sexual drive, for instance, but sexual activity affects hormone levels. An active brain seeks a stimulating environment, but living in a stimulating environment literally changes and enriches the brain. Fatigue and boredom cause poor performance on the job, but stultifying job conditions produce fatigue and boredom. Scientists and writers who reduce our personalities, problems, and abilities to biology thereby tell only half the story, and miss half the miracle of how human biology works.

Ruth Bleier, ... a neuroscientist, put the whole matter in perspective this way:

> Such efforts directed at the callosum (or any other particular structure in the brain, for that matter) are today's equivalent of 19th-century craniology: if you can find a bigger bump here or a smaller one there on a person's skull, if you can find a more bulbous splenium here or a more slender one there ... you will know something significant about their intelligence, their personality, their aspirations, their astrological sign, their gender and race, and their status in society. We are still mired in the naive hope that we can find something that we can *see* and *measure* and it will explain everything. It is silly science and it serves us badly.

POSTSCRIPT

Are Gender Differences Rooted in the Brain?

Kimura believes that there is substantial evidence to show that early exposure to sex hormones has permanent effects on brain functioning. She maintains that men perform better than women on spatial tasks and mathematical reasoning tests and that women perform better than men in perceptual speed and verbal fluency. She thinks that these differences are so great that they cannot be explained by socialization; they must be genetic and based on the way the brain is organized.

Tavris states that even though scientists have found no differences in the brains of men and women, they still continue to look. She cites studies that have examined hundreds of brains and found no differences based on gender. Tavris continues to refute the theory by reporting that studies do not show gender differences in verbal abilities and that females have better mathematical skills than males when they are compared to the general population. Tavris illustrates how biology and behavior form a two-way street. The brain seeks a stimulating environment, but living in a stimulating environment changes and enriches the brain.

It seems prudent to examine how nature and nurture interact to impact children. How does heredity combine with family environment and learning opportunities to affect a child's intellectual ability? Do adoption and twin studies provide adequate answers to the controversy?

In spring 1995, Shaywitz and Shaywitz, researchers at Yale University School of Medicine, released the results of a study that found the first definitive evidence that men and women *use* their brains differently. This study has added more fuel to the debate on sex differences in the brain.

SUGGESTED READINGS

Emde, R. (1992). Temperament, emotion, and cognition at fourteen months: The MacArthur longitudinal twin study. *Child Development, 63,* 1437–1455.

Plomin, R., Reiss, D., Hetherington, E. M., & Howe, G. (1994). Nature and nurture: Genetic contributions to measures of the family environment. *Developmental Psychology, 30,* 32–43.

Seligman, M. E. P. (1994, May/June). What you can change... what you cannot. *Psychology Today, 27,* 34–41, 70–74, 84.

Shaywitz, S. E., and Shaywitz, B. A. (1995, February 16). Sex differences in the functional organization of the brain for language. *Nature, 373,* 607–609.

ISSUE 3

Should Hospitals Continue Early Discharge Policies for Newborns?

YES: John R. Britton, Helen L. Britton, and Susan A. Beebe, from "Early Discharge of the Term Newborn: A Continued Dilemma," *Pediatrics* (September 1994)

NO: Elizabeth H. Thilo and Susan F. Townsend, from "What Are the Pitfalls of Early Discharge?" *Contemporary OB/GYN* (January 1997)

ISSUE SUMMARY

YES: John B. Britton, Helen L. Britton, and Susan A. Beebe, all affiliated with the Department of Pediatrics at the University of Utah Medical Center in Salt Lake City, reviewed the available data on the appropriate time to discharge a newborn. They summarize some of the studies that promote early discharge.

NO: Elizabeth H. Thilo, associate professor of pediatrics, and Susan F. Townsend, assistant professor of pediatrics, both medical directors, are concerned that the recently recommended 48-hour hospital stay for newborns may still not be long enough to catch some of the medical problems that infants could develop.

In 1995 there was an uproar in the medical community, which spread to the public, concerning the common practice of discharging mothers and newborns from the hospital 12–24 hours after birth. Many insurance policies were paying for hospital costs for only the first 24 hours after childbirth. Outrage at releasing babies from the hospital before it was considered medically safe by many health care professionals led to legislation in several states and eventually to the U.S. Senate. Laws were passed that required insurance companies to extend their coverage from 12–24 hours to 48 hours after birth when recommended by the doctor. It was concluded that 48 hours, not 24 hours, was a more reasonable amount of time to ensure the health of the newborn baby. Yet a 48-hour discharge is still considered an "early discharge."

It is becoming a more common practice for insurance companies to cover hospital costs for a 48-hour hospital stay, but is 48 hours long enough to ensure the health and safety of a newborn? Some physicians question the efficacy of discharging newborns only 48 hours after birth, whereas others say that this would not create health problems for healthy newborns. Early discharge saves money and, according to some researchers, is associated with a better outcome than staying in the hospital longer.

The roots of this issue can be traced back to the 1960s and 1970s, when families fought to be released from the hospital sooner than the traditional five to seven days. Many mothers wanted to go home where they felt more comfortable and could save on costs. This movement snowballed until the 1990s, when 12–24 hours became a common hospital stay after childbirth.

The authors of both selections agree that the decision about when to release a newborn from the hospital should be determined on a case-by-case basis, with the physician and parents considering a variety of factors. Health care professionals seldom mention insurance companies or legislative bodies as partners in the decision of early discharge. Should insurance companies have the power to interfere in a medical decision? If insurance companies do not get involved in health care costs, will our premiums go through the roof? Are there long-term effects related to early discharge of newborns or are potential problems merely short term?

Early discharge raises questions not only about the health and safety of babies, but about society as well. How much health care should a newborn receive? Who should decide? Shortening the hospital stay of newborns and their mothers by one day can save $4 billion per year, according to a 1997 study by Thilo and Townsend. This is a significant savings for everyone who pays insurance premiums. Is it appropriate to consider a cost savings in this situation? Should insurance companies be a partner in deciding when a newborn should be released from the hospital? Should state legislatures be involved in the decision? In our society, how does one juggle health issues and financial concerns with mandates from state legislatures? What are the implications for the later development of children who develop serious illnesses after leaving the hospital too soon?

Studies of the effects of early discharge of newborns have not settled the debate over how long newborns should stay in the hospital after birth. There are concerns over how these studies were conducted and their results. John R. Britton, Helen L. Britton, and Susan A. Beebe present findings of studies that support the practice of early discharge. Elizabeth H. Thilo and Susan F. Townsend believe that the "definitive study on the safety of early discharge has not yet been performed." They question how safe it is to let a newborn leave the hospital after only 48 hours.

YES

John R. Britton, Helen L. Britton, and Susan A. Beebe

EARLY DISCHARGE OF THE TERM NEWBORN: A CONTINUED DILEMMA

Although it has recently become common practice to discharge healthy term infants with their mothers at increasingly earlier postnatal ages,[1] current opinion varies widely regarding the desirability of this practice. Proponents of early discharge claim that it is safe and may be advantageous from both a medical and psychosocial standpoint. Opponents, on the other hand, argue that an element of risk may be involved because detection of significant illness may be either missed or delayed outside of the hospital.[2] To further complicate the issue, economic considerations often limit the choice of families and their physicians. Third party payers usually fund only the shortest possible inpatient hospital stays, thus constituting a driving force behind the trend to earlier discharge.[2]

The United States appears to have taken the lead in the practice of early discharge, and it is not uncommon in this country for a term newborn to leave the hospital at 12 to 24 hours postnatally. Recently, 1- to 3-day postnatal stays have also become more popular in other Western countries, such as the United Kingdom, Australia, and Scandinavia, where 6- to 10-day hospitalizations had been customary in the past.[3-7] Medical, social, and economic considerations have presumably influenced such trends, as they have in the United States.

Because of these changes, questions regarding the timing of hospital discharge of term infants are faced almost daily by practicing pediatricians throughout the world. In 1980, the American Academy of Pediatrics recommended criteria to be met by early discharge candidates,[8] and these continue to form the basis for their current guidelines.[9] However, few pediatricians are familiar with the limited information on this subject, which has never been reviewed in the pediatric literature. In this review, available data on early newborn discharge will be presented with particular emphasis upon the safety and benefits of this practice. Since published studies are heterogeneous with respect to methodology and study design, analytical approaches such as meta-analysis are unfortunately not applicable.[10] Moreover, almost

From John R. Britton, Helen L. Britton, and Susan A. Beebe, "Early Discharge of the Term Newborn: A Continued Dilemma," *Pediatrics*, vol. 94, no. 3 (September 1994), pp. 291–295. Copyright © 1994 by The American Academy of Pediatrics. Reprinted by permission of *Pediatrics*.

all published studies suffer from substantial methodological limitations, and only a few satisfy as many as three of the 11 criteria that have been suggested for adequacy of clinical study design by DerSimonian et al.[11] Accordingly, these methodological concerns will be discussed in a separate section....

PSYCHOSOCIAL ISSUES AND EARLY DISCHARGE

Proponents of early discharge often argue that this practice may be associated with a variety of psyche-social benefits, such as facilitation of bonding and attachment, increased breastfeeding, enhanced family interactions, and generally improved patient satisfaction. Although some studies lend support to these beliefs, others are less convincing of a beneficial effect.

In a randomized, controlled study at a tertiary maternity hospital in Vancouver, Carty and Bradley evaluated 131 women and their infants discharged at 12 to 24 hours, 25 to 48 hours, or 4 days postpartum.[12] As determined by a questionnaire, mothers in the two early discharge groups were significantly more satisfied with their care; those hospitalized longer demonstrated less confidence and greater depression as assessed by standardized psychological testing. In a Swedish study, mothers and fathers in an early discharge group were more satisfied with medical care than those undergoing a traditional 6-day postpartum stay.[7] Other reports have shown an association between early discharge and improved maternal postpartum adjustment[5] and increased time spent by fathers with their infants during days 2 to 4 postnatally.[13]

Several reports suggest that early discharge may foster enhanced breastfeeding. In a Swedish study,[14] infants discharged early were breastfed significantly more often on the third and fourth days postnatally than those staying in the hospital, although no difference in incidence of breastfeeding was observed during the subsequent 10 days. Among Canadian mothers, a significant association of early discharge with unsupplemented breastfeeding at 4 to 6 weeks postpartum was noted.[12]

Similar psychosocial benefits of early discharge were not observed in other early discharge reports. A study conducted in 1962 found decreased satisfaction among mothers discharged early from an inner-city hospital in New York.[15] In a randomized trial conducted at a California health maintenance organization,[16] no difference in satisfaction was noted between mothers discharged early and late. Two groups[13,17] observed no differences in the practice of breastfeeding as related to the time of newborn discharge.

One study compared simultaneous discharge of low-income mothers and their infants at 24 to 47 hours postnatally with maternal discharge at a similar time without their infants.[18] Simultaneous discharge was associated with higher maternal attachment scores, fewer concerns, and greater satisfaction than discharge with separation.

MORBIDITY AND MORTALITY: RELATIONSHIP TO TIME OF DISCHARGE

Although the Committee on the Fetus and Newborn of the American Academy of Pediatrics has stated that there is "an element of risk in early discharge",[8] this risk remains poorly defined. Among published series of infants discharged early, mortality rates are low and not significantly different from those of accompanying controls or the general population of infants from which the study groups were drawn.[15,19–21] Most early discharge studies have attempted to compare morbidity, expressed as rates of hospital re-admission, between infants discharged early and late.

The first early discharge program reported from New Orleans, LA, in 1943 suggested the safety of hospital discharge at 2 to 5 days postnatally.[22] In a report from Bradford, England, in 1959,[23] hospital re-admission rates during the first 14 days postnatally were evaluated among infants discharged at approximately 48 hours after birth. Although this practice of "early discharge" was considered a drastic step at the time, only four of 741 infants discharged early required re-admission to the hospital.[23] Subsequent reports from this center confirmed a low rate of re-admission (0.5% to 0.9%), as did those from other British hospitals during the 1960s.[19–21,24,25] Later reports from around the world suggested the medical safety of a 1- to 3-day postnatal stay.[26–28]

With the advent of even shorter hospital stays for newborns in more recent years, concern regarding the safety of this practice again arose, prompting further evaluation. A variety of institutions, ranging from university hospitals to free-standing birthing centers, reported discharge as early as the first day after birth, with re-admission rates ranging from 0% to 11%.[29–40] The few reports that have included a comparison group of infants discharged at a later age suggest similar rates of re-admission for early and late discharge groups.

Only three prospective, randomized controlled studies provide information regarding the medical safety of early discharge.[3,12,16] For these, discharge times varied, infant numbers were small and follow-up periods variable, making comparison difficult. In a study from the Kaiser-Permanente Medical Center in San Francisco, 44 infants discharged at a median age of 26 hours were compared to a control group of 44 infants discharged at a median age of 68 hours.[16] The two groups were similar with respect to ethnicity, socioeconomic status, and parenting characteristics. Almost half of the infants in the early discharge group actually went home prior to 24 hours postnatally. Only two infants in the group discharged early required rehospitalization, compared to four infants in the late discharge group that required a prolonged stay for medical problems. There were no significant differences in morbidity between groups within the first 6 weeks postnatally. A confusing aspect of this study was considerable overlap in discharge times between early and control (late) discharge groups. In a report from a Swedish hospital,[3] expectant mothers were invited to participate in a study in which they were randomized prenatally to either early discharge (24 to 48 hours) with domicilliary visits or a traditional stay (control group, average length, 6 days). There were 50 infants in the early discharge group and 54 controls. One infant from each group was re-admitted to a neonatal unit within the first week because of feeding and/or respiratory problems; no infant required re-admission for jaundice. There were no differences between groups on follow-up through the 6th postnatal week. In Vancouver, Carty and Bradley[12] randomized mothers and their infants prenatally to discharge at 12 to 24 hours (44 infants), 25 to 48 hours (49 infants), and 4 days after birth (38 infants). One infant was re-admitted to the hospital from each of he early discharge groups during the first 6 postnatal weeks; there were no re-admissions from the control group.

Although criteria for re-admission undoubtedly vary widely among centers, reported re-admission diagnoses appear quite similar. Hyperbilirubinemia requiring phototherapy is the most common, accounting for approximately three-fourths of all cases.[3,12,15,16,26-40] Because of the recent increased popularity of home phototherapy, a lower figure might be expected in a more current study. Other commonly reported re-admission diagnoses include infection, apnea, respiratory disorders, and feeding problems.[3,12,15,16,26-40]

Published studies have focused upon morbidity and mortality associated with early discharge, yet possible negative complications of a prolonged hospital stay have not been adequately investigated. In one report, infants remaining in the hospital had a higher rate of admission to a level II nursery than did those discharged early.[41] Increased exposure to nosocomial pathogens and the imposition of artificial schedules by the hospital environment have been suggested as possible detrimental effects of a prolonged stay.[15] Perhaps overly aggressive assessment of normal variations in newborn physiology may be incurred in the hospital, such as frequent bilirubin drawings on mildly jaundiced infants, with a consequent increase in cost and iatrogenic risk. These possibilities deserve further exploration.

SOCIOECONOMIC FACTORS AND EARLY DISCHARGE

From an economic perspective, financial saving and more optimal utilization of health care resources are often cited as advantages of early discharge, yet published studies vary in their conclusions with respect to these issues. Several short-stay programs were motivated by limitations in numbers of obstetrical beds.[15,21-23] However, McIntosh[42] found that although an early discharge program in Alberta, Canada, was effective in reducing length of hospital stay and costs, it did not actually reduce pressure on bed space in a maternity unit. Yanover and coworkers[16] noted that the costs incurred for infants discharged early with home follow-up were comparable to those of a similar group kept in the hospital. Other reports suggest that substantial financial savings may be achieved by early discharge.[18,29,37,43] The magnitude of such savings may very likely depend upon the relative expense incurred by follow-up and rehospitalization.

Unfortunately, many families for whom early discharge is either financially attractive or mandated by third party payers may also be at risk for inadequate follow-up or recognition of medical problems. In a study of low-income mothers discharged with their infants 24 to 36 hours postpartum, 10% failed to return for a follow-up visit within 48 hours, even though they had signed a contract agreeing to do so.[41] This population had been carefully screened for medical risk factors, yet still had a high rate of hospital readmission. Possibly, similar low-income groups who are less carefully screened might be at even greater risk for unidentified medical or social problems. Limitations of public health support or resources may further enhance this risk.

It is possible that early discharge may provide a safer and more attractive alternative to home birth for those mothers who are opposed to hospitalization.

Unfortunately, this question has not been adequately addressed in the literature.

METHODOLOGICAL ASPECTS OF EARLY DISCHARGE STUDIES

Most published studies on early discharge describe outcomes of specific individual programs, each with its own particular and often unique characteristics. Socioeconomic factors, geography, nationality, ethnicity, birth setting, and other population characteristics vary widely, as do criteria for determining an infant's candidacy for early discharge. Varied methods of risk screening and parental education have been utilized, maternal support systems at home differ widely, and mechanisms of follow-up vary from phone calls to home and office visits. The definition of early discharge differs considerably among studies: infants discharged in the "late" group in one study may actually go home at an earlier postnatal age than the "early" group of another. As a result, it is often difficult to compare data from different reports or to generalize results from one program to other settings.

Most reports state or imply that the infant is well at discharge, but few stipulate requirements for ascertaining health or selection criteria used to establish early discharge candidacy. Often, neither the period of follow-up nor the number of patients lost to follow-up are given, and in some cases the readmission rate is either unstated or difficult to discern.[5,37–40] Only a few of the reports that include a control group have employed randomization in group assignment.[3,12,16] Bias in patient selection thus constitutes a major obstacle in the interpretation of such studies. In some, the decision to discharge early was prompted by bed space limitations[15,18];

in others, mothers chose early discharge. In the few prospective randomized studies, mothers were recruited prenatally to participate in trials in which they might have a chance to leave the hospital earlier than otherwise.[3,12,16] In these cases, evaluation of psychosocial outcomes, such as parental satisfaction, depression, or anxiety, may be biased depending upon the extent of realization of parental expectations. Similarly, recruitment of mothers to participate in early discharge studies may select those with greater parenting capabilities, and mothers that choose early discharge may have enhanced home support mechanisms, more personal resources, and stronger motivation to succeed in the endeavor than women forced to leave the hospital earlier than desired.[39,40,44] Finally, reports of psychosocial outcomes, with only one exception,[18] have assessed the effects of combined early discharge of both mother and infant, closely related factors that are difficult to separate in study design.

A major concern regarding most studies involves the definition of morbidity. Details of individual cases are rarely given, and the age of presentation of medical problems is usually not stated. Criteria for medical concern are likely to vary considerably among practitioners, especially for problems such as jaundice, and it is possible that an infant re-admitted at one center might be followed as an outpatient at another. Moreover, in comparison studies the interpretation of outcome measures manifested beyond the time of discharge of both early and late groups may be difficult because of an inability to determine whether outcomes are related to the duration of initial hospitalization or factors arising during the interim. This is especially true for long observation periods after discharge. For example, the finding in one report that early and late discharge groups had similar rates of re-admission over a 6-week period does not support meaningful conclusions regarding safety of the time of discharge,[45] since medical problems presenting later (in this report, 68% were infections) commonly arise de novo and are often unrelated to events of the immediate newborn period. Conversely, assessing re-admission rates during a period after discharge that is short in comparison to the initial hospitalization may also be misleading: that infants kept in the hospital for greater than 48 hours should have lower rates of re-admission during the first week than those discharged at 24 to 36 hours might be expected,[41] because the portion of that week spent as an outpatient is correspondingly less. As a result, such a finding does not necessarily reflect differences in morbidity between the two discharge groups.

Because rates of re-admission are low, large numbers of infants would be needed in a controlled trial to detect differences in risk of rehospitalization between early and late discharge groups.[46] For example, assuming a minimum incidence of problems requiring re-admission in the population to be 1%, 38 211 infants would be needed in each group to detect a difference in outcome of 25% ($\alpha = .05$; $\beta = .1$). It is unlikely that a study of this magnitude could be performed at a single center, and a multi-center effort would be needed. Most published reports have included only small groups of infants, and consequently sufficient statistical power is lacking. Because groups are small a single additional re-admission in either early or late discharge groups could, in many cases, affect the overall outcome of the study.

CONCLUSION AND RECOMMENDATIONS

Available data regarding early discharge of the term newborn is thus fraught with bias and methodological flaws, and consequently guidelines regarding this issue have been difficult to establish. Possible risks of early discharge remain of concern to many physicians, who feel that early signs of disease will be missed out of the hospital. On the other hand, the superiority of a longer hospitalization in facilitating improved outcomes has not been established, and arguments that continued hospitalization poses increased risk are equally tenable. In the absence definitive medical data, current practices remain based upon clinical judgment, and economic considerations continue to emerge as directive forces behind the trend to discharge early.

Considering the very low incidence of morbidity among term newborns, it would seem that discharge as early as the first day postnatally may be safe if adequate psychosocial support and appropriate follow-up are available. Although as yet unvalidated, the guidelines for early discharge initially recommended by the American Academy of Pediatrics in 1980[8] still seem appropriate today.[9] These criteria include term delivery, appropriate growth for gestational age, normal physical examination, and a minimum of 6, preferably 12 hours of hospitalization, during which thermal homeostasis and successful feeding have occurred. Appropriate screening (cord blood type and coombs) and follow-up at 2 to 3 days postnatally were also recommended. Based upon observations that an uneventful transitional period was predictive of subsequently low neonatal morbidity, we have advocated careful monitoring during this period as a means of ascertaining health prior to discharge.[43] Finally, assessment of the adequacy of social environment and parenting skills should play an important part in the decision-making process. Until more definitive data are available, the decision regarding when to discharge the well term newborn must remain an individual one, made by the practioner based upon the medical, social, and economic aspects of each case.

REFERENCES

1. Norr KF, Nacion K. outcomes of postpartum early discharge, 1960–1986. A comparative review. *Birth.* 1987;14:135–141

2. Eidelman AI. Early discharge—early trouble. *J Perinatol.* 1992;12:101–102

3. Waldenstrom U, Sundelin C, Lindmark G. Early and late discharge after hospital birth. Health of mother and infant in the postpartum period. *Uppsala J Med Sci.* 1987;92:301–314

4. Gee A. Transfer home—two aspects of transfer home of mother and baby. *Midwives Chronicle & Nursing Notes.* 1984;97:8–9

5. James ML, Hudson CN, Gebski VJ, et al. An evaluation of planned early postnatal transfer home with nursing support. *Med J Australia.* 1987;127:434–438

6. Verbrugge HP. Youth health care in the Netherlands: a bird's eye view. *Pediatrics.* 1990;66:1044–1047

7. Waldenstrom U. Early discharge with domiciliary visits and hospital care. Parents' experiences of two modes of post-partum care. *Scan J Caring Sci.* 1987;1:51–58

8. Committee on Fetus Newborn, American Academy of Pediatrics. Criteria for early infant discharge and follow-up evaluation. *Pediatrics.* 1980;65:651

9. American Academy of Pediatrics, American College of Obstetricians and Gynecologists. *Guidelines for Perinatal Care,* Third Edition, 1992, pp 108–109

10. Fisher LD, Van Belle G. *Biostatistics: A Methodology for the Health Sciences.* New York: John Wiley Sons, Inc; pp 893–897

11. DerSimonian R, Charette J, McPeek B, Mosteller F. Reporting on methods in clinical trials. *New Eng J Med.* 1982;306:1332–1337

12. Carty EM, Bradley CF. A randomized, controlled evaluation of early postpartum hospital discharge. *Birth.* 1990;17:199–204

13. Waldenstrom U. Early and late discharge after hospital birth: father's involvement in infant care. *Early Human Dev.* 1988;17:19–28

14. Waldenstrom U, Sundelin C, Lindmark G Early and late discharge after hospital birth breastfeeding. *Acta Paediatr Scand,* 1987;76:727-732

15. Hellman LM, Kohl SG, Palmer J. Early hospital discharge in obstetrics. Lancet. 1962;1:227–232

16. Yanover MJ, Jones DJ, Miller MD. Perinatal care of low-risk mothers and infants: early discharge with home care. *N Engl J Med.* 1976;294:702–705

17. Arborelius E, Lindell D. Psychological aspects of early and late discharge after hospital delivery *Scand J Soc Med.* 1989;17:103–107

18. Norr KF, Nacion KW, Abramson R. Early discharge with home follow-up; impacts on low-income mothers and infants. *JOGN Nurs* 1988;22:133–141

19. Pinker GD, Fraser AC. Early discharge of maternity patients. *Br Med J.* 1964;7:99–100

20. Theobald GW. Weekly antenatal care and home on the second day. *Lancet.* 1962;4:735–737

21. Arthturton MW, Bamford FN. Paediatric aspects of the early discharge of maternity patients. *Br Med J.* 1976;3:517–520

22. Guerriero WF. A maternal welfare programme for New Orleans. *Am J Obstet Gynecol* 1943;46:312–313

23. Theobald GW. Home on the second day: The Bradford experiment. *Br Med J.* 1959;2:1364–136?

24. College of General Practitioners, Bradford Group. A survey of 100 early discharge cases. *Lancet.* 1961;1:536–540

25. Craig GA, Muirhead JMB. Obstetric aspects of the early discharge of maternity patients. *Br Med J.* 1967;3:520–522

26. Power DJ, Wolf E, Van Coeverden de Grooot HA. Early discharge from maternity units in Cape Town. *S Afr Med J.* 1980;58:893–895

27. Thurston NE, Dundas JB. Evaluation of an early post partum discharge program. *Can J Public Health.* 1985;76:384–387

28. Jansson P. Early postpartum discharge. *Am Nursing.* 1985;5:547–550

29. Cottrell DG, Pittala B, Hey D. One day maternity care: a pediatric view. *J Am Osteopath Assoc* 1986;83:216–221

30. Rollins AJ, Kaplan JA, Ratkay ME, et al. A homestyle delivery program in a university hospital. *J Fam Practice.* 1979;9:407–414

31. Barton JJ, Rovner S, Puls K, Read PA. Alternative birthing center: experience in a teaching obstetric service. *Am J Obstet Gynecol.* 1980;137:377–384

32. Avery MD, Fournier LC, Jones PL, Sopovi CP. An early postpartum hospital discharge

program. Implementation and evaluation. *JOGN Nurs.* 1982;11:233–235

33. Scupholme A. Postpartum early discharge: an inner city experience. *J Nurs Mid.* 1981;26:19–22

34. Neuenschwander F, Meier M, Witschi M. Die ambulante Geburt: Erfahrungen und Organisation. *Ther Umsch.* 1981;38:981–984

35. Dudenhausen JW, Stauber M. Erfahrungen mit der sogenannten ambulanten Geburt in der Klinik. *Arch Gynecol.* 1983;235:617–623

36. Berryman GK. An early discharge program. *Mil Med.* 1991;156:583–584

37. Waskerwitz S, Fournier L, Jones P, Meier W. A comparative analysis of newborn outcome in a hospital-based birthing center. *Clin Pediatr.* 1985;24:273–277

38. Mehl LE, Peterson GH, Sokolosky W, Whitt MC. Outcomes of early discharge after normal birth. *Birth and Family J.* 1976;3:101–107

39. Patterson PK. A comparison of postpartum early traditional discharge groups. *Q Rev Bull.* 1987;13:365–371

40. Lemmer CM. Early discharge: outcomes of primiparas and their infants. *JOGN Nurs.* 1987;16:230–236

41. Conrad PD. Wilkening RB, Rosenberg AA. Safety of newborn discharge in less than 36 hours in an indigent population. *Am J Dis Child.* 1989;143:98–101

42. McIntosh ID. Hospital effects of maternity early discharge. *Med Care.* 1984;22:611–619

43. Britton HL, Britton JR. Efficacy of early newborn discharge in a middle-class population. *Am J Dis Child.* 1984;138:1041–1046

44. Waldenstrom U, Lindmark G. Early and late discharge after hospital birth. A comparative study of parental background characteristics. *Scand J Soc Med.* 1987;15:159–167

45. Pittard WB, Geddes KM. Newborn hospitalization: a closer look. *J Pediatr.* 1988;112:257–262

46. Detsky AS, Sackett DL. When was a 'negative' clinical trial big enough? *Arch Intern Med.* 1985;145:709–712

NO

Elizabeth H. Thilo and Susan F. Townsend

WHAT ARE THE PITFALLS OF EARLY DISCHARGE?

What constitutes the ideal hospital stay for a healthy term infant? Who should decide whether mother and baby are ready for discharge—the mother, the doctor, or the insurer? What follow-up arrangements are needed when babies are discharged early? How early is "early"? And what effect does early discharge have on newborn screening for metabolic disease?

These questions have become increasingly newsworthy in recent months. Reports of bilirubin encephalopathy and severe dehydration in newborns discharged after short hospital stays have attracted public attention, and a number of state legislatures have passed laws requiring third-party-payers to cover longer postpartum stays.

In the 1970s, when early new-born discharge first attracted public attention, it was a parent-driven request: Well-educated parents with good support systems at home wanted to shorten the typical postpartum stay from 4 or more days to 2 or less. More recently, early newborn discharge has evolved into an insurer-driven quest to cut health-care costs. Childbirth is the most common reason for hospitalization in the US. With some 4 million births per year, savings from shortening the hospital stay by 1 day per birth have been estimated at nearly $4 billion a year. But as short stays become standard practice, the question of safety is crucial.

DEVELOPING STANDARDS FOR SAFETY

The Committee on the Fetus and Newborn of the American Academy of Pediatrics (AAP) published updated and detailed minimum criteria for early newborn discharge in 1995 (Table 1).[1] The Committee suggests that all criteria be fulfilled before the newborn is discharged, and says this is "unlikely" in a hospital stay of less than 48 hours.

From Elizabeth H. Thilo and Susan F. Townsend, "What Are the Pitfalls of Early Discharge?" *Contemporary OB/GYN*, vol. 42, no. 1 (January 1997), pp. 72–87. Copyright © 1997 by *Contemporary OB/GYN*. Reprinted by permission.

The new guidelines clarify safety standards considerably, but practical problems remain. For example, the guidelines state that "the mother's knowledge, ability, and confidence to provide adequate care for her baby are documented by the fact that she has received training sessions" in feeding and newborn care. Such training could be incorporated into childbirth education classes or prenatal visits, and not postponed until the brief postpartum hospital stay. But what if the mother doesn't feel confident and knowledgeable after such training? Should her continued hospital stay be covered by insurance? What about newborns whose home environment is considered too risky for discharge? Should insurers pay for care until, as the guidelines put it, "a plan to safeguard the infant is in place"? If the answer to questions like these is yes, how can insurers be made to comply?

One approach is to mandate coverage for a minimum length of stay. The states of Massachusetts, New Jersey, and North Carolina now have laws requiring postpartum hospital insurance to cover a minimum 48-hour hospital stay for an uncomplicated vaginal delivery, and 96 hours for a cesarean section. Maryland law permits discharge of a mother and newborn infant if AAP and the American College of Obstetricians and Gynecologists (ACOG) medical stability criteria are met, which is now equivalent to a 48-hour recommendation. Similar laws have been introduced in the US Senate and are pending in 20 states.[2] In a somewhat different approach, insurers in Colorado were persuaded to allow a 48-hour stay in a compromise with legislators so as to avoid specific legislation.

It's too early to tell what effect legislation will have on average length of stay and costs, or to what extent new parents will take advantage of these laws. In addition, both AAP and ACOG endorse collaborative decision-making between physicians and parents in determining the length of hospital stay, not timetables mandated by legislators or insurers.[1,2]

RESEARCH GIVES LIMITED GUIDANCE

Published findings on early discharge of term newborns are limited by methodological variability and flaws in study design. One finding that seems secure is that an uncomplicated transition period (first 6 hours) is important in predicting short-term outcome.[4] In a retrospective study of a middle-class population, one team reported that the majority of newborn illnesses were present in the first 6 hours; a normal transition period predicted continued wellness 98% of the time (99% when jaundice was excluded).[4] Only 1% of infants who were initially well (17 of 1,583) became ill with a problem other than jaundice between 6 hours and 2 weeks of age. However, this study did not address the question of optimal timing of discharge for infants who achieved a successful transition.

The definitive study on the safety of early discharge has not yet been performed, although several authors have recently published comprehensive reviews.[5-7] Some investigators have concluded that the literature supporting the safety and efficacy of early discharge is "fraught with bias," that the studies available are too small to have statistical power, and that guidelines recommended by the AAP in 1980 still seem reasonable.[5] They also note that no evidence supports the notion that longer

Table 1

Criteria for Early Newborn Discharge

Uncomplicated antepartum, intrapartum, and postpartum course for baby and mother
Single birth
Vaginal delivery
Term gestation (38–42 wk), with birthweight appropriate for gestational age by appropriate growth curve, with normal exam
Baby shows normal, stable vital signs for 12 hr preceding discharge
    Thermal homeostasis (axillary temperature 36.1°C–37°C in open crib)
    Respiratory rate < 60/min
    Heart rate 100–160 beats/min
Baby has voided and stooled; if circumcised, no excess bleeding for ≥ 2 hr
Baby has fed at least twice, demonstrating coordinated suck, swallow, and breathing
No significant jaundice in first 24 hr of life
Mother has adequate knowledge to care for her newborn, documented by training in:
    Breastfeeding or bottle feeding—trained staff should assess breastfeeding
    Knowledge of normal urine and stool frequency
    Cord, skin, infant genital care
    Recognition of common signs of infant illness, especially jaundice
    Infant safety issues (car safety seats, sleep positioning)
Support (family members or health-care providers) available to mother and baby for first few days after discharge. Supporters:
    Familiar with newborn care and knowledgeable about lactation
    Able to recognize jaundice and dehydration
Laboratory data obtained and reviewed as normal or negative, including:
    Maternal testing for syphilis and hepatitus B
    Cord/infant blood type, direct Coombs' test if indicated
Newborn screening sample obtained according to state regulations; if sample obtained before 24 hr of milk feedings, follow-up testing is assured
Initial hepatitus B vaccine given or scheduled within first week
Physician-directed source of continuing care identified:
    If discharged at < 48 hr, definite appointment for exam within next 48 hr
    Examiner competent in newborn assessment, reports to physician on day of visit
Family, environmental, and social risk factors assessed, including but not limited to:
    Substance abuse, history of child abuse or neglect, no fixed home, teen mother, lack of social support (especially for single, first-time mother), domestic violence
If risk factors are present, discharge delayed until a plan to safeguard the baby is in place

Source: AAP Committee on Fetus and Newborn[1]

stays would improve outcome. They calculate that, because readmission rates are low (around 1%), a comparison of early and late discharge outcomes would require more than 38,000 infants in each category to detect a difference of 25%. They recommend a minimum of 12 rather than 6 hours of hospitalization so that feeding can begin to be established, and suggest that decisions about when to discharge a well, term newborn be made on an individual basis determined by "the medical, social, and economic aspects of each case."

Another group addressed the short-omings in the current literature.[6] No adequately designed studies have evaluated early discharge in the absence of additional, routine follow-up services, or example. Also, limited information is available about compliance with follow-up visits. Most studies concluding that early discharge is "safe" were too small to detect significant adverse outcomes, were conducted under restricted conditions, or showed clear bias in how results were interpreted. After analyzing more than 0 studies, the authors stated that "the currently available literature provides little scientific evidence to guide discharge planning for most apparently well newborns and their mothers." In addition, they said that there is "no evidence to support the general safety or advisability of early discharge in the absence of stringent selection criteria and post-discharge nurse home visits." This view reinforces the need to be selective about which infants to discharge early and the need for prompt follow-up in the home.

In another evaluation of the literature, one researcher examined only experimental or quasi-experimental studies.[7] One noted the methodological flaws cited above—small sample size and restrictive protocols that included well-defined follow-up. Interestingly, the definition of "early" discharge in the studies he examined varied from 2 hours to 5 days. He also pointed out that most studies used readmission of the infant or mother as the only measure of health outcome, probably because readmission is the easiest outcome to measure. Other possible outcomes, such as success at breastfeeding, parent satisfaction, and compliance, have not been evaluated.

These reviews indicate that available data are too limited to predict a length of stay that would guarantee safety and optimal outcome for most newborns. However, most clinicians agree on the major safety issues associated with early discharge: avoiding severe jaundice, providing adequate follow-up, and screening accurately for congenital disorders.

JAUNDICE REDUX

Jaundice is the most common cause for hospital readmission in the first 2 weeks of life. In recent years, a gentler approach to nonhemolytic jaundice in well, term infants has coincided with the trend to shorter newborn hospital stays, resulting in the return of kernicterus.[8–11] The shorter the hospital stay, the higher the readmission rate in the first 2 weeks of life for severe jaundice and dehydration.[12]

At the time of discharge, neonatal jaundice is not apparent; in the absence of hemolysis, it rarely is at 24 hours of age. Intake during the hospital stay may have been inadequate, although the feeding pattern in the first 24 hours is often sluggish and it's difficult to judge whether the infant is getting enough to eat. The infant goes home, often breastfeeding, perhaps with inadequate intake over the next several days that is not recognized by the mother. After 4 to 8 days, the baby returns to the hospital with excessive weight loss, dehydration, and hyperbilirubinemia.

Although not usually life threatening on its own, marked hyperbilirubinemia should not be ignored. It is often the most easily recognized sign of problems with breastfeeding intake.... Specific instructions for the breastfeeding mother may help her recognize problems in the baby. We tell mothers to contact their health provider if they do not see signs of adequate intake, and advise them to supplement breastfeeding with expressed milk or formula if the baby shows signs of dehydration.

FOLLOW-UP IS CRUCIAL

Clearly, as length of stay decreases, the importance of follow-up increases. The traditional 2-week checkup is too late to pick up serious jaundice, dehydration, and excessive weight loss in a baby who is not breastfeeding well, and the occasional infant with serious congenital heart disease or a metabolic problem that was not apparent at the time of early discharge.

The AAP as part of routine preventive care, recommends a follow-up visit 2 to 4 days after discharge for any newborn who goes home before 48 hours, but there are difficulties in providing this service. Some insurers don't cover an office visit at this time, and some parents have trouble with transportation in the days after birth.[13] For these reasons, home visits by nurses have been widely endorsed, particularly in the lay press. Many insurers who mandate 24-hour discharge include a home nurse visit in their reimbursement package. The problems with home visits are a lack of standardization in the background, training, and experience of the personnel performing these duties, and a lack of consistency in the evaluation of the infant. In the Denver area, the Kaiser Permanente system has solved these problems by employing a group of nurses with experience in perinatal care who do only newborn home visits. If such a specialized group of personnel is not available, home nursing visits can be structured to follow specific guidelines, with explicit instructions to contact the primary care provider for certain indications.

A follow-up visit that conforms to these guidelines will provide consistent assessments and allow the visiting nurse to recognize problems with lactation and jaundice before the baby is compromised. The only specialized equipment needed is a well-calibrated scale. A careful history of intake and elimination should be obtained, and the infant observed while breastfeeding if possible. In our opinion, the visiting nurse should undress the infant completely for the examination and weigh the baby. The nurse should report any heart murmur immediately and arrange for a physician examination without delay. The visiting nurse should have a working knowledge of normal newborn vital signs, normal patterns of weight loss following birth, normal elimination patterns, and common breastfeeding problems, in order to discuss the findings with the physician and make referrals to a lactation specialist when necessary.[14] The nurse should fax a summary of the visit to the primary care provider the same day as the home visit.

For such a program to succeed, both home health nurses and primary care physicians need more instruction in lactation. A 1995 survey of recently trained pediatricians, obstetricians, and family physicians revealed a serious lack of breastfeeding knowledge and training, with fewer than 50% of senior residents and 75% of practicing physicians feeling that their training in breastfeeding issues was adequate.[15] Only 50% to 60% of respondents knew the appropriate interventions for low milk supply or jaundice in the breastfeeding newborn. Clearly, training and continuing education programs for physicians and others who work with new breastfeeding mothers should give more attention to these issues. This is particularly critical because specialized lactation-support services are likely to be early casualties when hospitals cut their budgets.[16]

WHAT ABOUT SCREENING?

What are the effects of early newborn discharge on newborn screening tests? Should testing be done even when discharge before 12 or 24 hours is anticipated? One group recommends drawing the newborn screen sample before discharge regardless of the baby's age, since this may be the only opportunity to detect a problem, and many of the results will be reliable.[17] Early sampling does not affect the results of hemoglobin electrophoresis, galactosemia testing, and testing for biotinidase deficiency, since these tests rely upon a protein marker (hemoglobin S, for example) or the absence of an enzyme. Tests that depend on the accumulation of a metabolite or rapid changes in hormone levels at birth, however, may be affected. These include screens for hypothyroidism, congenital adrenal hyperplasia, maple syrup urine disease, homocystinuria, and phenylketonuria (PKU). Although the exact effects of the timing of the sample are not known for most of these, research has been done on PKU and hypothyroidism.[17,18]

Phenylaline levels will be reliably elevated by 24 hours of age, even in breastfed infants.[17] Therefore, if the PKU screen is drawn after 24 hours, it will not need to be repeated. However, since laboratories in most states do not do quantitative phenylalanine levels, but rather the less sensitive Guthrie test, a bioassay, a second PKU screen will be required if the first sample is obtained at less than 24 hours of age.[18]

Thyroid screening may need to be repeated, depending on the screening method used in your region. There is normally a surge of TSH at birth, with normal T_4 levels. If your screening method relies on TSH testing, samples taken within the first day of life will yield many false positives. Programs that rely on T_4 measurements generally also include TSH testing on the lowest 10% of samples, and therefore will also have higher recall rates for early discharge infants with low normal T_4 who have a mildly elevated TSH level. The AAP recommends that any infant with a TSH level greater than 40 mU/L be considered hypothyroid until proven otherwise, and to repeat testing in those with mildly elevated TSH levels between 20 and 40 mU/L.[19]

WHERE DO WE STAND?

Early discharge has led to unforeseen problems in some patients. Experience shows that many infants fare well if discharged at 24 hours or even less, while a few go on to develop problems with feeding, jaundice, or, rarely, infection or cardiac symptoms. To avert these problems, reliable, knowledgeable follow-up within 48 to 72 hours of discharge is imperative. This early follow-up ensures that repeat PKU screening will occur, adequacy of breastfeeding will be assessed, and the infant will be evaluated for jaundice and other medical problems. Efforts to improve prenatal education in breastfeeding and newborn care should also be pursued and could be incorporated into prenatal visits. With a systematic approach to parent and physician education, and appropriately guided early follow-up, the physician and mother can work together to determine the best length of stay for that mother-infant pair.

REFERENCES

1. AAP Committee on Fetus and Newborn: Hospital stay for healthy term newborns. Pediatrics 1995;96:788
2. Annas G: Women and children first. N Engl J Med 1995;333:1647
3. Algeo D: Insurers' agreement kills hospital-stay bill. The Denver Post, January 30, 1996
4. Britton HL, Britton JR: Efficacy of early newborn discharge in a middle class population. Am J Dis Child 1984;138:1041
5. Britton JR, Britton HL, Beebe SA: Early discharge of the term newborn: A continued dilemma. Pediatrics 1994;94:291
6. Braveman P, Egerter S, Peral M, et al: Early discharge of newborns and mothers: A critical review of the literature. Pediatrics 1995;96:716
7. Margolis LH: A critical review of studies of newborn discharge timing. Clin Pediatr 1995;34(12):626
8. Newman TB, Maisels MJ: Evaluation and treatment of jaundice in the term newborn: A kinder, gentler approach. Pediatrics 1992;89:809
9. AAP Provisional Committee for Quality Improvement and Subcommittee on Hyperbilirubinemia: Practice parameter: Management of hyperbilirubinemia in the healthy term newborn. Pediatrics 1994;94:558
10. Sola A: Changes In clinical practice and bilirubin encephalopathy in "healthy term newborns." Pediatr Res 1995;37:145A
11. Hansen TWR: Kernicterus in a full-term infant: The need for increased vigilance (Letter). Pediatrics 1995;95:798
12. Lee K-S, Perlman M. Ballantyne M, et al: Association between duration of neonatal hospital stay and readmission rate. J Pediatr 1995;127:758
13. AAP Committee on Practice and Ambulatory Medicine: Recommendations for preventive pediatric health care. Pediatrics 1995;96(2):insert
14. Freed GL, Landers S, Schanier RJ: A practical guide to successful breast-feeding management. Am J Dis Child 1991;145:917
15. Freed GL, Clark SJ, Sorenson J, et al: National assessment of physicians' breastfeeding knowledge, attitudes, training, and experience. JAMA 1995;273:472
16. Eicher D: Breastfeeding program dealt a blow: Cutbacks, changes trim services. The Denver Post, January 29,1996
17. Doherty LB, Rohr FJ, Levy HL: Detection of phenylketonuria in the very early newborn blood specimen. Pediatrics 1991;87:240
18. Early discharge from the newborn nursery: A potential threat to effective newborn screening (editorial). Screening 1994;3:45
19. AAP section on Endocrinology and Committee on Genetics, and American Thyroid Association Committee on Public Health: Newborn screening for congenital hypothyroidism: Recommended guidelines. Pediatrics 1993;91:203

POSTSCRIPT

Should Hospitals Continue Early Discharge Policies for Newborns?

Britton, Britton, and Beebe concede that there are methodological flaws in the studies on early discharge, but that there is evidence to show early discharge is safe for the majority of babies. The three physicians wrote their selection before the mandatory 48-hour hospital stay for newborns was instituted, but their summary of available data of the appropriate time for hospital discharge of term newborns provides valuable research on the subject. They report studies that show psychosocial benefits of early discharge. These include a facilitation of bonding, attachment, increased breast-feeding, enhanced family interactions, and overall improved patient satisfaction.

Thilo and Townsend detail the minimum criteria for early newborn discharge, which has been published by the Committee on the Fetus and Newborn of the American Academy of Pediatrics. Although the criteria for discharge seem clear, there are some vague areas that are difficult to measure. Is 48 hours enough time for the doctor to ascertain that the baby will stay healthy? Thilo and Townsend state that there is little evidence to show that all of these criteria can be met within 48 hours.

SUGGESTED READINGS

Braveman, P., Egerter, S., Pearl, M., Marchi, K., & Miller, C. (1995, October). Problems associated with early discharge of newborn infants. Early discharge of newborns and mothers: A critical review. *Pediatrics, 96*(4), 716–726.

Carty, E., & Bradley, C. (1990). A randomized, controlled evaluation of early postpartum hospital discharge. *Birth, 17*, 199–204.

Hammonds, K. (1996, January). Newborn babies, bawling moms. *Business Week (Industrial/Technology Edition), 40*(3457).

Kyong-Soon, L., Periman M., Ballantyne, M., Ailed, I., & To, T. (1995, November). Association between duration of neonatal hospital stay and readmission rate. *Journal of Pediatrics, 127*(5), 758–766.

Margolis, L. (1995, December). A critical review of studies of newborn discharge timing. *Clinical Pediatrics, 34*(12), 626–634.

Oh, W. (1995, October). Hospital stay for healthy term newborns. *Pediatrics, 96*(4), 788–790.

Survival of drive-through babies same as others—study. (1996, September). *American Medical News, 39*(33), 11.

ISSUE 4

Is the Welfare of Our Disadvantaged Children Improving?

YES: Lisbeth B. Schorr, from "Making the Most of What We Already Know," *Public Welfare* (Spring 1994)

NO: William J. Bennett, from "What to Do About the Children," *Commentary* (March 1995)

ISSUE SUMMARY

YES: Lisbeth B. Schorr, author and director of the Harvard University Project on Effective Services, contends that organized intervention programs are working to circumvent social problems such as teen pregnancy, juvenile crime, and school dropout rates. She cites specific examples of these and sees much hope for the future.

NO: William J. Bennett, former secretary of education and former director of the Office of National Drug Control Policy, argues that children have many problems that will probably not be solved in the near future. Regardless of the many social programs aimed at helping disadvantaged children, the educational achievement of children has dropped, and rates of child abuse and neglect have skyrocketed. He sees the decline of the two-parent family and moral confusion as primary reasons for children's poor living conditions.

Since the 1960s social programs have been established by schools, civic organizations, local agencies, and the federal government to reduce the risk factors that disadvantaged youth face. These programs provide intervention treatments such as after-school activities, counseling programs, and tutoring to reduce the incidence of juvenile delinquency, teen pregnancy, and dropping out of school. Some of these programs, such as Head Start and, more recently, the midnight basketball program, have become well known, but others are less familiar to the public. All the programs have good intentions and some have evaluation results to confirm their success, but questions are being raised about their efficacy. Are intervention programs really improving the lives of disadvantaged children or are they a band-aid, masking a larger societal problem?

The Federal Interagency Forum on Child and Family Statistics issued a report in July 1997 on key national indicators of child well-being. Not only are the results of the report useful, but this marked the first time that national agencies collaborated on trends on the health and education of America's children. The forum was founded in 1994 and includes the Departments of Agriculture, Commerce, Health and Human Services, Housing and Urban Development, Justice, and Labor; the National Science Foundation; and the Office of Management and Budget. Specifically, the National Institute of Child Health and Human Development, National Maternal and Child Health Bureau, and National Center for Education Statistics were listed as contributors to the report.

On a positive note, the report states that more children know where their next meal is coming from, more children are being read to by parents, more children are being enrolled in preschool programs and also graduating from college, immunization rates are up, and the rate of infant and childhood deaths has decreased. Not all the trends for children were positive. The use of illicit drugs and cigarette smoking is up and the incidence of youth as victims of crime has increased. Children in families with annual incomes below $15,000 were 22 times more likely to experience abuse and neglect than families with annual incomes above $30,000.

In the following selections, Lisbeth B. Schorr reports that programs for disadvantaged children are working and have the support of those in power in Washington, D.C. She lists a number of intervention programs that have met their goals and are considered worth the money being spent on them. William J. Bennett takes an opposing view of the status of children in America and points to many societal ills that continue to keep children in the lower class and underclass at a disadvantage.

YES

Lisbeth B. Schorr

MAKING THE MOST OF
WHAT WE ALREADY KNOW

Human-service administrators probably have the toughest jobs in America. When I reviewed the agenda for your meeting [of the American Public Welfare Association], I was delighted that both welfare reform and health care reform would be so expertly covered, so that I would be free to talk about what we know about the needs of children and families that go beyond income, employment, and access to health care, as well as my favorite subject: what we know about what works in meeting those needs.

I began collecting information that sheds light on this subject almost by accident. In the early 1980s, I was struck with a prevailing sense of helplessness in the face of urgent social problems; and I set out to find examples of programs that worked. I wanted to show that organized interventions—in early education, schooling, health services, social services, and family supports—did indeed change life outcomes among disadvantaged children.

I decided at the outset that I would look for programs that were successful in dealing with problems of consequence—problems that were seen as important because of the enormous toll they take on individual youngsters, their families, and society as a whole: school-age child-bearing, school dropout, delinquency, and long-term welfare dependence. I called these "rotten outcomes."

I then looked at the risk factor research and discovered a strong convergence around the finding that because risk factors interact and multiply the effects of one another, the reduction of any risk factor improves the odds of a favorable outcome. The more risk factors in a particular situation, the greater the damaging impact of each. But the impact is not just additive—risk factors multiply one another's destructive effects.

Youngsters who become pregnant or delinquent or who drop out of school already have been in trouble for many years; many of the troubles that surface in adolescence can be predicted from poor school performance and truancy as early as third or fourth grade. We also know that trouble in elementary

From Lisbeth B. Schorr, "Making the Most of What We Already Know," *Public Welfare*, vol. 52 (Spring 1994), pp. 22–26. Copyright © 1993 by Lisbeth B. Schorr. Reprinted by permission.

school correlates with a number of antecedent risk factors. In addition to poverty, these include

- being born unwanted or to a teenage mother;
- low weight at birth;
- untreated childhood health problems;
- lack of language, reasoning, and coping skills at school entry; and
- failure to develop trusting relationships with reliable and protective adults early in life.

The important news about these risk factors is that every one of them has been successfully attacked through interventions we know how to provide. We now have evidence of

- school-based health clinics that have reduced the rate of teenage childbearing, raised the average age at which youngsters became sexually active, and reduced the number of unwanted births;
- comprehensive prenatal care and nutrition programs that have reduced the proportion of low birth weight babies;
- intensive family support, nurse home-visiting, and childcare programs that have resulted in lower rates of child abuse, fewer children removed from their homes, and fewer mothers dependent on welfare;
- quality preschool programs whose participants, when they become young adults, include fewer dropouts, fewer delinquents, fewer teenage mothers, and fewer youngsters without jobs; and
- reformed elementary schools that were able to so change the climate of the school that whole populations of children who had been failing began to succeed.

As one synthesizes the evidence, it becomes clear that the contention that in the world of social programs "nothing works" is in fact a canard—a myth that cannot be maintained in the face of the research and experience now at hand.

COMMON ELEMENTS

The good news, then, is not only that there are programs that work, but that we now know a lot about how and why they work. As I analyzed the information I had collected to identify common patterns among successful programs, several characteristics emerged:

Successful programs are comprehensive, intensive, flexible, and responsive. Staffs in these programs have extensive repertoires and extensive community networks. They have the capacity to respond flexibly to concrete needs for help with food or housing or a violent family member. Sister Mary Paul, who runs a family services program in Brooklyn, says that no one in her program ever says, "This may be what you need, but helping you get it is not part of my job."

Many of these programs provide their staffs with a pool of flexible funds, which they can use at their discretion to help a family buy a wheelchair or a washing machine or to get the car repaired. They respond to the needs of families at times and places that make sense to the family, often at home, at school, or in neighborhood centers and at odd hours, rather than in distant offices once a week on Wednesday afternoons. Job descriptions are broad, boundaries are permeable, and professionalism is redefined.

In my book, *Within Our Reach: Breaking the Cycle of Disadvantage*, I tell the story of a Homebuilders family preservation worker who appeared at the front door of a family in crisis, only to be greeted by a mother's declaration that the one thing she did not need in her life was one more social worker telling her what to do. What she needed, she said, was to get her house cleaned up. The Homebuilders therapist, a master's-level clinical psychologist with supplemental training by Homebuilders, responded by asking the mother if she wanted to start with the kitchen. After they worked together for an hour, the two women were able to talk about the issues that were at the heart of the family's difficulty. It may have been an unorthodox way of forging a therapeutic alliance, but it worked.

I told this story at a meeting some months ago, and a distinguished professor of psychology interrupted to say that that was going too far. What the psychologist had done, she claimed, was unprofessional.

In a sense, of course, she was quite right. In most professions, highest status is conferred on those who deal with issues from which all human complexity and messiness have been removed. Narrowly drawn boundaries that limit what is expected of a professional may be the traditional essence of professionalism, yet they often interfere with professional effectiveness.

Successful programs deal with children as parts of families. They recognize that a mother's needs cannot be dealt with in isolation from her children's, and vice versa. They work not alone with one generation, but with two, and often three. Successful Head Start programs and family support centers nurture parents so they can better nurture their children.

Successful programs take into account the real world of those they serve. The clinician treating an infant for recurrent diarrhea sees beyond the patient on the examining table to whether the family needs help from a public health nurse or social worker to obtain nonmedical services. I visited a health center in Mississippi that actually delivers clean water to families who cannot get it any other way.

The effective job-training program knows that unstable childcare can stop a transition to self-sufficiency cold, and that poor-quality child care is likely to interfere powerfully with a young child's chances to climb out of poverty.

Successful programs deal with families as parts of neighborhoods and communities. Most successful programs have deep roots in the community. They are not imposed from without—they are not "parachuted" into communities—but are carefully integrated with specific local community needs and strengths so that local communities have a genuine sense of ownership, and programs are in fact designed to respond to the real needs of that particular community.

Staff in successful programs have the time, skills, and support to build relationships of trust and respect with children and families. They work in settings that allow them to develop meaningful personal relationships over time and to provide services respectfully, ungrudgingly, and collaboratively. Psychiatrist James Comer points out that relationship issues are particularly important among low-income people who have given up on helping systems.

None of the programs that succeed are "lean and mean." They have been able to establish a climate that is warm, welcoming, and supportive. The quality and continuity of relationships and support are what make many other activities effective. Home visitors say that respectful, trusting relationships make parent education work.

A careful evaluation of an enhanced prenatal care program in Washington, D.C., found that the most important element that kept women in the program and utilizing health services properly was not the program's cash incentives or even easy access to care; rather it was the "friendly support" of "someone to talk to about pregnancy and other life stresses" that was valued most highly.

Smallness of scale at the point of service delivery also seems to be crucial. Large schools, massive outpatient clinics, and large caseloads vastly complicate the job of personalizing services to respond to individual and family needs. For many children, life trajectories have been changed through a relationship with a caring, attentive adult. And, as those who work as volunteers or as professionals can attest, a caring, attentive adult can come in many forms.

Successful programs have long-term, preventive orientations and continue to evolve over time. The people responsible for these programs have no illusion that they can implement the perfect model program. They allow their programs to evolve continually to maintain their responsiveness to individual, family, and community needs over time and to respond to feedback from both front-line staff and participants.

Successful programs combine a highly flexible mode of operation with a clearly articulated sense of mission. They operate in an organizational culture that is outcome oriented rather than rule bound. Their approach is long-term, inclusive, preventive, and empowering.

COUNTERING THE SYSTEM

The successes of these interventions are of enormous importance despite the fact that many of the most successful programs operate in special—and sometimes idiosyncratic—circumstances. But these successes show that something can be done to address social problems previously considered intractable. They provide a vision of what can be achieved. They refute the contention that families in the so-called underclass are beyond the reach of organized services. They show that when high-risk populations get the best of services rather than the worst, life trajectories change. And, by revealing the attributes of success, they contain the information we need to take successful programs to scale.

These attributes of success, of course, are neither counterintuitive nor surprising. When I go around the country making speeches about how effective programs are characterized by flexibility, comprehensiveness, responsiveness, front-line discretion, a family focus, community rootedness, and respectful relationships, practitioners never seem surprised. This is the stuff that most people on the front lines know works—the stuff they know is important.

It is also the stuff that the good ones have to lie, cheat, and connive in order to be able to do.

Recently I received a letter from the director of a community health center who had heard me discuss the attributes of effective programs. She wrote that these attributes describe precisely what she does each day—and that they are precisely the opposite of what she's told to do each day by the large hospital under whose auspices her center operates.

Marc Tucker of the National Center on Education and the Economy says, "When you find an individual school that works, it's almost always because it's running against the grain. You find a teacher or a principal who really doesn't give a damn about the system. They are willing to ignore or subvert every rule in the book in order to get the job done for the kids." You hear the same thing from child protection workers and the staff of job training programs.

Unless we come to grips with the mismatch between the attributes of effective programs and the pressures placed on programs by prevailing systems, successful models will continue to flourish briefly and then disappear or become diluted when special funding and special political protection end, or when they can no longer find a leader who combines the talents of a Mother Theresa, a Machiavelli, and a certified public accountant.

The attributes of effective programs that are now supported by theory, a convergent body of research, and front-line experience in many different disciplines turn out to be totally at odds with the systems within which most programs must function—and which chief executive officers must administer. Successful programs remain the exception and not the rule because existing systems undermine precisely the elements that are the hallmarks of effective programs.

With the tools you are issued, which include categorical financing, rigid rules, hierarchical management techniques, and input-based accountability, of course the front-line practitioners complain that they cannot provide comprehensive, flexible, family-centered, responsive services.

BRIGHT PROSPECTS

So what are the prospects for change, the prospects that you will get some help in operating systems in which ordinary people can achieve superior outcomes, in which effective programs can b sustained—systems that do not depen on a single charismatic leader?

I think the prospects are bright—eve though money may be short. Let me tel you why I believe this:

First, I think we have the best shot w have had in a generation to break th cycle of disadvantage, because we hav the information we need to do better; an we have a growing consensus that w must do better.

There is increasing recognition tha teenage pregnancy, violence, and schoo failure are not isolated problems tha have either isolated or standardize solutions. We know we have the element of past success to build on, and we kno that we cannot do it at bargain basemen prices and that we cannot do it overnigh But we can be certain that if it is done wel it will make a difference in the life of thi nation.

Marian Wright Edelman of the Chi dren's Defense Fund likes to say that w are at a point in this country today whe doing what is right coincides with wha we have to do to save our national skins The people who are committed to socia justice can join with those whose highes priority is a workforce that can increas American productivity and win the inter national economic competition.

Second, I am optimistic about wha can be done because human service ad ministrators now have a lot of friend in Washington. From the president o down, the new leadership in Washing ton is not only competent, but it is re spectful of state competence. They see th differences among states and communi ties not as inconvenient impediments t standardized rule making but rather a critical strengths.

So we have the president declaring

We're going to give the states, the counties, and the cities the right to design what we call "bottoms-up" initiatives. In other words, you decide what it is you need, tell us what you need, and if it's in a grant proposal that's anywhere under $10 million—or over $10 million if you get approval for it—we will design something to give you the money you need instead of you having to figure out how to walk through the hoops of all the rules and regulations of the hundreds and hundreds of grants in the federal government.

To carry out this charge, the president has created a "community enterprise board" to identify neighborhoods across America, both urban and rural, that are in trouble. These neighborhoods, in the president's words, "will say what they want done. Then my cabinet will sit down and work together and figure out how to do it—not how to tell them how to comply with our rules, but how to do what people need done at the local level."

As columnist Neal Pierce points out, when a city is struggling to assist homeless people, for example, it will now be able to capture not only federal funds earmarked for the homeless, but also monies appropriated for housing, transportation, job training, childcare, health, mental health, and alcohol and drug abuse—keeping just one set of books and adhering to one set of rules.

In exchange for greater flexibility, we will surely see a greater emphasis on outcome accountability, which I think we should welcome. I believe that accountability based on outcomes that reflect common sense and common understanding—such as increasing rates of healthy births, school readiness, and school success—may be the most powerful force to

- focus attention on the mission rather than on the rules,
- permit flexibility and autonomy at the front end,
- encourage cross-systems collaboration,
- promote a community-wide "culture of responsibility" for children and families, and
- provide evidence to funders and the public that programs are indeed achieving their intended purposes.

I believe that efforts to obtain new funds, especially public funds, and to use old funds under new and more flexible rules will succeed only if they are coupled with clear commitments that effectiveness will ultimately be demonstrated in improved outcomes. Especially if one considers discretion at the frontlines as critical, and if one believes that local programs must be able to evolve over time to meet unique local needs, the old ways of ensuring accountability become counterproductive. Legislation or regulations that attempt to ensure quality by imposing detailed procedural protocols interfere profoundly with a program's ability to operate flexibly. But the demands for accountability cannot be dismissed; and the most reasonable way of ensuring that funds are in fact accomplishing their intended purposes, while allowing for front-line creativity, is by documenting results in terms of important, real-world outcomes.

In an outcome-oriented climate, it would be easier to combine publicly funded efforts with the initiatives that several national foundations, including The Ford Foundation, The Pew Charitable Trusts, the Rockefeller Foundation, and the Annie E. Casey Foundation, are now targeting on cross-systems, neighborhood-based efforts to turn around both neighborhood and family disintegration in areas of persistent poverty and social dislocation.

The provision of effective services to populations that heretofore have been neglected or poorly served requires collaboration among individuals and agencies that have previously worked in isolation. But collaboration alone will not improve outcomes. Because fragmentation is such a big problem in existing services, many have come to see the coordination and integration of services as the solution.

Collaboration is hard, and it's a crucial step in solving many current problems; but it is futile to put together services that are of mediocre quality, that are rendered grudgingly, or that are rendered by professionals who do not persevere or do not know how to work collaboratively with families.

Whether we are talking about school-based services, one-stop shopping, or new links between education and other human services, putting together formerly isolated services is essential. But we should not be so dazzled by the feat of putting together formerly isolated pieces of service that we forget to pay attention to the contents of those elements.

That is why I attach so much importance to the many... geographically based initiatives that would match the concentration of social problems in urban communities and depleted rural areas with a similar magnitude of fiscal resources and problem-solving capabilities. The factors implicated in persistent poverty and concentrated social dislocation are too intertwined and pervasive for narrow, one-shot interventions. What is needed is a broad attack on many fronts at once. This approach combines comprehensive and responsive services and restructured schools with community development and economic development, sometimes even with reforms to improve housing and public safety, so that they will interact synergistically to achieve a visible level of effectiveness in an entire threatened community.

It is virtually impossible for any child to grow up whole in neighborhoods that society has abandoned, that are left without decent health care, schools, parks, libraries, theaters, youth centers, or even washing machines—neighborhoods where no one can count on being able to land a legal job that will support a family and where no one feels safe.

Everyone agrees that it takes a village to raise a child. But in the inner city, the village has disintegrated. That is why we need bold and comprehensive strategies. Incrementalism will not do it. There are chasms you cannot cross one step at a time. So my third reason for feeling confident is that bold thinking is in.

It became hard, in the last decade, to think boldly. We learned to think small and to content ourselves with fiddling at the margins. But it is rapidly becoming clear that some of our most urgent problems will not be solved unless we dare to adopt a bolder vision—a vision that is built on a shared understanding that we cannot allow the richest country in the world to declare bankruptcy in our civic life. That vision could transform into action—public-private, national, state, and local—the widespread yearning that I see in so many American communities to make life better for all of America's children and families.

NO

William J. Bennett

WHAT TO DO ABOUT THE CHILDREN

At the dawn of the 20th century there was every reason to believe that ours would be (in the title of a best-selling book at the time) "the century of the child." From the early part of the 1900's through the 1950's, despite ups and downs, despite Depression and war, things got better in almost every area touching the welfare of American children: economic security improved, material earnings increased, medicine progressed, family structure was stable, children occupied a valued place in society, and our civic institutions were strong and resilient. In retrospect, it seems as if the midpoint of the century was a high point for the well-being of children.

By the 1960's, however, America began a steep and uninterrupted slide toward what might be called decivilization. Although every stratum of society has been affected, the worst problems have been concentrated within America's inner cities. No age group has remained untouched, but the most punishing blows have been absorbed by children.

In assessing conditions today, it is important to keep perspective: America is *not* in danger of becoming a third-world country; the vast majority of children do not live in sewers of disease and depravity; and most are not violent, sexually promiscuous, or drug-takers. At the same time, however, there is no question that as we approach the end of the last decade of this "American century," the condition of too many of our children is not good. The indicators are well-known: low educational achievement, the decline of the two-parent family, moral confusion, and, for a sizable and increasingly large minority, abuse, neglect, and very bleak prospects for the future.

Consider some real-world facts:

- From 1960 to 1991, the rate of homicide deaths among children under the age of 19 more than quadrupled. Among black teenagers, homicide is now by far the leading cause of death.

From William J. Bennett, "What to Do About the Children," *Commentary*, vol. 99 (March 1995), pp. 23–28. Copyright © 1995 by *Commentary*. Reprinted by permission. All rights reserved.

- Since 1965, the juvenile arrest rate for violent crimes has tripled, and the fastest-rowing segment of the criminal population is made up of children.
- Since 1960, the rate at which teenagers take their own lives has more than tripled.
- The rate of births to unmarried teenagers has increased by almost 200 percent in three decades; the number of unmarried teenagers getting pregnant has nearly doubled in the past two decades.
- Today, 30 percent of all births and almost 70 percent of all black births are illegitimate. By the end of the decade, according to the most reliable projections, 40 percent of all American births and 80 percent of all minority births will be out-of-wedlock.
- During the last 30 years there has been a tripling of the percentage of children living in single-parent families. According to some projections, only 30 percent of white children and only 6 percent of black children born in 1980 will live with both parents through the age of 18.

A useful historical reference point may be 1965, when Daniel P. Moynihan, then an Assistant Secretary of Labor, wrote *The Negro Family: The Case for National Action.* Then, one-quarter of all black children were born out of wedlock; one-half of all black children lived in broken homes at some time before they reached age 18; and 14 percent of black children were on welfare. Moynihan considered this "tangle of pathologies" to be a social catastrophe, and so it was. Today, however, were we to achieve such figures in even one of our major urban centers, we would consider it a stunning accomplishment.

As the figures above demonstrate, these problems are by no means limited to lower-class or minority populations. In addition to everything else, divorce, rampant in all social classes, causes over one million children annually to end up, at least temporarily, in single-parent families. And wherever they live, American children today—especially the teenagers among them—spend relatively minuscule amounts of time with either their fathers or their mothers—or their homework—and vastly greater amounts of time on other things from crime to television.

A few years ago a special commission of political, medical, educational, and business leaders issued a report on the health of America's teenagers titled *Code Blue.* In the words of this report. "Never before has one generation of American teenagers been less healthy, less cared for, or less prepared for life than their parents were at the same age." According to the sociologist David Popenoe, today's generation of children is the first in our nation's history to be less well-off psychologically and socially than its parents.

Nor is the concern limited to the experts. When asked in a recent Family Research Council poll, "Do you think children are generally better off today or worse off than when you were a child?," 60 percent of all Americans—and 77 percent of all black Americans—said children today are "worse off." They are right.

II

The greatest long-term threat to the well-being of our children is the enfeebled condition—in some sectors of our society, the near-complete collapse—of our character-forming institutions. In a free society, families, schools, and churches have primary responsibility for shaping the moral sensibilities of the young. The influence of these institutions is determinative; when they no longer provide moral instruction or lose their moral authority, there is very little that other auxiliaries—particularly the federal government—can do.

Among those three institutions, the family is preeminent; it is, as Michael Novak of the American Enterprise Institute once famously said, the original and best department of health, education, and welfare. But the family today is an agency in disrepair. Writes David Popenoe:

This period [the 1960's through the 1990's] has witnessed an unprecedented decline of the family as a social institution. Families have lost functions, social power, and authority over their members. They have grown smaller in size, less stable, and shorter in life span.... Moreover, there has been a weakening of child-centeredness in American society and culture. Familism as a cultural value has diminished.

And so, too, has fatherhood. Each night in America, four out of ten children go to sleep without fathers who live in their homes, and upward of 60 percent will spend some major part of their childhood without fathers.

In the past, the typical cause of fatherlessness was divorce; its new face is homes headed by never-married mothers. This is "the most socially consequential family trend of our generation" (in the words of David Blankenhorn of the Institute for American Values), and it has seismic social implications. Moynihan warned [more than] 30 years ago that a society which allows a large number of young men to grow up without fathers in their lives asks for and almost always gets chaos. We have come to the point in America where we are asking prisons to do for many young boys what fathers used to do.

* * *

There are other signs of decay, particularly of the cultural variety. Television shows make a virtue of promiscuity, adultery, homosexuality, and gratuitous acts of violence. Rap music celebrates the abuse and torture of women. Advertisements are increasingly erotic, even perverse. And many of our most successful and critically-acclaimed movies celebrate brutality, casual cruelty, and twisted sex.

None of these trends takes place in a moral or cultural vacuum. During the last 30 years we have witnessed a profound shift in public attitudes. The pollster Daniel Yankelovich finds that we Americans now place less value on what we owe others as a matter of moral obligation; less value on sacrifice as a moral good, on social conformity, respectability, and observing the rules; less value on correctness and restraint in matters of physical pleasure and sexuality—and correlatively greater value on things like self-expression, individualism, self-realization, and personal choice.

How does all this affect young children? A single, simple statistic tells much: if, in 1951, 51 percent of Americans agreed with the statement, "Parents who don't get along should not stay together for the children," in 1985 that figure had risen to 86 percent.

The social historian Barbara Dafoe Whitehead has observed that the Hallmark company now offers two lines of divorce cards: one set for the newly single adults, the other for children of divorced parents. For the latter, a typical message is piercing in its casualness: "I'm sorry I'm not always there when you need me but I hope you know I'm always just a phone call away." By contrast, one adult card reads, "Think of your former marriage as a record album. It was full of music—both happy and sad. But what's important now is... YOU! the recently released HOT NEW SINGLE! You're going to be at the TOP OF THE CHARTS!" As Whitehead comments, What had once been regarded as hostile to children's best interests is now considered essential to adults' happiness."

If the self, in the late Allan Bloom's withering assessment, has become "the modern substitute for the soul," we are also living in an era in which it has become unfashionable to make judgments on a whole range of behaviors and attitudes. This unwillingness to judge has resulted in unilateral moral disarmament, as harmful in the cultural realm as its counterpart is in the military. With the removal of social sanctions in the name of "tolerance" and "open-mindedness," and the devaluing of the idea of personal responsibility, is it any wonder, for instance, that in a recent survey 70 percent of young people between the ages of 18 and 34 said that people who generate a baby out-of-wedlock should not be subject to moral reproach *of any sort?*

It would be supererogatory at this late date to catalogue the role of government in giving form and force to these ideas and beliefs through law and policy. Suffice it to say that from the area of criminal justice, to education, to welfare policy, to the arts, to a whole tangle of sexual and family issues, government has increasingly put itself on the side of the forces of decomposition, not on the side of the forces of restoration. The consequence is that the moral universe we are sending our children into today is more harsh, more vulgar, more coarse, and more violent than the moral universe most of us grew up in—and they are less equipped to deal with it.

We should not flinch from admitting this unsettling truth: we live in a culture which seems dedicated to the corruption of the young, to assuring the loss of their innocence before their time. "It dawned on me recently," the anthropologist David Murray has written, "that we have now become the kind of society that in the 19th century almost every Christian denomination felt compelled to missionize."

III

If the problem is one of moral breakdown, it would be fatuous to suggest that it can be fixed by government intervention. There is, after all, one proposition which has been tested repeatedly over the last three decades and just as repeatedly been found wanting—namely, that we can spend our way out of our social problems. Instead of encouraging government, we need to relimit it—not only, or even primarily, for fiscal reasons, but because the "nanny state" has eroded self-reliance and encouraged dependency, crowding out the character-forming institutions and enfeebling us as citizens.

Still, there are a number of actions government *can* take that would amount to constructive and far-reaching, even radical, reforms. A number of these ideas have been on the table for quite some time, but as the results of the November 1994 elections suggest, Americans may be more ready for fundamental reform today than at any other point in recent history. So we suddenly find ourselves presented with an extraordinary opportunity.

Before getting down to particulars, I would stipulate two general points that should guide any discussion of public-policy solutions to the problems faced by children in America. One of them I borrow from an old principle of medicine: *primum non nocere*—first, do no harm. In many, many cases, the best thing government can do is (to quote Myron Magnet of the *City Journal*) "to *stop* doing what makes the problem worse."

As for the second point, it was well expressed by Alexander Hamilton, who in *The Federalist No. 17* questioned whether "all those things... which are proper to be provided for by local legislation [should] ever be desirable cares of a general jurisdiction." To state this in terms of our present situation, there are many responsibilities which would be better handled by states and localities but which have fallen under the jurisdiction of the federal government; they should be devolved back to the smaller "laboratories of democracy."

Within those constraints, government, at one level or another, does have a role to play in improving conditions for the young. Let us look at a few key areas, beginning with the link between welfare and illegitimacy.

Between 1962 and 1992, welfare spending in the United States increased by over 900 percent in 1992 dollars. At the same time, the poverty rate dropped by less than 5 percent—and illegitimacy rates increased over 400 percent. Children are the real victims in this national tragedy. They are being conditioned into the same habits of dependence they are surrounded by, resulting in an almost unbreakable cycle of welfare and "the tangle of pathologies" associated with it.

John J. DiIulio, Jr. of Princeton has put this last point well:

> The problem *is* that inner-city children are trapped in criminogenic homes, schools, and neighborhoods where high numbers of teenagers and adults are no more likely to nurture, teach, and care for children than they are to expose them to neglect, abuse, and violence.... Children cannot be socialized by adults who are themselves unsocialized (or worse), families that exist in name only, schools that do not educate, and neighborhoods in which violent and repeat criminals circulate in and out of jail....

Quite a number of serious and thoughtful proposals have been advanced for restructuring the entire system of welfare benefits, of which Charles Murray's is among the most thoroughgoing.[1] In a similar spirit, I would endorse full-scale and far-reaching plans to send welfare back to the states, which have proved the best settings for innovative reform and experimentation.

As for the problem of illegitimacy in particular, one year after legislation is enacted I would recommend ending direct welfare payments to women who have children out of wedlock; enforcing existing child-support laws; and terminating the increase in benefits for women who have children while participating in welfare programs. The success of such reforms, it seems to me, depends critically on their sweep and magnitude; incremental steps will not do the necessary job of altering fundamental assumptions and expectations.

To turn to a point that has been heavily controverted since the elections of November 8 [1994]: in my view, situations will arise which may warrant the removal of a child from the care of his parent(s). To be sure, this should only happen in desperate circumstances and as a last resort. But we cannot ignore the plain fact that there are more and more horrifying cases of abuse, neglect, and parental malfeasence.

While adoption is the best alternative in such circumstances, the concept of orphanages, or group-care homes, should not be dismissed. Such institutions pretty much disappeared from the national scene when government began distributing money in the expectation that poor parents, with federal assistance, would do a better job of raising their children. But in far too many cases that expectation has been resoundingly refuted by experience.

When parents cannot care for their children's basic material, psychological, medical, and moral needs, it is time to look to other institutions. The orphanage —call it a boarding school without tuition —may then be in their best interest. Can anyone seriously argue that some boys would be worse off living in Boys Town than in, say, the Cabrini Green housing project in Chicago, considered by its residents a virtual war zone?

* * *

But adoption is certainly preferable. Only 50,000 children are adopted each year in the United States; half are healthy infants and half are older children or children with disabilities. At any given time, however, one to two million homes are waiting to adopt. Provided only the child is young enough, there is, in effect, no such thing as an unwanted child, and this goes even for babies who are not fully healthy. Unfortunately, most potential adopters (and adoptees) are hamstrung by needless barriers.

In addition to the high cost of a private adoption, often as much as $10,000, many couples are automatically excluded from consideration due to race, financial background, age, disability, or home size. Other potential adopters are scared away by lax confidentiality laws, nonbinding adoptions, and the expanded rights of the biological father to reclaim legal custody.

The barriers to adoption are only one side of the problem. Availability is also severely limited. Unwed mothers are often denied information about adoption in prenatal counseling; others decide to abort their pregnancy for economic reasons. (Indeed, it may be partly for this reason that abortion has increasingly become a problem of juveniles: of the one million teenage pregnancies each year about 400,000 now end in abortion.) Finally, and perhaps most importantly, with the stigma of illegitimacy all but gone in this country, for many young, unwed, pregnant women single motherhood has become a more attractive option than giving a child up for adoption.

Again, there is a limit to what government can do. But again, too, the greatest hope lies in reforms at the state level, such as:

- prohibiting the use of race and/or ethnicity as a disqualification for would be foster or adoptive parents (in practice this has affected whites seeking to adopt nonwhite babies);
- expediting adoption procedures for infants and children who have been abandoned by their parents and are living in limbo in hospitals, group homes, and/or foster care;
- terminating parental rights and thus making a child available for adoption if by the age of six months—in the case of infants born with positive toxicology

—maternal drug use has not ceased, or if a child has been severely abused by its parents;

- enacting model legislation that will require courts to consider the best interests of the child first in all cases concerning custody;

- establishing uniform rules making voluntary surrender/adoption irrevocable at any point past 72 hours after birth;

- restricting payments to biological parents by adoptive parents to necessary expenses related directly to the pregnancy and adoption;

- ensuring that adoptive families are treated with the same respect as other families, free of the fear of intrusion by the state or other parties after an adoption has been finalized.

* * *

Then there is divorce—which, in terms of damage to children, can be the most devastating circumstance of all, yet which is conspicuous by its absence from the agenda of policy-makers.

As Karl Zinsmeister of the *American Enterprise* has written: "We talk about the drug crisis, the education crisis, and the problems of teen pregnancy and juvenile crime. But all these ills trace back predominantly to one source: broken families."

The statistics, indeed, are chilling. Children of single-parent families are twice as likely to drop out of high school, or, if they remain in school, have lower grade-point averages, lower college aspirations, and poorer attendance records than the general population. Girls living with only one parent are two-and-a-half times more likely to become teenage mothers. When it comes to crime, accord-

ing to some studies, 70 percent of juveniles now incarcerated in state-reform institutions have lived either in single-parent homes or with someone other than their natural parents, and 75 percent of adolescent murderers come from single-parent homes.

The divorce rate has nearly doubled since 1960—not coincidentally, the same period in which no-fault divorce laws became popular. Previously, before a divorce was granted, the law had required a showing of fault, such as cruelty, abuse, adultery, or desertion. The recision of these conditions not only significantly increased the number of divorces but transformed marriage into a simple business contract.

Though the incidence of divorce cannot significantly be addressed through public policy, its effects can perhaps be curbed to some degree. My suggestions include braking mechanisms when children are involved, such as mandatory and substantial "cooling-off" periods as well as mandatory counseling; reinstituting fault as an absolute requirement for divorce and in determining the terms of a settlement; and classifying all property as family property, which would affect the distribution of assets in cases where children are involved.

* * *

This brings us to institutions outside the home, starting with the schools. Parents all over the country are increasingly aware that the public-education system in America is an embarrassment. As the federal government has taken over more responsibilities for the nation's schools, the quality of education has plummeted. The response of the education establishment and of the teachers' unions to this situation, and to the growing movement for greater parental involvement and local control that has arisen in response to it, has been to advocate pumping more money into the system. This has only served to perpetuate and even escalate the problem.

The signs of failure are everywhere, and need not be reiterated here.[3] Fortunately, there are many potentially good solutions—though more money is not among them. Instead, and yet again, a devolution is in order: the first step toward genuine education reform should be to rein in the federal government. In my judgment, legislation is called for which would restore decision-making responsibilities to state and local authorities, enabling the federal government to give states a block grant with virtually no strings attached. The state, local school districts, and parents would then be in a better position to make their own decisions regarding curriculum, books, standards, discipline. etc. Not only would this lead to a system more accountable to parents, but it would encourage innovation and experimentation.

The next step is to implement reforms at the state level which would foster excellence in the education system. These include open enrollment; charter schools; privatization; performance-testing for students and teachers; a merit-pay system for teachers and administrators; and, above all, school choice, complete with vouchers redeemable at public, private, and religious schools. And to prevent a future trend toward regulatory authority, the federal Department of Education should be dismantled. The limited functions of the department should be carried out by the executive branch in an office of education policy.

* * *

What about crime? Between 1985 and 1991, the annual rate at which young men aged 15 to 19 were being killed increased by 154 percent, far surpassing the rate of change in any other group. Twenty percent of high-school students now carry a knife, razor, firearm, or other weapon on a regular basis. As James Q. Wilson recently pointed out, "Youngsters are shooting at people at a far higher rate than at any time in recent history."[4] Or, in the words of Senator Bill Bradley, "The murderers are younger, the guns more high-powered, and the acts themselves occur more and more randomly." This problem will almost certainly get worse before it gets better, as by the end of the decade there will be a half-million more American males between the ages of 14 and 17 than there are today, 30,000 of whom will probably become high-rate offenders.

The justice system spends $20 billion a year to arrest, rehabilitate, and jail juvenile offenders, only to watch 70 percent of them commit crimes again. Here, too, money is evidently not the panacea. Genuine reform of our juvenile-justice laws, which for the most part should take place on the state level, would involve keeping records of juvenile arrests, fingerprinting offenders, and making these records available to adult courts to prevent juvenile criminals from being treated as first-time offenders when they reach the age of 18. I would also strongly recommend legislation at the state level to allow juveniles, 14 or older, to be charged as adults for certain crimes—such as murder, rape, armed robbery, and assault with a firearm.

Genuine reform would also establish consistent, graduated punishments for every offense. It would insist on building and maintaining the facilities needed to keep violent offenders off the streets. It would speed up the criminal-justice system by enacting and enforcing realistic trial provisions. It would prohibit irresponsible judges from unilaterally imposing measures (such as "prison caps") which release violent and repeat offenders back onto the streets. It would require offenders to pay restitution to their victims. And it would create extended sentences in institutional boot camps for repeat offenders and those who failed to participate in the community-service and public-works programs to which they had been sentenced.

* * *

A special subcategory of the overall crime problem is drugs. From the mid-1980's until 1991, significant progress was made on the drug front, with researchers tracking a sharp decline in overall use. But in 1991 use began to rise, and drugs are still a major problem among the young.

According to the latest study from the University of Michigan's Institute for Social Research, one in four students has used illegal drugs before reaching high school; among 8th graders, 13 percent say they have smoked marijuana in the last year, *double* the rate of 1991; and over 40 percent of all 10th graders and nearly 50 percent of all 12th graders have used some illicit drug, including LSD, inhalants, stimulants, barbiturates, and cocaine and crack. This, in the words of the study's principal investigator, Lloyd D. Johnston, is "a problem that is getting worse at a fairly rapid pace," and it is being abetted by a decline in peer disapproval and a general softening of teenagers' attitudes toward drug use.

While the Clinton administration has not formally abandoned the war against drugs, it has abandoned it for all practical purposes. This could have a dire effect on what has already been achieved, incomplete as that is. If we mean to continue our efforts, we will need to do a number of things. They include allowing communities to choose their own antidrug priorities by combining federal antidrug support with that from states and localities; putting the U.S. military in charge of stopping the flow of illegal drugs from abroad, and giving the military control over the entire interdiction process; establishing trade and diplomatic sanctions and eliminating aid to cocaine-source countries that fail to reduce their production of cocaine by 10 percent per year, and by at least 50 percent in five years; and requiring the Attorney General first to identify all major drug-trafficking organizations known to be operating in the U.S. and then to create a plan to dismantle them.

IV

Drawing up laundry lists of public policy may seem a tedious and academic exercise. It is nevertheless an instructive one, if for no other reason than that it glaringly exposes how *little* has been done, on the most commonsensical level, to address the terrible problems that confront us, and that have accumulated in both number and intensity over the past 30 years. In this sense, thinking concretely about specific, practical reforms offers the hope that, by a concerted national effort, we might yet begin to alleviate some of the worst manifestations of these ills, and even, in time, to reverse course.

And yet, to repeat, even if we were to enact each and every one of the desired reforms in each and every area, we would still be a long way from having healed the broken families of America. Smart, intelligent public policies can and do make a difference. But political solutions are not, ultimately, the answer to problems which are at root moral and spiritual.

"Manners," wrote Edmund Burke two centuries ago,

> are of more importance than laws. Upon them, in a great measure, the laws depend. The law touches us but here and there, and now and then. Manners are what vex or soothe, corrupt or purify, exalt or debase, barbarize or refine us, by a constant, steady, uniform, insensible operation, like that of the air we breathe in. They give their whole form and color to our lives. According to their quality, they aid morals, they supply them, or they totally destroy them.

Can government supply manners and morals if they are wanting? Of course it cannot. What it can supply, through policy and law, is a vivid sense of what we as a society expect of ourselves, what we hold ourselves responsible for, and what we consider ourselves answerable to. There can be little doubt that in this last period of time the message our laws have been sending our young people and their parents has been the profoundly demoralizing one

that we expect little, and hold ourselves answerable for still less.

By changing and improving our laws, we might not thereby bring about, but we would certainly *help* to bring about, a climate that would make it easier rather than harder for all of us to grow more civilized; easier rather than harder for us to keep our commitments to one another; easier rather than harder for us to recapture the idea of personal and civic responsibility. This, in turn, would make it easier rather than harder for us to raise our children in safety to adulthood —something which at the moment we are not doing very well at all.

NOTES

1. "What To Do About Welfare," *Commentary,* December 1994.

2. Although abortion *per se* is not one of my subjects in this article, let me register here my belief that 1.5 million abortions a year—of which the overwhelming majority are performed on perfectly healthy women in order to prevent the birth of perfectly healthy children—is a national catastrophe. There is no doubt that such a number must also have a coarsening effect on adults' attitudes toward children and what they need from us.

3. Chester E. Finn, Jr., in "What To Do About Education: The Schools" *Commentary,* October 1994 provides a long list of the appalling details.

4. "What To Do About Crime," *Commentary,* September 1994.

POSTSCRIPT

Is the Welfare of Our Disadvantaged Children Improving?

Schorr collected information on social programs aimed at reducing risk factors for children in the areas of school-age childbearing (teen parenting), school dropouts, delinquency, and long-term welfare dependence. Programs that are working had some common elements such as flexibility in responding to family needs, dealing with the whole family system, and community ownership.

Both Schorr and Bennett use statistics to support their views on social intervention results for disadvantaged children. Their views reflect the current discussions being conducted on a larger scale about America's welfare system. Welfare reform proponents are asking social programs to be held accountable for their expenditure of funds and their success rates.

The goals of welfare reform are to reduce the amount of time some families can receive public assistance and to build incentives to motivate families to improve their own lives. Proponents assume that in the absence of welfare payments, parent(s) will find a job, support the family, and develop a sense of pride, initiative, and self-esteem, but are these goals realistic for the people involved? Similarly, proponents of social intervention programs for disadvantaged children believe that their programs will work to reduce risk factors and motivate children to seek a better life, but are their goals realistic? Can they be successful within the context of the larger society? Can the long-term effects of these programs be documented, and is the cycle of poverty and family dysfunction ended by these interventions?

SUGGESTED READINGS

Barry, V. (1995, Winter). What will happen to the children? *Policy Review, 71,* 7–14.

Besharov, D. J. (1996, May). Child abuse reporting. *Society, 33,* 40–46.

Edelman, M. W. (1996, June). Taking a stand. *Emerae, 7,* 58–63.

Murphy. P. T. (1995, May). Preserving chaos. *Commonweal, 122,* 12–15.

Peter, V. J. (1995, November). Welfare reform, the American family, and orphanages: What's best for the children? *USA Today: The Magazine of the American Scene, 124,* 56–60.

Sorenson, S. B. (1994, April). Traumatic child death and documented maltreatment history. *American Journal of Public Health, 84,* 623–627.

Stoesz, D. (1996, June). Suffer the children. *Washington Monthly, 28,* 20–25.

On the Internet . . .

http://www.dushkin.com

National Network for Child Care (NNCC)

Resources for raising children from the Cooperative Extension system are provided and include additional Web sites designed especially for children, activities for children, nutrition information, and parent involvement issues.
http://www.iastate.edu

Educational Resources Information Center (ERIC)

This Web site is sponsored by the U.S. Department of Education and leads to numerous documents related to elementary and early childhood education, as well as other curriculum topics and issues.
http://www.ed.gov

Child Welfare Review

Child Welfare Review is a forum for inquiry into issues related to the welfare of children. It contains conflicting and contrasting viewpoints.
http://www.childwelfare.com/kids/news.htm

Creating Peaceable Families

Ben and Jerry's Ice Cream Company, cosponsored by Educators for Social Responsibility, has created this Web site. It is composed of guidelines and ideas for resolving conflicts with children both at home and school.
http://www.benjerry.com/esr/peaceable-index.html

Children Now

Children Now focuses on improving conditions for children who are poor or at risk. Articles include information on education, influence of media, health, and security.
http://www.childrennow.org/

Corporal Punishment Bibliography

This is a collection of references on corporal punishment from independent researchers, government institutions, and universities.
http://wsu.edu/publications/corporal/index.html

PART 2

Early Childhood

The period of early childhood is sometimes referred to as the preschool years. It generally encompasses ages two or three through four or five. This is a time when children become much more adept at taking part in physical activities, satisfying curiosities, and learning from experience. Preschoolers play more frequently with other children, become increasingly skilled in daily tasks, and are much more responsive to people and things in their environment. Many children begin school during their preschool years, an experience that gives them their first extended contacts with a social institution other than the family. Changing attitudes about discipline, family size, divorce, and the mass media all have implications on a child's development. This section examines some of the choices families make in rearing their preschool children.

■ Is Spanking Detrimental to Children?

■ Are Only Children Less Independent Than Firstborn Children?

■ Does Divorce Create Long-Term Negative Effects for Children?

■ Is Television Viewing Harmful for Children?

ISSUE 5

Is Spanking Detrimental to Children?

YES: Murray A. Straus, from *Beating the Devil Out of Them: Corporal Punishment in American Families and Its Effects on Children* (Lexington Books, 1994)

NO: John K. Rosemond, from *To Spank or Not to Spank: A Parent's Handbook* (Andrews and McMeel, 1994)

ISSUE SUMMARY

YES: Murray A. Straus, a social researcher, believes that frequent spanking teaches children aggressiveness. He has conducted numerous studies that found a direct relationship between the physical punishment that children experienced and increased violent acts during the teen and adult years.

NO: John K. Rosemond, a family psychologist, author, and speaker, contends that research on the effects of spanking is skewed. Spankings, not beatings, should be administered at the discretion of loving parents and should not be considered child abuse.

The topic of spanking (also known as corporal punishment) provokes highly emotional responses from many family practitioners, parents, and researchers. Were you spanked when you were a child? What was used to spank you? bare hand? hairbrush? ruler? switch? Do you think the spankings affected you negatively or did they teach you how to act appropriately? Parents and children often quote the following to support the ritual of spanking: "Spare the rod and spoil the child; I was spanked and I turned out OK; spankings teach children how to act; kids need spankings to know who's boss."

If you were not spanked, what was used to correct your misbehavior? Was the misbehavior explained? Were your good deeds rewarded as your bad deeds were punished? Perhaps verbal abuse or a slap in the face was used to correct your behavior, or maybe you were ignored altogether; these techniques are similar to spanking and, in fact, are often considered by researchers to have the same effects as spanking. What about children who were not spanked or corrected in any way? Would these children necessarily turn out spoiled or out of control?

A public opinion poll commissioned by the National Committee for the Prevention of Child Abuse (Brown, 1994) asked parents how they disciplined their children in the past year. Parents responded by naming more than one method. Denying privileges was used by 79 percent, confining in a room was used by 59 percent, 49 percent spanked or hit their child, and 45 percent used insults or swore at their child. What was most notable about the statistics was that for the first time a majority (51 percent) of parents reported that they did not spank their children.

Spanking is a popular form of correction in the United States; Wisconsin and Maryland have tried to pass laws to outlaw spanking, but none to date have been passed into legislation. Five other countries have outlawed spanking. Austria, Norway, Denmark, Sweden, and Finland have banned physical punishment of children. Proponents of spanking are quick to point out that some of these countries' child abuse rates have not declined as a result of the spanking ban.

Spanking has been associated with violence, which is receiving overwhelming attention in the media. Violence is perceived as a social ill that has infiltrated our institutions such as schools, post offices, medical facilities, and restaurants (all of which have been the sites for mass shooting sprees). Do spankings in childhood lead to increased violent behavior in the teen and adult years?

Many parents solve the problem of misbehavior by hitting their children. As children are spanked, hit, or otherwise physically punished, can they see spanking as an acceptable problem-solving option? When parents spank their children, are they guiding them or controlling them? If parents do not spank, how do they teach their children right from wrong? Does any kind of punishment, such as yelling or taking away privileges, help shape appropriate behavior? What message are parents sending? What is the best way to help children become responsible, moral adults?

In the following selections, Murray A. Straus, who has made a career out of linking all kinds of negative outcomes to spanking or corporal punishment, contends that spanking is detrimental both to children and to society as a whole. John K. Rosemond points out the fallacies in Straus's research on spanking. He cautions parents to distinguish between beatings and spankings; beatings indeed send a violent message to the child.

YES

Murray A. Straus

TEN MYTHS THAT PERPETUATE CORPORAL PUNISHMENT

[H]itting children is legal in every state of the United States and 84 percent of a survey of Americans agreed that it is sometimes necessary to give a child a good hard spanking.... [A]lmost all parents of toddlers act on these beliefs. Study after study shows that almost 100 percent of parents with toddlers hit their children. There are many reasons for the strong support of spanking. Most of them are myths.

MYTH 1: SPANKING WORKS BETTER

There has been a huge amount of research on the effectiveness of corporal punishment of animals, but remarkably little on the effectiveness of spanking children. That may be because almost no one, including psychologists, feels a need to study it because it is assumed that spanking is effective. In fact, what little research there is on the effectiveness of corporal punishment of children agrees with the research on animals. Studies of both animals and children show that punishment is *not* more effective than other methods of teaching and controlling behavior. Some studies show it is less effective.

Ellen Cohn and I asked 270 students at two New England colleges to tell us about the year they experienced the most corporal punishment. Their average age that year was eight, and they recalled having been hit an average of six times that year. We also asked them about the percent of the time they thought that the corporal punishment was effective. It averaged a little more than half of the times (53 percent). Of course, 53 percent also means that corporal punishment was *not* perceived as effective about half the time it was used.

LaVoie (1974) compared the use of a loud noise (in place of corporal punishment) with withdrawal of affection and verbal explanation in a study of first- and second-grade children. He wanted to find out which was more effective in getting the children to stop touching certain prohibited toys. Although the loud noise was more effective initially, there was no difference over a longer period of time. Just explaining was as effective as the other methods.

From Murray A. Straus, *Beating the Devil Out of Them: Corporal Punishment in American Families and Its Effects on Children* (Lexington Books, 1994), pp. 149–164. Copyright © 1994 by Jossey-Bass, Inc., Publishers. Reprinted by permission. Notes and some references omitted.

A problem with LaVoie's study is that it used a loud noise rather than actual corporal punishment. That problem does not apply to an experiment by Day and Roberts (1983). They studied three-year-old children who had been given "time out" (sitting in a corner). Half of the mothers were assigned to use spanking as the mode of correction if their child did not comply and left the corner. The other half put their non-complying child behind a low plywood barrier and physically enforced the child staying there. Keeping the child behind the barrier was just as effective as the spanking in correcting the misbehavior that led to the time out.

A study by Larzelere (in press) also found that a combination of non-corporal punishment and reasoning was as effective as corporal punishment and reasoning in correcting disobedience.

Crozier and Katz (1979), Patterson (1982), and Webster-Stratton et al. (1988, 1990) all studied children with serious conduct problems. Part of the treatment used in all three experiments was to get parents to stop spanking. In all three, the behavior of the children improved after spanking ended. Of course, many other things in addition to no spanking were part of the intervention. But, as you will see, parents who on their own accord do not spank also do many other things to manage their children's behavior. It is these other things, such as setting clear standards for what is expected, providing lots of love and affection, explaining things to the child, and recognizing and rewarding good behavior, that account for why children of non-spanking parents tend to be easy to manage and well-behaved. What about parents who do these things and also spank? Their children also tend to be well-behaved,

but it is illogical to attribute that to spanking since the same or better results are achieved without spanking, and also without adverse side effects.

Such experiments are extremely important, but more experiments are needed to really understand what is going on when parents spank. Still, what Day and Roberts found can be observed in almost any household. Let's look at two examples.

In a typical American family there are many instances when a parent might say, "Mary! You did that again! I'm going to have to send you to your room again." This is just one example of a non-spanking method that did *not* work.

The second example is similar: A parent might say, "Mary! You did that again! I'm going to have to spank you again." This is an example of spanking that did *not* work.

The difference between these two examples is that when spanking does not work, parents tend to forget the incident because it contradicts the almost-universal American belief that spanking is something that works when all else fails. On the other hand, they tend to remember when a *non*-spanking method did not work. The reality is that nothing works all the time with a toddler. Parents think that spanking is a magic charm that will cure the child's misbehavior. It is not. There is no magic charm. It takes many interactions and many repetitions to bring up children. Some things work better with some children than with others.

Parents who favor spanking can turn this around and ask, If spanking doesn't work any better, isn't that the same as saying that it works just as well? So what's wrong with a quick slap on the wrist or bottom? There are at least three things that are wrong:

- Spanking becomes less and less effective over time and when children get bigger, it becomes difficult or impossible.
- For some children, the lessons learned through spanking include the idea that they only need to be good if Mommy or Daddy is watching or will know about it.
- ... [T]here are a number of very harmful side effects, such as a greater chance that the child will grow up to be depressed or violent. Parents don't perceive these side effects because they usually show up only in the long run.

MYTH 2: SPANKING IS NEEDED AS A LAST RESORT

Even parents and social scientists who are opposed to spanking tend to think that it may be needed when all else fails. There is no scientific evidence supporting this belief, however. It is a myth that grows out of our cultural and psychological commitment to corporal punishment. You can prove this to yourself by a simple exercise with two other people. Each of the three should, in turn, think of the most extreme situation where spanking is necessary. The other two should try to think of alternatives. Experience has shown that it is very difficult to come up with a situation for which the alternatives are not as good as spanking. In fact, they are usually better.

Take the example of a child running out into the street. Almost everyone thinks that spanking is appropriate then because of the extreme danger. Although spanking in that situation may help *parents* relieve their own tension and anxiety, it is not necessary or appropriate for teaching the child. It is not necessary because spanking does not work better than other methods, and it is not appropriate because of the harmful side effects of spanking. The only physical force needed is to pick up the child and get him or her out of danger, and, while hugging the child, explain the danger.

Ironically, if spanking is to be done at all, the "last resort" may be the worst. The problem is that parents are usually very angry by that time and act impulsively. Because of their anger, if the child rebels and calls the parent a name or kicks the parent, the episode can escalate into physical abuse. Indeed, most episodes of physical abuse started as physical punishment and got out of hand (see Kadushin and Martin, 1981). Of course, the reverse is not true, that is, most instances of spanking do not escalate into abuse. Still, the danger of abuse is there, and so is the risk of psychological harm.

The second problem with spanking as a last resort is that, in addition to teaching that hitting is the way to correct wrongs, hitting a child impulsively teaches another incorrect lesson—that being extremely angry justifies hitting.

MYTH 3: SPANKING IS HARMLESS

When someone says, I was spanked and I'm OK, he or she is arguing that spanking does no harm. This is contrary to almost all the available research. One reason the harmful effects are ignored is because many of us (including those of us who are social scientists) are reluctant to admit that their own parents did something wrong and even more reluctant to admit that we have been doing something wrong with our own children. But the most important reason may be that it is difficult to see the harm. Most of the harmful effects do not become visible right away, often not for years. In addition, only a relatively small percentage of spanked children experience obviously harmful effects....

Another argument in defense of spanking is that it is not harmful if the parents are loving and explain why they are spanking. The research does show that the harmful effects of spanking are reduced if it is done by loving parents who explain their actions. However,... a study by Larzelere (1986) shows that although the harmful effects are reduced, they are not eliminated. The... harmful side effects include an increased risk of delinquency as a child and crime as an adult, wife beating, depression, masochistic sex, and lowered earnings.

In addition to having harmful psychological effects on children, hitting children also makes life more difficult for parents. Hitting a child to stop misbehavior may be the easy way in the short run, but in the slightly longer run, it makes the job of being a parent more difficult. This is because spanking reduces the ability of parents to influence their children, especially in adolescence when they are too big to control by physical force. Children are more likely to do what the parents want if there is a strong bond of affection with the parent. In short, being able to influence a child depends in considerable part on the bond between parent and child (Hirschi, 1969). An experiment by Redd, Morris, and Martin (1975) shows that children tend to avoid caretaking adults who use punishment. In the natural setting, of course, there are many things that tie children to their parents. I suggest that each spanking chips away at the bond between parent and child....

Contrary to the "spoiled child" myth, children of non-spanking parents are likely to be easier to manage and better behaved than the children of parents who spank. This is partly because they tend to control their own behavior on the basis of what their own conscience tells them is right and wrong rather than to avoid being hit. This is ironic because almost everyone thinks that spanking "when necessary" makes for better behavior.

MYTH 4: ONE OR TWO TIMES WON'T CAUSE ANY DAMAGE

The evidence in this book indicates that the greatest risk of harmful effects occurs when spanking is very frequent. However, that does not necessarily mean that spanking just once or twice is harmless. Unfortunately, the connection between spanking once or twice and psychological damage has not been addressed by most of the available research. This is because the studies seem to be based on this myth. They generally cluster children into "low" and "high" groups in terms of the frequency they were hit. This prevents the "once or twice is harmless" myth from being tested scientifically because the low group may include parents who spank once a year or as often as once a month. The few studies that did classify children according to the number of times they were hit by their parents... show that even one or two instances of corporal punishment are associated with a slightly higher probability of later physically abusing your own child, slightly more depressive symptoms, and a greater probability of violence and other crime later in life. The increase in these harmful side effects when parents use only moderate corporal punishment (hit only occasionally) may be small, but why run even that small risk when the evidence shows that corporal punishment is no more effective than other forms of discipline in the short run, and less effective in the long run.

MYTH 5: PARENTS CAN'T STOP WITHOUT TRAINING

Although everyone can use additional skills in child management, there is no evidence that it takes some extraordinary training to be able to stop spanking. The most basic step in eliminating corporal punishment is for parent educators, psychologists, and pediatricians to make a simple and unambiguous statement that hitting a child is wrong and that a child *never*, ever, under any circumstances except literal physical self-defense, should be hit.

That idea has been rejected almost without exception everytime I suggest it to parent educators or social scientists. They believe it would turn off parents and it could even be harmful because parents don't know what else to do. I think that belief is an unconscious defense of corporal punishment. I say that because I have never heard a parent educator say that before we can tell parents to never *verbally* attack a child, parents need training in alternatives. Some do need training, but everyone agrees that parents who use *psychological* pain as a method of discipline, such as insulting or demeaning, the child, should stop immediately. But when it comes to causing *physical* pain by spanking, all but a small minority of parent educators say that before parents are told to stop spanking, they need to learn alternative modes of discipline. I believe they should come right out, as they do for verbal

attacks, and say without qualification that a child should *never* be hit....

This can be illustrated by looking at one situation that almost everyone thinks calls for spanking: when a toddler who runs out into the street. A typical parent will scream in terror, rush out and grab the child, and run to safety, telling the child, No! No! and explaining the danger —all of this accompanied by one or more slaps to the legs or behind.

The same sequence is as effective or more effective *without the spanking*. The spanking is not needed because even tiny children can sense the terror in the parent and understand, No! No! Newborn infants can tell the difference between when a mother is relaxed and when she is tense (Stern, 1977). Nevertheless, the fact that a child understands that something is wrong does not guarantee never again running into the street; just as spanking does not guarantee the child will not run into the street again....

Of course, when the child misbehaves again, most spanking parents do more than just repeat the spanking or spank harder. They usually also do things such as explain the danger to the child before letting the child go out again or warn the child that if it happens again, he or she will have to stay in the house for the afternoon, and so on. The irony is that when the child finally does learn, the parent attributes the success to the spanking, not the explanation.

MYTH 6: IF YOU DON'T SPANK, YOUR CHILDREN WILL BE SPOILED OR RUN WILD

It is true that some non-spanked children run wild. But when that happens it is not because the parent didn't spank. It is because some parents think the alternative to spanking is to ignore a child's misbehavior or to replace spanking with verbal attacks such as, Only a dummy like you can't learn to keep your toys where I won't trip over them. The best alternative is to take firm action to correct the misbehavior without hitting. Firmly condemning what the child has done and explaining why it is wrong are usually enough. When they are not, there are a host of other things to do, such as requiring a time out or depriving the child of a privilege, neither of which involves hitting the child.

Suppose the child hits another child. Parents need to express outrage at this or the child may think it is acceptable behavior. The expression of outrage and a clear statement explaining why the child should never hit another person, except in self-defense, will do the trick in most cases. That does not mean one such warning will do the trick, any more than a single spanking will do the trick. It takes most children a while to learn such things, whatever methods the parents use.

The importance of how parents go about teaching children is clear from a classic study of American parenting —*Patterns of Child Rearing* by Sears, Maccoby, and Levin (1957). This study found two actions by parents that are linked to a high level of aggression by the child: permissiveness of the child's aggression, namely ignoring it when the child hits them or another child, and spanking to correct misbehavior. The most aggressive children ... are children of parents who permitted aggression by the child and who also hit them for a variety of misbehavior. The least aggressive children are ... children of parents who clearly condemned acts of aggression and who, by not spanking,

acted in a way that demonstrated the principle that hitting is wrong.

There are other reasons why, on the average, the children of parents who do not spank are better behaved than children of parents who spank:

- Non-spanking parents pay more attention to their children's behavior, both good and bad, than parents who spank. Consequently, they are more likely to reward good behavior and less likely to ignore misbehavior.

- Their children have fewer opportunities to get into trouble because they are more likely to child-proof the home. For older children, they have clear rules about where they can go and who they can be with.

- Non-spanking parents tend to do more explaining and reasoning. This teaches the child how to use these essential tools to monitor his or her own behavior, whereas children who are spanked get less training in thinking things through.

- Non-spanking parents treat the child in ways that tend to bond the child to them and avoid acts that weaken the bond. They tend to use more rewards for good behavior, greater warmth and affection, and fewer verbal assaults on the child (see Myth 9). By not spanking, they avoid anger and resentment over spanking. When there is a strong bond, children identify with the parent and want to avoid doing things the parent says are wrong. The child develops a conscience and lets that direct his or her behavior. That is exactly what Sears et al. found.

MYTH 7: PARENTS SPANK RARELY OR ONLY FOR SERIOUS PROBLEMS

Contrary to this myth, parents who spank tend to use this method of discipline for almost any misbehavior. Many do not even give the child a warning. They spank before trying other things. Some advocates of spanking even recommend this. At any supermarket or other public place, you can see examples of a child doing something wrong, such as taking a can of food off the shelf. The parent then slaps the child's hand and puts back the can, sometimes without saying a word to the child. John Rosemond, the author of *Parent Power* (1981), says, "For me, spanking is a first resort. I seldom spank, but when I decide ... I do it, and that's the end of it."

The high frequency of spanking also shows up among the parents [studied]. The typical parent of a toddler told us of about 15 instances in which he or she had hit the child during the previous 12 months. That is surely a minimum estimate because spanking a child is generally such a routine and unremarkable event that most instances are forgotten. Other studies, such as Newson and Newson (1963), report much more chronic hitting of children. My tabulations for mothers of three- to five-year-old children in the National Longitudinal Study of Youth found that almost two-thirds hit their children during the week of the interview, and they did it more then three times in just that one week. As high as that figure may seem, I think that daily spanking is not at all uncommon. It has not been documented because the parents who do it usually don't realize how often they are hitting their children.

MYTH 8: BY THE TIME A CHILD IS A TEENAGER, PARENTS HAVE STOPPED

As we have seen, parents of children in their early teens are also heavy users of corporal punishment, although at that age it is more likely to be a slap on the face than on the behind.... [M]ore than half of the parents of 13- to 14-year-old children in our two national surveys hit their children in the previous 12 months. The percentage drops each year as children get older, but even at age 17, one out of five parents is still hitting. To make matters worse, these are minimum estimates.

Of the parents of teenagers who told us about using corporal punishment, 84 percent did it more than once in the previous 12 months. For boys, the average was seven times and for girls, five times. These are minimum figures because we interviewed the mother in half the families and the father in the other half. The number of times would be greater if we had information on what the parent who was not interviewed did.

MYTH 9: IF PARENTS DON'T SPANK, THEY WILL VERBALLY ABUSE THEIR CHILD

The scientific evidence is exactly the opposite. Among the nationally representative samples of parents [surveyed], those who did the least spanking also engaged in the least verbal aggression.

It must be pointed out that non-spanking parents are an exceptional minority. They are defying the cultural prescription that says a good parent should spank if necessary. The depth of their involvement with their children probably results from the same underlying characteristics that led them to reject spanking. There is a danger that if more ordinary parents are told to never spank, they might replace spanking by ignoring misbehavior or by verbal attacks. Consequently, a campaign to end spanking must also stress the importance of avoiding verbal attacks as well as physical attacks, and also the importance of paying attention to misbehavior.

MYTH 10: IT IS UNREALISTIC TO EXPECT PARENTS TO NEVER SPANK

It is no more unrealistic to expect parents to never hit a child than to expect that husbands should never hit their wives, or that no one should go through a stop sign, or that a supervisor should never hit an employee. Despite the legal prohibition, some husbands hit their wives, just as some drivers go through stop signs, and a supervisor occasionally may hit an employee.

If we were to prohibit spanking, as is the law in Sweden (see Deley, 1988; and Haeuser, 1990), there still would be parents who would continue to spank. But that is not a reason to avoid passing such a law here. Some people kill even though murder has been a crime since the dawn of history. Some husbands continue to hit their wives even though it has been more than a century since the courts stopped recognizing the common law right of a husband to "physically chastise an errant wife" (Calvert, 1974).

A law prohibiting spanking is unrealistic only because spanking is such an accepted part of American culture. That also was true of smoking. Yet in less than a generation we have made tremendous progress toward eliminating smoking. We can make similar progress toward eliminating spanking by showing parents that spanking is dangerous, that their children will be easier to bring up if they do not spank, and by clearly saying that a child should *never*, under any circumstances, be spanked.

NO

John K. Rosemond

TO SPARE OR NOT TO SPARE

In the spring of 1993, in a hotel room somewhere in America and desperate for the sound of a human voice, I turned on the television. Up popped Oprah, who was orchestrating a politically correct hoot 'n' holler over spanking. I know how these things work because I've been on several such free-for-alls (never again, I assure you). The producer, acting on behalf of the host, assembles a panel of people who are expected, perhaps even coached, to express a certain opinion. The illusion of "balance" is quickly dispelled as one realizes the host has an agenda. In this case, Ms. Winfrey's clearly was to promote to public acceptance the idea that the act of spanking is, without exception, child abuse and should be made illegal. That's right, as in *against the law!*

At one point in this ersatz discussion, Oprah approached a man in the audience whom I immediately pegged as a "plant." This very professional-looking gentleman, in response to a rogue's gallery of parents who had all confessed to spanking their children (and their intention to continue doing so), reeled off something to the effect that spankings instill a violent bent into the psyches of children and, furthermore, amount to a mixed message. The fact that parents can hit a child, yet the child cannot hit them back, he said, is horribly confusing and destructive to self-esteem. The audience roared on cue, Oprah smiled knowingly, and all was well in Talk Show Land.

With this scene fresh in mind, I subsequently asked the 250 members of an audience in Pueblo, Colorado, "Please raise a hand if you were spanked as a child." Close to 250 hands went up. "Now," I continued, "keep your hand up if you remember that as a child you were confused over or resented the fact that although your parents felt free to spank you, you were not allowed to hit them." Immediately, all hands went down.

I replicated this demonstration with several other audiences that same spring. The results were always the same. I occasionally tacked on the request that those who were spanked as kids raise their hands again if they ever recall feeling that the fact their parents spanked them meant that hitting someone in anything other than self-defense was okay. Never once did anyone raise a hand. Either the people who attend my presentations are atypical, or the

From John K. Rosemond, *To Spank or Not to Spank: A Parent's Handbook* (Andrews and McMeel, 1994), pp. 17–35. Copyright © 1994 by John K. Rosemond. Reprinted by permission politically correct rhetoric concerning the effects of spanking on children is dead wrong.

I've seen the research on spanking. In fact, this being a relatively fascinating topic, I dare say I've kept closely abreast of the research. Some of it paints an ominous picture: A person who was spanked as a child is more likely to commit violent crimes as an adult, be physically abusive toward his or her spouse and children, suffer from low self-esteem... in short, become a misfit in every possible sense.

One of the most outspoken, oft-quoted critics of spanking is sociologist Murray Straus of the University of New Hampshire Family Research Laboratory. Straus's opinions have significantly informed and shaped the rhetoric of the antispanking movement. In fact, it can legitimately be said that he is its "guru."

In a 1994 article (which appears in *Debating Children's Lives*, Mason and Gambrill, eds., Sage Publications), Dr. Straus asserts that "research showing the harmful effects of spanking is one of the best-kept secrets of American child psychology" because it implies that "almost all American parents are guilty of child abuse, *including those who write books of advice for parents* [emphasis mine, and yes, I stand accused]."

Citing a study which found that nearly all parents of toddlers spank, more than half of parents of teens spank, and 41 percent of parents feel a spanking is appropriate in the case of a child hitting another child, Straus says these parents send their children a double message: Hitting another person is bad, but it is not bad to hit someone who's done something bad. His conclusion: "Corporal punishment therefore teaches the morality of hitting."

Another aspect of spanking's "hidden curriculum," as Straus calls the supposedly irrevocable lessons he sees embedded in the act of swatting a child's rear end, is the message "those who love you, hit you." Spankings also teach, says Straus, that it is "morally acceptable to hit those you love when they 'do wrong.'" This aspect of the "hidden curriculum" is "almost a recipe for violence between spouses later in life."

After citing the results of surveys which supposedly demonstrate that spankings place children at greater risk for eventual criminal behavior, alcoholism, suicide, drug use, and lower occupational achievement, Straus comes to his point, which is a call for laws prohibiting the spanking of children *under any circumstances*. Straus firmly believes that antispanking laws will result in a "healthier, less violent, wealthier" society. He points to the fact that spanking has been against the law in Sweden since 1979. (For quite some time, Sweden has been plagued with alarmingly high rates of alcoholism, divorce, and illegitimacy. These longstanding crises, which are a direct result of Sweden's socialist politics, have contributed greatly to unusually high levels of stress in Swedish families—many of which are single-parent. As a result, Sweden's child abuse rate was —and continues to be—relatively high, prompting passage of an antispanking law which has not been shown to have reduced child abuse one iota.)

Straus proposes, however, that parents who violate these proposed laws should *not* be punished. Rather, as is the case in Sweden, the fact that they spank their children should be taken as a sign they need help, and the help should be provided. In fact, the "help" Straus refers to amounts to forced intervention into the family on the part of the state. In the case of parents who refuse this "help," the state will then be free to take clearly punitive measures, all under the guise of protecting the children, including removing them from the home, possibly permanently.

Straus's research and conclusions are full of gaping holes:

• First, his studies fail to demonstrate that spankings per se cause any problems—psychological, behavioral, or otherwise. His conclusions are based in large part on data collected from adults who report having been spanked *as teenagers.* Straus claims to have discovered that the more frequently a person was spanked as a teen, the more likely it is that as an adult that person will assault his wife, abuse his or her children, use alcohol to problematic excess, and think about committing suicide. But the mere fact that parents are spanking a teenager, and frequently at that, suggests that the teen's behavior may already be antisocial. At the very least, it speaks of serious family problems. In other words, rather than proving a link between spanking and later antisocial behavior, Straus simply demonstrates what common sense will tell us: that spankings at this age are a red flag indicating that serious problems already exist in the teen's life—in other words, that he or she is "at risk." To extend this line of thinking: We might also discover that in addition to being frequently spanked as teens, lots of criminals, wife beaters, etc., cannot remember ever being hugged or kissed or told they were loved by their parents. In that case, what "caused" their later antisocial behavior? Being spanked as children? Being starved of affection? We'll never know. All we know is that these individuals didn't have happy childhoods and that

an unhappy childhood is predictive of later problems. Common sense.

• A second major problem with Straus's conclusions is that he fails—as is the case with all of the research I've ever seen that reaches blanket antispanking conclusions—to distinguish between a *beating* and a *spanking.* In effect, Straus and other antispankers feel that such a distinction does not exist. In their view, the moment a parent strikes a child—regardless of where on the child's body the strike lands, regardless of the force behind the strike, regardless of whether the parent uses a hand or some other implement, such as a belt—the parent has committed child abuse. Period. As a result of Straus's unwillingness to distinguish between a beating and a spanking (a difference which will be clearly spelled out in the next chapter), his results are skewed to the negative by the life histories of people who, as children, suffered unspeakable abuse. No doubt about it, if you're beaten on as a child, you're more likely, as an adult, to pass it on. This, too, is common sense.

• Straus's spanking-leads-to-wife-beating hypothesis is contradicted by the fact that whereas the overwhelming majority of males in my generation were spanked as children, the number who beat their wives is extremely small, albeit problematic. This is yet another example of Straus's overall tendency to oversimplify extremely complex social situations, a trait that is hardly conducive to conducting worthwhile sociological study.

• Straus cannot even come close to proving his claim that spanking's "hidden curriculum" teaches children that "those who love you, hit you" and that violence is a just response to a maddening social situation. This is rhetoric, pure and simple. It is, however, emotionally seductive (which is, after all, the point of rhetoric), but in the final analysis it is nothing more than undiluted psychobabble—a construction of language, not of fact.

• Straus and other antispankers frequently argue that parents always have options other than to spank. That goes without saying, but again, the existence of other options doesn't prove that spanking is abusive or even ineffective. The question is whether any of the options, in any given situation, would be as effective as a spanking or in combination *with* a spanking. Psychologist Robert Larzelere, director of research at a residential treatment facility for children and youth and an adjunct faculty member of the University of Iowa, has found that the effectiveness of two frequently mentioned disciplinary options—verbal reprimand and time-out—actually *improves* in combination with a mild spanking, especially with children between the ages of two and six. This suggests, says Larzelere, that parents who enhance their discipline with occasional *mild* spankings during their children's earlier years may have better-behaved teens. That is certainly consistent with my own observations.

• Straus also makes the mistake of taking spanking out of context of a parent's total disciplinary style. A very well-known study which sought to determine the outcomes of various parenting styles found that children of *authoritative* parents—characterized by firm control and high nurturance—were more socially responsible and exercised greater individual initiative than children of either permissive (low control, high nurturance) or authoritarian (excessive control, low nurturance) parents. *Authoritative* parents, furthermore, were generally willing to occasionally spank. The con-

clusion reached was that spanking per se was not harmful, but rather that the *total pattern* of parental behavior was of utmost importance in determining the effectiveness of any disciplinary method, including spanking.

Having been trained in the scientific method, Straus is well aware that his research proves nothing. The fact that he pretends it does reveals the lack of objectivity he brings to this issue. In further fact, it suggests that Straus (and this is a problem common to antispanking "research") isn't doing research at all. He's attempting to promote a point of view. In effect, Straus is cloaking a propaganda effort in the trappings of "science."

In an interview with the *Philadelphia Inquirer* (November 1993), Straus identifies several "myths" concerning spanking, including: *I was spanked and I'm okay.* After pointing out that a *small* percentage of spanked children experience harmful effects, he asks, "Why chance it?" Again, Straus is wrong. It is *not* a myth that the overwhelming majority of people who were spanked as kids are okay as adults. In fact, he disproves his own contention by admitting that the number who do not turn out okay is small. (Keep in mind that Straus does not distinguish between a beating and a spanking. Therefore, it's probably correct to assume that the small percentage of children he refers to as being harmed come primarily from the ranks of those who were beaten.) To cite my personal example, I was spanked as a kid. I'm comfortable with myself, enjoy positive relations with my wife, children, and friends, and am satisfyingly productive. (Straus might say, however, that the fact I spanked my children proves I'm not okay at all.) In fact, I was often spanked with a belt. So was my wife: We're both okay. We spanked both of our children (albeit never with anything other than our hands), and the evidence is overwhelmingly in favor of concluding that both of our kids, as young adults, are very okay. The same can be said for the vast majority of people who were spanked as children. Straus asks, "Why chance it?" I ask, if the risk is—by his own admission—small, and the connection between being spanked and developing later problems is tenuous, and we already have laws concerning the blatant abuse of children, why do we need a law against spanking? Straus's argument here is akin to proposing that since a small number of people die during heart transplants, heart transplants should be made illegal.

Most people would, no doubt, agree that certain instances of parents striking children are, indeed, abusive. Likewise, verbal reprimands can be abusive. According to the "logic" of the antispanking argument, in the interest of not "chancing it," we should ban the use of all "negative language" when addressing children. Or, since confining a child to his room may put the child at greater risk for claustrophobia, parents should be prohibited, by law, from exercising this "more risky" form of discipline. To some degree—at least at present—these scenarios are nothing more than absurd parodies of the antispanking mentality. I for one, however, am becoming increasingly convinced that we're talking about people who, if given an inch in the social policy realm, will want a mile. These are, I fear, social engineers of the worst kind, itching to impose their influence upon the American family.

According to Straus and his cohorts in the antispanking movement, slapping a child's rear end is abuse. Only the enlightened few see through the wall of denial American parents—with the assistance of many child-rearing authorities—have erected to shield themselves from this national disgrace. Since the rest of us are unwilling to admit the error of our ways (or our advice!), the only option is to pass laws which will turn the average parent into a criminal. Not to worry, however, because offending parents won't be punished. They will be given "help." And who, pray tell, will provide this help? Why "helping professionals," of course. I think it's safe to assume that these individuals, despite their altruistic mission, will expect to be compensated for their services.

The possibility of such legislation raises a host of very conceivable possibilities, none of which is consistent with democratic principles or the privacy and stability of families. I can envision, for example, "family living education" classes in schools which would have the intended effect of encouraging children to report instances of having been "mis-parented," including having been spanked. At present, there is hardly an elementary school counselor in America who has not had a child complain that a mild spanking from his or her parents was, in the child's immature mind, abusive. Imagine the number of children who will line up outside the offices of school counselors around the country if the day comes that even a mild a spanking is, by legal definition, abuse.

Along these lines, the National Committee to Prevent Child Abuse recently published (with funds from Kmart Corporation) a Spider-Man comic book in which Spider-Man helps a father see that one reason his son is getting into fights at school is because the boy is receiving spankings at home. On page 5, Spider-Man tells the youngster that any time he is "hit" he should tell a grown-up, and keep on telling grown-ups until he finds someone who will listen and do something about it. On page 6, a spanking from a parent is equated with hitting.

In a letter to me, Richard Wexler, author of *Wounded Innocents* (Prometheus Books, 1990), had this to say about Spider-Man's message:

> Now imagine this scenario: A child gets a spanking and, following Spider-Man's advice, tells his teacher he's been "hit" by his parent. The teacher is required to report any suspicion of "child abuse." She makes such a report and a caseworker is sent to the home to investigate.... At a minimum, the child is in for a traumatic interrogation and, quite possibly, a strip-search as the worker looks for bruises. At worst, the worker will remove the child [from the home] on the spot.

By the time the book you hold in your hands is published, NCPCA's Spider-Man comic will have been distributed to thousands of children in public schools across America and discussed in many a classroom.

Amazingly enough, NCPCA denies that one of the intents of the comic is to equate spanking with abuse. During an April 1994 phone conversation and in a subsequent letter, Ann Cohn Donnelly, NCPCA's executive director, assured me they have no official position favoring anti-spanking legislation and do not feel that spankings per se are abusive. When I pointed out that their Spider-Man comic not only equates being spanked by parents with being "hit" by peers or teachers and suggests that children who are spanked should report their parents to authorities, Donnelly replied that "some people might interpret it that way" but denied that the comic was meant to imply that any and all spankings administered by parents are inappropriate. Don-

nelly was being evasive. The comic's introduction, written by her and addressed to children, reads:

> The stories you are about to read are about hitting and why we believe that people are not for hitting—and children are people, too. The stories are about children who are being hit by adults they know or by other children. They tell you what to do if someone is hitting you. Perhaps you or someone you know has been the object of someone else's violence....

Nowhere does the comic differentiate between being slapped in the face by, say, a teacher and being spanked on the buttocks by a parent. Quite the contrary, they are both examples of "hitting." In either case, says NCPCA, the child in question should tell adults until one listens. Regardless of Donnelly's disclaimer, the message to children reading the comic is clear: If your parents spank you, you should report them to other adult authority figures.

According to Richard Wexler, NCPCA has consistently refused to distinguish between physical abuse and corporal punishment and has gone on record as opposing any effort to do so. According to NCPCA, any statement that might be construed as condoning spanking "doesn't belong in a child abuse prevention presentation."

In 1990, NCPCA published a brochure entitled "How to Teach Your Children Discipline." It states that spanking is not a useful approach to discipline because it "is used to directly control children's behavior," teaches children "to solve problems by hitting others," and teaches children "to be afraid of the adult in charge." The brochure also implies that spankings are violent acts of "lashing out" by parents who are out of control.

Strictly speaking, Ann Cohn Donnelly is correct. NCPCA has never *explicitly* stated that spankings and child abuse are one and the same, but it is equally true that they have never taken any pains to distinguish between spankings and behaviors which are clearly abusive, such as slapping, punching, kicking, etc. Furthermore, as Richard Wexler points out, they refuse to do so, citing as rationale the sort of "data" generated by Murray Straus and like-minded ideologues. NCPCA's position statement on physical punishment, adopted May 1989, reads:

> Although physical punishment of children is prevalent in the United States, numerous studies have demonstrated that hitting, spanking, slapping, and other forms of physical punishment are harmful methods of changing children's behavior....

Ignoring for the moment the fact that this statement is not true, the tone and content of NCPCA's propaganda clearly leads to the conclusion that spanking a child on the buttocks is in the final analysis no different from slapping the child in the face.

Donnelly also told me that she didn't think antispanking legislation would ever fly in the United States because it would be regarded as too intrusive. That's true, but again, she's being disingenuous. At the present time, NCPCA knows that it would be political suicide for any legislator, state or national, to sponsor a law *specifically prohibiting parental spanking*. The prohibition, should it ever come, will more likely be the result of a judicial ruling rather than a legislative act. A group calling itself The National Task Force for Children's Consti-tutional Rights (NTFCCR), whose advi-sory board consists of a number of promi-nent individuals from the fields of law, psychology, medicine, and family socia-work, believes that the best way to protec-children from mistreatment within thei-own families is through an amendmen-to the Constitution of the United States-The proposed wording of this amend-ment would open a judicial Pandora'-box that could well lead to antispanking-rulings in the courts:

> Section 1
> All citizens of the United States who are fifteen years of age or younger shall enjoy the right to live in a home that is safe and healthy... and the right to the care of a loving family or a substitute thereof....

One of NTFCCR's cofounders, Con-necticut Superior Court Judge Charles D-Gill, gives approximately fifty speeches a-year in which he issues the clarion cal-for a children's rights movement to be-modeled on the women's movement. In a 1991 article for the *Ohio Northern Uni-versity Law Review*, Gill equates a Chil-dren's Rights Amendment with the Equa-Rights Amendment. Conceding that ER/-was defeated, he notes that "nearly half o-our states have enacted an Equal Right-Amendment" and "nearly all state legis-latures have passed legislation that alter-the status of women."

In other words, Gill is saying tha-while a Children's Rights Amendmen-to the Constitution might not fly a-present, it might be possible to galvaniz-enough public support behind such a-concept to implement its equivalent or-a state-by-state basis. If such legislatior-is eventually enacted, it would only-be a matter of time before an attorney-acting on behalf of a child would file a-suit asserting that a parent who spanks is failing to provide a "safe, healthy, and loving" environment, thus violating the child's protected rights. If a judge concurred, a de facto law prohibiting parental spanking would be on the books.

Support for a Children's Rights Amendment is growing. In 1991, the National Committee for the Rights of the Child (NCRC) was formed in Washington, D.C. According to Judge Gill, dozens of national groups, representing millions of Americans, met to initiate "The Next Great Movement in America."

The United Nations is even in on the act. In 1989, the UN Convention on the Rights of the Child was unanimously adopted. Article 19 of its charter states: "Parties shall take all appropriate legislative, administrative, social and educational measures to protect the child from all forms of physical or mental violence, injury or abuse... while in the care of parents, legal guardians or any other person who has the care of the child." While this does not specifically define spanking as "physical violence," the intent of the framers is to include parental spanking in that rather broad category (Radda Barnen—Sweden's Save the Children—was intimately involved in drafting and implementing the Swedish law banning parental spanking as well as in drafting the wording of Article 19 of the UN Convention on the Rights of the Child.) The convention went into force as international law on September 2, 1990, when it was ratified by the twentieth nation. Close to one hundred nations have now ratified, thus affirming that they are legally bound by its standards. One notable holdout: the United States of America.

But an international organization calling itself End Physical Punishment of Children (EPOCH) is working diligently to enlighten American diplomats and lawmakers as to the rights of children. EPOCH's worldwide aim is that of "ending all physical punishment of children by education and legal reform." In their literature, they state that "hitting children is a violation of their fundamental rights as people and a constant confirmation of their low status," and they make it perfectly clear that spanking is hitting. As of 1992, EPOCH was able to boast that largely as a result of their efforts, physical punishment of children by parents had been legally proscribed in Sweden, Finland, Denmark, Norway, and Austria. In addition, similar bills are up for consideration in Germany, the United Kingdom, Canada, and Bolivia.

Completing the circle, the cofounder of the American chapter of EPOCH, Adrienne Hauser, is on National Staff at the National Committee to Prevent Child Abuse. (During the writing of this book, I left several messages asking Ms. Hauser to call me, but she never responded.) So although NCPCA may publicly disavow support for antispanking legislation, strong connections exist between themselves and organizations like EPOCH, the National Committee for the Rights of Children, and the National Task Force for Children's Constitutional Rights, which are working toward that end.

As reflected in much of NCPCA's literature, the distinct possibility exists that antispanking legal rulings would be just one stage in the ever-broadening legal definition of child abuse. Once spankings are defined as abusive, it's quite conceivable that raising one's voice to a child (yelling) would be next on the list of parenting behaviors to be deemed abusive (in a letter which appeared in

"Dear Abby" in April of 1994, Joy Byers, an NCPCA spokesperson, writes: "Never raise your voice, or your hand, in anger") followed by banishing a child to his or her room. (If you think the latter prospect is absurd, think again. A considerable number of helping professionals are presently of the opinion that restricting a child to his room causes the development of "negative feelings" concerning what should be a "positive environment," thus increasing the risk of onset of separation anxieties, phobias, sleep disturbances, and the like, not to mention lowered self-esteem.)

Where does this end? The answer: It doesn't, for it is the inherent nature of institutional bureaucracies not only to perpetuate themselves but to expand their influence—their "mandate"—within society. As child abuse laws are liberalized, it is inevitable that the numbers of children removed from their homes and placed in the care of the state would increase, as would the number of terminations of parental rights. As one concerned reader of my syndicated newspaper column recently wrote: "I am genuinely frightened concerning the attempts of well-intentioned social engineers to effect the 'redistribution' of children to 'better' parents. The ultimate outcome is the destruction of the family as we know it." Paranoia? Keep in mind that just forty years ago, the average citizen would have regarded someone who warned of the coming of antispanking laws as nothing less than hysterical, in both senses of the term.

Murray Straus says that, under his proposed legislation, parents who spanked would not be punished, only helped. That's if, and only if, they admitted they needed help. What if, as a matter of principle, a parent refused to make such a confession? At present, if a parent clearly abuses a child and refuses to admit that his or her actions toward the child are wrong, the child is almost always immediately removed from the home until the parent's discipline has undergone successful rehabilitation. The very real possibility that this policy would be extended to parents who administer mild spankings yet refuse to confess the error of their ways is downright scary.

Straus tells us that antispanking laws will transform us into a "healthier, less violent, and wealthier society." This grand vision serves to distract from the more insidious aspects of such laws, including that for many otherwise law-abiding American parents, receiving professional "help" would no longer be a matter of choice. In short, the specter raised is one of a totalitarian family policy, one that puts the autonomy of the American family at tremendous risk.

There is evidence, furthermore, that an antispanking law might be profoundly counterproductive. It is significant to note that the outlawing of spanking in Sweden may have actually *increased* the incidence of child abuse. One study—done a year after Sweden enacted antispanking laws—found that the Swedish rate of beating a child or threatening to use or using a weapon of some sort against a child was *two to four times that of the rate in the United States*. This is especially telling of the ultimate effect of anti-spanking laws, since Sweden is by other measures a far less violent society than the United States. Their murder rate, for example, is less than half that of our own. To explain this paradox, psychologist Larzelere posits that occasional mild spankings may serve as a safety valve of sorts, preventing escalations of misbehavior and parental frustration of the sort that lead to physical explosions. He further suggests—and I second his emotion —that providing parents who intend to spank with guidelines for spanking appropriately and effectively may do more to reduce child abuse than laws which prohibit spanking altogether.

When all is said and done, this argument isn't about spanking; it's about people, zealous professionals, politics, and political correctness. It's about people who feel morally superior and therefore justified in their desire to impose their ideology on everyone, by hook or crook. The more frustrated they become, the more outrageous and dangerous they become. That's the problem with moral superiority in any form. Frustrated, it inclines toward totalitarianism.

The problem with spanking is not spanking per se. Again, it's people—people who use corporal punishment inappropriately. It's a people problem that will *not* be solved through legislation. It will, in all likelihood, never be completely solved, only mitigated. It can be mitigated through education. So let's begin the education, keeping in mind that the best, most effective educators, the ones that cause people to truly want to listen, inquire, and learn, don't promote extremist points of view.

POSTSCRIPT

Is Spanking Detrimental to Children?

Child development professionals Lee Salk, T. Berry Brazelton, and Penelope Leach agree with Straus that spanking is never appropriate for children and has too many long-term consequences to justify the short-term goal of getting children "to mind." Straus also believes that any physical punishment of children contributes to a cycle of violence. He found that children whose parents spank them are more aggressive, have higher juvenile delinquency, higher rates of spouse abuse, lower economic achievement, and show higher drug and alcohol abuse rates, when compared to unspanked peers. By spanking, parents model the norm of violence and legitimize it as a way to solve problems.

Straus's 10 myths of spanking further explain that even one or two spankings can lead to poor relationships between parents and children. He contends that any spanking is harmful; it leads to depression, anxiety, aggression, and uncontrollable behavior. The more parents use explanation, redirection, and rewards for positive behavior, the more likely their children will act appropriately.

Rosemond uses his public speaking audiences to illustrate how prevalent and harmless he believes spanking to be. Hundreds of people admit they were spanked, but at the same time agree that parents have a right to spank and that spanking was not harmful to them. Spanking is something many parents do and many children accept as part of a normal childhood. According to Rosemond, spankings that have just cause and are done by a loving parent are an acceptable form of discipline. James Dobson, author of *The New Dare to Discipline*, agrees with Rosemond and goes further by promoting spanking as part of an overall parenting plan. Child care authorities Alvin Poussaint and James Comer do not necessarily endorse spanking but concede that there are well-adjusted adults who were spanked as children and have shown no obvious harm to their later development. Rosemond admits that parents can create violent children if children grow up in a violent home, but does not think that occasional spankings make a home a violent place.

Rosemond suggests flaws in Straus's research on spanking. He questions whether it is spanking or the lack of love exhibited in the home that later causes violent teen behavior. Much of Straus's research is on children who have been spanked as teens. Rosemond contends that spanking teens is a red flag in itself; much more dysfunctional parenting than spanking is going on in these types of situations. Rosemond says that there is a difference between a spanking and a beating; beating causes problems related to violence and inappropriate behavior, but spanking does not create later problems for the child. He points to research that claims a combination of time out, verbal reprimand, and spanking in early childhood actually improves teen behavior.

Spanking is a popular child-rearing technique in America. If one believes that spanking is effective in guiding children, are the possible long-term effects of anxiety, depression, and aggression worth the trade-off? If spanking leads to increased violence in children and adults, then what other form of guidance can parents use? After all, we do not want a generation of uncontrollable, self-centered individuals leading our country. Some child development experts agree that reasoning, talking, and listening to children works well in teaching right from wrong as well as preserving the child's self-concept. They admit that this child-rearing approach takes more time, but the benefits outweigh the costs. Other child-rearing authorities feel that spankings that are correctly administered within the context of a loving home are effective in positively shaping a child's behavior.

SUGGESTED READINGS

Brown, C. (1994, April 22–24). To spank or not to spank. *USA Weekend*, pp. 4–7.

Corner, J., & Poussaint, A. (1992). *Raising black children*. New York: Plume.

Dobson, J. (1992). *The new dare to discipline*. Wheaton, IL: Tyndale House.

Ellison, C., & Sherkat, D. (1993, February). Conservative Protestantism and support for corporal punishment. *American Sociological Review, 58,* 131–144.

Giles-Sims, J., Strauss, M., & Sugarman, D. (1995, April). Child, maternal, and family characteristics associated with spanking. *Family Relations, 44,* 170–176.

Hastier, A. (1990). Can we stop physical punishment of children? *Education Digest, 56,* 67–69.

Leach, P. (1994). *Children first*. New York: Alfred A. Knopf.

Mercury, C. (1994, December). Elementary school's answers to corporal punishment. *Education Digest, 60,* 25–28.

Samalin, N. (1992, July). What's wrong with spanking? *Parents' Magazine. 67*(7), 56–61.

Simmonds, B. (1991, Winter). Ban the hickory stick. *Childhood Education, 68*(2), pp. 69–70.

Survey says some mothers still believe that spanking is good discipline. (1995, January). *Jet, 87,* 14–18.

ISSUE 6

Are Only Children Less Independent Than Firstborn Children?

YES: Barbara Byrd, Arnold P. DeRosa, and Stephen S. Craig, from "The Adult Who Is an Only Child: Achieving Separation or Individuation," *Psychological Reports* (August 1993)

NO: Steven Mellor, from "How Do Only Children Differ from Other Children?" *The Journal of Genetic Psychology* (June 1990)

ISSUE SUMMARY

YES: Barbara Byrd, Arnold P. DeRosa, and Stephen S. Craig, professors at Seton Hall University, conclude from a study of college students that only children are less autonomous than firstborn children.

NO: Steven Mellor, a psychology professor at Pennsylvania State University, reports that only children are similar to firstborns as well as children from two-child families in terms of their developmental path.

For many years research on the birth order, or ordinal position of children in a family, has suggested that there are certain personality traits that can be attributed to oldest, middle, and youngest children. Only children and firstborns had been thought to be very similar in personality characteristics. Researchers define as *firstborn* the first child in a family, the last child born if there is a significant time lapse between siblings' births, or the only child in a one-child family. Only children and firstborns have been labeled perfectionists, high achievers, and conformists. Almost all of the original astronauts and many of the world's leaders, for example, were firstborn or only children.

But some contemporary researchers believe that only children are significantly different from firstborns in terms of their ability to separate from their families. These scientists posit that only children get more attention from their parents for the duration of their childhoods than do firstborns. Moreover, only children can become more dependent on their parents for emotional support than children who have siblings. Consequently, these factors might slow the rate at which only children individuate from their families as compared to children from families with more than one child. Similarly, researchers argue that firstborns may have more success individuating from their parents due in part to the "dethroning process" that takes place within the family system upon the arrival of the second child. This process, which is briefly discussed by Barbara Byrd and her colleagues, refers to the firstborn's loss of exclusive parental attention with the addition of a sibling and the ways in which the firstborn adjusts to the change.

The debate that follows presents two studies that investigate whether or not being an only child can impact a person's ability to achieve independence from the family system. As you read them, think about your own family. Where are you in terms of ordinal position? Do you think birth order influences the development of self-sufficiency or individuation from one's family of origin?

YES Barbara Byrd, Arnold P. DeRosa, and Stephen S. Craig

THE ADULT WHO IS AN ONLY CHILD: ACHIEVING SEPARATION OR INDIVIDUATION

Summary.—60 women and 60 men between the ages of 18 and 45 years ($M = 30.5$, $SD = 9.6$) were categorized by sex, age, and birth order (only child, firstborn, lastborn) to assess the differences among the adult only-child, the youngest child, and the oldest child in autonomous characteristics and cohesiveness in family interaction. Analysis of the responses on a biographical data sheet, the California Psychological Inventory, and the Family Adaptability Cohesion Scales III showed that main effects for birth order and sex are significant in the process of separation-individuation and that the only child is less autonomous than the oldest child.

Family Systems and Differentiating Influences

Maintaining relatedness, yet allowing independence of its members is a primary task that challenges the well functioning family throughout the life cycle. There has been increased interest on the part of family theorists and researchers in recent years concerning issues of differentiation, autonomy, and individuation (Bowen, 1978; Grotevant & Cooper, 1986; Haley, 1980; Minuchin, 1974; Sabatelli & Mazor, 1985). Of particular relevance to issues of autonomy is Bowen's construct of differentiation of self. Bowen uses this formulation to define the functioning and experience both of individuals and of family relationships. In Bowenian theory, individual and family functioning are seen as a direct consequence of the differentiation achieved between emotionality and intellect. Individuals with low differentiation are unable to separate themselves from their family system. From this perspective, the farther a person is along the continuum toward differentiation, the healthier is that person. A family's differentiation influences how interpersonal distances are regulated among the family members. For Bowen (1976) the "triangle" is the basic foundation of any family emotional system. Ideally, a family should

From Barbara Byrd, Arnold P. DeRosa, and Stephen S. Craig, "The Adult Who Is an Only Child: Achieving Separation or Individuation," *Psychological Reports*, vol. 73, no. 1 (August 1993), pp. 171–177. Copyright © 1993 by *Psychological Reports*. Reprinted by permission.

consist of differentiated individuals; however, since one-to-one relationships are difficult to maintain, parents will typically triangulate around a child. The concept of triangulation is especially relevant to the only-child family wherein this natural threesome may be particularly vulnerable to fusion of this kind.

Researchers interested in the process of leaving home have demonstrated ways that dysfunctional parent-adolescent relationships curtail the successful attainment of autonomy. Stierlin, Levi, and Savard (1971) stress issues concerning families that are too tightly bound together. He found that this binding mode keeps the adolescent locked within the parental orbit and thwarts opportunities for individuation. Haley (1980), focusing on a population of dysfunctional young adults with psychosomatic illnesses who were unable to leave home, posited complex parent-child dynamics that prevent healthy separation. These formulations coincide with the earlier work of Masterson (1976), who studied borderline adolescents and attributed certain family interactions to the disrupted individuation of these teenagers. While these theorists have concentrated on a clinical population, elements of similar family dynamics may be in operation in modified forms of most family units.

Blos (1979), as a corollary to Mahler, Pine, and Bergman's (1975) work, has proposed that the transition from adolescence into adulthood requires a second separation-individuation. While Josselson (1980) views individuation as a life-long process, she stresses that there is a prominent acceleration during adolescence. For identity formation to proceed, the main tasks of individuation during adolescence involve (1) psychological separation from the "reality" parents and

(2) the separation from the introjected parents (Josselson, 1980, p. 193). Consistent with this is the relational perspective of Grotevant and Cooper (1986), who proposed that there is a co-occurrence of individuality and connectedness in family relationships that contribute to the adolescent's ability to explore identity-related choices (p. 96). From these perspectives, issues of personal autonomy cannot be understood apart from the family as a whole, since it is only relative and reciprocally shared by all.

Siblings and Issues of Separation-Individuation

Bank and Kahn (1975) view the sibling relationship as a life-long process, influential throughout the life cycle which often is overlooked when studying family functioning. Both authors view identification as the "glue" of the sibling relationship. "Identification with brothers and sisters are more abundant than the possibilities for parent-child identification, but the motivation (love, protection, relief of guilt) may be less" (p. 320). This implies that sibling identifications are apt to be more spontaneous and less encumbered than parent-child identifications. Bank and Kahn (1975) also point out that the sibling experience helps foster differentiations, which can serve as an inhibitor against fusion within a family. This mutually regulatory process is common among brothers and sisters, which can provide an "observing ego" for siblings that is not present in most parent-child relationships.

Neubauer (1982, 1983), in his studies on the importance of siblings' interaction, makes many of the same observations and further adds that, because siblings often share a similar psychic organization, they are responsive to one another with respect to drive manifestations and fluctuations between progression and regression. "Experimentation, sexual curiosity, and displacement of aggression can provide special, shared nontraumatic experiences that go far beyond the identification with the parents they share" (1983, p. 334). Neubauer views issues of rivalry, jealousy, and envy among siblings in nonpathological or traumatic settings as a positive contribution to emotional development. He sees these dynamics as an expression of the interactions of all psychic structural components, facilitating comparisons promoting the differentiation of object and self.

METHOD

Subjects

Subjects, 552 undergraduate and graduate students at a private university, were sampled from which 120 were randomly drawn for inclusion in the study. Among the original 552, 284 were firstborn, 200 lastborn, and 68 only children. Of the 284 firstborn, 171 were younger (18 to 30 years old) firstborn, and 113 older (31 to 45 years old) firstborn. Of the 68 only children, 38 were younger and 30 older only children. Of the 200 lastborn, 112 were younger and 88 older lastborn. Twenty subjects (10 men and 10 women) were randomly selected from each of the six categories so defined for inclusion in the study. Subjects whose childhood included either divorce or death of a parent were eliminated from the pool from which the final sample were selected.

Procedure

Biological data sheets, the California Psychological Inventory (30 items of the Independence scale) and the Family Adaptability and Cohesion Evaluation Scales (FACES III) were distributed in packets to 200 subjects. Each completed packet was assigned a number from 1 to 200. Subjects ($N = 120$) were placed into subgroups based on age, sex, and birth-order categories, placing 20 men and 20 women in each of the three categories.

Biographical data sheet. The biographical data sheet was devised to provide information about each subject's birth-order position, family status, age, sex, and number of members in the family.

The Family Adaptability Cohesion Evaluation Scales III (Olson, Portner, & Lavee, 1985). Family Adaptability Cohesion Evaluation Scales (FACES III) is a 20-item instrument used to measure cohesion and adaptability. The instrument is designed to assess how family members see their family (perceived) and how they would like it to be (ideal) (Olson, *et al.*, 1985). The instrument addresses four levels of family cohesion, namely, disengaged, separated, connected, and enmeshed (Minuchin, 1974).

Each item of the FACES III has a five-point response option. The subject is asked to describe his family as it is or was and how ideally he would like it to be or have been. The difference between the two should give an inverse estimate of one's family satisfaction (Olson, *et al.*, 1985). The higher the cohesion scores the more enmeshed is a family. Reliability (N = 242) was reported as .77 for the 10-item cohesion scale, and .68 for the Total FACES III scores.

California Psychological Inventory (Gough, 1987). From the California Psychological Inventory the Independence Scale was used to measure autonomy, higher independence (55 to 70T) indicating self-sufficiency, resourcefulness, and detachment, lower independence (30 to 45T) indicating lack of self-confidence and support-seeking behavior. Reliability coefficients for the Independence Scales were .69 for men and .67 for women.

RESULTS

A completely randomized factorial analysis of variance was used to investigate the differences in autonomy, as measured by the Independence Scale, across the three birth orders and two genders. The analysis indicated significant main effects for both birth order ($F_{2,114} = 2.93$, $p = .06$) and gender ($F_{1,114} = 5.13$, $p = .03$) but no significant interaction for birth order × gender. Effect sizes based on formulas suggested by Cohen (1988) and Rosnow and Rosenthal (1988) for both birth order, .3, and gender, .4, were rather low. The effect size of .4 for gender indicates that variable accounted for approximately 4% of the variance in autonomy while the effect size of .3 for birth order indicates that variable accounted for approximately 3% of the variance in autonomy.

Post hoc analysis using Tukey's test indicated that men evidenced higher autonomy than did women and oldest siblings evidenced higher autonomy than did only children. . . .

Scores on the Cohesion scale of FACES III were used to classify subjects' families as disengaged, separated, connected, or enmeshed. Chi-squared analysis indicated that among the only children more subjects rated their families of origin as enmeshed than would be expected by chance ($x^2 = 8.33$, $p < .05$).

DISCUSSION

The purpose of the present investigation was to examine the relationship between birth order and autonomous functioning. The position advanced was based on the orientation that there is a continuous interplay between individuality and connectedness in family relationships. Differences in scores on autonomy, as measured on the California Psychological Inventory's Independence Scale, were significantly associated with birth order. The results, therefore, show that only children were less independent than oldest children. In addition, men exhibited greater independence than women.

The present data showed that firstborn children were significantly more independent than only children. While lastborn children had a higher mean independence score than only children, this difference was not significantly greater. It might be hypothesized that the "dethronement process," in which the firstborn must relinquish only-child status at the birth of a sibling, is instrumental in fostering independence. Unique to the oldest child is the status of having been first and foremost, a rank which may produce a sense of entitlement and even superiority. It is also likely that the loss of exclusive parental attention reduces the later tendency for dependent and potentially guilt-producing relationships. Taylor and Kogan (1973) observed that mothers may withdraw emotionally from a first child in anticipation of and immediately following the birth of their second child so the firstborn's relationship to the parents must be redefined. There is a repeated "rapprochement crisis" when there is another birth in the family. However, it may be that for the firstborn the resolution of the crisis is a more individuated state characterized by greater autonomous functioning. Furthermore, it may be that with the birth of a sibling assertive behavior becomes necessary and even reinforced, and the firstborn is propelled to achieve independence from his parents. One might suggest that for the oldest child the inevitable dethronement process can be a positive and useful adaptation in the attainment of autonomy.

The data indicated that youngest children were more independent than only children and that only children were significantly less independent than firstborns. Adler (Ansbacher & Ansbacher, 1984) described the youngest child as " . . . a pampered child . . . all the family spoils them. A spoiled child can never be independent" (p. 381). Adler's comments are consistent with findings of Blane and Barry (1973) who reported heightened conflict between dependency and independent striving in lastborn males.

The data showed only children to be less independent than firstborns. This finding is consistent with the observations of both Feldman (1981) and Forer (1977) who attribute a prolonged Oedipal triangle as an obstacle that created a fixated dependent relationship for the only child and his parents. An important aspect of the separation-individuation phase is the ability to neutralize aggression towards the parental objects. The only child would seem to have greater difficulty with this task because the parent-child relationship is exclusive. Sibling aggression is adaptive in nature and is an integral part of the give and take relationship of siblings, as well as a healthy avenue for the expression of conflict and frustration. Minuchin (1974) views sibling rivalry as a stabilizing force in the system of many families. Clearly, the only child is lacking in this experi-

ence, a factor which could contribute to greater anxiety with aggressive feelings and increased dependency.

REFERENCES

Ansbacher, H. L., & Ansbacher, R. (Eds.) (1984) *The individual psychology of Alfred Adler: a systematic presentation in selections from his writings.* New York: Basic Books.

Bank, S. P., & Kahn, M. D. (1975) Sisterhood-brotherhood is powerful: sibling subsystems and family therapy. *Family Process,* 14, 317–319.

Blane, H. T., & Barry, H. III. (1973) Birth order and alcoholism. *Quarterly Journal of Studies on Alcohol,* 34, 837–852.

Blos, P. (1979) *The adolescent passage: developmental issues.* New York: International Universities Press.

Bowen, M. (1976) Theory and practice in psychotherapy. In P. J. Guerin (Ed.), *Family therapy: theory and practice in psychotherapy.* New York: Gardner Press. Pp. 42–90.

Bowen, M. (1978) *Family therapy in clinical practice.* New York: Jason Aronson.

Cohen, J. (1988) *Statistical power analysis for the behavioral sciences.* (2nd ed.) Hillsdale, NJ: Erlbaum.

Feldman, G. C. (1981) Three's company: family therapy with only child families. *Journal of Marital and Family Therapy,* 7, 43–46.

Forer, L. K. (1977) Use of birth order information in psychotherapy. *Journal of Individual Psychology,* 33, 105–118.

Gough, H. G. (1987) *California Psychological Inventory.* Palo Alto, CA: Consulting Psychologists Press.

Grotevant, H. D., & Cooper, C. R. (1986) Individuation in family relationship. *Human Development,* 29, 82–100.

Haley, J. (1980) *Leaving home: the therapy of disturbed young people.* New York: McGraw-Hill.

Josselson, R. L. (1980). Ego development in adolescence. In J. Adelson (Ed.), *Handbook of adolescent psychology.* New York: Wiley, Pp. 188–210.

Mahler, M. (1968) *On human symbiosis and the vicissitudes of individuation.* Vol. 1. *Infantile psychosis.* New York: International Universities Press.

Mahler, M., Pine, F., & Bergman, A. (1975) *The psychological birth of the human infant.* New York: Basic Books.

Masterson, J. (1976) *Psychotherapy of the borderline adult: a developmental approach.* New York: Brunner/Mazel.

Minuchin, S. (1974) *Families and family therapy.* Cambridge, MA: Harvard Univer. Press.

Neubauer, P. B. (1982) Rivalry, envy and jealousy. In A. J. Solnit (Ed.), *Psychoanalytic study of the child.* Vol. 37. New Haven, CT: Yale Univer. Press, Pp. 121–142.

Neubauer, P. B. (1983) The importance of the sibling experience. In A. J. Solnit (Ed.), *Psychoanalytic study of the child.* Vol. 38. New Haven, CT: Yale Univer. Press. Pp. 325–336.

Olson, D., Portner, J., & Lavee, Y. (1985) *FACES III.* St. Paul, MN: Family Social Science.

Rosnow, R. L., & Rosenthal, R. (1988) Focused tests of significance and effect size estimates in counseling psychology. *Journal of Counseling Psychology,* 59, 217–224.

Sabatelli, R. M., & Mazor, A. (1985) Differentiation, individuation and identity formation: the integration of family system and individual developmental perspectives. *Adolescence,* 20, 619–633.

Stierlin, H., Levi, L., & Savard, R. (1971) Parental perceptions of separating children. *Family Process,* 10, 411–427.

Taylor, L., & Kogan, K. (1973) Effects of birth of a sibling on mother-child interactions. *Child Psychiatry and Human Development,* 4(1), 53–58.

NO

Steven Mellor

HOW DO ONLY CHILDREN DIFFER FROM OTHER CHILDREN?

ABSTRACT. Developmental outcomes of only and non-only children, categorized by birth order and by family size, were investigated. Multiple hypotheses based on meta-analyses of the only-child literature (Falbo & Polit, 1986) were tested with independent comparison techniques. Results indicated that developmental outcomes of only children were similar to outcomes for firstborns and children from two-child families but dissimilar to outcomes for later borns and children from larger families. Furthermore, outcomes were more positive for only children, firstborns, and children from two-child families than for all other comparison groups. In agreement with Falbo and Polit, only-child deprivation and only-child uniqueness explanations for outcome differences were not supported in favor of an explanation that emphasizes qualities of the parent–child relationship. Results suggest that future comparisons to only-child outcomes should preserve the independence of contrast results and expand the only-child category to include data from firstborns and others from two-child families.

How do only children differ from other children? Falbo and Polit (1986) reported the results of six meta-analyses of the research literature on the only child since 1925 and concluded that several of the developmental outcomes of only children were similar to the outcomes for firstborn children and children from two-child families but dissimilar to outcomes for children from three- or four-child families and children from five- or more child families. Despite dissimilarities between only children and a group of non-only children, Falbo and Polit ruled out explanatory mechanisms relating to only-child deprivation and only-child uniqueness in favor of theoretical propositions that emphasized qualities of the parent–child relationship. Although Falbo and Polit are probably correct in their conclusion that the developmental paths of only children have more in common with the paths of children from smaller families, we believe that theoretical propositions based on meta-analyses are

From Steven Mellor, "How Do Only Children Differ from Other Children?" *The Journal of Genetic Psychology*, vol. 151, no. 2 (June 1990), pp. 221–230. Copyright © 1990 by The Helen Dwight Reid Educational Foundation. Reprinted by permission of Heldref Publications, 1319 18th Street, NW, Washington, DC 20036-1802. Some notes omitted.

tenuous at best and require support from independent comparison techniques designed to test multiple hypotheses.

Falbo and Polit (1986) searched through the sibling relationship, birth order, and family size literature for studies that included only-child comparison groups. These studies variously defined the only child as firstborn, last born or as a one-child family. Of 200 studies reviewed for inclusion in the meta-analyses, 115 survived a 6-point quality rating system based on sample size, controls for extraneous variables, and other indices of methodological rigor. Other studies were omitted because effect sizes (based on Cohen's d) could not be computed from reported correlations or because data for only borns were combined with data for firstborns or others from small families. On the basis of included studies, with total sample sizes ranging from 50 to over 600,000, Falbo and Polit formed a series of contrasts between only children and a non-only comparison group (anyone who had a sibling), and between only children and comparison groups defined in terms of birth order (firstborns or later borns from multichild families) and family size—small (two-child), medium (three- or four-child), or large (five- or more child) families.

A broad variety of developmental outcomes found in the literature were classified into 14 categories (e.g., academic progress/grades, self-esteem, personal control/autonomy, IQ/standardized ability tests, and affiliation need/extraversion). Because of the uneven number of studies represented by these categories, outcomes were grouped into five general developmental categories: achievement, adjustment, character, intelligence, and sociability. The outcome groups were used as dependent variable measures

for five separate meta-analyses involving contrasts between only children and non-only children and comparison groups defined by birth order and by family size.[1] Mean effect sizes reliably differed from zero (based on nonorthogonal t tests) for achievement, character, and intelligence outcomes. For achievement and intelligence, only children had more desirable outcomes than comparison groups of all non-only borns, children from medium and large families, and later borns, but had similar outcomes to groups of firstborns and children from small families. In the character area, only children had more desirable outcomes than groups of all non-only borns and groups of children from medium and large families but similar outcomes to all other comparison groups. None of the mean effect sizes for sociability and adjustment outcomes were reliably different from zero ($p < .05$).

Meta-analysis results were used by Falbo and Polit (1986) to suggest that only borns had higher levels of achievement and intelligence than children from medium and large families, had more desirable personalities, and were as sociable and adjusted as peers with siblings. Because no data were uncovered that revealed a single significant disadvantage for only borns across developmental outcomes, and because only borns were not found to be reliably different from all other comparison groups, Falbo and Polit argued that explanatory mechanisms that employ only-child deprivation and uniqueness were less feasible than a mechanism that emphasizes the parent–child relationship. Indirect support for this mechanism came from the finding that, across all meta-analyses, comparison between only borns and firstborns, and comparisons between only borns and children from small families, never yielded reliable outcome differences. Falbo and Polit suggested that, because both only borns and firstborns were their parents' first child, at least for awhile, both were only borns, and concluded that the parent–child mechanism that produces only child outcomes was probably at work in producing similar firstborn and small-family outcomes.

Our central concern was with Falbo and Polit's (1986) theoretical proposition that two explanatory mechanism have been excluded in favor of one that can explain how only children differ from others on general developmental outcomes. At the very least, Falbo and Polit's use of nonorthogonal t tests (36 at $p < .05$) to evaluate contrasts between comparison groups (when independent mean comparison tests are preferable) calls for replication; a task we address with a new sample in our study. But, we also believed that theoretical propositions ruling out other mechanisms must find support from procedures designed to test multiple hypotheses and preserve outcome probability levels. Thus, our study was designed to retest hypotheses that follow from Falbo and Polit's meta-analyses and to further clarify a number of the similar and dissimilar developmental outcomes of only and non-only borns.

METHOD

Subjects
The sample consisted of 434 students (239 males and 195 females) recruited from six junior and senior high schools and one community college in the Los Angeles area. Subjects' ages ranged from 11 to 19 years, with a mean age of 15.9 years. Adolescents and young adults were targeted as subjects to approximate the mean age

of subjects (16.6 years) and the majority of age groups (56%) included in Falbo and Polit's (1986) sample. Seventy-nine percent were Caucasian, 11% were Black, 8% were Hispanic, and 2% were Asian, an ethnic mix proportional to current national percentages ("The Nation," 1988).

Subjects were first categorized by birth order and then by family size. Eight percent were only borns, 32% were firstborns, and 60% were later borns. In terms of family size, 8% percent were from one-child families, 38% were from small (two-child) families, 38% were from medium (three- or four-child) families and 15% were from large (five- or more child) families. The distribution of gender within categories for birth order and family size was proportional to the distribution in the total sample, and mean ages did not significantly differ from one category to the next ($p < .05$).

Procedure
Measures were administered in random order to students in "home" classroom by undergraduates earning course credits. Informed consent forms were used to brief subjects on the nature of the project to request voluntary participation, and to assure subjects of anonymity. Completed measures were received from 89% of the students contacted. Feedback on group results were sent to subjects through their home classroom instructors.

Measures
The Erikson Psychosocial Stage Inventory (EPSI; Rosenthal, Gurney, & Moore 1981) was selected to measure general developmental outcomes included in Falbo and Polit's (1986) meta-analyses. The EPSI is a measure of negative and positive resolutions to identity crises as defined by Erikson, and many of the res

olutions are thought to play a critical role in influencing the outcomes grouped by Falbo and Polit. For example, outcomes related to affiliation need, personal control/autonomy, and academic progress/grades overlap with resolutions to the crises of trust versus mistrust, autonomy versus shame, and industry versus inferiority (cf. Hamachek, 1988). One important shortcoming for this claim is in the area of intelligence. The EPSI does not include standardized items designed to measure ability per se, but arguments can be launched that suggest that achievement and intelligence are highly correlated with respect to developmental outcomes (cf. Fitzgerald & Mellor, 1988).

The EPSI is a 72-item self-report inventory consisting of six 12-item subscales that assess degrees of negative to positive resolutions to six of Erikson's identity crises in childhood, adolescence, and early adulthood (trust vs. mistrust, autonomy vs. shame, initiative vs. guilt, industry vs. inferiority, identity vs. identity confusion, and intimacy vs. isolation). Items are rated on a 5-point scale ranging from *hardly ever true* (1) to *almost always true* (5). Subscale scores are represented by mean item scores. High mean scores for each subscale indicate positive resolutions to crises. Rosenthal et al. (1981) reported internal reliability (alpha) coefficients for subscales ranging from .57 to .81. Alpha coefficients for the present sample ranged from .74 to .86. Supportive validity can be found in Rosenthal, Moore, and Taylor (1983), and further subscale uses can be found in Moore and Rosenthal (1984), Pickar and Tori (1986), and Mellor (1989).[2]

Sociobiographic measures also were included to assess subject gender, age, educational level (indexed by grade level), ethnic mix, vocabulary, and socioeco-

nomic status (SES). A variety of other measures were used to determine birth order and family size. Form Z of the Basic Word Vocabulary Test (BWVT; Dupey, 1974) was used as the measure of vocabulary, and SES was based on Hollingshead's (1975) Four-Factor Index of Social Status, adjusting for combined parental income. Along with age and educational level, the latter two measures were given to check for covariation affects on birth-order and family-size differences reported in the only-child literature (cf. Claudy, 1984; Falbo, 1984; Gecas & Pasley, 1983; Mednick, Baker, & Hocevar, 1985).

RESULTS

The results of primary interest are the outcomes of sets of orthogonal planned comparisons computed on the data of all subjects. Comparison sets were constructed within Gender × Birth Order (only borns, firstborns, later borns) and Gender × Family Size (one-child, small, medium, large), analyses of variance. Analyses were repeated for EPSI subscales as separate dependent variable measures. Weights were assigned to birth-order and family-size groups to ensure that contrast results were independent within sets, despite the fact that some contrast results were redundant within analyses.

Four sets of contrasts (two per analysis) were performed to retest contrasts indicated by Falbo and Polit (1986)....

Comparison results indicated that only predicted contrasts within sets yielded reliable differences between group means or group mean combinations on dependent variable measures. All other group contrasts failed to reach significance ($p < .05$). Furthermore, reliable mean differences were consistent with high-low predictions. Within the first contrast set for birth–order groups, reliable differences were not found between only borns and firstborns, but differences were found between only borns and later borns on autonomy, $F(1,411) = 4.84$, $p < .03$, initiative, $F(1,405) = 5.00$, $p < .03$, and industry, $F(1,413) = 3.79$, $p < .05$. Mean differences for these groups indicated that only borns had significantly higher mean scores (4.12, 3.93, 3.88) than later borns (3.87, 3.69, 3.64). Within the second set for birth–order groups, group combination differences were not detected between means for only borns and average means for firstborns and later borns, but differences were detected between average means for only borns and first-borns and means for later borns on autonomy, $F(1,411) = 4.26$, $p < .04$, initiative, $F(1,405) = 3.86$, $p < .05$, industry, $F(1,413) = 5.36$, $p < .02$, and identity, $F(1,404) = 3.97$, $p < .05$. Mean differences for these latter contrasts indicated that mean scores for only borns and firstborns were significantly higher (4.02, 3.82, 3.82, 3.84) than mean scores for later borns (3.87, 3.69, 3.64, 3.69).

For the third and fourth contrast sets, we noted a consistent pattern of comparison results. Within the third contrast set for family-size groups, only contrasts between only-child and medium family groups, and between only-child and large family groups, yielded reliable differences on dependent variable measures. Significant mean differences between only-child and medium family groups were recorded on autonomy, $F(1,409) = 4.03$ $p < .04$, and initiative, $F(1,403) = 4.26$ $p < .04$. Mean differences for these contrasts indicated that only-child scores were significantly higher (4.12, 3.93) than medium-family scores (3.88, 3.70). Reliable mean differences between only-child and large-family groups were recorded on initiative, $F(1,403) = 3.75$, $p < .05$, and identity, $F(1,402) = 6.20$, $p < .01$. Mean differences for the latter contrasts indicated that only-child scores were significantly higher (3.93, 3.88) than large-family scores (3.57, 3.53).

The most reliable differences between comparison groups occurred with the fourth set for family size. Although no other contrasts between group combinations were significant, average means for only-child and small-family groups were reliably different from average means for medium- and large-family groups on trust, $F(1,404) = 3.99$, $p < .05$, autonomy, $F(1,409) = 5.95$, $p < .01$, initiative, $F(1,403) = 7.92$, $p < .005$, industry, $F(1,411) = 7.39$, $p < .007$, and identity, $F(1,402) = 4.54$, $p < .03$. Mean differences for these combined groups indicated that only-child and small-family mean scores were significantly higher (3.55, 4.02, 3.83, 3.82, 3.82) than medium- and large-family mean scores (3.39, 3.83, 3.63, 3.59, 3.65).

Within all contrast sets, we also found reliable differences between male and female groups on intimacy, $F(1,408) = 27.28$, $p < .001$. Mean differences for these groups indicated that females' mean scores were significantly higher (3.86) than males' mean scores (3.52). In addition, we repeated analyses for all sets, controlling for the influence of age, grade level, SES, and vocabulary. Results for separate and multiple analyses of covariance with adjusted probability levels ($p < .05$) produced similar results, and reported significant effects were unchanged. Furthermore, across all analyses, we failed to find a single significant interaction effect between gender and birth order or gender and family size.

DISCUSSION

The data of this study support Falbo and Polit's (1986) conclusion that the developmental paths of only children are similar to the paths of firstborns and children from two-child families but dissimilar to paths of children from larger families. In fact, on the basis of developmental outcomes related to resolutions of developmental crises in childhood, adolescence, and early adulthood, the crucial outcome differences appear precisely between the only child, whether defined as only born or firstborn, and the later-born child on the birth-order variable, and precisely between children from two-child families and three-child families on the family-size variable.

We believe that our results provide much clearer support for the hypotheses revealed in Falbo and Polit's meta-analyses. Although the procedures they used to construct the analyses appeared sound, the use of non-orthogonal t tests to test comparison group differences failed to preserve the independence of contrast results and protect against inflated outcome probability levels. As such, the theoretical propositions offered by Falbo and Polit were tenuous at best.

In contrast with techniques used by Falbo and Polit (1986), we retested multiple hypotheses related to only-child uniqueness and deprivation, and the parent–child relationship, with orthogonal contrasts that ensured that comparison results were independent and outcome probability levels were fixed as stated. The only-child uniqueness hypothesis was not supported. Only-children resolution outcomes were not reliably different from outcomes for all non-only comparison groups, whether defined by birth order or by family size.

Comparisons revealed that, across outcomes, the positive-negative resolutions of only children did not significantly differ from the resolutions of firstborns or children from small families.

The only-child deprivation hypothesis also was not supported. Only children had significantly higher positive outcomes to crises than did later borns and children from medium and large families. Furthermore, group means indicated that the positive outcomes of only borns were higher across the board than the positive outcomes for all other comparison groups, including first-borns and children from small families.

Our findings were consistent with the parent–child hypothesis simply because we failed to find significant outcome differences between group combinations of only children and firstborns or between group combinations of only children and children from small families. In contrast, we did find significant outcome differences between combinations of only children and later borns and others from medium and large families. Although we did not directly test the parent–child hypothesis, qualities of the parent–child relationship are apparently similar for only children, firstborns, and children from two-child families but dissimilar to qualities of the parent–child relationship for later borns and others from larger families. On the basis of the outcome differences found in this study, we would suggest that the definition of the only child be expanded to include firstborns and others from two-child families in future studies that use the parent–child mechanism to explain the outcome differences of only children.

We found differences in resolution outcomes between birth-order groups and between family-size groups. Findings that suggest that only children, compared with non-only children, are generally more autonomous in terms of personal control, have higher levels of initiative or personal aspiration or motivation, are more industrious in terms of educational or occupational achievement, and have stronger identities (as indexed by self-esteem or adjustment levels) are not new in the only-child literature (cf. Falbo, 1984, 1987 for reviews). Inconsistencies often appear with respect to each of these findings, however, and a consensus of thought about only-child outcome advantages and disadvantages is far from established. We suggest that profitable meta-analyses for future research include sets of orthogonal comparisons of developmental outcomes of an only-child group (defined as only borns, first-borns, and others from two-child families) with outcomes of various non-only child groups. We believe that outcome differences will be consistent with the present results and that a stronger consensus can be reached in terms of the similarities and dissimilarities of the developmental paths of the only child.

NOTES

1. A sixth meta-analysis was conducted on 19 studies that included various ratings of the quality of the parent–child relationship (keyed toward more positive relationships). Results indicated mean effect sizes reliably different from zero (based on multiple t tests) for comparisons between only children and all non-only borns, and between only children and children from large families. Because mean effect sizes were positive, Falbo and Polit suggested that only children had more positive relationships with their parents than did other children.

2. Additional psychometric information on the EPSI, including factor structure results and inter-subscale correlations may be found in Rosenthal (1982).

3. A detailed explanation for male-female outcome differences relating to intimacy may be found in Mellor (1989).

REFERENCES

Claudy, J. G. (1984). The only child as a young adult: Results from Project Talent. In T. Falbo (Ed.)., *The single-child family* (pp. 211–252). New York: Guilford Press.

Dupey, H. J. (1974). The rationale, development, and standardization of the Basic Word Vocabulary Test. *Vital and Health Statistical Series 2, 60,* 1–71.

Falbo, T. (1984). Only children: a review. In T. Falbo (Ed.)., *The single-child family* (pp. 1–24). New York: Guilford Press.

Falbo, T. (1987). Only children in the United States and China. In S. Oskamp (Ed.), *Annual social psychology* (Vol. 7, pp. 159–183). Beverly Hills: Sage.

Falbo, T., & Polit, D. F. (1986). Quantitative review of the only child literature: Research evidence and theory development. *Psychological Bulletin, 100,* 176–189.

Fitzgerald, J. M., & Mellor, S. (1988). How do people think about intelligence? *Multivariate Behavioral Research, 23,* 143–157.

Gecas, V., & Pasley, K. (1983). Birth order and self-concept in adolescence. *Journal of Youth and Adolescence, 12,* 521–535.

Hamachek, D. E. (1988). Evaluating self-concept and ego development within Erikson's framework: A formulation. *Journal of Counseling and Development, 66,* 354–360.

Hollingshead, A. B. (1975). *Four-Factor Index of Social Status.* Unpublished manuscript, Department of Sociology, Yale University, New Haven, CT.

Mednick, B. R., Baker, R. L., & Hocevar, D. (1985). Family size and birth order correlates of intellectual, psychosocial, and physical growth. *Merrill-Palmer Quarterly, 31,* 67–84.

Mellor, S. (1989). Gender differences in identity formation as a function of self-other relationships. *Journal of Youth and Adolescence, 18,* 361–375.

Moore, S. M., & Rosenthal, D. A. (1984). Balance versus main effects androgyny: Their relationship to adjustment in three ethnic groups. *Psychological Reports, 54,* 823–831.

Pickar, D. B., & Tori, C. D. (1986). The learning disabled adolescent: Eriksonian psychological development, self-concept, and delinquent behavior. *Journal of Youth and Adolescence, 15,* 429–440.

Rosenthal, D. A., (1982). *The Erikson Psychosocial Stage Inventory.* Unpublished manuscript. University of Melbourne, Department of Psychology, Victoria, Australia.

Rosenthal, D. A., Gurney, R. M., & Moore, S. M. (1981). From trust to intimacy: A new inventory for examining Erikson's stages of psychosocial development. *Journal of Youth and Adolescence, 10,* 525–537.

Rosenthal, D. A., Moore, S. M., & Taylor, M. J. (1983). Ethnicity and adjustment: A study of the self-image of Anglo-, Greek-, and Italian-Australian working class adolescents. *Journal of Youth and Adolescence, 12,* 117–135.

The Nation. (1988, September). *The Chronicle of Higher Education Almanac,* p. 3.

POSTSCRIPT

Are Only Children Less Independent Than Firstborn Children?

Byrd, DeRosa, and Craig measured college students' level of self-sufficiency and resourcefulness and found that firstborn children, as well as youngest children, were more independent than only children. Additionally, men displayed greater individuation than women. The researchers speculated that only children have less need for assertive behavior than firstborns who have brothers and sisters. Not only do firstborns adapt to the family by developing more autonomy, but parents support their independent behavior by reinforcing it. Because only children have an exclusive relationship with their parents and do not have to compete with anyone for their attention, they do not achieve the same level of independence as firstborns.

Mellor studied the way that children aged 11 to 19 responded to psychoanalyst Erik Erikson's identity crises. Children were rated on their reactions to developmental crises such as autonomy versus shame and identity versus identity confusion. He found that firstborn children and only children responded similarly and had more positive outcomes to the crises than laterborn children or children from medium and large families. Only children and firstborns were also similar to children from two-child families in their responses to Erikson's developmental crises.

Although research continues on the effects of birth order on personality, there are societal influences that may change future results on the subject, such as smaller family size, more employed mothers, increased use of day care for children, and a greater incidence of stepfamily situations. Today families in the United States have fewer children than families in the past. As a result, parents often spend as much time with the younger children as with the older ones. Will this increased attention from adults create the same personality characteristics in younger children as firstborns?

More mothers are working outside the home than ever before; thus, more children are spending their early years in child-care centers. Not only are these children less likely to spend time with adults, but they are also being socialized by other children. Will this decrease in adult interaction and increase in child interaction change the personality characteristics previously assigned to firstborns and only children?

What about the stepfamily effect? When parents remarry and families blend together, ordinal positions in the family change. In the original family, for example, a child could have been the firstborn or an only child. Now, with the addition of a stepparent and an older sibling, the child is neither the firstborn nor the only child. While previous research on this subject has been useful in understanding children's development, future studies will likely reflect these changes in our society.

SUGGESTED READINGS

Bernstein, L. (1994, February). What's new about the oldest child? *Working Mother, 17*, 60–64.

Bohmer, P., & Sitton, S. (1993, Summer). The influence of birth order and family size on notable American women's selection of careers. *The Psychological Record, 43*, 375–380.

Falbo, T. (1984). Only children: A review. In T. Falbo (Ed.), *The single-child family* (pp. 1–24). New York: Guilford Press.

Hudson, V. (1990, September). Birth order of world leaders: An exploratory analysis of effects on personality and behavior. *Political Psychology, 11*, 583–601.

Leman, K. (1985). *The birth order book.* New York: Dell.

Marzollo, J. (1990, December). What birth order means. *Parents, 65*, 84–91.

Segal, J. (1992, May). The firstborn child. *Parents, 67*, 219.

ISSUE 7

Does Divorce Create Long-Term Negative Effects for Children?

YES: Karl Zinsmeister, from "Divorce's Toll on Children," *The American Enterprise* (May/June 1996)

NO: David Gately and Andrew I. Schwebel, from "Favorable Outcomes in Children After Parental Divorce," *Journal of Divorce and Remarriage* (vol. 18, nos. 3–4, 1992)

ISSUE SUMMARY

YES: Karl Zinsmeister, editor in chief of the *American Enterprise*, presents a case for parents staying together for the sake of the children. He argues that divorce causes damage from which children never recover. The conflict within a marriage will not cause the same amount of problems for children that the breakup of a marriage creates.

NO: David Gately and Andrew I. Schwebel, both university educators, contend that children of divorce are not doomed to failure; they often display positive characteristics such as enhanced levels of maturity, self-esteem, empathy, and adaptability. Divorce itself does not cause problems in children's behavior and development.

According to some reports, children from divorced homes are more likely to become divorced themselves. Conversely, other studies explain that the quality of the postdivorce home is more responsible for subsequent development in children than the divorce itself. Is society setting children up for failed marriages by condoning divorce? Or is divorce simply a way to solve the problem of choosing the wrong marriage partner, giving individuals and families a way to correct that mistake? Does the event of divorce spell disaster for children as they grow into adulthood or are there other explanations for the problems that children from divorced homes exhibit?

There is a movement in the 1990s to do away with no-fault divorce, which has spawned a renewed interest in the topic of divorce's effects on children. As the divorce debate evolved from the 1960s to the 1980s, many professionals began viewing divorce as an acceptable alternative to living in an unhappy home. Now family scientists, therapists, and researchers are questioning the belief that children can eventually adjust to the effects of divorce and that it is better for children to live in a divorced home than in an unhappy, intact home.

How does divorce affect children? Do children perceive it as positive or negative? How would their lives have differed if their parents had worked out their problems and stayed together? How do the children from divorced families compare with those who grew up in an unhappy, intact family? Do both groups have similar characteristics or are they different? These are some of the questions related to the study of divorce's effects on children.

There are many studies of divorce's effects on children. Some of these studies show that children benefit from a family's divorce, whereas others show it as the worst thing that ever happened to children. On the positive side, children from divorced families can reap positive benefits as a consequence of their divorce experience, particularly if the parents model responsible coping skills. Some children do better in a home without the constant tension and fighting that an unhappy, intact home exhibits. These children appear more mature, are more realistic about life, and are more flexible.

On the other hand, problems for children in divorced families are well documented. These children are caught in a situation that they cannot control. Their parents split legally but not emotionally. Such families might ride an emotional roller coaster for years after the initial divorce decree. One parent pitted against the other with the children in the middle is not uncommon. This family turmoil may result in children doing poorly in school, beginning to have sex at an early age, and displaying delinquent behavior. Children are not consulted in the decision to divorce but must live through the instability and confusion that the breakup causes.

In the following two selections, arguments are made about the negative and positive effects of divorce on children. Karl Zinsmeister uses studies of children and divorce to argue against the claim by many parents that it is better to divorce than to rear children in a marriage with conflict. He believes that children's sense of stability and family structure supersedes parental needs. David Gately and Andrew I. Schwebel use a different set of studies of divorce and children; their interpretations of the results and methods of those studies are quite different from those of Zinsmeister.

YES
Karl Zinsmeister

DIVORCE'S TOLL ON CHILDREN

Originally, notes family historian John Sommerville, marriage arose to create "security for the children to be expected from the union." Yet nowadays "the child's interest in the permanence of marriage is almost ignored." During the divorce boom that began in the mid-1960s, divorces affecting children went up even faster than divorces generally, and today *most* crack-ups involve kids. Since 1972, more than a million youngsters have been involved in a divorce *each year.*

The result is that at some time before reaching adulthood, around half of today's children will go through a marital rupture. Most of these youngsters will live in a single-parent home for at least five years. A small majority of those who experience a divorce eventually end up in a step-family, but well over a third of them will endure the extra trauma of seeing that second marriage break up.

The typical divorce brings what researcher Frank Furstenberg describes as "either a complete cessation of contact between the non-residential parent and child, or a relationship that is tantamount to a ritual form of parenthood." In nine cases out of ten the custodial parent is the mother, and fully half of all divorce-children living with their mom have had no contact with their father for at least a full year. Only one child in 10 sees his non-custodial parent as often as once a week. Overall, only about one youngster in five is able to maintain a close relationship with both parents.

Joint child custody receives a lot of publicity (it is now allowed in about half the states), but it remains unusual. In California, where it is much more common than anywhere else, only 18 percent of divorced couples have joint physical custody. Most divorced children still live solely with their mothers.

"For most men," sociologist Andrew Cherlin notes, "children and marriage are part of a package deal. Their ties to their children depend on their ties to their wives." Studies show that remarriage makes fathers particularly likely to reduce involvement with the children from their previous marriage.

Even when divorced parents do maintain regular contact with their children, truly cooperative child rearing is very rare. Most often, research shows, the estranged parents have no communication or mutual reinforcement. As

From Karl Zinsmeister, "Divorce's Toll on Children," *The American Enterprise*, vol. 7, no. 3 (May/June 1996) pp. 39–44. Copyright © 1996 by *The American Enterprise* Reprinted by permission.

a result, mother and father frequently undercut each other, intentionally or not, and parent-child relations are often unhealthy.

A series of interviews with children of divorce conducted by author/ photographer Jill Krementz illustrates this phenomenon. "My relationship with my parents has changed because now my mother does all the disciplining," says 14-year-old Meredith, "and sometimes she resents it—especially when we tell her how much fun we have with Dad. It's as if it's all fun and games with him because we're with him so little." Ari, also 14, confides, "I really look forward to the weekends because it's kind of like a break —it's like going to Disneyland because there's no set schedule, no 'Be home by 5:30' kind of stuff. It's open. It's free. And my father is always buying me presents." Zach, age 13, reports "whenever I want to see my other parent I can, and if I have a fight with one of them, instead of having to take off . . . I can just go eat at my Mom's house or my Dad's."

Other youngsters feel torn in two after a divorce, particularly in cases of joint custody where they must physically bounce back and forth between two houses. "It's hello, goodbye, hello, goodbye all the time," says one father. Gary Skoloff, chairman of the American Bar Association's family law section, explains that "joint custody was going to be a great panacea, the ultimate solution. . . . But it turned out to be the world's worst situation." The lack of a stable home has proved so harmful to children that several states, including California where the practice was pioneered, have recently revoked statutes favoring joint custody.

FEAR AND LOATHING OF DIVORCE AMONG THE YOUNG

Children's view of divorce is unambiguous: it's a disaster. In 1988, professor Jeanne Dise-Lewis surveyed almost 700 junior high school students, asking them to rate a number of life events in terms of stressfulness. The only thing students ranked as more stressful than parental divorce was death of a parent or close family member. Parental divorce received a higher rating than the death of a friend, being "physically hit" by a parent, feeling that no one liked them or being seriously injured.

The "fairy tale" believed by adults, says University of Michigan psychologist and divorce expert Neil Kalter, is that if they simply present new family set-ups to their children in a calm, firm way, the children will accept them. Actually, he says, that "is seen by the kids as a lot of baloney." Among the hundreds of children he's worked with in setting up coping-with-divorce programs for schools, "there are very few who have anything good to say about divorce." "Children are generally more traditional than adults," agrees Judith Wallerstein. "Children want both parents. They want family." If children had the vote, she says, there would be no such thing as divorce.

Indeed, Gallup youth surveys in the early 1990's show that three out of four teenagers age 13 to 17 think "it is too easy for people in this country to get divorced." Go into a typical high school today and ask some students what their most important wish for the future is and a surprising number will answer "that there wouldn't be so many divorces." Young Arizonan Cynthia Coan has lots of company when she says, "as a child of divorce, I cannot help but hope that the next generation of children will be spared what mine went through."

You'll sometimes hear the claim that divorce doesn't hurt children as much as conflict in a marriage. This is not supported by the evidence. "For kids," reports Kalter, "the misery in an unhappy marriage is usually less significant than the changes" after a divorce. "They'd rather their parents keep fighting and not get divorced." Even five years later, few of the youngsters in Wallerstein's study agreed with their parents' decision to separate. Only ten percent were more content after the split than before.

Contrary to popular perceptions, the alternative to most divorces is not life in a war zone. Though more than 50 percent of all marriages currently end in divorce, experts tell us that only about 15 percent of all unions involve high levels of conflict. In the vast number of divorces, then, there is no gross strife or violence that could warp a youngster's childhood. The majority of marital break-ups are driven by a quest for greener grass—and in these cases the children will almost always be worse off.

Many mothers and fathers badly underestimate how damaging household dissolution will be to their children. A 1985 British study that quizzed both parents and children found that the children reported being far more seriously upset by their parents' separation than the parents assumed. Despite the common perception that the best thing parents can do for their children is to make themselves happy, the truth is that children have their own needs that exist quite apart from those of their parents. One may argue that a parent should be allowed to rank his own needs above those of his children (though this is not the traditional understanding of how families should work). But one ought not cloak that decision with the false justification that one is thereby serving the children's best interests.

Wade Horn, former commissioner of the U.S. Administration for Children, Youth, and Families, illustrates how parents can be deluded in this way:

> Families used to come to me when I was practicing psychology, seeking advice about how to divorce. They would say, "We want a divorce because we really don't get along very well any more, and we understand that our child will be better off after we divorce than if we stay together." Rarely, if ever, did I hear a family say, "We're having conflict, but we have decided to work as hard as we can at solving our problems because we know that children of divorce are more disturbed than children of intact families."

A major reason parents are making this mistake is because that is what some authorities and many ideologues in the cause of family "liberation" have been telling them. "For years experts said, 'Once the initial trauma wears off, kids make adjustments,'" complains psychologist John Guidubaldi, past president of the National Association of School Psychologists. While it's true that kids make adjustments, Guidubaldi notes in the *Washington Post*, "so do people in prisons and mental institutions. The pertinent question is: Are those adjustments healthy? And the weight of the evidence has become overwhelming on the side that they aren't."

SHORT- AND LONG-TERM EFFECTS OF DIVORCE ON CHILDREN

The longer-term effects of divorce on children are something we've learned a lot about over the last decade. Guidubaldi, who orchestrated one of the large studies documenting these effects, concludes from his work that "the old argument of staying together for the sake of the kids is still the best argument.... People simply aren't putting enough effort into saving their marriages." Family scholar Nicholas Zill points out that "if you looked at the kind of long-term risk factors that divorce creates for kids and translated them to, say, heart disease, people would be startled."

In the early months after divorce, young children are often less imaginative and more repetitive. Many become passive watchers. They tend to be more dependent, demanding, unaffectionate, and disobedient than their counterparts from intact families. They are more afraid of abandonment, loss of love, and bodily harm. A significant number—in some studies a quarter—say they blame themselves for their parents' smash-up.

A small study conducted some years ago by University of Hawaii psychiatrist John McDermott sorted preschoolers who had been involved in a divorce a few months earlier into three categories. Three out of 16 children were judged to have weathered the initial storm essentially unchanged. Two of 16 became what he called "severely disorganized" and developed gross behavior problems. The rest, more than two-thirds, he categorized as "the sad, angry children." They displayed resentment, depression, and grief, were restless, noisy, possessive and physically aggressive.

In Judith Wallerstein's landmark study, almost half of the pre-schoolers still displayed heightened anxiety and aggression a full year after their parents' divorce. Forty-four percent "were found to be in significantly deteriorated psy-chological condition." All of the two- and three-year-olds showed acute regression in toilet training. They displayed unusual hunger for attention from strangers. Older pre-schoolers had become more whiny, irritable, and aggressive, and had problems with play.

Wallerstein's study also returned to its subjects five and 10 years later, and the collected results were quite staggering. In overview they look like this: initially, two-thirds of all the children showed symptoms of stress, and half thought their life had been destroyed by the divorce. Five years down the road, over a third were still seriously disturbed (even more disturbed than they had been initially, in fact), and another third were having psychological difficulties. A surprisingly large number remained angry at their parents.

After a decade, 45 percent of the children were doing well, 14 percent were succeeding in some areas but failing in others, and 41 percent were still doing quite poorly. This last group "were entering adulthood as worried, underachieving, self-deprecating, and sometimes angry young men and women." In addition to their emotional problems and depression, many felt sorrow over their childhoods and fear about their own marriage and childrearing prospects. About a third of the group had little or no ambition at the 10-year mark. Many expressed a sense of powerlessness, neediness, and vulnerability. Most of the ones who had reached adult age regarded their parents' divorce as a continuing major influence in their lives.

It should be noted that the 131 children in the study experienced divorce in what Wallerstein and associates call the "best of circumstances." Most of their parents were college educated, and at the beginning these children were achievers in school. None of the participants was initially being treated for psychiatric disorder. Most of the families were white and middle class; half regularly attended church or synagogue.

Even in families with all these advantages, divorce wreaks havoc among the young. Summarizing her findings on the offspring of broken marriages, Wallerstein has written that "it would be hard to find any other group of children—except, perhaps, the victims of a natural disaster—who suffered such a rate of sudden serious psychological problems." Other long-term studies teach similar conclusions. "Divorce," says psychiatrist McDermott, "is now the single largest cause of childhood depression." Marital disruption, quite clearly, can wound children for years.

A CATALOGUE OF BEHAVIORAL CHANGES

Let's look more specifically at some of the changes in behavior that affect children of divorce. John Guidubaldi and Joseph Perry found in their survey of 700 youngsters that children of divorced parents performed worse than children of intact families on 9 of 30 mental health measures, showing, among other things, more withdrawal, dependency, inattention, and unhappiness, plus less work effort. Divorced students were more likely to abuse drugs, to commit violent acts, to take their own life, and to bear children out of wedlock.

A University of Pittsburgh study in the late 1980s found that there were 30 percent more duodenal ulcers and 70 percent more suicide attempts—both symptoms of serious psychological stress —among children who had lost a parent.

In Wallerstein's middle-class sample, one-third of the girls with divorced parents became pregnant out of wedlock, and 8 percent had at least two abortions. Two-thirds of the girls had a history of delinquency, and almost 30 percent of the boys had been arrested more than once.

The National Survey of Children showed that more than 30 percent of the individuals whose parents separated or divorced before they were eight years old had received therapy by the time they were teenagers. Divorce-children are two to four times as numerous in psychiatric care populations as they are in society at large. In fact, more than 80 percent of the adolescents in mental hospitals, and 60 percent of the children in psychiatric clinics, have been through a divorce. And what is being treated in most cases is much more than just a short-term reaction: the average treatment takes place five years after their parents' marital breakup. At the fully adult age of 23, middle-class women whose mother and father had divorced were three times likelier to have a psychological problem than counterparts from intact families, according to a massive multi-year British study.

Schooling is another problem area. Children exposed to divorce are twice as likely to repeat a grade, and five times likelier to be expelled or suspended. (Fully 15 percent of all teenagers living with divorced mothers have been booted from school at least temporarily, according to the National Survey of Children.) Even in Wallerstein's middle-class sample, 13 percent of the youngsters had dropped out of school altogether. Barely half of Wallerstein's subjects went on to college, far less than the 85 percent average for students in their high schools. Wallerstein concludes that 60 percent of the divorce-children in her study will fail to match the educational achievements of their fathers.

Children of divorce also frequently have problems with sexual identity. In most studies, boys seem to be harder hit than girls. Pre-school boys tend to be unpopular with male peers, to have difficulty gaining access to play groups, to spend more time with younger compatriots and females, and to engage in more activities traditionally considered to be feminine. Young boys tend to be more vehemently opposed to the divorce, to long more for their father, to feel rejected by him, and to feel uncertain about their masculinity. They are more likely than girls to become depressed and angry. Many later have problems developing intimacy, and build lifestyles of solitary interests and habits.

For girls there is a "sleeper effect"—beginning at adolescence, seemingly well-adjusted individuals often develop serious problems with sexuality, self-control, and intimacy. Kalter found higher rates of substance abuse, running away, and sexual activity among girls who had been through divorce, particularly when the father had departed early on. Wallerstein found that a "significant minority" of girls expressed insecurity, anger, or lack of self-respect in promiscuity, some gravitating to older men or a series of aimless sexual relationships. "I'm prepared for anything. I don't expect a lot," said one 20-year-old. "Love is a strange idea to me. Life is a chess game. I've always been a pawn."

Mavis Hetherington of the University of Virginia has found that girls have special problems when their divorced mothers remarry. She has also shown that the pattern of low self-respect and sexual precocity among girls with a divorced mother does *not* hold true among girls living with a solo mother due to death of the father—apparently it is active alienation from the father, more than his simple absence, that causes the disturbance. This fits well with psychologist Erik Erikson's view that it is less deprivation *per se* that is psychologically destructive than deprivation without redeeming significance.

Wallerstein points out that teenage girls often view their absent fathers with a combination of idealization and distrust.

> The idealized father that the young adolescent girl imagines is the exact opposite of the image that later becomes prominent in her mind as she grows older—namely, the father as betrayer.... Because daughters of divorce often have a hard time finding out what their fathers are really like, they often experience great difficulty in establishing a realistic view of men in general, in developing realistic expectations, and in exercising good judgment in their choice of partner.

Researcher Conrad Schwarz has hypothesized that children who are allied only with their same-sex parent (as a girl growing up with a divorced mother would be) tend to hold a chauvinistic and alienated view of the opposite sex. Conversely, he suggests, children growing up with only opposite-sex parents (like boys living with divorced mothers) tend to have problems with gender identity and self-esteem. One study that fits this hypothesis found that college-age women who had experienced divorce in childhood were more prone to see men as unfeeling and weak than counterparts from intact families.

Female children of divorced parents are more likely to choose "inadequate husbands" and to have marital problems of their own. They are substantially likelier to have extensive premarital sexual experience and twice as likely to cohabit before marriage. They are more frequently pregnant at their weddings.

And both male and female children of divorce see their own marriages dissolve at significantly higher rates than counterparts who grew up in intact families. Partly this is attitudinal: One eight-year study of 1,300 men and women found that people who had watched their own parents divorce were much more tolerant of the idea of divorce, and that this tolerance translated into increased marital break-up.

The other thing that childhood divorce encourages, of course, is the avoidance of marriage. "My mom got remarried and divorced again, so I've gone through two divorces so far. And my father's also gotten remarried—to someone I don't get along with all that well. It's all made me feel that people shouldn't get married," 14-year-old Ari explained to Jill Krementz.

Divorces involving children thus set a whole train of losses into motion, transporting unhappy effects not only over the years but even across generations. And not even children fortunate enough to live in stable homes are wholly insulated from the turmoil. As writer Susan Cohen observes:

> Although I am not divorced and live in a conventional nuclear family with a husband and two children... divorce has been part of my daughter Sarah's life since she was two or three. Divorce is in her books, on her television programs, in her lessons as school, in her conversations with her friends, and in her questions to me.

Indeed, divorce is in the very air our children breathe—with lasting significance for their later views of love, families, and life.

NO

David Gately and
Andrew I. Schwebel

FAVORABLE OUTCOMES IN CHILDREN AFTER PARENTAL DIVORCE

SUMMARY. The present paper is based on a review of the literature that considers the short- and long-term effects parental divorce has on children. Most studies in this literature have identified unfavorable outcomes that develop in many areas of children's lives as they struggle to cope with their changed family situations. However, as children adjust to the challenges they face before, during, and after parental divorce, neutral and favorable outcomes are also possible in one or more areas of their lives. In fact, the literature review indicated that many investigators have identified certain strengths in children who had experienced parental divorce. In particular they have observed that following the divorce of their parents some children, in comparison to peers or their own pre-divorce development, have shown enhanced levels of functioning in four areas: maturity, self-esteem, empathy, and androgyny.

Over ten million divorces were granted in the United States during the 1980s (U.S. Bureau of the Census, 1990). The great number of people affected by divorce in the second half of the 20th century stimulated scholarly interest in this area. One topic that received considerable attention is the effects of parental divorce on children, a group affected at a rate of about one million per year since the mid 1970s (U.S. Bureau of Census, 1990).

Findings consistently show that children experience distress during the process of parental separation and divorce and that it is associated with a variety of short- and long-term negative outcomes (see reviews by Anthony, 1974; Fry & Addington, 1985; Kelly, 1988; Kurdek, 1981; Long & Forehand, 1987; Lopez, 1987; Santrock, 1987). Wallerstein and Blackeslee (1989) stated, "Almost all children of divorce regard their childhood and adolescence as having taken place in the shadow of divorce. . . . Almost half of the children entered adulthood as worried, underachieving, self-deprecating, and sometimes angry young men and women" (pp. 298–299).

From David Gately and Andrew I. Schwebel, "Favorable Outcomes in Children After Parental Divorce," *Journal of Divorce and Remarriage*, vol. 18, nos. 3–4, (1992), pp. 57–63, 66–78. Copyright © 1992 by The Haworth Press, Inc. Reprinted by permission.

In fact, studies indicate that children may experience difficulties in interpersonal relationships, school behavior, academic achievement, self-esteem, in future life outlook, etc. Besides delineating the wide range of unfavorable outcomes that can develop in children before, during, and after the divorce, the literature also identifies factors that can moderate and exacerbate the problems children face.

Although much of the literature discusses children's struggle to cope with parental divorce and the unfavorable outcomes they may experience in one or more aspects of their lives, some children in adjusting to their changed circumstances before, during, and after parental divorce may also become strengthened in one or more areas. These individuals develop competencies or grow psychologically because of what they learn while undertaking the divorce-related challenges they face and/or because of the changes they experience in self-view as a result of successfully meeting the challenges.

Decades ago Bernstein and Robey (1962) suggested that successful coping with the demands presented by parental divorce can spur emotional and personality growth in children. Since then a number of investigators have found these favorable outcomes in youngsters relative either to their pre-divorce status or to matched peers from intact family backgrounds. (These include: Grossman, Shea, & Adams, 1980; Hetherington, 1989; Kelly & Wallerstein, 1976; Kurdek & Siesky, 1979, 1980a, 1980b, 1980c; MacKinnon, Stoneman & Brody, 1984; Reinhard, 1977; Richmond-Abbott, 1984; Rosen, 1977; Santrock & Warshak, 1979; Slater, Stewart, & Linn, 1983; Springer & Wallerstein, 1983; Wallerstein, 1984, 1985a, 1987; Wallerstein & Kelly,

1974, 1976, 1980b; Warshak & Santrock, 1983; Weiss, 1979).

The present paper is based on a comprehensive review of the literature that investigated post-divorce outcomes in children. The review included literature generated from computer searches of the Psychological Abstracts and Family Resources and Educational Resources Information Center data bases. Manual searches of the Psychological Abstracts, The Inventory of Marriage and Family Literature, and the Social Sciences Index bases were conducted to supplement the computer searches. Finally, empirical and theoretical contributions published in books, chapters, and Dissertation Abstracts were reviewed. Following a brief assessment of this body of literature, the present paper focuses on those studies that reported favorable outcomes in children following parental divorce.

Most of the earliest investigations used a pathogenic model that viewed the divorced family as a deviation from the traditional 2-parent family, and attempted to link this "inferior" family structure to negative effects on children's adjustment and psychosocial development (Levitin, 1979). The picture of the effects of parental divorce on children were further colored in a negative way because these projects typically employed clinical samples and studied the crisis period immediately following divorce (Bernstein & Robey, 1962; Kalter, 1977; McDermott, 1968; Westman, 1972).

Later studies employing non-clinical samples showed that, although divorce is associated with an initial crisis reaction in most children, long-term consequences are variable (Hetherington, Cox, & Cox, 1982; Hetherington, 1989). While longitudinal studies demonstrated that parental divorce may have long-term negative effects on the social, emotional, and cognitive functioning of children (Guidubaldi & Cleminshaw, 1985; Hetherington, Cox, & Cox, 1985), they also showed that children may escape long-term negative outcomes if the crisis of divorce is not compounded by multiple stressors and continued adversity (Hetherington, 1979, 1989; Hetherington et al., 1982, 1985).

The finding that divorce does not necessarily result in long-term dysfunction led to a search for individual, family, and environmental factors that moderate children's adjustment. Researchers found the quality of adjustment related to: the child's gender and age at the time of separation/divorce (Guidubaldi & Perry, 1985; Hetherington et al., 1982, 1985; Kalter & Rembar, 1981; Wallerstein & Kelly, 1980a); the child's temperament, locus of control, interpersonal knowledge, and level of coping resources (Ankerbrandt, 1986; Hetherington, 1989; Kurdek & Berg, 1983; Kurdek, Blisk, & Siesky, 1981; Kurdek & Siesky, 1980a); the amount of interparental conflict prior to, during, and following separation/divorce (Emery, 1982; Hetherington et al., 1982; Jacobson, 1978; Wallerstein & Kelly, 1980b); the quality of parent-child relationships (Hess & Camara, 1979; Hetherington, Cox, & Cox, 1982; Wallerstein & Kelly, 1980a); the parents' mental and physical health (Guidubaldi & Cleminshaw, 1985; Guidubaldi & Perry, 1985); the type of custody arrangement (Ambert, 1984; Lowery & Settle, 1985; Santrock & Warshak, 1979; Santrock, Warshak, & Elliot, 1982; Warshak & Santrock, 1983; Wolchik, Braver, & Sandler, 1985); parental remarriage (Clingempeel & Segal, 1986; Hetherington et al., 1982; Santrock, Warshak, Lindbergh & Meadows, 1982); the number of major life changes experienced following divorce (Hetherington et al., 1985; Stolberg, Camplair, Currier, & Wells, 1987), including the amount of financial decline experienced by the post-divorce family (Desimone-Luis, O'Mahoney, & Hunt, 1979); and the social support available to both the parents and children (Isaacs & Leon, 1986).

Drawing upon the concept of stress, Wallerstein (1983a) and Peterson, Leigh, & Day (1984) developed models that could account for the absence of negative outcomes in children. For example, Wallerstein conceived of divorce as an acute social stressor that had consequences and made unique demands on children (differing from those associated with stressors like the death of a parent). Although families experiencing divorce and the loss of a parent pass through similar transitional stages (Schwebel, Fine, Moreland & Prindle, 1988), studies comparing the short- and long-term effects on children of separation/divorce and death of a parent support Wallerstein's contention (Boyd & Parish, 1983; Felner, Stolberg, & Cowen, 1975; Hetherington, 1972; Mueller & Cooper, 1986; Rozendal, 1983).

Wallerstein (1983a, 1983b) described the sequence of adjustments a child must make: (1) acknowledge the marital disruption, (2) regain a sense of direction and freedom to pursue customary activities, (3) deal with loss and feelings of rejection, (4) forgive the parents, (5) accept the permanence of divorce and relinquish longings for the restoration of the pre-divorce family, and (6) come to feel comfortable and confident in relationships. The successful completion of these tasks, which allows the child to stay on course developmentally, depends on the child's coping resources and the degree of support available to help in dealing with the stressors. Of course, the divorce process also may include pre-separation distress, family conflict, and compromised parenting which both place children at risk and call for them to make adjustments well before the time when the legal divorce is granted (Block, Block & Gjerde, 1986).

Reports describing protective factors that could mitigate negative outcomes for children following parental divorce complemented findings being described in stress research. More specifically, several authors (Garmezy, 1981, Rutter, 1987; Werner, 1989; Werner & Smith, 1982) found that some children, although exposed to multiple stressors that put them at risk, did not experience negative outcomes. Protective factors diminished the impact of these stressors. Although these investigators studied different stressors, their findings were remarkably similar and suggested that the factors which produce "resilience" in children-at-risk fit into three categories: (1) positive personality dispositions (e.g., active, affectionate, socially responsive, autonomous, flexible, intelligent; possessing self-esteem, an internal locus of control, self-control, and a positive mood); (2) a supportive family environment that encourages coping efforts; and (3) a supportive social environment that reinforces coping efforts and provides positive role models (Garmezy, 1981).

These protective factors reduce the likelihood of negative outcomes by means such as: decreasing exposure to or involvement with risk factors; opening of opportunities for successful task accomplishment and growth; and promoting self-esteem and self-efficacy through secure, supportive personal relationships (Rutter, 1987). Besides helping children avoid short-term harm, these resiliency-building factors strengthen children so they will cope more effectively with and master the stressful life events they will encounter in the future. This "steeling" effect is a favorable outcome that develops after an exposure to stressors of a type and degree that is manageable in the context of the child's capacities and social situation (Rutter, 1987).

The number of studies that identify favorable outcomes of any type of children following parental divorce is small in contrast to the number of studies that have reported unfavorable outcomes. To state the obvious, this difference in the volume of research reports primarily reflects the reality of what children face before, during, and after their parents' divorce. However, a small yet significant part of the difference may be due to the way science has addressed the question of children's outcomes. Specifically, the content of the literature has certainly been shaped, in part, by the fact that neither the pathological nor the stress models heuristically guide researchers to search for favorable outcomes (Kanoy & Cunningham, 1984; McKenry & Price, 1984, 1988; Scanzoni, Polonko, Teachman, & Thompson, 1988) and the fact that the research methods which have been typically employed are more likely to detect negative consequences than positive ones (Blechman, 1982; Kanoy & Cunningham, 1984). For instance, the wide use of measures that identify weaknesses (Blechman, 1982; Kanoy & Cunningham, 1984) and of subjects drawn from clinical samples, who are more maladjusted than their peers (Isaacs, Leon, & Donohue, 1987), makes the likelihood of detecting favorable outcomes unlikely (Kanoy & Cunningham, 1984).

A similar issue is presented by the tendency among researchers to neglect children as a source of data while, at the same time electing to use informants (eg., parents, teachers, clinicians) aware of children's family status (Kanoy & Cunningham, 1984). Although parents' ratings of their elementary school children's adjustment is not related to the children's assessment of the emotional support they are receiving, the children's self-rating of their adjustment are significant (Cowen, Pedro-Carroll & Alpert-Gillis, 1990). Teachers hold more negative expectations for children from divorced families than for their counterparts from intact families (Ball, Newman, & Scheuren, 1984) while parents and clinicians, in contrast to the children, tend to overestimate the negative effects of the divorce (Forehand, Brody, Long, Slotkin, & Fauber, 1986; Wolchik, Sandler, Braver, & Fogas, 1985). In fact, correlations between children's ratings of their own post-divorce adjustment and their parent's ratings are typically low (Kurdek & Siesky, 1980b), a finding consistent with correlations found between children's self-ratings and the ratings of adult informants in other areas of the literature (Achenbach, McConaughy & Howell, 1987)....

The review of... the divorce-adjustment literature suggested four areas, in particular, in which children may experience favorable outcomes following their parents' divorce: in maturity, self-esteem, empathy, and androgyny. Each is discussed below.

Maturity

Intact families have an "echelon structure" in which parents form the executive unit. In the single-parent home this structure is replaced by a parent-child partnership that encourages children to assume more self and family responsibility and to participate more fully in important family decisions (Weiss, 1979). Such involvement fosters maturity which is evidenced by increased levels of responsibility, independence, and awareness of adult values and concerns.

Studies employing nonclinical samples have supported Weiss's conclusions. Kurdek and Siesky (1980a) reported that about 80% of the 132 5–19 year-old children they sampled (four years post-separation) believed they had assumed increased responsibilities after the divorce and learned to rely on themselves more. Their parents agreed, with about 75% of the 74 parents sampled rating their children as more mature and independent (Kurdek & Siesky, 1980b). Similar findings were reported by Rosen (1977), who assessed children 6–10 years after parental divorce, and by Reinhard (1977), who surveyed 46 adolescents three years post-divorce.

Children from single-parent families spend more time working in the home and taking care of siblings (Amato, 1987; Bohannon & Erikson, 1978; Hetherington, 1989; Zakariya, 1982). These chores can foster maturity in children, if they are age-appropriate and if the children receive adequate support. The maturity may exhibit itself in the form of an increased level of independence, realism, or identity development (Grossman et al., 1980). Single-parents further foster maturity when they (1) involve children in appropriate decision making and in a healthy range of other responsibilities in the post-divorce family (Bohannon & Erickson, 1978; Devall, Stoneman, & Brody, 1986; Hetherington, 1989; Kurdek & Siesky, 1979, 1980a; Reinhard, 1977; Wallerstein, 1985a; Weiss, 1979; Zakariya, 1982), and (2) allow children appropriate access to feelings that they, the adult caretakers, have as vulnerable individuals who may not always be able to meet the children's needs (Springer & Wallerstein, 1983; Wallerstein & Kelly, 1974).

Finally, a distinction is needed between pseudomaturity, a precocious adoption of adult roles and responsibilities, and maturity, an adaptive development that helps individuals cope more effectively. Pseudomaturity is seen in females from divorced families who display flirtatious and attention-seeking behavior with male interviewers (Hetherington, 1972), who engage in earlier and more frequent sexual activity (Boss, 1987; Hetherington, 1972; Kinnaird & Gerard, 1986) and who possess a greater likelihood of premarital pregnancy (Boss, 1987) than counterparts from intact families. Pseudomaturity is also found in both males and females from divorced families who engage in earlier and more frequent dating activity (Booth, Brinkerhoff & White, 1984; Hetherington, 1972) and marry earlier (Boss, 1987; Glenn & Kramer, 1987) than peers from intact families.

Self-Esteem

Children may experience increased self-esteem in the aftermath of parental divorce because they cope effectively with changed circumstances, are asked to assume new responsibilities, successfully perform new duties, and so forth. Santrock and Warshak (1979) studied 6–11 year-old children, three years after their parents' divorce, and matched youngsters from intact, mother-custody and father-custody families. Father-custody boys demonstrated higher levels of self-esteem and lower levels of anxiety than intact family boys, while the opposite was true for girls. Slater et al. (1983) studied matched adolescents and found that boys from divorced family backgrounds possessed significantly higher levels of self-esteem than boys from intact and girls from both intact and divorced family backgrounds. Girls from divorced family backgrounds had lower levels of self-esteem than their counterparts from intact families. These results are consistent with Wallerstein and Kelly's (1980a).

One circumstance that appears to foster boys' increased self-esteem in post-divorce families is that they may be more heavily relied upon by custodial parents (most of whom are women) than girls, and as a result may gain a new position of increased responsibility and status. A study of children raised during the Great Depression indicated that older children were strengthened by assuming domestic responsibilities and part-time work (Elder, 1974).

Besides developing as a result of an individual's accomplishments, feelings of self-efficacy may also evolve from vicarious experience, verbal persuasion, and a reduction in the level of fear associated with performing particular behaviors (Bandura, Adams, and Beyer, 1977). Concretely, this suggests that divorcing parents benefit their children by modeling adaptive coping behavior (Kaslow & Hyatt, 1982) and by persuading children to be less fearful and to cope more effectively. Children are most likely to develop hardiness in facing post-divorce challenges if the demands upon them are moderate, if their parents support their efforts to perform new responsibilities, and if family members hold a positive view of divorce-related changes (Maddi & Kobasa, 1984).

Empathy

Some children in divorced and single-parent families show increased concern for the welfare of family members (Kurlek & Siesky, 1980b; Reinhard, 1977; Veiss, 1979). For example, Hetherington 1989) found older girls in divorced families, in contrast to peers, are more often involved in supportive and nurturing eaching, play, and caretaking activities vith younger sisters and tend to help and hare more frequently. Likewise, about 5% of Rosen's (1977) South African children sample reported they had gained greater understanding of human emoions as a result of their parent's divorce to 10 years earlier.

Although Wallerstein (1985b) suggested that children's increase in empathy does not extend beyond the parent-hild relationship, Hetherington (1989) believes the increased empathy and sensitivity may reflect a more general orientation. The conditions prevalent during children's adjustment may determine the extent to which empathy develops nd generalizes. If children are encouraged to provide age-appropriate emoional and practical support to family members, they may be able to extend hemselves, gaining an understanding of thers' feelings and, in this way, practice and refine their role- and perspective-aking skills. Hetherington and Parke 1979) suggested that more advanced ole-taking skills are related to increased ltruism, prosocial behavior, communiation skills, moral standards, and empathetic understanding.

Androgyny

Necessity, encouragement from others, nd the observation of models are among he factors that can lead children to shift way from stereotypical sex-role thinking nd behavior and toward androgyny. This shift, in turn, can result in increased ognitive and behavioral flexibility (Bem,

1975; Bem & Lenney, 1976; Bem, Martyna, & Watson, 1976).

MacKinnon et al. (1984) investigated the effects of marital status and maternal employment on sex-role orientations in matched groups of mothers and children between 3 and 6 years old. While employment influenced mother's sex-role views, divorce appeared related to children's sex-role views. These authors suggested that the more androgynous sex-role views of the children in the post-divorce homes may stem from the mothers modeling more generalized sex-role behavior, or from the children assuming more nontraditional responsibilities.

Kurdek & Siesky (1980c) investigated the sex-role self-concepts of divorced single parents and their 10 to 19 year-old children, approximately four years post-separation. They found that custodial and noncustodial parents and their children possessed higher levels of self-reported androgyny, when compared to published norms, and that the boys and girls possessed more androgynous sex-role self-concepts than a comparison group of children from intact family backgrounds.

Richmond-Abbott (1984) found that the sex-role attitudes of children, ages 8 to 14, tended to reflect the liberal ones of their divorced, single-parent mothers. However, although the mothers stated that they wanted their children to behave in nontraditional ways, children were encouraged to pursue and tended to prefer sex-stereotyped chores and activities. This fits with the failure of others to find an effect of divorce on preadolescent female's sex-role orientation (Kalter, Riemer, Brickman & Chen, 1985; Hetherington, 1972). Another finding, that the girls in the sample did foresee themselves engaging in nontraditional behaviors and occupations in the future, supports a conclusion that clear post-divorce increases in androgynous attitudes and behaviors may not emerge until children cope with adolescent identity issues.

Stevenson and Black (1988) conducted a meta-analysis of 67 studies that compared the sex-role development of children in father-present and father-absent homes. The applicability of their findings to the present issue are limited, however, by the fact that father absence because of divorce was not treated separately from father absence because of death or other reasons. Nonetheless, some conclusions they drew fit well with points made above. Specifically, father-absent female adolescents and young adults were slightly but consistently less feminine than their father-present peers in measures of traditionally feminine characteristics such as nurturance and expressiveness. Similarly, father-absent preschool boys, compared to their father-present peers, made fewer stereotypically sex-typed choices in picking toys and activities. However, older father-absent boys were more stereotypical than their father-present peers in their overt behavior, particularly in the expression of aggression. This latter difference could be reflecting the fact that in a mother-headed household an older boy may be asked to assume "man-of-the-house" duties.

In conclusion, the literature suggests that increased androgyny in children may develop following divorce if parents model nontraditional attitudes and behaviors or if children, by necessity and/or with parental encouragement, engage in nontraditional activities following divorce. While children in adolescence may struggle with androgynous thoughts, feelings, and behaviors, by their late teens and early twenties many will have worked through the issues. For example, two studies used by Stevenson and Black (1988) showed that college men who had experienced father absence reported fewer stereotypical vocational preferences. Finally, methodology has affected findings: While data collected from parents and teachers suggests that father-absent boys' behavior is more stereotypical than father-present boys', self-report measures indicate the opposite. In this connection, teachers' assessments have differed depending on whether they thought they were rating a child from a divorced or an intact home (Ball et al., 1984; Santrock & Tracy, 1978).

RESEARCH AND TREATMENT IMPLICATIONS

Research is needed to identify a full list of favorable outcomes that can emerge following children's adjustment to parental divorce. Longitudinal studies would be desirable, especially those using matched comparison groups of intact family children while controlling for possible confounding variables, including parental conflict and family SES.

Hurley, Vincent, Ingram, and Riley (1984) categorize interventions designed to cope with unfavorable consequences in children following parental divorce as either therapeutic or preventative. The therapeutic approaches, which include psychodynamic and family systems interventions, focus on treating psychopathology, while the preventative approaches help healthy children avoid significant dysfunction by coping effectively with the normal post-divorce crisis reaction. Preventative interventions take the form of school-based support groups for children (Cantor, 1977; Gwynn & Brantley, 1987; Moore & Sumner, 1985;

Pedro-Carroll & Cowen, 1985) or school and community-based support groups for parents (Davidoff & Schiller, 1983; Omizo & Omizo, 1987) and families (Magid, 1977; Stolberg, & Cullen, 1983). Outcome studies show that parents, children, and group leaders believe support groups decrease distress and dysfunction in children (Cantor, 1977; Freeman, 1984; Gwynn & Brantly, 1987; Magid, 1977; Omizo & Omizo, 1987; Pedro-Carroll & Cowen, 1985). At this point, mental health workers could draw from the literature and design a third type of intervention: ones aimed at promoting favorable outcomes in children who must adjust to their parents' divorce.

REFERENCES

Achenbach, T. M., McConaughy, S. H., & Howell, C. T. (1987). Child/adolescent behavioral and emotional problems: Implications of cross-informant correlations for situational specificity. *Psychological Bulletin, 101*, 213–232.

Amato, P. R. (1987). Family processes in one-parent, stepparent, and intact families: The child's point of view. *Journal of Marriage and the Family, 49*, 327–337.

Ambert, A. M. (1984). Longitudinal changes in children's behavior toward custodial parents. *Journal of Marriage and the Family,* (May), 463–467.

Ankenbrandt, M. J. (1986). Learned resourcefulness and other cognitive variables related to divorce adjustment in children. *Dissertation Abstracts International, 47* B, DA8628750, 5045.

Anthony, E. J. (1974). Children at risk from divorce: A review. In E. J. Anthony & C. Koupernik (Eds.) *The child in his family: Children at psychiatric risk* (Vol. 3), 461–478. N.Y. John Wiley & Sons.

Ball, D. W., Newman, J. M., Scheuren, W. J. (1984). Teachers' generalized expectations of children of divorce. *Psychological Reports, 54*, 347–352.

Bandura, A., Adams, N. E., & Beyer, J. (1977). Cognitive processes mediating behavioral changes. *Journal of Personality and Social Psychology, 35*, 125–139.

Bem, S. L. (1975). Sex-role adaptability: One consequence of psychological androgyny. *Journal of Personality and Social Psychology, 31*, 634–643.

Bem, S. L. & Lenney, E. (1976). Sex typing and the avoidance cross-sex behavior. *Journal of Personality and Social Psychology, 33*, 48–54.

Bem, S. L., Martyna, W., & Watson, C. (1976). Sex typing and androgyny: Further explorations of the expressive domain. *Journal of Personality and Social Psychology, 34*, 1016–1023.

Bernstein, N., & Robey, J. (1962). The detection and management of pediatric difficulties created by divorce. *Pediatrics, 16*, 950–956.

Blechman, E. A. (1982). Are children with one parent at psychiatric risk? A methodological review. *Journal of Marriage and the Family, 44*, 179–195.

Block, J. H., Block, J., & Gjerde, P. F. (1986). The personality of children prior to divorce: A prospective study. *Child Development, 57*, 827–840.

Bohannon, P., & Erickson, R. (1978, Jan.) Stepping in. *Psychology Today, 11*, 53–59.

Booth, A., Brinkerhoff, D. B., White, L. K. (1984). The impact of parental divorce on courtship. *Journal of Marriage and the Family, 46*, 85–94.

Boss, E. R. (1987). The demographic characteristics of children of divorce. *Dissertation Abstracts International, 48* 1026A, DA8714900.

Boyd, D. A. & Parish T. (1983). An investigation of father loss and college students' androgyny scores. *The Journal of Genetic Psychology, 145*, 279–280.

Cantor, D. W. (1977). School based groups for children of divorce. *Journal of Divorce, 1*, 183–187.

Clingempeel, W. G., & Segal, S. (1986). Stepparent-stepchild relationships and the psychological adjustment of children in stepmother and stepfather families. *Child Development, 57*, 474–484.

Cowen, E., Pedro-Carroll, J., & Alpert-Gillis, L. (1990). Relationships between support and adjustment among children of divorce. *Journal of Child Psychology and Psychiatry, 31*, 727–735.

Davidoff, I. F. & Schiller, M. S. (1983). The divorce workshop as crisis intervention: A practical model. *Journal of Divorce, 6*, 25–35.

Desimone-Luis, J., O'Mahoney, K., & Hunt, D. (1979). Children of separation and divorce: Factors influencing adjustment. *Journal of Divorce, 3*, 37–41.

Devall, E., Stoneman, Z., & Brody, G. (1986). The impact of divorce and maternal employment on pre-adolescent children. *Family Relations, 35*, 153–159.

Elder, G. H. (1974). *Children of the great depression.* Chicago: University of Chicago Press.

Emery, R. E. (1982). Interparental conflict and the children of discord and divorce, *Psychological Bulletin, 92*, 310–330.

Felner, R. D., Stolberg, A., & Cowen, E. L. (1975). Crisis events and school mental health referral patterns of young children. *Journal of Consulting and Clinical Psychology, 3*, 305–310.

Forehand, R., Brody, G., Long, N., Slotkin, J., & Fauber, R. (1986). Divorce/divorce potential and interparental conflict: The relationship to early adolescent social and cognitive functioning. *Journal of Adolescent Research, 1,* 389–397.

Freeman, R. (1984). Children in families experiencing separation and divorce: An investigation of the effects of brief intervention. Family Service Association of Metropolitan Toronto (Ontario).

Fry, P. S. & Addington, J. (1985). Perceptions of parent and child adjustment in divorced families. *Clinical Psychology Review, 5,* 141–157.

Garmezy, N. (1981). Children under stress: Perspective on antecedents and correlates of vulnerability and resistance to psychopathology. In A. I. Rabin, J. Arnoff, A. N. Barclay, & R. A. Zucker (Eds.), *Further explorations in personality* (pp. 196–269). N.Y.: Wiley.

Glenn, N. D. & Kramer, K. B. (1987). The marriage and divorce of children of divorce. *Journal of Marriage and the Family, 49,* 811–825.

Grossman, S. M., Shea, J. A. & Adams, G. R. (1980). Effects of parental divorce during early childhood on the ego development and identity formation of college students. *Journal of Divorce, 3,* 263–271.

Guidubaldi, J. & Cleminshaw, H. (1985). Divorce, family health, and child adjustment. *Family Relations, 34,* 35–41.

Guidubaldi, J. & Perry, J. D. (1985). Divorce and mental health sequelae for children: A two-year follow-up of a nationwide sample. *Journal of American Academy of Child Psychiatry, 24* (5), 531–537.

Gwynn, C. A. & Brantley, H. T. (1987). Effects of a divorce group intervention for elementary school children. *Psychology in the Schools, 24,* 161–164.

Hess, R. D. & Camara, K. A. (1979). Post-divorce family relationships as mediating factors in the consequences of divorce for children. *Journal of Social Issues, 35* (4), 79–95.

Hetherington, E. M. (1972). Effects of father absence on personality development in adolescent daughters. *Developmental Psychology, 7,* 313–326.

Hetherington, E. M. (1979). Divorce a child's perspective. *American Psychologist, 34,* 851–858.

Hetherington, E. M. (1989). Coping with family transitions: Winners, losers, and survivors. *Child Development, 60,* 1–14.

Hetherington, E. M., Cox, M., & Cox, R. (1982). Effects of divorce on parents and children. In M. Lamb (Ed.), *Nontraditional families: Parenting and child development* (233–288). Hillsdale, N.J.: Erlbaum.

Hetherington, E. M., Cox, M., & Cox, R. (1985). The long-term effects of divorce and remarriage on the adjustment of children. *Journal of the American Academy of Child Psychiatry, 24* (5), 518–530.

Hetherington, E. M. & Parke, R. D. (1979). *Child psychology: A contemporary viewpoint.* New York: McGraw-Hill Inc.

Hurley, E. C., Vincent, L. T., Ingram, T. L., & Riley, M. T. (1984). Therapeutic interventions for children of divorce. *Family Therapy, 9,* 261–268.

Isaacs, M. B. & Leon, G. (1986). Social networks, divorce, and adjustment: A tale of three generations. *Journal of Divorce, 9,* 1–16.

Isaacs, M. B., Leon, G., & Donohue, A. M. (1987). Who are the "normal" children of divorce? On the need to specify population. *Journal of Divorce, 10,* 107–119.

Jacobson, D. S. (1978). The impact of marital separation/divorce on children: II. Interparental hostility and child adjustment. *Journal of Divorce 2*(1), 3–19.

Kalter, N. (1977). Children of divorce in an outpatient psychiatric population. *American Journal of Orthopsychiatry, 47,* 40–51.

Kalter, N., & Rembar, J. (1981). The significance of a child's age at the time of divorce. *American Journal of Orthopsychiatry, 51,* 85–100.

Kalter, N., Riemer, B., Brickman, A., & Chen, J. W. (1985). Implications of parental divorce for female development. *Journal of the American Academy of Child Psychiatry, 24,* 538–544.

Kanoy, K. W. & Cunningham, J. L. (1984). Consensus or confusion in research on children and divorce: Conceptual and methodological issues. *Journal of Divorce, 74,* 45–71.

Kaslow, F. & Hyatt, R. (1982). Divorce: A potential growth experience for the extended family. *Journal of Divorce, 6,* 115–126.

Kelly, J. B. (1988). Longer-term adjustment in children of divorce: Converging findings and implications for practice. *Journal of Family Psychology, 2,* 119–140.

Kelly, J. B. & Wallerstein, J. S. (1976). The effects of parental divorce: Experiences of the child in early latency. *American Journal of Orthopsychiatry, 46,* 20–32.

Kinnaird, K. L. & Gerrard, M. (1986). Premarital sexual behavior and attitudes toward marriage and divorce among young women as a function of their mothers' marital status. *Journal of Marriage and the Family, 48,* 757–765.

Kurdek, L. A. (1981). An integrative perspective on children's divorce adjustment *American Psychologist, 36,* 856–866.

Kurdek, L. A. & Berg, B. (1983). Correlates of children's adjustment to their parents' divorce. In L. A. Kurdek (Ed.). *Children and Divorce* (pp. 47–60). San Francisco: Jossey-Bass Inc., Publishers.

Kurdek, L. A., Blisk, D., & Siesky, A. E. (1981). Correlates of children's long-term adjustment to their parents' divorce. *Developmental Psychology, 17,* 565–579.

Kurdek, L. A. & Sieksy, A. E. (1979). An interview study of parents' perceptions of their children's reactions and adjustment to divorce. *Journal of Divorce, 3,* 5–17.

Kurdek, L. A. & Siesky, A. E. (1980a). Children's perceptions of their parents' divorce. *Journal of Divorce, 3,* 339–379.

Kurdek, L. A. & Siesky, A. E. (1980b). Effects of divorce on children: The relationship between parent and child perspectives. *Journal of Divorce, 4,* 85–99.

Kurdek, L. A. & Siesky, A. E. (1980c). Sex-role self-concepts of single divorced parents and their children. *Journal of Divorce, 3,* 249–261.

Levitin, T. E. (1979). Children of divorce. *Journal of Social Issues, 35,* 1–25.

Long, N. & Forehand, R. (1987). The effects of parental divorce and parental conflict on children: An overview. *Developmental and Behavioral Pediatrics, 8,* 292–296.

Lopez, F. G. (1987). The impact of parental divorce on college student development. *Journal of Counseling and Development, 65,* 484–486.

Lowery, C. R. & Settle, S. A. (1985). Effects of divorce on children: Differential impact of custody and visitation patterns. *Family Relations, 34,* 455–463.

MacKinnon, C. E., Stoneman, Z., & Brody, G. H. (1984). The impact of maternal employment and family form on children's sex-role stereotypes and mothers' traditional attitudes. *Journal of Divorce, 8,* 51–60.

Maddi, S. R. & Kobasa, S. C. (1984). *The hardy executive: Health under stress.* Chicago: Dorsey Professional Books.

Magid, K. M. (1977). Children facing divorce: A treatment program. *Personnel and Guidance Journal, 55,* 534–536.

McDermott, J. F. (1968). Parental divorce in early childhood. *American Journal of Psychiatry, 124,* 1424–1432.

McKenry, P. C. & Price, S. J. (1984). The present state of family relations research. *Home Economics Journal, 12,* 381–402.

McKenry, P. C. & Price, S. J. (1988). Research bias in family science: Sentiment over reason. *Family Science Review, 1,* 224–233.

Moore, N. E. & Sumner, M. G. (1985). *Support group for children of divorce: A family life enrichment group model.* Paper presented at Annual Meeting of the National Association of Social Workers, New Orleans.

Mueller, D. & Cooper, P. W. (1986). Children of single parent families: How they fare as young adults. *Family Relations, 35,* 169–176.

Omizo, M. M. & Omizo, S. A. (1987). Effects of parents' divorce group participation on child-rearing attitudes and children's self-concepts. *Journal of Humanistic Education and Development, 25,* 171–179

Pedro-Carroll, J. L. & Cowen, E. L. (1985). The children of divorce intervention program: An investigation of the efficacy of a school based prevention program. *Journal of Consulting and Clinical Psychology, 53,* 603–611.

Peterson, G., Leigh, G. K., & Day, R. D. (1984). Family stress theory and the impact of divorce on children. *Journal of Divorce, 7,* 1–20.

Reinhard, D. (1977). The reaction of adolescent boys and girls to the divorce of their parents. *Journal of Clinical Child Psychology, 6,* 21–23.

Richmond-Abbott, M. (1984). Sex-role attitudes of mothers and children in divorced, single-parent families. *Journal of Divorce, 8,* 61.

Rosen, R. (1977). Children of divorce: What they feel about access and other aspects of the divorce experience. *Journal of Clinical Child Psychology, 6,* 24–27.

Rozendal, F. G. (1983). Halos vs. stigmas: Long-term effects of parent's death or divorce on college students' concepts of the family. *Adolescence, 18,* 948–955.

Rutter, M. (1987). Psychosocial resilience and protective mechanisms. *American Journal of Orthopsychiatry, 57,* 316–331.

Santrock, J. W. (1987). The effects of divorce on adolescence: Needed Research perspectives. *Family Therapy, 14,* 147–159.

Santrock, J. W. & Tracy, R. L. (1978). Effects of children's family structure status on the development of stereotypes by teachers. *Journal of Educational Psychology, 70,* 754–757.

Santrock, J. W. & Warshak, R. A. (1979). Father custody and social development in boys and girls. *Journal of Social Issues, 35,* 112–125.

Santrock, J. W., Warshak, R. A., & Elliot, G. L. (1982). Social development and parent child interactions in father-custody and stepmother families. In M. Lamb (Ed.), *Nontraditional families: Parenting and child development.* Hillsdale, N.J.: Erlbaum, 289–314.

Santrock, J. W., Warshak, R. A., Lindbergh, C., & Meadows, L. (1982). Children's and parents' observed social behavior in stepfather families. *Child Development, 53,* 472–480.

Scanzoni, J., Polonko, K., Teachman, J. T., & Thompson, L. (1988). *The sexual bond: Rethinking families and close relationships.* Newbury Park, CA: Sage Publications Inc.

Schwebel, A. I., Fine, M., Moreland, J. R., & Prindle, P. (1988). Clinical work with divorced and widowed fathers: The adjusting family model. In P. Bronstein & C. Cowen (Eds.), *Fatherhood today: Men's changing role in the family.* New York: Wiley, 299–319.

Slater, E. J., Stewart, K., & Linn, M. (1983). The effects of family disruption on adolescent males and females. *Adolescence, 18,* 933.

Springer, C. & Wallerstein, J. S. (1983). Young adolescents' responses to their parents' divorce. In L. A. Kurdek (Ed.), *Children and divorce*. San Francisco: Jossey-Bass, 15–27.

Stevenson, M. R. & Black, K. N. (1988). Paternal absence and sex-role development: A meta-analysis. *Child Development, 59*, 795–814.

Stolberg, A., Camplair, C., Currier, K., & Wells, M. (1987). Individual, familial, and environmental determinants of children's post-divorce adjustment and maladjustment. *Journal of Divorce, 11*, 51–70.

Stolberg, A. L. & Cullen, P. M. (1983). Preventive interventions for families of divorce: The divorce adjustment project. *New Directions for Child Development, 19*, 71–81.

U.S. Bureau of the Census (1990). *Statistical abstract of the U.S.: 1990*. Washington, D.C.

Wallerstein J. (1983a). Children of divorce: Stress and developmental tasks. In N. Garmezy and M. Rutter (Eds.), *Stress, coping, and development*. New York: McGraw-Hill Inc., 265–302.

Wallerstein, J. (1983b). Children of divorce: The psychological tasks of the child. *American Journal of Orthopsychiatry, 53*, 230–243.

Wallerstein, J. (1984). Children of divorce: Preliminary report of a ten-year follow-up of young children. *American Journal of Orthopsychiatry, 54*(3), 444–458.

Wallerstein, J. (1985a). Children of divorce: Preliminary report of a ten-year follow-up of older children and adolescents. *Journal of American Academy of Child Psychiatry, 24*(5), 545–553.

Wallerstein, J. (1985b). The overburdened child: Some long-term consequences of divorce. *Social Work, 30*(2), 116–123.

Wallerstein, J. (1987). Children of divorce: Report of a ten-year follow-up of early latency-age children. *American Journal of Orthopsychiatry, 57*, 199–211.

Wallerstein, J. & Blackeslee, S. (1989). *Second chances*. New York: Ticknor & Fields.

Wallerstein, J., & Kelly, J. (1974). The effects of divorce: The adolescent experience. In J.

Anthony & C. Koupernik (Eds.), *The child in his family: Children at psychiatric risk* (Vol. 3). N.Y.: Wiley.

Wallerstein, J., & Kelly, J. (1976). The effects of divorce: Experiences of the child in later latency. *American Journal of Orthopsychiatry, 46*(2), 256–269.

Wallerstein, J., & Kelly, J. (1980a). *Surviving the Breakup*. New York: Basic Books Inc.

Wallerstein, J., & Kelly, J. (1980b, Jan.) California's children of divorce. *Psychology Today*, 67–76.

Warshak, R. & Santrock, J. W. (1983). The impact of divorce in father-custody and mother-custody homes: The child's perspective. In L. Kurdek (Ed.), *Children and divorce*, San Francisco: Jossey-Bass Inc., Publishers, 29–45.

Weiss, R. (1979). Growing up a little faster: The experience of growing up in a single-parent household. *Journal of Social Issues, 35*(4), 97–111.

Werner, E. E. (1989). High-risk children in young adulthood: A longitudinal study from birth to 32 years. *American Journal of Orthopsychiatry, 59*, 72–81.

Werner, E. E. & Smith, B. S. (1982). *Vulnerable but invincible: A study of resilient children*. New York: McGraw-Hill Inc.

Westman, J. C. (1972). Effect of divorce on child's personality development. *Medical Aspects of Human Sexuality, 6*, 38–55.

Wolchik, S. A., Braver, S., Sandler, I. (1985). Maternal versus joint custody: Children's postseparation experiences and adjustment. *Journal of Clinical Child Psychology, 14*, 5–10.

Wolchik, S. A., Sandler, I., Braver, S., & Fogas, B. (1985). Events of parental divorce: Stressfulness ratings by children, parents, and clinicians. *American Journal of Community Psychology, 14*, 59–74.

Zakariya, S. B. (1982, Sept.). Another look at the children of divorce: Summary report of school needs of one-parent children. *Principal, 62*, 34–38.

POSTSCRIPT

Does Divorce Create Long-Term Negative Effects for Children?

Zinsmeister proposes that parents stay together for the sake of the children. According to some studies, children rate divorce second only to the death of a parent as the most stressful event in their lives, and most of them end up not having a close relationship with one of their parents.

Although the number of studies that show negative divorce effects outweighs studies with positive results, Gately and Schwebel use them to illustrate the children's resilience. These children developed traits such as a positive personality, self-control, self-reliance, and empathy for others, probably as a result of the divorce situation.

Is it divorce that creates problems for children, or is it the poverty, family disorganization, and unmet needs that accompany most divorces, which cause long-term problems? A common complaint of these children is that there is no adult in whom they can confide.

SUGGESTED READINGS

Amato, P. R. (1994, Spring). Life span adjustment of children to their parents' divorce. *The future of children* (143–164). Los Altos, CA: Center for the Future of Children.

Cherlin, A. (1993, Winter). Nostalgia as family policy (emotional and economic effects of divorce on children). *The Public Interest, 110*, 77–85.

Ehrenreich, B. (1996, April 8). In defense of splitting up. *Time, 147*, 80.

Gill, R. (1992, Spring). For the sake of the children (effects of divorce on children). *The Public Interest, 108*, 81–97.

Jones, S. (1993, May). The two-parent heresy (divorce and single parent families can adversely affect children). *Christianity Today, 37*, 20–22.

Jost, K., & Robinson, M. (1991, June). At issue: Does divorce always have long-term effects on children? *CQ Researcher, 1*, 351–367.

Lehrman, K. (1993, May). Growing up with divorce. *Vogue, 193*, 182–186.

Robinson, K. (1994, May/June). Which side are you on? *Networker, 18*, 19–23, 26–30.

Roe, C. (1994, Summer). The pros and cons of divorce. *Single Parent, 37*, 26–28.

Wallerstein, J., & Blakeslee, S. (1990). *Second chances: Men, women, and children a decade after divorce—who wins, who loses—and why*. New York: Ticknor and Fields.

ISSUE 8

Is Television Viewing Harmful for Children?

YES: Brandon S. Centerwall, from "Television and Violent Crime," *The Public Interest* (Spring 1993)

NO: Brian Siano, from "Frankenstein Must Be Destroyed: Chasing the Monster of TV Violence," *The Humanist* (January/February 1994)

ISSUE SUMMARY

YES: Brandon S. Centerwall, an epidemiologist, explains that children have an instinctive desire to imitate behavior. However, they do not possess the instinct for determining the appropriateness of the behavior—for determining whether or not a given behavior should be imitated. As a consequence, children act out the violence they see on television shows and carry the violent behaviors into adulthood. This is one reason why violent crimes such as homicide, rape, and assault have been increasing.

NO: Brian Siano, a writer and researcher, says that while we should constantly strive for quality programming, we should not attempt to indiscriminately eliminate all violence from television. He argues that children with non-nurturing parents and those who least identify with their parents tend to be the most aggressive. These variables are more influential than TV violence in affecting aggression in children.

Ask any group of people you meet today about violence in contemporary society and the responses you get will likely be remarkably similar: "Violence is epidemic"; "there is a lot more violence out on the streets now than when I was a kid"; "it's just not safe to be out anymore"; "we live in such violent times." The anecdotes we hear about violence and the nostalgia that people express for a more peaceful past seem to be commonplace. However, the unison with which society decries the rise in violence begins to disintegrate once the discussion turns to the causes for the increase in violence.

Television, particularly television programming for children, is regularly targeted as a key contributor to the rise in violence in U.S. society. There is considerable debate over whether or not television is too violent. It has been suggested, for example, that a child will witness in excess of 100,000 acts of simulated violence on television before graduating from elementary school. Poor children may view even more. Many researchers suggest that television violence is at least partly responsible for the climbing rates of violent crime because children tend to imitate in life what they observe on television. On the other side, critics argue that it is not what is on television that bears responsibility for the surge in violence. Programming is merely reflective of the level of violence in contemporary society. The argument is that while television watching may be associated with violence, it does not mean that it causes violence. For example, some social scientists have suggested that aggressive children tend to watch more aggressive television programming than their relatively passive counterparts. But does the aggressive nature of the child predispose the child to be interested in aggressive programming, or does the programming *cause* the aggression? This is a question that has sparked hotly contested debates.

Those who believe television viewing is at least partly responsible for aggressive behavior in children want the United States Congress to take action and regulate the amount of violence shown on television and the time slots within which programs containing violence can be broadcast. Those on the other side of the issue point out that such legislation would be an infringement on First Amendment rights of freedom of expression.

The two selections that follow are typical of the debate that surrounds violence and television and its effects on children. Brandon S. Centerwall presents a compelling argument, documented with carefully selected research, that violence in children's television programming must be limited. Brian Siano suggests that although adults who seek to regulate television are well intentioned, they are missing the mark by misinterpreting research on the topic and seeing the issue through adult eyes rather than those of a child.

YES

Brandon S. Centerwall

TELEVISION AND VIOLENT CRIME

Children are born ready to imitate adult behavior. That they can, and do, imitate an array of adult facial expressions has been demonstrated in newborns as young as a few hours old, before they are even old enough to know that they have facial features. It is a most useful instinct, for the developing child must learn and master a vast repertoire of behavior in short order.

But while children have an instinctive desire to imitate, they do not possess an instinct for determining whether a behavior ought to be imitated. They will imitate anything, including behavior that most adults regard as destructive and antisocial. It may give pause for thought, then, to learn that infants as young as fourteen months demonstrably observe and incorporate behavior seen on television.

The average American preschooler watches more than twenty-seven hours of television per week. This might not be bad if these young children understood what they were watching. But they don't. Up through ages three and four, most children are unable to distinguish fact from fantasy on TV, and remain unable to do so despite adult coaching. In the minds of young children, television is a source of entirely factual information regarding how the world works. There are no limits to their credulity. To cite one example, an Indiana school board had to issue an advisory to young children that, no, there is no such thing as Teenage Mutant Ninja Turtles. Children had been crawling down storm drains looking for them.

Naturally, as children get older, they come to know better, but their earliest and deepest impressions are laid down at an age when they still see television as a factual source of information about the outside world. In that world, it seems, violence is common and the commission of violence is generally powerful, exciting, charismatic, and effective. In later life, serious violence is most likely to erupt at moments of severe stress—and it is precisely at such moments that adolescents and adults are most likely to revert to their earliest, most visceral sense of the role of violence in society and in personal behavior. Much of this sense will have come from television.

From Brandon S. Centerwall, "Television and Violent Crime," *The Public Interest,* no. 111 (Spring 1993), pp. 56–71. Copyright © 1993 by National Affairs, Inc. Reprinted by permission.

THE SEEDS OF AGGRESSION

In 1973, a remote rural community in Canada acquired television for the first time. The acquisition of television at such a late date was due to problems with signal reception rather than any hostility toward TV. As reported in *The Impact of Television* (1986), Tannis Williams and her associates at the University of British Columbia investigated the effect of television on the children of this community (which they called "Notel"), taking for comparison two similar towns that already had television.

The researchers observed forty-five first- and second-graders in the three towns for rates of inappropriate physical aggression before television was introduced into Notel. Two years later, the same forty-five children were observed again. To prevent bias in the data, the research assistants who collected the data were kept uninformed as to why the children's rates of aggression were of interest. Furthermore, a new group of research assistants was employed the second time around, so that the data gatherers would not be biased by recollections of the children's behavior two years earlier.

Rates of aggression did not change in the two control communities. By contrast, the rate of aggression among Notel children increased 160 percent. The increase was observed in both boys and girls, in those who were aggressive to begin with an in those who were not. Television's enhancement of noxious aggression was entirely general and not limited to a few "bad apples."

In another Canadian study, Gary Granzberg and his associates at the University of Winnipeg investigated the impact of television upon Indian communities in northern Manitoba. As described in *Television and the Canadian Indian* (1980), forty-nine third-, fourth-, and fifth-grade boys living in two communities were observed from 1973, when one town acquired television, until 1977, when the second town did as well. The aggressiveness of boys in the first community increased after the introduction of television. The aggressiveness of boys in the second community, which did not receive television then, remained the same. When television was later introduced in the second community, observed levels of aggressiveness increased there as well.

In another study conducted from 1960 to 1981, Leonard Eron and L. Rowell Huesmann (then of the University of Illinois at Chicago) followed 875 children living in a semirural U.S. county. Eron and Huesmann found that for both boys and girls, the amount of television watched at age eight predicted the seriousness of criminal acts for which they were convicted by age thirty. This remained true even after controlling for the children's baseline aggressiveness, intelligence, and socioeconomic status. Eron and Huesmann also observed second-generation effects. Children who watched much television at age eight later, as parents, punished their own children more severely than did parents who had watched less television as children. Second- and now third-generation effects are accumulating at a time of unprecedented youth violence.

All seven of the U.S. and Canadian studies of prolonged childhood exposure to television demonstrate a positive relationship between exposure and physical aggression. The critical period is preadolescent childhood. Later exposure does not appear to produce any additional effect. However, the aggression-enhancing effect of exposure in pre-adolescence extends into adolescence and adulthood. This suggests that any interventions should be designed for children and their caregivers rather than for the general adult population.

These studies confirmed the beliefs of most Americans. According to a Harris poll at the time of the studies, 43 percent of American adults believe that television violence "plays a part in making America a violent society." An additional 37 percent think it might. But how important is television violence? What is the effect of exposure upon entire populations? To address this question, I took advantage of an historical accident—the absence of television in South Africa prior to 1975.

THE SOUTH AFRICAN EXPERIENCE

White South Africans have lived in a prosperous, industrialized society for decades, but they did not get television until 1975 because of tension between the Afrikaner- and English-speaking communities. The country's Afrikaner leaders knew that a South African television industry would have to rely on British and American shows to fill out its programming schedule, and they felt that this would provide an unacceptable cultural advantage to English-speaking South Africans. So, rather than negotiate a complicated compromise, the government simply forbade television broadcasting. The entire population of two million whites—rich and poor, urban and rural, educated and uneducated—was thus excluded from exposure to television for a quarter century after the medium was introduced in the United States.

In order to determine whether exposure to television is a cause of violence, I compared homicide rates in South Africa,

Canada, and the United States. Since blacks in South Africa live under quite different conditions than blacks in the United States, I limited the comparison to white homicide rates in South Africa and the United States, and the total homicide rate in Canada (which was 97 percent white in 1951).[1] I chose the homicide rate as a measure of violence because homicide statistics are exceptionally accurate.

From 1945 to 1974, the white homicide rate in the United States increased 93 percent. In Canada, the homicide rate increased 92 percent. In South Africa, where television was banned, the white homicide rate declined by 7 percent.

CONTROLLING FOR OTHER FACTORS

Could there be some explanation other than television for the fact that violence increased dramatically in the U.S. and Canada while dropping in South Africa? I examined an array of alternative explanations. None is satisfactory:

- **Economic growth.** Between 1946 and 1974, all three countries experienced substantial economic growth. Per capita income increased by 75 percent in the United States, 124 percent in Canada, and 86 percent in South Africa. Thus differences in economic growth cannot account for the different homicide trends in the three countries.
- **Civil Unrest.** One might suspect that anti-war or civil-rights activity was responsible for the doubling of the homicide rate in the United States during this period. But the experience of Canada shows that this was not the case, since Canadians suffered a doubling of the homicide rate without similar civil unrest.

Other possible explanations include changes in age distribution, urbanization, alcohol consumption, capital punishment, and the availability of firearms. As discussed in *Public Communication and Behavior* (1989), none provides a viable explanation for the observed homicide trends.

In the United States and Canada, there was a lag of ten to fifteen years between the introduction of television and a doubling of the homicide rate. In South Africa, there was a similar lag. Since television exerts its behavior-modifying effects primarily on children, while homicide is primarily on adult activity, this lag represents the time needed for the "television generation" to come of age.

The relationship between television and the homicide rate holds *within* the United States as well. Different regions of the U.S., for example, acquired television at different times. As we would expect, while all regions saw increases in their homicide rates, the regions that acquired television first were also the first to see higher homicide rates.

Similarly, urban areas acquired television before rural areas. As we would expect, urban areas saw increased homicide rates several years before the occurrence of a parallel increase in rural areas.

The introduction of television also helps explain the different rates of homicide growth for whites and minorities. White households in the U.S. began acquiring television sets in large numbers approximately five years before minority households. Significantly, the white homicide rate began increasing in 1958, four years before a parallel increase in the minority homicide rate.

Of course, there are many factors other than television that influence the amount of violent crime. Every violent act is the result of a variety of forces coming together—poverty, crime, alcohol and drug abuse, stress—of which childhood TV exposure is just one. Nevertheless, the evidence indicates that if, hypothetically, television technology had never been developed, there would today be 10,000 fewer homicides each year in the United States, 70,000 fewer rapes, and 700,000 fewer injurious assaults. Violent crime would be half what it is.

THE TELEVISION INDUSTRY TAKES A LOOK

The first congressional hearings on television and violence were held in 1952, when not even a quarter of U.S. households owned television sets. In the years since, there have been scores of research reports on the issue, as well as several major government investigations. The findings of the National Commission on the Causes and Prevention of Violence, published in 1969, were particularly significant. This report established what is now the broad scientific consensus: Exposure to television increases rates of physical aggression.

Television industry executives were genuinely surprised by the National Commission's report. What the industry produced was at times unedifying, but physically harmful? In response, network executives began research programs that collectively would cost nearly a million dollars.

CBS commissioned William Belson to undertake what would be the largest and most sophisticated study yet, an investigation involving 1,565 teenage boys. In *Television Violence and the Adolescent Boy* (1978), Belson controlled for one hundred variables, and found that teenage boys who had watched above-average quantities of television violence before adolescence were committing acts of serious violence (e.g., assault, rape, major vandalism, and abuse of animals) at a rate 49 percent higher than teenage boys who had watched below-average quantities of television violence. Despite the large sum of money they had invested, CBS executives were notably unenthusiastic about the report.

ABC commissioned Melvin Heller and Samuel Polsky of Temple University to study young male felons imprisoned for violent crimes (e.g, homicide, rape, and assault). In two surveys, 22 and 34 percent of the young felons reported having consciously imitated crime techniques learned from television programs, usually successfully. The more violent of these felons were the most likely to report having learned techniques from television. Overall, the felons reported that as children they had watched an average of six hours of television per day—approximately twice as much as children in the general population at that time.

Unlike CBS, ABC maintained control over publication. The final report, *Studies in Violence and Television* (1976), was published in a private, limited edition that was not released to the general public or the scientific community.

NBC relied on a team of four researchers, three of whom were employees of NBC. Indeed, the principal investigator, J. Ronald Milavsky, was an NBC vice president. The team observed some 2,400 schoolchildren for up to three years to see if watching television violence increased their levels of physical aggressiveness. In *Television and Aggression* (1982), Milavsky and his associates reported that television violence had no effect upon the children's behavior. However, every independent investigator who has examined their data has concluded that, to the contrary, their data show that television violence did cause a modest increase of about 5 percent in average levels of physical aggressiveness. When pressed on the point, Milavsky and his associates conceded that their findings were consistent with the conclusion that television violence increased physical aggressiveness "to a small extent." They did not concede that television violence actually caused an increase, but only that their findings were consistent with such a conclusion.

The NBC study results raise an important objection to my conclusions. While studies have repeatedly demonstrated that childhood exposure to television increases physical aggressiveness, the increase is almost always quite minor. A number of investigators have argued that such a small effect is too weak to account for major increases in rates of violence. These investigators, however, overlook a key factor.

Homicide is an extreme form of aggression—so extreme that only one person in 20,000 committed murder each year in the United States in the mid-1950s. If we were to rank everyone's degree of physical aggressiveness from the least aggressive (Mother Theresa) to the most aggressive (Jack the Ripper), the large majority of us would be somewhere in the middle and murderers would be virtually off the chart. It is an intrinsic property of such "bell curve" distributions that small changes in the average imply major changes at the extremes. Thus, if exposure to television causes 8 percent of the population to shift from below-average aggression to above-average aggression, it follows that the homicide rate will double. The findings of the NBC study and the doubling of the homicide rate are two sides of the same coin.

After the results of these studies became clear, television industry executives lost their enthusiasm for scientific research. No further investigations were funded. Instead, the industry turned to political management of the issue.

THE TELEVISION INDUSTRY AND SOCIAL RESPONSIBILITY

The television industry routinely portrays individuals who seek to influence programming as un-American haters of free speech. In a 1991 letter sent to 7,000 executives of consumer product companies and advertising agencies, the president of the Network Television Association explained:

> Freedom of expression is an inalienable right of all Americans vigorously supported by ABC, CBS, and NBC. However, boycotts and so-called advertiser "hit lists" are attempts to manipulate our free society and democratic process.

The letter went on to strongly advise the companies to ignore all efforts by anyone to influence what programs they choose to sponsor. By implication, the networks themselves should ignore all efforts by anyone to influence what programs they choose to produce.

But this is absurd. All forms of public discourse are attempts to "manipulate" our free society and democratic process. What else could they be? Consumer boycotts are no more un-American than are strikes by labor unions. The Network Television Association is attempting to systematically shut down all discourse between viewers and advertisers, and between viewers and the television industry. Wrapping itself in patriotism, the television industry's response to uppity viewers is to put them in their place. If the industry and advertisers were to actually succeed in closing the circle between them, the only course they would leave for concerned viewers would be to seek legislative action.

In the war against tobacco, we do not expect help from the tobacco industry. If someone were to call upon the tobacco industry to cut back production as a matter of social conscience and concern for public health, we would regard that person as simple-minded, if not frankly deranged. Oddly enough, however, people have persistently assumed that the television industry is somehow different—that it is useful to appeal to its social conscience. This was true in 1969 when the National Commission on the Causes and Prevention of Violence published its recommendations for the television industry. It was equally true in 1989 when the U.S. Congress passed an anti-violence bill that granted television industry executives the authority to hold discussions on the issue of television violence without violating antitrust laws. Even before the law was passed, the four networks stated that there would be no substantive changes in their programming. They have been as good as their word.

For the television industry, issues of "quality" and "social responsibility" are peripheral to the issue of maximizing audience size—and there is no formula more tried and true than violence for generating large audiences. To television executives, this is crucial. For if advertising revenue were to decrease by just 1 percent, the television industry would stand to lose $250 million in revenue annually. Thus, changes in audience size that appear trivial to most of us are regarded as catastrophic by the industry. For this reason, industry spokespersons have made innumerable protestations of good intent, but nothing has happened. In the more than twenty years that levels of television violence have been monitored, there has been no downward movement. There are no recommendations to make to the television industry. To make any would not only be futile but could create the false impression that the industry might actually do something constructive.

On December 11, 1992, the networks finally announced a list of voluntary guidelines on television violence. Curiously, reporters were unable to locate any network producers who felt the new guidelines would require changes in their programs. That raises a question: Who is going to bell the cat? Who is going to place his or her career in jeopardy in order to decrease the amount of violence on television? It is hard to say, but it may be revealing that when Senator Paul Simon held the press conference announcing the new inter-network agreement, no industry executives were present to answer questions.

MEETING THE CHALLENGE

Television violence is everybody's problem. You may feel assured that your child will never become violent despite a steady diet of television mayhem, but you cannot be assured that your child won't be murdered or maimed by someone else's child raised on a similar diet.

The American Academy of Pediatrics recommends that parents limit their children's television viewing to one to two hours per day. But why wait for a pediatrician to say it? Limiting children's exposure to television violence should become part of the public health agenda, along with safety seats, bicycle helmets,

immunizations, and good nutrition. Part of the public health approach should be to promote child-care alternatives to the electronic babysitter, especially among the poor.

Parents should also guide what their children watch and how much. This is an old recommendation that can be given new teeth with the help of modern technology. It is now feasible to fit a television set with an electronic lock that permits parents to preset the channels and times for which the set will be available; if a particular program or time of day is locked, the set will not operate then. Time-channel locks are not merely feasible; they have already been designed and are coming off the assembly line.

The model for making them widely available comes from closed-captioning circuitry, which permits deaf and hard-of-hearing persons access to television. Market forces alone would not have made closed-captioning available to more than a fraction of the deaf and hard-of-hearing. To remedy this problem, Congress passed the Television Decoder Circuitry Act in 1990, which requires that virtually all new television sets be manufactured with built-in closed-captioning circuitry. A similar law should require that all new television sets be manufactured with built-in time-channel lock circuitry—and for a similar reason. Market forces alone will not make this technology available to more than a fraction of households with children and will exclude most poor families, the ones who suffer the most from violence. If we can make television technology available to benefit twenty-four million deaf and hard-of-hearing Americans, surely we can do no less for the benefit of fifty million American children.

A final recommendation: Television programs should be accompanied by a violence rating so that parents can judge how violent a program is without having to watch it. Such a rating system should be quantitative, leaving aesthetic and social judgments to the viewers. This approach would enjoy broad popular support. In a *Los Angeles Times* poll, 71 percent of adult Americans favored the establishment of a TV violence rating system. Such a system would not impinge on artistic freedom since producers would remain free to produce programs with high violence ratings. They could even use high violence ratings in the advertisements for their shows.

None of these recommendations would limit freedom of speech. That is as it should be. We do not address the problem of motor vehicle fatalities by calling for a ban on cars. Instead, we emphasize safety seats, good traffic signs, and driver education. Similarly, to address the problem of television-inspired violence, we need to promote time-channel locks, program rating systems, and viewer education about the hazards of violent programming. In this way we can protect our children and our society.

NOTES

1. The "white homicide rate" refers to the rate at which whites are the victims of homicide. Since most homicide is intra-racial, this closely parallels the rate at which whites commit homicide.

REFERENCES

William A. Belson, *Television Violence and the Adolescent Boy*. Westmead, England: Saxon House (1978).

Brandon S. Centerwall, "Exposure to Television as a Cause of Violence," *Public Communication and Behavior*, Vol. 2. Orlando, Florida: Academic Press (1989), pp. 1–58.

Leonard D. Eron and L. Rowell Huesmann, "The Control of Aggressive Behavior by Changes in Attitudes, Values, and the Conditions of Learning," *Advances in the Study of Aggression*. Orlando, Florida: Academic Press (1984), pp. 139–171.

Gary Granzberg and Jack Steinbring (eds.), *Television and the Canadian Indian*. Winnipeg, Manitoba: University of Winnipeg (1980).

L. Rowell Huesmann and Leonard D. Eron, *Television and the Aggressive Child*. Hillsdale, New Jersey: Lawrence Erlbaum Associates (1986), pp. 45–80.

Candace Kruttschnitt, et al., "Family Violence, Television Viewing Habits, and Other Adolescent Experiences Related to Violent Criminal Behavior," *Criminology*, Vol. 24 (1986), pp. 235–267.

Andrew N. Meltzoff, "Memory in Infancy," *Encyclopedia of Learning and Memory*. New York: Macmillan (1992), pp. 271–275.

J. Ronald Milavsky, et al., *Television and Aggression*. Orlando, Florida: Academic Press (1982).

Jerome L. Singer, et al., "Family Patterns and Television Viewing as Predictors of Children's Beliefs and Aggression," *Journal of Communication*, Vol. 34, No. 2 (1984), pp. 73–89.

Tannis M. Williams (ed.), *The Impact of Television*. Orlando, Florida: Academic Press (1986).

NO

Brian Siano

FRANKENSTEIN MUST BE DESTROYED: CHASING THE MONSTER OF TV VIOLENCE

Here's the scene: Bugs Bunny, Daffy Duck, and a well-armed Elmer Fudd are having a stand-off in the forest. Daffy the rat-fink has just exposed Bugs' latest disguise, so Bugs takes off the costume and says, "That's right, Doc, I'm a wabbit. Would you like to shoot me now or wait until we get home?"

"Shoot him now! Shoot him now!" Daffy screams.

"You keep out of this," Bugs says. "He does not have to shoot you now."

"He does *so* have to shoot me now!" says Daffy. Full of wrath, he storms up to Elmer Fudd and shrieks, "And I *demand* that you shoot me now!"

Now, if you *aren't* smiling to yourself over the prospect of Daffy's beak whirling around his head like a roulette wheel, stop reading right now. This one's for a very select group: those evil degenerates (like me) who want to corrupt the unsullied youth of America by showing them violence on television.

Wolves' heads being conked with mallets in Tex Avery's *Swing Shift Cinderella*. Dozens of dead bodies falling from a closet in *Who Killed Who?* A sweet little kitten seemingly baked into cookies in Chuck Jones' *Feed the Kitty*. And best of all, Wile E. Coyote's unending odyssey of pain in *Fast and Furrious* and *Hook, Line, and Stinker*. God, I love it. The more explosions, crashes, gunshots, and defective ACME catapults there are, the better it is for the little tykes.

Shocked? Hey, I haven't even gotten to "The Three Stooges" yet.

* * *

The villagers are out hunting another monster—the Frankenstein of TV violence. Senator Paul Simon's hearings in early August 1993 provoked a fresh round of arguments in a debate that's been going on ever since the first round of violent kids' shows—"Sky King," "Captain Midnight," and "Hopalong Cassidy"—were on the air. More recently, Attorney General Janet Reno has taken a hard line on TV violence. "We're fed up with excuses," she told

From Brian Siano, "Frankenstein Must Be Destroyed: Chasing the Monster of TV Violence," *The Humanist*, vol. 54, no. 1 (January/February 1994). Copyright © 1994 by The American Humanist Association. Reprinted by permission.

the Senate, arguing that "the regulation of violence is constitutionally permissible" and that, if the networks don't do it, "government should respond." ...

Simon claims to have become concerned with this issue because, three years ago, he turned on the TV in his hotel room and was treated to the sight of a man being hacked apart with a chainsaw.... This experience prompted him to sponsor a three-year antitrust exemption for the networks, which was his way of encouraging them to voluntarily "clean house." But at the end of that period, the rates of TV violence hadn't changed enough to satisfy him, so Simon convened open hearings on the subject in 1993....

The debate becomes even more impassioned when we ask how children might be affected. The innocent, trusting little tykes are spending hours bathed in TV's unreal colors, and their fantasy lives are inhabited by such weirdos as Wolverine and Eek the Cat. Parents usually want their kids to grow up sharing their ideals and values, or at least to be well-behaved and obedient. Tell parents that their kids are watching "Beavis and Butt-head" in their formative years and you set off some major alarms.

There are also elitist, even snobbish, attitudes toward pop culture that help to rationalize censorship. One is that the corporate, mass-market culture of TV isn't important enough or "art" enough to deserve the same free-speech protection as James Joyce's *Ulysses* or William Burrough's *Naked Lunch*. The second is that rational, civilized human beings are supposed to be into Shakespeare and Scarlatti, not Pearl Jam and "Beavis and Butt-head." Seen in this "enlightened" way, the efforts of Paul Simon are actually for *our own good*. And so we

define anything even remotely energetic as "violent," wail about how innocent freckle-faced children are being defiled by such fare as "NYPD Blue," and call for a Council of Certified Nice People who will decide what the rest of us get to see. A recent *Mother Jones* article by Carl Cannon (July/August 1993) took just this hysterical tone, citing as proof "some three thousand research studies of this issue."

Actually, there aren't 3,000 studies. In 1984, the *Psychological Bulletin* published an overview by Jonathan Freedman of research on the subject. Referring to the "2,500 studies" figure bandied about at the time (it's a safe bet that 10 years would inflate this figure to 3,000), Freedman writes:

> The reality is more modest. The large number refers to the complete bibliography on television. References to television and aggression are far fewer, perhaps around 500.... The actual literature on the relation between television violence and aggression consists of fewer than 100 independent studies, and the majority of these are laboratory experiments. Although this is still a substantial body of work, it is not vast, and there are only a small number of studies dealing specifically with the effects of television violence outside the laboratory.

The bulk of the evidence for a causal relationship between television violence and violent behavior comes from the research of Leonard Eron of the University of Illinois and Rowell Huesmann of the University of Michigan. Beginning in 1960, Eron and his associates began a large-scale appraisal of how aggression develops in children and whether or not it persists into adulthood. (The question of television violence was, originally, a side issue to the long-term study.) Unfortunately, when the popular press writes about Eron's work, it tends to present his methodology in the simplest of terms: *Mother Jones* erroneously stated that his study "followed the viewing habits of a group of children for twenty-two years." It's this sort of sloppiness, and overzealousness to prove a point, that keeps people from understanding the issues or raising substantial criticisms. Therefore, we must discuss Eron's work in some detail.

* * *

The first issue in Eron's study was how to measure aggressiveness in children. Eron's "peer-nominated index" followed a simple strategy: asking each child in a classroom questions about which kids were the main offenders in 10 different categories of classroom aggression (that is, "Who pushes or shoves children?"). The method is consistent with other scales of aggression, and its one-month test/retest reliability is 91 percent. The researchers also tested the roles of four behavioral dimensions in the development of aggression: *instigation* (parental rejection or lack of nurturance), *reinforcement* (punishment versus reward), *identification* (acquiring the parents' behavior and values), and *sociocultural norms*.

Eron's team selected the entire third-grade population of Columbia County, New York, testing 870 children and interviewing about 75 to 80 percent of their parents. Several trends became clear almost immediately. Children with less nurturing parents were more aggressive. Children who more closely identified with either parent were less aggressive. And children with low parental identification who were punished tended to be *more* aggressive (an observation which required revision of the behavioral model).

Ten years later, Eron and company tracked down and re-interviewed about half of the original sample. (They followed up on the subjects in 1981 as well.) Many of the subjects—now high-school seniors—demonstrated a persistence in aggression over time. Not only were the "peer-nominated" ratings roughly consistent with the third-grade ratings, but the more aggressive kids were three times as likely to have a police record by adulthood.

Eron's team also checked for the influences on aggression which they had previously noted when the subjects were eight. The persistent influences were parental identification and socioeconomic variables. Some previously important influences (lack of nurturance, punishment for aggression) didn't seem to affect the subjects' behavior as much in young adulthood. Eron writes of these factors:

> Their effect is short-lived and other variables are more important in predicting later aggression. Likewise, contingencies and environmental conditions can change drastically over 10 years, and thus the earlier contingent response becomes irrelevant.

It's at this stage that Eron mentions television as a factor:

> One of the best predictors of how aggressive a young man would be at age 19 was the violence of the television programs he preferred when he was 8 years old. Now, because we had longitudinal data, we could say with more certainty, on the basis of regression analysis, partial correlation, path analysis, and so forth, that there indeed was a cause-and-effect relation. *Continued research, however, has indicated that the causal effect is probably bidirectional: Aggressive children prefer violent television,*

and the violence on television causes them to be more aggressive. [italics added]

Before we address the last comment, I should make one thing clear. Eron's research is sound. The methods he used to measure aggression are used by social scientists in many other contexts. His research does not ignore such obvious factors as the parents' socioeconomic status. And, as the above summary makes clear, Eron's own work makes a strong case for the positive or negative influence of parents in the development of their children's aggressiveness.

Now let's look at this "causal effect" business. Eron's data reveals that aggressive kids who turn into aggressive adults like aggressive television. But this is a correlation; it is not proof of a causal influence. If aggressive kids liked eating strawberry ice cream more often than the class wusses did, that too would be a predictor, and one might speculate on some anger-inducing chemical in strawberries.

Of course, the relation between representational violence and its influence on real life isn't as farfetched as that. The problem lies in determining precisely the nature of that relation, as we see when we look at the laboratory studies conducted by other researchers. Usually, the protocol of these experiments involves providing groups of individuals with entertainment calibrated for violent content, and studying some aspect of behavior after exposure—response to a behavioral test, which toys the children choose to play with, and so forth. But the results of these tests have been somewhat mixed. Sometimes the results are at variance with other studies, and many have methodological problems. For example, which "violent" entertainment is chosen? Bugs Bunny and the "Teenage Mutant Ninja Turtles" present action in very different contexts, and in one study, the Adam West "Batman" series was deemed nonviolent, despite those *Pow! Bam! Sock!* fistfights that ended every episode.

Many of the studies report that children do demonstrate higher levels of interpersonal aggression shortly after watching violent, energetic entertainment. But a 1971 study by Feshbach and Singer had boys from seven schools watch preassigned violent and nonviolent shows for six weeks. The results were not constant from school to school—and the boys watching the *nonviolent* shows tended to be more aggressive. Another protocol, carried out in Belgium as well as the United States, separated children into cottages at an institutional school and exposed certain groups to violent films. Higher aggression was noted in *all* groups after the films were viewed, but it returned to a near-baseline level after a week or so. (The children also rated the less violent films as less exciting, more boring, and sillier than the violent films —indicating that maybe kids *like* a little rush now and then.) Given the criticisms of the short-term-effects studies, and alternate interpretations of the longitudinal studies, is this matter really settled?

Eron certainly thinks so. Testifying before Simon's committee in August, he declared that "the scientific debate is over" and called upon the Senate to reduce TV violence. His statement did not include any reference to such significant factors as parental identification—which, as his own research indicates, can change the way children interpret physical punishment. And even though Rowell Huesmann concurred with Eron in similar testimony before a House subcommittee, Huesmann's 1984 study of 1,500 youths in the United States, Finland, Poland, and

Australia argued that, assuming a causal influence, television might be responsible for 5 percent of the violence in society. At *most*.

This is where I feel one has to part company with Leonard Eron. He is one of the most respected researchers in his field, and his work points to an imperative for parents in shaping and sharing their children's lives. But he has lent his considerable authority to such diversionary efforts as Paul Simon's and urged us to address, by questionable means, what only *might* be causing a tiny portion of real-life violence.

Some of Eron's suggestions for improving television are problematic as well. In his Senate testimony, Eron proposed restrictions on televised violence from 6:00 AM to 10:00 PM—which would exclude pro football, documentaries about World War II, and even concerned law-person Janet Reno's proudest moments. Or take Eron's suggestion that, in televised drama, "perpetrators of violence should not be rewarded for violent acts." I don't know what shows Eron's been watching, but all of the cop shows I remember usually ended with the bad guys getting caught or killed. And when Eron suggests that "gratuitous violence that is not necessary to the plot should be reduced or abandoned," one has to ask just *who* decides that it's "not necessary"? Perhaps most troubling is Eron's closing statement:

> For many years now Western European countries have had monitoring of TV and films for violence by government agencies and have *not* permitted the showing of excess violence, especially during child viewing hours. And I've never heard complaints by citizens of those democratic countries that their rights have been violated. If something

doesn't give, we may have to institute some such monitoring by government agencies here in the U.S.A. If the industry does not police itself, then there is left only the prospect of official censorship, distasteful as this may be to many of us.

* * *

The most often-cited measure of just how violent TV programs are is that of George Gerbner, dean of the Annenberg School of Communications at the University of Pennsylvania. Few of the news stories about TV violence explain how this index is compiled, the context in which Gerbner has conducted his studies, or even some criticisms that could be raised.

Gerbner's view of the media's role in society is far more nuanced than the publicity given the violence profile may indicate. He sees television as a kind of myth-structure/religion for modern society. Television dramas, situation comedies, news shows, and all the rest create a shared culture for viewers, which "communicates much about social norms and relationships, about goals and means, about winners and losers." One portion of Gerbner's research involves compiling "risk ratios" in an effort to discern which minority groups—including children, the aged, and women—tend to be the victims of the aggressors in drama. This provides a picture of a pecking order within society (white males on top, no surprise there) that has remained somewhat consistent over the 20-year history of the index.

In a press release accompanying the 1993 violence index, Gerbner discusses his investigations of the long-term effects of television viewing. Heavy viewers were more likely to express feelings of living in a hostile world. Gerbner adds, "Violence is a demonstration of power.

It shows who can get away with what against whom."

In a previous violence index compiled for cable-television programs, violence is defined as a "clear-cut and overt episode of physical violence—hurting or killing or the threat of hurting and/or killing —in any context." An earlier definition reads: "The overt expression of physical force against self or other compelling action against one's will on pain of being hurt or killed, or actually hurting or killing." These definitions have been criticized for being too broad; they encompass episodes of physical comedy, depiction of accidents in dramas, and even violent incidents in documentaries. They also include zany cartoon violence; in fact, the indexes for Saturday-morning programming tend to be substantially higher than the indexes for prime-time programming. Gerbner argues that, since he is analyzing cultural norms and since television entertainment is a deliberately conceived expression of these norms, his definition serves the purposes of his study.

The incidents of violence (total number $= R$) in a given viewing period are compiled by Gerbner's staff. Some of the statistics are easy to derive, such as the percentage of programs with violence, the number of violent scenes per hour, and the actual duration of violence, in minutes per hour. The actual violence index is calculated by adding together the following stats:

$\%P$—the *percentage* of programs in which there is violence;

$2(R/P)$—twice the number of violent episodes per program;

$2(R/H)$—twice the number of violent episodes per *hour*;

$\%V$—percentage of *leading characters* involved in violence, either as victim or perpetrator; and

$\%K$—percentage of leading characters involved in an actual *killing*, either as victim or perpetrator.

But if these are the factors used to compile the violence profile, it's difficult to see how they can provide a clear-cut mandate for the specific content of television drama. For example, two of the numbers used are averages; why are they arbitrarily doubled and then added to percentages? Also, because the numbers are determined by a definition which explicitly separates violence from dramatic context, the index says little about actual television content outside of a broad, overall gauge. One may imagine a television season of nothing but slapstick comedy with a very high violence profile.

This is why the violence profile is best understood within the context of Gerbner's wider analysis of media content. It does not lend itself to providing specific conclusions or guidelines of the sort urged by Senator Paul Simon. (It is important to note that, even though Simon observed little change in prime-time violence levels during his three-year antitrust exemption, the index for all three of those years was *below* the overall 20-year score.)

*   *   *

Finally, there's the anecdotal evidence—loudly trumpeted as such by Carl Cannon in *Mother Jones*—where isolated examples of entertainment-inspired violence are cited as proof of its pernicious influence. Several such examples have turned up recently. A sequence was edited out of the film *The Good Son* in which McCaulay

Culkin drops stuff onto a highway from an overhead bridge. (As we all know, nobody ever did this before the movie came out.) The film *The Program* was re-edited when some kids were killed imitating the film's characters, who "proved their courage" by lying down on a highway's dividing line. Perhaps most notoriously, in October 1993 a four-year-old Ohio boy set his family's trailer on fire, killing his younger sister; the child's mother promptly blamed MTV's "Beavis and Butt-head" for setting a bad example. But a neighbor interviewed on CNN reported that the family didn't even have cable television and that the kid had a local rep as a pyromaniac months before. This particular account was not followed up by the national media, which, if there were no enticing "Beavis and Butt-head" angle, would never have mentioned this fire at a low-income trailer park to begin with.

Numerous articles about media-inspired violence have cited similar stories —killers claiming to be Freddy Kreuger, kids imitating crimes they'd seen on a cop show a few days before, and so forth. In many of these cases, it is undeniably true that the person involved took his or her inspiration to act from a dramatic presentation in the media—the obvious example being John Hinckley's fixation on the film *Taxi Driver.* . . . But stories of media-inspired violence are striking mainly because they're so *atypical* of the norm; the vast majority of people don't take a movie or a TV show as a license to kill. Ironically, it is the *abnormality* of these stories that ensures they'll get widespread dissemination and be remembered long after the more mundane crimes are forgotten.

Of course, there are a few crazies out there who will be unfavorably influenced by what they see on TV. But even assuming that somehow the TV show (or movie or record) shares some of the blame, how does one predict what future crazies will take for inspiration? What guidelines would ensure that people write, act, or produce something that *will not upset a psychotic?* Not only is this a ridiculous demand, it's insulting to the public as well. We would all be treated as potential murderers in order to gain a hypothetical 5 percent reduction in violence.

* * *

In crusades like this—where the villagers pick up their torches and go hunting after Frankenstein—people often lose sight of what they're defending. I've read reams of statements from people who claim to know what television does to kids; but what do *kids* do with television? Almost none of what I've read gives kids any credit for thinking. None of these people seems to remember what being a kid is like.

When *Jurassic Park* was released, there was a huge debate over whether or not children should be allowed to see it. Kids like to see dinosaurs, people argued, but this movie might scare them into catatonia. . . . These objections were actually taken seriously. But kids like dinosaurs because they're big, look really weird, and scare the hell out of everything around them. Dinosaurs *kick ass.* What parent would tell his or her child that dinosaurs were *cute?* . . .

Along the same lines, what kid hasn't tried to gross out everyone at the dinner table by showing them his or her chewed-up food? Or tried using a magnifying glass on an anthill on a hot day? Or clinically inspected the first dead animal he or she ever came across? Sixty years ago, adults were terrified of *Frankenstein* and fainted at the premiere of *King Kong*. But today, *Kong* is regarded as a fantasy story, *Godzilla* can be shown without the objections of child psychologists, and there are breakfast cereals called Count Chocula and Frankenberry. Sadly, there are few adults who seem to remember how they identified more with the monsters. Who wanted to be one of those stupid villagers waving torches at Frankenstein? That's what our *parents* were like.

But it's not just an issue of kids liking violence, grossness, or comic-book adventure. About 90 percent of the cartoon shows I watched as a child were the mass-produced sludge of the Hanna-Barbera Studios—like "Wacky Races," "The Jetsons," and "Scooby Doo, Where Are You?" I can't remember a single memorable moment from any of them. But that Bugs Bunny sequence as the beginning of this article (from *Rabbit Seasoning*, 1952, directed by Chuck Jones) was done from memory, and I have no doubt that it's almost verbatim.

I know that, even at the age of eight or nine, I had some rudimentary aesthetic sense about it all. There was something hip and complex about the Warner Bros. cartoons, and some trite, insulting *sameness* to the Hanna-Barbera trash, although I couldn't quite understand it then. Bugs Bunny clearly wasn't made for kids according to some study on social-interaction development. Bugs Bunny was meant to make adults laugh as much as children. Kids can also enjoy entertainment ostensibly created for adults—in fact, that's often the most rewarding kind. I had no trouble digesting *Jaws*, James Bond, and Clint Eastwood "spaghetti westerns" in my preteen years. And I'd have no problems with showing a 10-year-old *Jurassic Park*, because I know how much he or she would love it. . . .

I don't enjoy bad television with lots of violence, but I'd rather not lose *decent* shows that use violence for good reason. Shows like "Star Trek," "X-Men," or the spectacular "Batman: The Animated Series" can give kids a sense of adventure while teaching them about such qualities as courage, bravery, and heroism. Even better, a healthy and robust spirit of irreverence can be found in Bugs Bunny, "Ren and Stimpy," and "Tiny Toons." Some of these entertainments—like adventure stories and comic books of the past—can teach kids how to be really *alive*.

Finally, if we must have a defense against the pernicious influence of the mass media, it cannot be from the Senate's legislation or the pronouncements of social scientists. It must begin with precisely the qualities I described above—especially irreverence. One good start is Comedy Central's "Mystery Science Theater 3000," where the main characters, forced to watch horrendous movies, fight back by heckling them. Not surprisingly, children love the show, even though most of the jokes go right over their curious little heads. They recognize a kindred spirit in "MST 3000." Kids want to stick up for themselves, maybe like Batman, maybe like Bugs Bunny, or even like Beavis and Butt-head—but always against a world made by adults.

You know, *adults*—those doofuses with the torches, trying to burn up Frankenstein in the old mill.

POSTSCRIPT

Is Television Viewing Harmful for Children?

For those who think that television viewing is harmful, a simple solution to the problems that they think are associated with television watching and violence and child development would be to unplug the "tube." We could go back to the days when reading, listening to the radio, and swapping stories while sitting by the fireplace were the most common forms of at-home entertainment. On the other hand, there are those who argue that television is merely the next step in the evolution of communication technology and, consequently, we should just go with the flow, grin and bear it, for television is surely here to stay. We should stop worrying about watching television; after all, it is ultimately harmless.

What should be done, and by whom, to effectively address this question? Is it realistic to revert back to the days prior to the television era? Should everyone just relax and stop worrying about television? Are children resilient enough that they can eventually understand TV's impact on their lives? How much truth lies in Siano's contention that if parents were more involved with their children, especially while they are watching television, then what children watch would not be a problem? Would American society end up forfeiting quality programming if Congress were authorized to more closely censor television programming? How do you respond to Centerwall's contention that children are incapable of discriminating between what they should and should not imitate?

Critics of television do not see televised violence as the only potential harm to children. School-age children, for example, are a prime target audience for advertisers. This is evident in the fact that there are more commercial breaks per hour for children's programming than for any other. Additionally, with the growth of cable television, many children now have access to an even greater amount of adult programming. Furthermore, some research suggests that children who spend excessive amounts of time watching television tend to do poorly in school. Interestingly, research also indicates that children who spend a moderate amount of time watching television perform better scholastically than those who do not watch television at all.

Perhaps if all parents could accept the inevitable, that television is here to stay and that viewing choices are expanding almost daily, we, as a society, could move past this dichotomy of thinking that television is either good or bad. Television viewing could be thought of as an active endeavor rather than a passive one. Parents could become more involved with their children as they watch television. Through modeling, parents could teach children to be skeptical about television advertisements, point out the differences between fantasy and reality, and argue the moral values being portrayed on the tube when they differ from the values that are important to the parents.

Parents can use television watching to teach their children how to make decisions. Within limits set by the parents, children can be permitted to choose what they want to watch. Parents can discuss the programs that they watch with their children, always with an eye toward having children express their views while the parents gently challenge opinions and actions that may be different from the values they hold and want to develop in their children. To maximize choices in quality programming, parents can use VCRs (videocassette recorders) to tape-record programs and then find convenient times to watch special programs with their children.

SUGGESTED READINGS

Centerwall, B. S. (1989). Exposure to television as a cause of violence. *Public Communication and Behavior, 2,* 1–58.

Eron, L. D., & Huesmann, L. R. (1984). The control of aggressive behavior by changes in attitudes, values and the conditions of learning. *Advances in the Study of Aggression* (pp. 139–171). Orlando, FL: Academic Press.

Huesmann, L. R., & Eron, L. (1986). *Television and the aggressive child.* Hillsdale, NJ: Lawrence Erlbaum Associates.

Kolbert, E. (1994, December 14). Television gets closer look as a factor in real violence. *The New York Times (National),* D1, D20.

Kruttschnitt, C. (1986). Family violence, television viewing habits and other adolescent experiences related to violent criminal behavior. *Criminology, 24,* 235–267.

Kunkel, D. (1991, November/December). Crafting media policy. *American Behavioral Scientist, 35,* 181–202.

Kuney, J. (1992). Turn-off time? *Television Quarterly, 26,* 43–46.

Liebes, T. (1992, Fall). Television, parents and the political socialization of children. *Teacher's College Record, 94,* 73–86.

On the Internet . . .

http://www.dushkin.com

Council of Chief State School Officers

Officials who head the departments of elementary and secondary education in the states develop policy and consensus on major education issues which the council advocates before the U.S. president and Congress. Resources on the council's involvement in a number of issues from bilingual education to improvement in science and math opportunities are provided.
http://www.ccsso.org

The Children's Literature Web Guide

The Children's Literature Web Guide provides information useful in selecting literature suitable for children. It provides many literary alternatives to watching television.
http://www.ucalgary.ca/~dkbrown/index.html

School-Age Child Care Project

Directed by the Wellesley College Center for Research on Women, this project aims to improve the quality and quantity of school-age child care nationally.
http://www.wellesley.edu/WCW/CRW/SAC/

The Single Parent Resource

The Single Parent Resource focuses on issues concerning single parents and their children. Although the articles range from parenting children in infancy through adolescence, most of the articles deal with middle childhood.
http://www.parentsplace.com/readroom/spn/articles.html

National Black Child Development Institute

Resources for improving the quality of life for African American children through public education programs are provided.
http://www.nbcdi.org

PART 3

Middle Childhood

Middle childhood, or school age, is the period from ages five through twelve. The rate of a child's growth generally declines until the later part of this stage of development. Perhaps the most important experience during middle childhood is schooling. As a child progresses through this stage, new significant others outside the family emerge in the child's life. Children gain a broader understanding of the similarities and differences among them. The peer group (especially same-sex peers), teachers, and media personalities take on increased importance for the child. This section examines issues related to schooling, language development, and self-care.

■ Are Boys Better in Math Than Girls?

■ Are Children in Self-Care at a Disadvantage?

■ Is Home Schooling an Effective Method of Education?

■ Should Bilingual Education Programs Be Abandoned?

■ Will Stricter Dress Codes Improve the Educational Environment?

ISSUE 9

Are Boys Better in Math Than Girls?

YES: Carol J. Mills, Karen E. Ablard, and Heinrich Stumpf, from "Gender Differences in Academically Talented Young Students' Mathematical Reasoning: Patterns Across Age and Subskills," *Journal of Educational Psychology* (vol. 85, no. 2, 1993)

NO: American Association of University Women, from *How Schools Shortchange Girls: A Study of Major Findings on Girls and Education* (American Association of University Women, 1992)

ISSUE SUMMARY

YES: Carol J. Mills, Karen E. Ablard, and Heinrich Stumpf, all associates of the Center for Talented Youth Research at Johns Hopkins University, report that boys perform better than girls on tests for math reasoning ability.

NO: A report developed by the Center for Research on Women at Wellesley College for the American Association of University Women concludes that the differences in math achievement between boys and girls are not significant and are narrowing.

You may have heard the common assertion that "boys are better in math and girls are better in verbal skills." Does being born male automatically predispose a child to have a greater mathematical acuity? Are girls fated to go through life with perpetual math anxiety? Research results are divided on the question of gender and math ability. There are a number of studies that report that boys outperform girls in math. Other reports, based on analyses of over 100 studies, conclude that girls and boys perform equally on math tests.

Some of the reasons for the conflicting conclusions are due to the sample populations studied and the math skills that were tested. Some researchers argue that because boys are more likely to drop out of school than girls, the pool of boys and girls tested may be unequal. The boys left in school might be more likely to be above-average students than the girls. A boy's prior knowledge is also considered to be advantageous. For example, if boys are placed in more accelerated math courses than girls, they will probably perform better on standard math tests.

On the other hand, there are researchers who contend that there are no real differences in boys' and girls' ability or achievement in math. Math acuity could be more of a self-fulfilling prophecy issue: Boys are expected to be better in math and girls are not. So discrepancies in mathematical performance might simply be the result of children living up to expectations.

In the following selections you will read conflicting conclusions based on similar research studies. Mills, Ablard, and Stumpf conclude that there are clear and distinct differences in boys' and girls' math ability. The report of the American Association of University Women draws the opposite conclusion, that there are no gender differences when it comes to mathematics.

YES

Carol J. Mills, Karen E. Ablard, and Heinrich Stumpf

GENDER DIFFERENCES IN ACADEMICALLY TALENTED YOUNG STUDENTS' MATHEMATICAL REASONING: PATTERNS ACROSS AGE AND SUBSKILLS

When a sample of academically talented students in Grades 2–6 was given a test of mathematical reasoning ability, boys performed better overall than girls. The gender differences for mathematical ability appeared as early as 2nd grade in samples tested over a 7-year period but varied somewhat according to mathematical subskills. There were no substantial gender-related differences on tasks requiring students to identify whether enough information was provided to solve a task; however, boys performed better than girls on tasks requiring application of algebraic rules or algorithms, as well as on tasks in which the understanding of mathematical concepts and number relationships was required.

Speculation and research efforts concerning gender differences in cognitive abilities appear to be a "national preoccupation" (Jacklin, 1989). This is particularly true for differences in mathematical and spatial ability, whereas few consistent gender-related differences have been found for verbal ability.

One of the reasons for the tenacious interest in gender differences in mathematical ability is the possible relationship between mathematics performance and academic or career opportunities and performance (e.g., Sells, 1980). Research results suggest that gender differences in mathematical ability may be related to mathematics attitudes (Armstrong, 1985), self-confidence (Eccles et al., 1985; Fox, Brody, & Tobin, 1985), course choices (Benbow & Stanley, 1983), persistence in a mathematics discipline (Casserly & Rock, 1985), and career choices (Subotnik, Duschl, & Selmon, 1991). It has also been suggested that gender differences in ability combined with gender differences on a variety of other variables (including interests, values, and cognitive style) may

From Carol J. Mills, Karen E. Ablard, and Heinrich Stumpf, "Gender Differences in Academically Talented Young Students' Mathematical Reasoning: Patterns Across Age and Subskills," *Journal of Educational Psychology*, vol. 85, no. 2 (1993), pp. 340–346. Copyright © 1993 by The American Psychological Association. Reprinted by permission.

represent a particularly persistent constraint on equal representation of men and women across a variety of disciplines (Lubinski & Benbow, 1992; Mills, 1992).

General statements on gender differences in mathematical reasoning ability, however, are likely to be misleading because they mask the complexity of the issue. For example, the age at which gender differences first appear and the direction of such differences differ from one study or review article to another.

In general, small but reliable gender differences in favor of boys/men in mathematical reasoning ability have been consistently noted from adolescence onward (Hyde, Fennema, & Lamon, 1990; Maccoby & Jacklin, 1974; Weiner & Robinson, 1986). Some reviewers have concluded that the differences emerge only in the last 2 or 3 years of high school (Hyde et al., 1990; Meece, Parsons, Kaczala, Goff, & Futterman, 1982; Stage, Kreinberg, Eccles, & Becker, 1985).

Studies reporting gender differences at an earlier age (elementary school) have been based primarily on findings from achievement or knowledge tests as opposed to ability tests (Dossey, Mullis, Lindquist, & Chambers, 1988; Marshall & Smith, 1987). Some of these studies with younger students also have reported girls scoring higher than boys (Hilton & Berglund, 1971; Marshall & Smith, 1987). Overall, the point at which gender differences first appear and the direction they take seem to depend on the content and cognitive demands of the items used.

The appearance and nature of gender differences may also depend on the particular characteristics of the population studied. For example, gender-related differences in favor of boys/men appear to be even more pronounced in academically talented populations. In very select

but large samples tested over the past 11 years, boys have consistently scored higher as a group than girls on the mathematics section of the Scholastic Aptitude Test (SAT) as early as the seventh grade (Benbow, 1988; Benbow & Stanley, 1980; Durden, Mills, & Barnett, 1990).

Such differences in mathematical reasoning ability have not been clearly established, however, in academically talented samples at an earlier age. One of the obstacles in the past to such an endeavor has been the belief that the existing mathematical reasoning tests were inappropriate for assessing the ability in younger children (Benbow, 1988). The School and College Ability Test (SCAT), however, has been successfully used for a number of years in above-grade-level testing to identify academic talent in students of elementary school age (Durden, Mills, & Barnett, 1990). Because academically talented students, such as those tested in our study, have been shown to exhibit abstract reasoning ability and formal operational thinking at an earlier age than typically found in a general population of students (Ablard, Tissot, & Mills, 1992; Keating, 1975), gender differences may emerge earlier for these students than previous research has suggested. The nature of gender differences in mathematical reasoning ability in an elementary school population of academically talented students was, therefore, a major focus of the present study.

Another important issue surrounding gender differences in mathematical ability is the identification of subskills and the degree to which the performance of male and female students may differ on specific item types. Researchers such as Hyde et al. (1990), Marshall and Smith (1987), and Stage et al. (1985) have found that mathematical ability consists of several subskills, such as computation and problem solving, that differ in their degree of gender sensitivity.

Tests that predominantly measure computational skills are generally found to favor girls/women or show no gender-related differences at all, whereas tests involving the use of mathematical concepts or mathematical problem solving generally favor boys/men (Hyde et al., 1990). In a study of young adults, Klieme (1989) also found that tasks requiring the application of known mathematical algorithms did not show gender differences as large as did tasks requiring mathematical problem solving. These findings emphasize the need to differentiate between achievement or knowledge tests and tests of ability or aptitude. As Marshall and Smith (1987) have pointed out, it is equally important to examine gender patterns in performance on subcategories of items within a given test. This was also a focus of the present study.

The generalizability of all these findings, however, is challenged by the observation of some authors that gender-related differences in cognitive variables, such as mathematical and spatial ability, have declined during recent years (Emanuelsson & Svensson, 1986; Feingold, 1988; Hilton, 1985; Hyde et al., 1990; Linn, 1991; Rosenthal & Rubin, 1982; Stumpf & Klieme, 1989). Other recent studies (e.g., Cleary, 1991; Oosthuizen, 1991; Stanley, Benbow, Brody, Dauber, & Lupowski, 1991), however, have continued to find substantial differences between male and female students in these domains of cognitive functioning, so this matter is not as yet resolved.

In view of the research findings, three major questions were asked in the present study: (a) In a sample of academically talented elementary school children, do boys and girls differ in mathematical reasoning ability? (b) If a gender difference exists, does it differ by age or grade level? and (c) If gender differences are found for overall mathematical ability, does the pattern of results differ by subskills identified in the test of mathematical reasoning ability?

METHOD

Participants

The participants in our study were 2,586 students between 7 and 11 years of age. These students participated in eligibility testing (between 1985 and 1991) for special course work offered to elementary school children by the Center for Talented Youth at the Johns Hopkins University as part of a program introduced in 1985. Information on the racial, ethnic, and socioeconomic background of students attending the courses is obtained on a voluntary basis. Because such information is incomplete, analyses across subsamples are not reported in this article.[1]

All students had scored at or above the 97th percentile for either verbal or mathematical ability or achievement on a nationally normed test (such as the California Achievement Test) administered in their schools. Although all students could be considered academically talented, not all were talented specifically in mathematics. Therefore, we were able to obtain a sample with a relatively wide range of mathematical ability. Indeed, SCAT scores in the sample ranged across virtually all possible standard scores.

Procedure

Students identified as academically talented by their scores on a nationally normed mathematical or verbal aptitude test took the SCAT to apply for eligibility for advanced-level course work. Because the students had already shown high academic performance on a grade-appropriate test, a more challenging level of the SCAT (a level designed for students at least two grades above the participants' actual grade level) was administered to prevent ceiling effects and to make finer ability distinctions among these talented students. Testing took place in group sessions.

Two equivalent forms (X and Y) and three difficulty levels (elementary, intermediate, or advanced) of the SCAT were administered to accommodate the various age levels[2] and testing dates (Form X for fall administrations and Form Y for spring administrations). To make the scores on these forms and levels comparable, the raw scores were converted to standard scores as specified in the SCAT manual. The results reported here are predominantly based on the standard scores.

School and College Ability Test

The SCAT is a nationally normed standardized test developed by the Educational Testing Service; the SCAT Series III (Educational Testing Service, 1980) was used in this study. The test has two parts (subtests), verbal and quantitative, each of which consists of 50 items. Although students took both sections of the SCAT, only the results from the quantitative section were of interest for this article.

The quantitative subtest includes tasks covering a variety of content, such as estimation, fractions, proportions, and geometry. All items are quantitative comparison tasks: The student must decide which of two quantities is greater than the other, whether they are the same, or whether there is not enough information available to make a decision.

The questions on the SCAT III place minimum emphasis on reading and require more resourcefulness and insight than traditional computation items. Although some knowledge of arithmetic operations is necessary to answer the items correctly, no actual computations are required on the test. In fact, students who take the time to do the computations typically do less well and often do not complete the test within the time allowed. Because an "out-of-level" version (i.e., above the student's grade level) of the SCAT was administered to this group of students, thereby ensuring that most of them had not been formally exposed to many of the operations and concepts dealt with in the test, it seems reasonable to consider it a measure of high-level reasoning and problem-solving ability for this sample. Three sample items from the test are presented in the Appendix [at the end of this selection].

The SCAT Series III used in this study represents revisions of the SCAT Series II tests. It has been widely used since 1980 to assess the verbal and quantitative aptitude of 3rd- through 12th-grade students in both public and private schools (Educational Testing Service, 1980). In addition, a number of school districts currently use the SCAT to identify academically talented students for special programs.

The SCAT has been shown to predict scores on the SAT reasonably well (Educational Testing Service, 1980). In addition, the SCAT has successfully predicted how students progressed in advanced-level mathematics and humanities courses offered by the Center for Talented Youth over the past 7 years (Durden et al., 1990; Mills & Ablard, 1992). For more detailed psychometric evaluations of the SCAT, the reader is referred to Ahmann (1985) and Passow (1985).

RESULTS

Score differences for gender, grade level, and year of testing were examined for statistical significance with analyses of variance (ANOVAs). The regression approach within the Statistical Package for the Social Sciences (Norusis, 1988) was used for the ANOVAs. In this approach, all effects are assessed simultaneously, and each effect is adjusted for all other effects in the model. Given the occasionally observed difference in variance for male and female students, a test for homogeneity of variance (Cochran's test) was conducted. The results of this test indicated that the two variances were not significantly different ($C = .55$, $p > .001$). Because the sample was very large, a conservative criterion ($p < .001$) for classifying a difference as significant was adopted for all statistical tests.

In addition to the significance tests, the formula for unequal variances (Cohen, 1977, p. 44) was used to obtain effect-size estimates (d coefficients) for the differences between various groups. These estimates were useful for comparisons among group differences within the present study, as well as for comparisons with findings reported in the literature.

Grade Level

A 2 (gender) × 5 (grade level) ANOVA conducted for the quantitative subtest revealed significant main effects for gender and grade level, $F(1, 2576) = 99.10$, $p < .001$, and $F(4, 2576) = 448.62$, $p < .001$, respectively. The Scheffé test revealed that boys performed better than girls across all grade levels and that performance in-

creased with grade level for both boys and girls. The interaction effect for gender and grade level on mathematical reasoning performance, however, was not significant, $F(4, 2576) = 0.76$, $p > .05$, indicating that the gender effect did not vary across grade level.

The largest gender difference (for the fifth graders) was about one half of a standard deviation. Even among the youngest students, the second graders, the scores of the boys were higher than those for girls, as documented by means that differ by more than one third of a standard deviation. In view of the previous studies with young subjects (as summarized by Hyde et al., 1990), this finding suggests that gender differences in mathematics ability, at least in a population of highly able students, appear much earlier than thought and are relatively consistent across age levels.

Mathematical Subskills

Previous research has shown that the concept of mathematical reasoning ability can be broken down into concepts of more specific subskills required to solve mathematical problems. These subskills have been found to vary in the amount of gender-related differences they show (e.g., Hyde et al., 1990; Klieme, 1989). Higher level problem solving and understanding of mathematical concepts are believed to be more gender sensitive than computational skills, for which there is no difference at all or a slight superiority for females (Hyde et al., 1990). Factors underlying students' performance on the SCAT were examined, as well as the extent to which boys differed from girls on these factors....

Before the scores on the three factors were compared across gender (t tests), the factor structures for boys and girls (separately) were compared. Three factors were obtained for both sexes and rotated independently to an orthogonal simple structure. Coefficients of congruence (Harman, 1976, p. 344) were computed for each pair of factors from the two subgroups. These coefficients were .95, .94, and .92 for Factors 1, 2, and 3, respectively, thus indicating that the factor structures are basically the same and that it is meaningful to assume a common factor structure.

Factor 1 was characterized by high loadings of items that required the decision that not enough information was available to solve the task (seven of eight items). Although the items vary in format and content, their common element is that students must evaluate the sufficiency of the available information to solve the tasks. A sample item for this factor is provided in the Appendix as Item 1.

Factor 2 was dominated by tasks requiring the understanding of algebraic operations or handling expressions with an unknown quantity, especially when fractions and decimals were involved. A sample item for this factor is given as Item 2 in the Appendix.

Factor 3 was marked by tasks requiring the understanding of mathematical concepts (e.g., the concepts of whole numbers and even numbers) and relationships among numbers, especially when units, proportions (e.g., percentages), or simple statistics (e.g., the arithmetic mean) were to be evaluated. A sample item for this factor is given as Item 3 in the Appendix.

... [B]oys had higher scores than girls on all three factors, but only the differences on Factors 2, $t(685) = 4.18$, $p < .001$, and 3, $t(685) = 4.76$, $p < .001$, were significant; for Factor 1, $t(685) =$

2.50, $p > .01$. In terms of Cohen's (1977) classification, the differences on Factors 2 and 3 represent small effect sizes.

Although the difference of scores on Factor 1 was not significant, the "not enough information" response (Response D) was itself of interest in terms of differential responding by boys and girls. To determine whether boys and girls differed with respect to deciding whether enough information was available for solving a task, we examined gender differences for hits and false alarms.[3] ...

[B]oys had a slightly higher average of hits and a slightly smaller average of false alarms than did girls. Neither difference was statistically significant. As far as the discrimination score is concerned, however, the mean score for boys was significantly higher than that for girls, $t(685) = 3.53$, $p < .001$. Thus, boys were more accurate overall in deciding whether enough information was given to solve a problem. This male advantage for accurately choosing the not enough information response is obviously related to the slight (but nonsignificant) male advantage on Factor 1.

A final analysis was conducted to investigate a recent suggestion that gender-related differences on tests with time-limits may be related to gender differences in test-taking habits and confidence levels (Goldstein, Haldane, & Mitchell, 1990). Goldstein et al. suggested comparing conventional scores with ratio scores (number of items correctly answered divided by number of items attempted, multiplied by 100).

Using the largest subsample in our study, the students who had taken the intermediate level of SCAT Form X, we computed both the conventional and ratio scores and compared them for boys and girls. On the conventional number-correct scores, boys had a raw score mean of 28.12 (SD = 8.19) and girls had a mean of 24.19 (SD = 7.86), yielding a d coefficient of .49 for the gender-related difference. On the ratio scores, boys had a mean of 61.76 (SD = 15.76) and girls had a mean of 54.56 (SD = 16.03), which corresponds to a d value of .45. An examination of the d values reveals that the gender differences in this subsample of students are very similar according to either conventional or ratio scores, and they are consistent with the differences reported for all grade levels. Thus, only a small fraction of the gender differences found in the present study can be explained by the factors mentioned earlier and operationalized by the ratio score.

DISCUSSION

In contrast to studies that have reported a convergence in mental test scores of male and female students in recent years (Hyde et al., 1990; Linn, 1991), we found gender differences in mathematical ability.[4] We are not alone in our findings, because other recent studies have reported gender differences in mathematical ability (Cleary, 1991; Stanley et al., 1991).

The major purpose of this study, however, was not merely to revisit the gender difference issue but to help clarify and further understand such differences. Although an overall gender difference was found in our study, the more important findings are that (a) this difference was discovered as early as second grade in an academically talented population, (b) the magnitude of the gender difference was approximately the same across five grade levels, and (c) mathematical reasoning ability can be meaningfully broken down into several subsets of skills that differ somewhat in their gender sensitivity.

A unique contribution of our study is the finding of gender differences in mathematical reasoning ability in children at a much younger age than has previously been reported. This result was accompanied by the finding that the differences did not change appreciably across age or grade level.

To understand our findings, it is important to consider several related facts. First, we tested reasoning ability, which is rarely done with young elementary school students. Generally, standardized tests before seventh grade focus on specific knowledge and computational skills (achievement tests). Second, we used equivalent forms of the same test across all age levels, which meant that the type of ability tested did not change. Studies reporting changes in gender differences across age are often plagued by changes in test content, format, or focus when testing different age groups (e.g., Hyde et al., 1990; Marshall & Smith, 1987).

It is also important to consider the advanced cognitive development of the subjects in our study. Gender differences appear to be greatest for tasks involving problem solving and understanding of mathematical concepts that require higher level thinking (Hyde et al., 1990). Such differences generally first appear around the age of 12 years, when most children begin to develop formal operational thinking. Because academically talented students have been shown to exhibit performance indicative of formal operations well before 12 years of age (Ablard et al., 1992; Keating, 1975), it is not surprising that we found gender differences in mathematical reasoning at a younger age than has typically been found.

A side benefit of studying the development of reasoning and problem-solving ability in students who are cognitively advanced may be a resulting better understanding of general developmental patterns of such abilities. With the national push for reform in mathematics instruction to include more of an emphasis on problem solving and higher level reasoning in elementary school, an understanding of when and how gender differences in such skills develop takes on immediate importance.

The results of the factor analysis indicate, once again, that mathematical reasoning is not monolithic but can be broken down into several subskills. Our classification of subskills of mathematical reasoning ability, however, is purely post hoc. It is a description of the demands of various tasks, not an identification of cognitive processes involved in these tasks. More research is needed to arrive at a delineation of the basic cognitive processes underlying the specific sub-skills that make up mathematical reasoning ability, as well as how boys/men and girls/women may or may not differ in their development and use of such processes.

Although we found gender differences in favor of boys on two of the factors identified in the SCAT, on one factor significant differences did not emerge. This factor (Factor 1) contained mainly items requiring subjects to determine whether sufficient information was present to solve the task. However, in an analysis focusing on the discrimination between hits and false alarms on all not enough information responses given by students in our study, boys were more accurate.

Clearly, an understanding of the pattern of gender differences across subskills within what is called "mathematical reasoning ability" is still incomplete. Examining differences across subskills, however, may ultimately prove to be more useful than considering overall scores for understanding the cognitive development of males and females. A similar approach (Linn & Petersen, 1985) in the area of spatial ability proved to be useful in explaining inconsistencies in the literature. In addition, as Marshall and Smith (1987) suggested, an understanding of possible gender differences in the development of different skills may lead to useful educational recommendations for the teaching of mathematics.

Finally, it has been suggested that differences in test-taking styles and attitudes may be responsible for gender differences on tests exhibiting gender sensitivity (Goldstein et al., 1990). Specifically, researchers have hypothesized that female test takers are at a disadvantage on tests, such as the SCAT, that have time limits. A comparison of conventional and ratio scores, however, revealed that only a small fraction of the gender-related differences observed in this study could be explained by such factors.

One should, of course, never generalize from a select sample such as ours to the general population. One caution discussed recently by Feingold (1992) centers around the frequent finding over the years that the scores of male students on a large number of general ability tests have a larger variance than those of female students. Gender differences in the scores of a group selected from the right tail of the distribution may, therefore, show differences in the means even when the overall means are equal, for the simple reason that more high-scoring male students are likely to be selected than high-scoring female students. This may be one of the reasons why studies with select samples (Benbow, 1988; Benbow & Stanley, 1980, 1983; Hyde et al., 1990; Stanley et al., 1991) generally have found larger gender differences than have been found in a population with a full range of ability levels.

Even when such a generalization is explicitly avoided, however, a gender-related difference among highly talented students in the area of mathematical reasoning ability is a finding that needs to be described and explained in its own right. Although such gender differences in academically talented samples are usually small to moderate in magnitude and are not consistently found for all aspects of mathematical reasoning ability, they are consistently found for overall mathematical reasoning ability. In addition, these differences appear at a relatively young age (i.e., early elementary school), and they seem to be stable across age level and year of testing within a population from which future mathematicians and scientists are most likely to come.

NOTES

1. Most students are from a White or Asian background. African Americans and other minorities constitute a small percentage of the sample. The socioeconomic status of most families is middle class, although scholarships are available for students with financial need.

2. The elementary level of the SCAT (designed for mid-3rd-grade through mid-6th-grade students) was given to 2nd-, 3rd-, and 4th-grade students; the intermediate level (designed for mid-6th-grade through mid-9th-grade students) was given to 4th- and 5th-grade students; and the advanced level (designed for mid-9th-grade through 12th-grade students) was given to 6th-grade students.

3. A hit was defined as correctly responding that not enough information was available to solve the problem, whereas a false alarm was defined as indicating that not enough information was available when, in fact, there was. Both scores were standardized to a mean of 0 and a standard deviation of 1.

4. A trend analysis across years was considered because the data in this study were collected over a 7-year span. Most of the data, however, were collected during the last 5 years, a span considered to be too short for such an analysis.

REFERENCES

Ablard, K. E., Tissot, S. L., & Mills, C. J. (1992). *Academically talented students' precocious cognitive development and its predictors.* Unpublished manuscript, Johns Hopkins University, Baltimore.

Ahmann, J. S. (1985). Review of School and College Ability Tests, Series III. In J. V. Mitchell (Ed.), *The ninth mental measurements yearbook* (pp. 1315–1316). Lincoln: University of Nebraska Press.

Armstrong, J. M. (1985). A national assessment of participation and achievement of women in mathematics. In S. F. Chipman, L. R. Brush, & D. M. Wilson (Eds.), *Women and mathematics: Balancing the equation* (pp. 59–94). Hillsdale, NJ: Erlbaum.

Benbow, C. P. (1988). Sex differences in mathematical reasoning ability in intellectually talented preadolescents: Their nature, effects, and possible causes. *Behavioral and Brain Science, 11,* 169–183.

Benbow, C. P., & Stanley, J. C. (1980). Sex differences in mathematical reasoning ability: Fact or artifact? *Science, 210,* 1262–1264.

Benbow, C. P., & Stanley, J. C. (1983). Sex differences in mathematical reasoning ability: More facts. *Science, 222,* 1029–1031.

Casserly, P. L., & Rock, D. (1985). Factors related to young women's persistence and achievement in advanced placement mathematics. In S. F. Chipman, L. R. Brush, & D. M. Wilson (Eds.), *Women and mathematics: Balancing the equation* (pp. 225–247). Hillsdale, NJ: Erlbaum.

Cleary, T. A. (1991, October). *Sex differences in testing.* Paper presented at the invitational conference sponsored by the Educational Testing Service, New York.

Cohen, J. (1977). *Statistical power analysis for the behavioral sciences* (Rev. ed.). San Diego, CA: Academic Press.

Dossey, J. A., Mullis, I. V., Lindquist, M. M., & Chambers, D. L. (1988). *The mathematics report card.* Princeton, NJ: Educational Testing Service.

Durden, W. G., Mills, C. J., & Barnett, L. B. (1990). Aspects of gender differentiation in the Johns Hopkins University Center for Talented Youth. In W. Wieczerkowski & T. M. Prado (Eds.), *Highly talented young women* (pp. 166–185). Bad Honnef, Germany: K. H. Bock.

Eccles, J., Adler, T. F. Futterman, R., Goff, S. B., Kaczala, C. M., Meece, J. L., & Midgely, C. (1985). Self-perception, socializing influences, and the decision to enroll in mathematics. In S. F. Chipman, L. R. Brush, & D. M. Wilson (Eds.), *Women and mathematics: Balancing the equation* (pp. 95–121). Hillsdale, NJ: Erlbaum.

Educational Testing Service. (1979). *School and College Ability Tests: Intermediate Level Form X.* Monterey, CA: CTB/McGraw-Hill.

Educational Testing Service. (1980). *School and College Ability Tests (SCAT III): Manual and technical report.* Princeton, NJ: Author.

Emanuelsson, I., & Svensson, A. (1986). Does the level of intelligence decrease? A comparison between thirteen-year-olds tested in 1960, 1966, and 1980. *Scandinavian Journal of Educational Research, 30,* 25–37.

Feingold, A. (1988). Cognitive gender differences are disappearing. *American Psychologist, 43,* 95–103.

Feingold, A. (1992). Sex differences in variability in intellectual abilities: A new look at an old controversy. *Review of Educational Research, 62,* 61–84.

Fox, L. H., Brody, L., & Tobin, D. (1985). The impact of early intervention programs upon course-taking and attitudes in high school. In S. F. Chipman, L. R. Brush, & D. M. Wilson (Eds.), *Women and mathematics: Balancing the equation* (pp. 249–274). Hillsdale, NJ: Erlbaum.

Goldstein, G., Haldane, D., & Mitchell, C. (1990). Sex differences in visual-spatial ability: The role of performance factors. *Memory & Cognition, 18,* 546–550.

Harman, H. H. (1976). *Modern factor analysis.* Chicago: University of Chicago Press.

Hilton, T. L. (1985). *National changes in spatial-visual ability from 1960 to 1980* (Report No. RR-85-27). Princeton, NJ: Educational Testing Service.

Hilton, T. L., & Berglund, G. W. (1971). *Sex differences in mathematics achievement.* Princeton, NJ: Educational Testing Service.

Hyde, J. S., Fennema, E. F., & Lamon, S. J. (1990). Gender differences in mathematics performance: A meta-analysis. *Psychological Bulletin, 107,* 139–155.

Jacklin, C. N. (1989). Female and male: Issues of gender. *American Psychologist, 44,* 127–133.

Keating, D. P. (1975). Precocious cognitive development at the level of formal operations. *Child Development, 46,* 276–280.

Klieme, E. (1989). *Mathematisches Problemloesen als Testleistung* [Mathematical problem solving as test performance]. Frankfurt: Lang.

Linn, M. C. (1991, October). *Sex differences in educational achievement.* Paper presented at the invitational conference sponsored by the Educational Testing Service, New York.

Linn, M. C., & Petersen, A. C. (1985). Emergence and characterization of sex differences in spatial ability: A meta-analysis. *Child Development, 56,* 1479–1498.

Lubinski, D., & Benbow, C. P. (1992). Gender differences in abilities and preferences among the gifted: Implications for the math-science pipeline. *Current Directions in Psychological Science, 1(2),* 61–65.

Maccoby, E. E., & Jacklin, C. N. (1974). *The psychology of sex differences.* Stanford, CA: Stanford University Press.

Marshall, S. P., & Smith, J. D. (1987). Sex differences in learning mathematics: A longitudinal study with item and error analyses. *Journal of Educational Psychology, 79,* 372–383.

Meece, J. L., Parsons, J., Kaczala, C. M., Goff, S. B., & Futterman, R. (1982). Sex differences in math achievement: Toward a model of academic choice. *Psychological Bulletin, 91,* 324–348.

Mills, C. J. (1992, March). *Gender, personality, and academic ability.* Paper presented at the 15th annual meeting of the Eastern Educational Researchers Association, Hilton Head, SC.

Mills, C. J., & Ablard, K. E. (1992). *Academically talented young students' achievement in an individually-paced mathematics program.* Unpublished manuscript, Johns Hopkins University.

Norusis, M. (1988). *SPSS/PC+ V2.0 Base manual.* Chicago: SPSS.

Oosthuizen, S. (1991). Sex-related differences in spatial ability in a group of South African students. *Perceptual and Motor Skills, 73,* 51–54.

Passow, A. H. (1985). Review of School and College Ability Tests, Series III. In J. V. Mitchell (Ed.), *The ninth mental measurements yearbook* (pp. 1317–1318). Lincoln: University of Nebraska Press.

Rosenthal, R., & Rubin, D. B. (1982). Further meta-analytic procedures for assessing cognitive gender differences. *Journal of Educational Psychology, 74,* 708–712.

Sells, L. (1980). The mathematics filter and the education of women and minorities. In L. Fox, L. Brody, & D. Tobin (Eds.), *Women and the mathematical mystique* (pp. 66–75). Baltimore, MD: Johns Hopkins University Press.

Stage, E. K., Kreinberg, N., Eccles, J. R., & Becker, B. J. (1985). Increasing the participation and achievement of girls and women in mathematics, science, and engineering. In S. S. Klein (Ed.), *Handbook for achieving sex equity through education* (pp. 237–269). Baltimore, MD: Johns Hopkins University Press.

Stanley, J. C., Benbow, C. P., Brody, L. E., Dauber, S., & Lupowski, A. E. (1991). Gender differences on eighty-six nationally standardized aptitude and achievement tests. In N. Colangelo, S. G. Assouline, & D. Ambroson (Eds.), *National Research Symposium on Talent Development* (pp. 42–65). Iowa City: University of Iowa Press.

Stumpf, H., & Klieme, E. (1989). Sex-related differences in spatial ability: More evidence for convergence. *Perceptual and Motor Skills, 69,* 915–921.

Subotnik, R. F., Duschl, R. A., & Selmon, E. H. (1991, April). *Retention and attrition of science talent: A longitudinal study of Westinghouse science talent search winners.* Paper presented at the biennial meeting of the Society for Research in Child Development, Seattle, WA.

Weiner, N. C., & Robinson, S. E. (1986). Cognitive abilities, personality and gender differences in math achievement of gifted adolescents. *Gifted Child Quarterly, 30,* 83–47.

APPENDIX:
SAMPLE ITEMS FROM THE SCHOOL AND COLLEGE ABILITY TEST, INTERMEDIATE LEVEL

(Instructions and items were taken verbatim from the test; Educational Testing Service, 1979, pp. 6–8.)

Each of the following questions has two parts. One part is Column A. The other part is Column B.

You must find out if one part is greater than the other, or if the parts are equal, or if not enough information is given for you to decide. Then, find the row of spaces on your answer sheet which has the same number as the question. In this row mark

A if the part in Column A is greater,

B if the part in Column B is greater,

C if the two parts are equal,

D if not enough information is given for you to decide.

Column A

1. The number p if $p + q = 1$
2. A number, if one-half of it is 4
3. 0.11

Column B

1. The number q if $p + q = 1$
2. 5
3. $^{10}/_{11}$

American Association of
University Women

ACHIEVEMENT AND PARTICIPATION:
WHAT DO THE DATA SHOW?

There is considerable evidence that girls earn higher grades than boys throughout their school careers. Test scores, however, because they measure all students on exactly the same material and are available nationally, are the measures most often used to discuss sex differences in achievement. The latest work on achievement differences presents a rather different picture than much of what has been reported and accepted in the past. The traditional wisdom that girls are better in verbal areas while boys excel in quantitative skills is less true today. Data indicate a narrowing of sex differences in tested achievement on a variety of measures. However, a narrowing of differences is not an absence of differences. Important insights can be gained by looking carefully at the continuing gender gaps in educational achievement and participation. Furthermore, research that looks at sex, race, ethnicity, and socioeconomic status reveals critical vulnerabilities among various groups of girls.

VERBAL SKILLS: LANGUAGE ARTS AND READING

Research does not entirely support the still-common assumption that girls do better in verbal areas than do boys. Almost twenty years ago Eleanor Maccoby and Carol Jacklin challenged the prevailing view that girls performed better than boys on verbal measures in their early years. However, researchers continued to document that girls outscored boys on tests of verbal ability starting at grade five or six. Recent work indicates that sex differences in verbal abilities have decreased markedly. Researchers completing a meta-analysis comparing earlier studies of verbal abilities with more recent research conclude: "There are not gender differences in verbal ability at least at this time, in American culture, in the standard ways that verbal ability has been measured."

Some researchers argue that girls do have certain verbal advantages but that these are not adequately measured by most tests. Furthermore, although

From American Association of University Women, *How Schools Shortchange Girls: A Study of Major Findings on Girls and Education* (American Association of University Women, 1992). Copyright © 1992 by The American Association of University Women Educational Foundation, 1111 16th Street, NW, Washington, DC 20036, (202) 785-7700. Reprinted by permission. Notes omitted.

boys have outscored girls on the verbal section of the Scholastic Achievement Test (SAT) since 1972, some suggest this may merely reflect the inclusion of more scientifically oriented items on which boys often perform better than do girls. An additional difficulty with the SAT is that test-takers are not a nationally representative sample; they are a self-selected group.

READING

A review of three representative surveys of reading skills indicates a mixed picture. In two major surveys—the National Assessment of Educational Progress (NAEP) and the National Education Longitudinal Survey (NELS)—girls perform better than boys on reading tests. In the High School and Beyond Survey (HSB), boys perform better than girls on reading and vocabulary tests. In all three surveys, the sex differences are very small.

NAEP is the most comprehensive survey of achievement. A congressionally mandated project of the National Center for Education Statistics (NCES), it measures the proficiency of nine-year-olds, thirteen-year-olds, and seventeen-year-olds in a variety of disciplines. In all age groups, girls have consistently received higher test scores in reading and writing since the 1970s. Since 1971, however, boys have made gains relative to girls, particularly in the seventeen-year-old group.

The NELS is a longitudinal survey of eighth-graders also being conducted under the auspices of NCES. The first wave of eighth-graders were interviewed and tested in 1988. Mean test scores for girls were higher than those for boys, although the difference was modest. Girls were less likely to score below "basic" and more likely to be rated as "advanced" when compared to boys. This sex difference is found for all racial and ethnic groups.

The HSB, also sponsored by NCES, is a longitudinal study of high school sophomores and seniors begun in 1980. Contrary to the other studies, boys consistently score better than girls on the HSB reading tests. This is true of sophomores and seniors, and for whites, blacks, and Hispanics. One possible explanation for the differences in these surveys is that sex differences narrow as children grow older. This would be consistent with the very small difference found for seventeen-year-olds in the NAEP and the gains boys make relative to girls in the follow-up of the HSB cohort.

Another explanation is that these differences may reflect differences in the tests given for each survey. The HSB tests were shorter and the NAEP tests much more comprehensive. This could prove to be another case where apparent sex differences may instead reflect test differences rather than differences in the test-takers knowledge or ability.

Even within the NAEP reading test, the performance of boys relative to girls varied, depending on the type of reading exercise. Boys did as well as girls on the expository passages and were most disadvantaged relative to girls in the literary passages. This is consistent with the finding that boys read more nonfiction than girls, and girls read more fiction than boys. This is also consistent with the finding that boys do slightly better than girls on other NAEP tests in subjects requiring good skills in expository reading and writing: civics, history, and geography.

If, as some suggest, boys regard fiction as more "feminine," any advantage girls experience relative to boys in the NAEP may reflect culturally defined biases against boys' reading certain kinds of material. It has been suggested that even if the small gender difference favoring girls is *statistically significant*, it may not be *educationally significant*. Boys still do better than girls in almost every other subject tested by NAEP, and the difference in reading scores appears to narrow and possibly even favor boys in older age groups.

Finally, it has also been argued that gender differences in reading favoring girls may be more pronounced among low-achieving or low-income students. This is particularly relevant given the recent heightening of concern about the education of low-income minority boys. An examination of achievement by race, sex, and social class is presented later in this section.

WRITING

Writing skills are tested less frequently. NAEP data do indicate that girls consistently outperform boys on writing-skills assessment. Smaller studies of particular populations do not always support these national findings. A seven-year longitudinal study comparing the development of written language skills of boys and girls from kindergarten through grade six found that—at least in the population studied—neither sex had an advantage over the other.

MATHEMATICS AND SCIENCE

The past fifteen years have seen an explosion of research on the relationship between gender and mathematics. While there has been less study on the linkage of gender and science there still is sufficient information to draw preliminary

conclusions. However, the usual cautions apply. Most of the research does not break down the data by both race/ethnicity and gender. Furthermore, the interactions of race/ethnicity and gender are rarely studied, and most conclusions based on predominantly white respondents cannot be generalized to women and girls of color.

Achievement in Mathematics. Gender differences in mathematics achievement are small and declining. Recent meta-analyses have found only very small differences in female and male performance in mathematics. Furthermore, meta-analyses comparing recent research with studies done in 1974 indicate a significant decline in gender differences. The High School and Beyond study of high school sophomores and seniors also shows that gender differences favoring boys in mathematics are declining.

Gender differences in mathematics do exist but are related to the age of the sample, how academically selective it is, and which cognitive level the test is tapping. Indeed these three variables were found to account for 87 percent of the variance in one meta-analysis. For example, no gender differences were found in the problem-solving ability of elementary- and middle-school girls and boys, but moderate to small differences favoring males emerged in high school. Large research studies support these results, finding no gender differences in math performance at age nine, minimal differences at age thirteen, and a larger difference favoring males at age seventeen. The most recent National Assessment of Educational Progress (NAEP) report finds few gender-related differences in math ability in grades four and eight other than a higher average proficiency in measurement and estimation for boys. However, by grade twelve males showed a small advantage in every content area except algebra.

Larger differences are found at the higher academic and cognitive levels. For example, an earlier NAEP report stated that 8.2 percent of the males but only 4.5 percent of the females were at the highest math levels, while 54 percent of the males and 48 percent of the females could do moderately complex procedures and reasoning. The college Board reports that males in 1988 scored an average of 37 points higher than females on the Level I Math Advanced Placement Test and 38 points higher on the Level II Math Advanced Placement Test. Another study revealed that nearly all differences in math performance between girls and boys at ages eleven and fifteen could be accounted for by differences among those scoring in the top 10–20 percent, with boys more often in the top-scoring groups. However, in classroom work, girls' math grades are as high or higher than boys'.

Gender differences on the SAT-Math have decreased, although they are still large. Between 1978 and 1988 female scores increased by eleven points while male scores increased by four points. However, males still outscored females 498 to 455. The Educational Testing Service does test a demographically matched sample of girls and boys on the Preliminary Scholastic Aptitude Test (PSAT) each year. From 1960 through 1983 gender differences in math from this group declined, although males still slightly outscored females.

A smaller body of research tying both gender and ethnicity to math achievement indicates that the patterns may differ for various groups. A study in Hawaii found non-Caucasian girls outperforming boys in math and outnumbering boys in the highest-achieving groups. Other studies have reported fewer gender differences in mathematics for minority students than for white students.

Gender differences in tests of spatial skills are also declining. For example, a large study found that girls and boys gained equally from instruction in spatial-visualization skills, despite initial differences.

The research results reported here must be examined in light of the achievement of all American students, female and male, in mathematics. An international assessment of the mathematics skills of thirteen-year-olds found United States students scoring below students in the other four countries and four Canadian provinces participating. Korean students had the highest average score (567.8), while the U.S. students scored 473.9. In addition, the most recent National Assessment of Educational Progress reports that more than a quarter of fourth-graders failed to demonstrate the ability to do arithmetical reasoning, and only 5 percent of high school seniors demonstrated the skills needed for high technology or college-level work.

Achievement in Science. Gender differences in science achievement are not decreasing and may be increasing. While no meta-analyses of studies linking gender and science achievement have been done, the National Assessment of Educational Progress does track science performance. Its results indicate that for nine- and thirteen-year-olds, gender differences in achievement increased between 1978 and 1986, due to the combination of a lag in performance for females and significant increases in the perfornance of males. According to the NAEP, gender differences in science achievement are largest for seventeen-year-olds, and these differences have not changed since 1978. The areas of largest male advantage are physics, chemistry, earth science, and space sciences.

In addition, gender differences exist at various levels of achievement. NAEP found only 5 percent of seventeen-year-old girls as compared to 10 percent of seventeen-year-old boys scoring at or above NAEP's "highest cognitive level," defined as students' ability to integrate specialized knowledge. Advanced placement (AP) test scores show a similar pattern. The Educational Testing Service reports that in 1988, males scored on average 29 points higher than females on AP biology tests. This, incidentally, was the only science area tested by ETS where gender differences declined; the spread between male and female test scores shrunk eleven points from the forty-point gap measured in 1981. Males also scored about fifty-six points higher than females on the 1988 AP physics tests. However, once again girls receive grades in science that are as high or higher than those of boys.

As with gender differences in mathematics achievement, gender differences in science should be looked at in a larger context. American students, both female and male, are not doing well in science. Their low levels of scientific knowledge, even at the factual level, have been documented in both national and international studies. One international assessment of the science skills of thirteen-year-olds found United States students placing ninth among the twelve nations and provinces participating.

Mathematics Participation. Gender differences in math-course participation are small, occur only in higher-level courses, and appear to be stable. In 1989 the National Science Board of the National Science Foundation reported that from 1982 to 1987, the average number of math credits that a male high school student received increased from 2.61 to 3.04. During the same time period, the average number of math credits that a female student received increased from 2.46 to 2.93. In 1982 males received .15 more math credits than females; in 1987, .11 more. The National Science Board found that approximately the same percentages of females and males took the same math courses up to calculus, which was taken by 7.6 percent of the boys but only 4.7 percent of the girls. The 1991 NAEP reports that for the District of Columbia and the thirty-seven states participating in the study "Up to Algebra III/Pre-Calculus and Calculus" there were no gender differences in either course-taking or average proficiency." These results are similar to the findings of a 1990 survey by the Council of Chief State School Officers.

Science Participation. Gender differences in the number of science courses students take are small. However, the pattern of course-taking differs, with girls being more apt to take advanced biology and boys being more apt to take physics and advanced chemistry. In 1989 the National Science Board of the National Science Foundation reported that from 1982 to 1987, the average number of science and computer-science credits a male high school student received increased from 2.25 to 2.69. During the same time period the average number of science credits a female student received increased from 2.13 to 2.57. In both 1982 and 1987, males received .12 more science credits than did females. Another study based on 1987 data reports young women taking .2 fewer science courses than young men (2.93 versus 3.13). Using 1988 data, the National Science Foundation reported girls taking an average of 3.1 science courses compared to boys' 3.3.

All three studies found approximately the same numbers of females and males taking Biology I and Chemistry I but more males taking physics. In 1987 the National Science Board reported 25.3 percent of the males but only 15 percent of the females took physics. This is, however, an improvement. In 1982, 18.2 percent of the males but only 10 percent of the females enrolled in physics.

These results are mirrored by a 1991 survey by the Council of Chief State School Officers. The survey reports that 60 percent of the students enrolled in first-year high school physics are male and that 70 percent of second-year physics students are male.

Career Plans. Gender differences show up in career plans as well....

High school girls, even those with exceptional academic preparation in math and science, are choosing math/science careers in disproportionately low numbers. A study of Rhode Island seniors found that 64 percent of the male students who had taken physics and calculus were planning to major in science or engineering in college compared to only 18.6 percent of the female students who had taken these courses.

Girls who do go on in scientific fields after high school report that the encouragement provided by their teachers is very important. One study reports that girls who went on to study engineer-ing felt that teachers encouraged them; unfortunately they also felt that counselors discouraged them. Clearly, differential treatment on the basis of sex contributes to the student choices reported here, but there are other factors as well.

Math and Science Influences. As they grow, girls and boys have different science experiences. Girls are more apt to be exposed to biology-related activities and less apt to engage in mechanical and electrical activities. One study found that by third grade, 51 percent of boys and 37 percent of girls had used microscopes, while by eleventh grade 49 percent of males and 17 percent of females had used an electricity meter. Gender differences in science-related activities may be reinforced in schools if children are allowed always to select science topics based on familiarity or interest.

Eighth-grade boys have been found to use more science instruments in class, particularly physical-science tools, such as power supplies. Although nine-year-old girls express interest in many science activities, they do not *do* as many as boys. This gender difference continues through ages thirteen and seventeen and is paralleled by an increasingly negative view of science, science classes, and science careers on the part of girls.

Gender differences in confidence are strongly correlated with continuation in math and science classes. Math confidence is the surety a student has of her or his ability to learn and perform well in mathematics. Math confidence has been found to be more highly correlated with math performance than any other affective variable.

Females, more than males, have been found to doubt their confidence in math. The Educational Testing Service reports that gender differences in perceptions of being good at math increase with age. Third-grade girls and boys think they are good in math in about the same percentages (64 percent versus 66 percent); by seventh grade, 57 percent of the girls agree, compared to 64 percent of the boys; by eleventh grade the gap widens to 48 percent of girls versus 60 percent of boys. In a classic study, researchers Elizabeth Fennema and Julia Sherman found a strong correlation between math achievement and confidence. Their research revealed a drop in both girls' math confidence and their achievement in the middle-school years. The drop in confidence *preceded* a decline in achievement.

One result of this diminished confidence is a lowering of the role that competence plays in girls' decisions about continuing in math and science. Researchers have found that competence is a more important prerequisite for the attainment of male career ambitions than it is for females. That is, females and males abandon math and science for different reasons. Males who drop out of math and science tend to do so because of a lack of competence—they cannot do the work; many females who drop out do so even though they can do the work.

Other researchers have also found that males are more apt than females to attribute their success to ability, while females are more apt to attribute failure to lack of ability. As boys get older, those who do not like math are more likely to attribute this feeling to the subject itself: they don't like math, they say, because it is "not useful." Girls, instead, interpret their problems with math as personal failures.

Concern about the difficulty or competitiveness of the field can also be an issue.

One study found that the perceived competitiveness of engineering was seen by girls as a major barrier to women entering the field. This finding is supported by research that shows girls who see themselves as highly competitive to be more interested in taking math and science courses than other girls. For boys, the degree of competitiveness is not related to interest in taking math and science.

While most students who dislike math do so because they consider it too hard, most students who dislike science say science is "not interesting." Adolescent girls are more likely than adolescent boys to find science uninteresting. Adolescent boys are more likely than girls to discount the importance of science itself.

In general, students' interest in and enthusiasm for math and science decline the longer they are in school. The poll commissioned by the American Association of University Women in 1990 found that all students' enthusiasm for math and science was greatest in the elementary years and dropped as they got older. However, losses for girls were larger than were those for boys.

In addition, males are more apt than females to envision themselves using math as adults. In assessing what factors they used to decide whether or not to continue math study, students listed the usefulness of math, followed by their confidence in their ability and their enjoyment of the subject.

Gender stereotyping also appears to influence whether girls persist in mathematics. Data from the National Assessment of Educational Progress indicate that girls who reject traditional gender roles have higher math achievement than girls who hold more stereotyped expectations. Moreover, girls in advanced math classes tend not to see math as a "male" subject.

Meta-analysis of affective variables associated with taking math courses indicate that gender differences are all small with the exception of the view of math as "something men do." Boys see math as very "male." A longitudinal study that tested students at sixth, eighth, tenth, and twelfth grades found that for girls a view of math as "male" was negatively correlated with math achievement at each grade level. This was the only affective variable for which consistent gender differences were found.

IMPLICATIONS

It is important that equal attention be given to both girls and boys in teaching reading and writing skills. The assumption that boys are in greater need of instruction in these areas should not be made. Furthermore, girls need particular encouragement to read more broadly in nonfiction areas and boys should be encouraged to read more fiction.

The gender gap is closing in math achievement but not in science achievement. Issues of gender and math have received more attention than issues of gender and science. Much of the work that has been done in science—beyond counting who is taking what courses—has been done in biology, a field in which there are many women, as opposed to physics, a field with very few women.

Since the growing gender gap in science is clearly related to males' climbing test scores, we need to ask why reforms in science education are apparently working for males and not for females. Just as the SAT-Math has been studied and found to underpredict women's achieve-ment, science tests need to be checked for bias as well.

Building on the work done in math, we need to study more fully the possible causes of the gender gap in the sciences. Particular emphasis should be placed on issues of confidence.

Once students satisfy math and science requirements for graduation and college admission, gender differences in science and math course-taking emerge. More students are taking more science and math, but at the advanced levels the gender gap remains constant. It appears that messages about math and science as critical assets for later employment have been somewhat successful, at least for middle-school students. However, while we have more girls taking more math and science, the numbers and percentages of girls interested in careers in math and science is increasing minimally, if at all. During senior high school and college, female students drop out of the math/science pipeline because they choose not to pursue scientific careers.

Changing the public images of physics and chemistry to reflect the diversity of these fields and the way they tie in to our everyday lives can provide more girls with the "inside information" that daughters of scientists appear to get. Meeting, getting to know, and working with scientists also reduces negative and intimidating stereotypes about the field. Providing students, especially girls, with more real-life experiences with science and scientists may make a big difference.

Teaching methods to decrease to eliminate the gender gaps in math and science already exist. Having students read and try out math and science problems before they are covered in class appears to narrow the "experience" gap between girls and boys, thus helping to reduce gender differences in class performance. Providing a structure in which all students answer questions, pose questions, and receive answers, rather than one that emphasizes target students or those who call out answers loudest, increases girls' opportunities and interest. Girls also respond well to special programs where they work cooperatively in a relaxed atmosphere where math is fun. Such programs significantly increase the number of math and science courses girls take. However, while hands-on experience is more successful than the lecture approach, such experiences must allow sufficient time and opportunities for girls to reach the same level of performance that teachers expect from boys.

Schools can learn much from out-of-school programs that encourage girls in math and science. Girls are not required to take special out-of-school programs. Designers of successful out-of-school math and science programs have learned how to get girls to attend and, more important, how to keep them interested so that they will keep on attending. We need to continue and expand programs like those developed by Girls, Incorporated; the Girl Scouts; and several AAUW [American Association of University Women] branches. These offer unique opportunities for girls to learn together to overcome stereotypes. What's more, such programs also act as laboratories for developing effective techniques to keep girls involved in math and science. We can't rely on these programs alone, however. Compared to the school system, they can reach only small numbers of girls for relatively short periods of time. Since all girls go to school and go for many years, we must focus most of our effort there, incorporating techniques that work for girls throughout our schools, and doing so in ways that continue to work for girls systemwide.

POSTSCRIPT

Are Boys Better in Math Than Girls?

Mills, Ablard, and Stumpf tested mathematical reasoning ability in children in grades two through six. They found that boys performed better than girls at all five grade levels. This particular study differed from previous studies in that gender differences were found as early as second grade. This had not been previously reported. The researchers also found that math ability differences were more evident in academically talented students.

The AAUW report concluded that an analysis of studies done since 1975 shows that gender differences in math achievement have narrowed. Gender differences that do exist depend on the ages of the students tested, how academically selective the sample is, and what cognitive level the test is tapping. Math achievement and ability are correlated with confidence. Girls report having less confidence in their math ability and thus do not perform as well on math tests. In addition, because there are fewer girls in advanced math classes, they are not exposed to the same type of math education as boys.

When girls have trouble in math, is it considered normal? Why is there controversy over girls being discriminated against in math when boys are more likely to make lower grades in most other subjects, more likely to be in special education classes, and more likely to drop out of school?

What difference does it make if girls and boys differ in math skills? Math ability paves the way for a variety of lucrative careers; could there be a feeling of superiority in being able to master the skills of mathematics? Could this feeling be generalized to other aspects of a person's life? Whether a difference in math achievement is real or perceived, children are being done a disservice if their potential for learning in any subject is not maximized.

SUGGESTED READINGS

Arbetter, S. (1991, December). Boys and girls: Equal but not the same. *Current Health, 18*, 16–17.

Bracey, G. (1994, January). Sex and math revisited. *Phi Delta Kappan, 75*, 417–418.

Byrnes, J., & Takahira, S. (1993). Explaining gender differences on SAT-math items. *Developmental Psychology, 29*, 805–810.

Felson, R., & Trudeau, L. (1991). Gender differences in mathematics performance. *Social Psychology Quarterly, 54*, 113–126.

Goulding, M. (1992, February 21). Let's hear it for the girls (assessment of girls' performance in mathematics). *Times Educational Supplement*, 38–39.

Nichols, R., & Kurtz, V. R. (1994, January). Gender and mathematics contests. *Arithmetic Teacher, 41*, 238–239.

Viadero, D. (1991, April 17). Math "gender gap" may be narrowing, researchers report. *Education Week, 10*, 1, 12.

ISSUE 10

Are Children in Self-Care at a Disadvantage?

YES: Sherryll Kraizer et al., from "Children in Self-Care: A New Perspective," *Child Welfare* (November/December 1990)

NO: John L. Woodard and Mark A. Fine, from "Long-Term Effects of Self-Supervised and Adult-Supervised Child Care Arrangements on Personality Traits, Emotional Adjustment, and Cognitive Development," *Journal of Applied Developmental Psychology* (January–March 1991)

ISSUE SUMMARY

YES: Child advocate Sherryll Kraizer and her colleagues found that children in self-care, so-called latchkey children, did not respond to dangerous situations safely.

NO: Professors John L. Woodard and Mark A. Fine conclude that, under appropriate circumstances, self-care can be a positive learning experience for children.

How old should a child be before being left at home alone? Twelve? Fifteen? Is seven or eight years of age too young to be left without supervision? Of course the answer to this question depends upon many considerations: How long will the parent be gone? How safe is the environment? What are the capabilities of the child? There is a big difference between leaving a capable eight-year-old at home alone while a parent runs to the corner grocery store and leaving a nine-year-old alone overnight while parents work.

Child development specialists agree that by age eleven, most children have the intellectual and emotional maturity to stay home without adult supervision for short periods of time—two or three hours. Yet, in some states, it is illegal for parents to leave children under thirteen at home alone, and parents who do are at risk of being reported for child abuse and neglect. Conversely, it is not uncommon for parents to leave children as young as six at home alone from the time they get out of school until the parents get home from work. There seems to be a disparity between social and legal policies and parental practices on this issue.

Our society expects parents to be responsible for their children. At the same time, current economics frequently necessitates a two-worker family income to live even modestly. This makes it especially difficult for single-parent families. The educational system operates as if there is always one parent at home. Schools are usually open from 8:00 or 8:30 A.M. until 2:30 or 3:00 P.M. Most jobs are scheduled from 8:00 A.M. to 5:00 P.M., which means that it is possible for children to be alone for approximately one hour in the morning to two or three hours in the afternoon. The U.S. Census Bureau reports that 2.1 million children 5 to 13 years of age care for themselves after school. Estimates vary as to what percentage of the school-age population this number represents. Some studies report that 7 percent of school children care for themselves, whereas other studies show that 25 percent of school-age children are in self-care.

Being left at home without adult care has been useful to some children, but studies also show that self-care can mean that children are left in risky and neglectful situations. In the following two selections, the benefits and disadvantages of children caring for themselves after school are debated.

YES

Sherryll Kraizer et al.

CHILDREN IN SELF-CARE:
A NEW PERSPECTIVE

The inability of families to provide continuous care to children is not a new phenomenon in the United States. Since the 1950s, the need for nonparental child care has accelerated at an intimidating pace. Continuing changes in social structure, including a large increase in the proportion of women in the nation's labor force, increasing numbers of children living in single-parent households, the rise in family mobility and the decline of the availability of the extended family, have led professionals and policy makers to consider what these changes mean to the welfare of our nation's children [Galambos and Garbarino 1983; Long and Long 1982; Grollman and Sweder 1986; Robinson et al. 1986].

Although we know that many families leave their children unsupervised, it is not known precisely how many children are left in self-care, how and/or why the choice is made, and what the effects of self-care on the development and safety of the children may be.

Current estimates of the number of children in self-care range from 7% to 25% of the nation's 29 million school-age children [Long and Long 1982; Hofferth and Cain 1987; U.S. Bureau of the Census 1987; Vandell and Corasaniti 1985]. These large discrepancies in incidence exist partly because of inconsistent definitions and because parents are reluctant to give out information about their child care methods.

Researchers have had difficulty in acquiring sample populations to study due to the informal and undefined nature of the self-care arrangement and the low profile of children left without supervision [Long and Long 1982; Rodman et al. 1985; Jones 1980]. Guilt, social stigma, and awareness on the part of parents that leaving their children unattended may appear irresponsible and is considered a form of neglect in most states, have prevented parents from reporting their child care methods accurately.

More important than incidence, and more difficult to determine, are the effects self-care arrangements have on children. Few empirical studies exist, but recent studies of the attributes of children in self-care in rural and suburban settings suggest that unsupervised children do not differ significantly

From Sherryll Kraizer, Susan Witte, George E. Fryer, Jr., and Thomas Miyoshi, "Children in Self-Care: A New Perspective," *Child Welfare*, vol. 69, no. 6 (November/December 1990). Copyright © 1990 by Transaction Publishers. Reprinted by permission.

from supervised children in terms of academic achievement and school adjustment [Galambos and Garbarino 1983; 1985; Vandell and Corasaniti 1985], locus of control and self-esteem [Rodman et al. 1985; Steinberg 1986], or peer relations [Vandell and Corasaniti 1985; Steinberg 1986]. In striking contrast, studies of urban children in self-care suggest that children at home alone often feel bored, lonely, isolated, and terrified [Long and Long 1982], and that they have lower academic achievement and social adjustment than supervised children [Woods 1972].

Although these studies are important first steps in defining and exploring this important social problem, they do not resolve most issues associated with children in self-care. The studies vary widely in methodology and findings, and are characterized by small sample sizes, nonprobability sampling, short-term rather than long-term timelines, and the use solely of pencil and paper measures of such dependent variables as academic achievement, social adjustment, and personality characteristics [Robinson et al. 1986].

In response to this lack of scientific data, more definitive study to determine causes, patterns, and consequences of self-care has been called for by child development and child welfare researchers [Galambos and Garbarino 1983; Robinson et al. 1986; Rodman et al. 1985]. Experts cite the need for progressive research "in context," comparing groups of children in self-care in terms of family demographics, family histories, frequency and duration of unsupervised time, presence of siblings, and home structure imposed by absent parents [Galambos and Garbarino 1983; Robinson et al. 1986; Rodman et al. 1985].

Bronfenbrenner [1979] has put forth a model that encourages exploration of variables that can distinguish subgroups and causal factors in child care decisions, including the systems and settings of the child in self-care, the interaction between the child and various environments, family composition, social demographic characteristics, family power dynamics, communication styles, and sex roles.

Recognition of the need for more definitive research builds on the principal contribution of latchkey research to date, which is the conclusion that a great many variables seem to affect the experience and vulnerability of the child in a self-care setting [Garbarino 1981; Galambos and Garbarino 1983, 1985; Robinson et al. 1986]. Garbarino [1981] notes:

> It is the premature granting of responsibility, particularly when it occurs in a negative emotional climate, that seems to be damaging. No social event affects all children or youth equally. Nearly all experiences are mediated by the quality and character of the family. Thus, we know that some kids will thrive on the opportunity of being a latchkey child. Others will just manage to cope. Still others will be at risk, and still others will be harmed. It is often difficult to separate the specific effects of the latchkey situation from the more general condition of the family.

Studies to date have not provided precise definitions of supervised and unsupervised environments, including clarification of the terms latchkey and self-care. Steinberg [1986] notes:

> The most important conclusion from [his] study is that variations within the latchkey population—variations in the setting in which self-care takes place, variations in the extent to which absent parents maintain distal supervision of

children, and variations in patterns of child rearing—are more important than are variations between adult care and self-care.

Finally, the most glaring omission in studies to date is the determination of vulnerability to child abuse and neglect when children are left in unsupervised settings. This article reports on a needs assessment and pilot study of risk to children, in kindergarten through grade 3, which dramatically highlights the need to study carefully the existing patterns of self-care and to develop resources responsive to need.

METHODOLOGY

To assess the need for programming to teach prevention skills to children in self-care, the authors conducted a needs assessment survey and piloted a behavioral simulation as a measure of risk. The combination of the survey and the behavioral simulation enabled a clearer and more valid assessment of self-care patterns with children ages five to nine years old than had previously been obtained.

The pivotal element of this study was the use of two self-care simulations that sought to extend the application of "measurable behavior" to evaluation of actual risk in a self-care situation [Fryer et al. 1987a, 1987b; Kraizer et al. 1988, 1989]. The simulations gave children a real-life opportunity to demonstrate behavioral skills on two tests associated with risk in self-care: answering the telephone and answering the door to a stranger trying to deliver a package.

Rural, urban, and suburban parents of 447 children were surveyed by telephone to determine patterns of self-care, if any. Virtually all the parents reported at first that they did not leave their children alone, but after describing to them the simulation that would be used to measure risk for children in self-care, the parents began to discuss their actual patterns of leaving children alone.

RESULTS OF SELF-CARE SURVEY

The authors found that 42% of the sample of 447 children (grades k–3) in rural, urban and suburban settings were left in self-care at least "occasionally," if not "regularly." It was apparent that as children got older, parents were more and more willing to leave them without supervision. Thus, the percentage of children left alone either occasionally or regularly in kindergarten was 28%, in first grade 37%, in second grade 45% and in third grade 77%. These figures far exceed any previously published estimates. The finding that 42% of the total sample of children were left alone occasionally or regularly was significant new information, and analysis by rural, urban and suburban groupings provided further insights.

Urban children were far more frequently left unattended occasionally at the kindergarten (k = 42%) and first grade level (1st = 45%) than were rural children (k = 21%, 1st = 25%) and suburban children (k = 25%, 1st = 22%). Urban children were also far more likely to be left along regularly, particularly in first (1st = 18%) and second grade (2nd = 19%) than rural children (1st = 8%, 2nd = 8%) and suburban children (1st = 5%, 2nd = 3%).

The finding that so many young urban children were left without supervision brings to mind many questions about the relationship of circumstance to risk

In the interviews, these parents were matter-of-fact and pragmatic about their care decisions. They said they had no alternatives and were "doing the best they could." They consistently noted the resources they had tried to make available for their children, usually a neighbor or relative in an adjoining apartment or house.

Suburban parents were less likely to leave children in regular self-care situations but were considerably more likely to leave them unattended for the "occasional" trip to the grocery store (3% regularly vs. 35% occasionally). This is an interesting finding because these parents do not perceive themselves as leaving their children alone and were therefore less likely to have discussed safety issues with them. More traditional alternatives to self-care, such as day care, were not considered relevant by those parents who left their children alone spontaneously. This leaving young children without supervision provides its own special challenge to policymakers precisely because it appears to be spontaneous.

Although rural parents cited the relative isolation of the rural setting and the inability of younger children to get to a neighbor quickly as the reason for not leaving children alone regularly, the percentage of rural children left alone as young as kindergarten age (k = 21%) for the occasional errand was comparable to that of the suburban children (k = 25%). This once again brings into play the parental perception that a "quick trip" somehow puts children at less risk than does regular self-care.

ASSESSMENT OF RISK: BEHAVIORAL SIMULATION PILOT

Following the needs assessment portion of the study, and with parental permission and cooperation, the behavioral simulations were piloted with 16 children (human subjects' approval was obtained). Parents were contacted by telephone to establish a prearranged 15-minute block of them when their child would normally be home alone. During this 15-minute period, a member of the research team conducted the following simulations:

Telephone call: Call the children and ask to speak with their mother or father. Ask the children their name. Ask to leave a message and do so.

The optimal response in this situation is for the children to say that their mother or father cannot come to the phone, and that they would like to take a message. At no point should the children give their name.

The actual response of each child was recorded in detail. For example, the children may reveal that they are home alone, refuse to give their name but take a message, or simply not answer the telephone.

Package delivery: Go to each child's home, knock on the door. If the child opens the door, deliver the package for the parent and leave. If the child asks, through the door, "Who is it?" say, "I have a package for your mother (or father)." If the child opens the door, deliver the package and leave. If the child does not open the door, say "I'll drop by another time," or put the package where instructed by the child and leave.

The optimal response in this situation is that the child would go to the door, say, "Who is it?" without opening the door, and then handle the request. For example, "My mother can't come to the door right now, please leave the package on the porch."

Once again, the actual response of each child was recorded in detail. For example, the child may open the door and take the package, not respond to the knock, or respond to the individual without opening the door and handle the request without revealing that she or he is home alone.

RESULTS OF SIMULATIONS

Although these simulations were extremely time and labor intensive, they were invaluable for assessing actual risk. Only two of the 16 children performed well on the telephone portion of the simulation, handling the call properly. All other children readily engaged in conversation with the evaluator, offering information including their name and that they were at home alone.

None of the children handled the package delivery portion of the simulation effectively. Thirteen of the 16 children opened the door and took the package, leaving themselves at risk to whoever the adult at the door happened to be. Two pretended they were not home (this increases the risk to the child in the event of illegal entry once a perpetrator believes no one is home), and one, who was playing in the street, walked up to announce that his parents weren't home and he'd be happy to take the package. In this particular case, the child had been instructed not to leave the house and his mother was unaware that he played outside. Other parents, in the debriefing interview, constantly expressed surprise at their child's performance on the simulation. Not one of them had expected the child would open the door and take the package.

Although the sample in this pilot is small, the findings are compellingly clear. At the very least, these children are at risk, vulnerable to individuals from the outside. And it must be anticipated that they are also at risk in other ways. If parents have not prepared their children to handle telephone calls and people at the door, we must question their preparation for other problems, including emergencies.

In addition, the striking difference between the parents' expectation of their child's performance on the simulations and the actual performance of the child tells us that parents are not realistically assessing their children's ability to handle even the most common occurrences.

The number of children participating in the pilot of the simulations was substantially smaller than expected. Completion of the simulation protocol took over two hours per participant. The survey calls with parents became quite lengthy because they discussed not only their care arrangements but also their reasons for these arrangements, as well as other concerns about self-care. Arranging the simulation at a time when the child would be alone and the parents could expect that the simulation would take place often required several scheduling attempts. The simulation involved going to the vicinity of the child's home, making the telephone call, then making the delivery effort. Follow-up calls were also lengthy; parents wanted to talk about their surprise that their child had failed to handle the simulation properly, and to learn what steps they could take to prepare their child more adequately for future self-care. Researchers wishing to replicate or follow up on these findings should not underestimate the considerable time and resources that must be committed to each participant.

DISCUSSION

The results of this initial effort demand that we take a closer look at the thinking of parents and their children, the resources available to them, and the process by which so many families come to leave very young children without supervision and without adequate training to minimize risk.

Further research is needed to identify causal factors and patterns clearly, to formulate interventions, and to assess more fully the actual risks to children left without supervision. A preliminary assessment of need, as reported here, has been accomplished. The findings lay the groundwork for a more comprehensive and detailed analysis of need that would yield quantifiable data and establish operational definitions from which to shape future policy and initiatives.

The following are questions the authors recommend for further study:

1. What are the identifiers for families who leave young children without supervision?
2. What is the actual level of risk to these children in terms of outside elements, such as perpetrators and emergency situations, and to their personal well-being, considering effects such as fear, anxiety, and self-esteem?
3. What alternatives exist or could be provided within the framework of the realities these parents face, including economics, transportation, quality of care, and so on?
4. What role can the school system play in providing preventive education and alternatives to "regular" before- and after-school self-care?

With a thorough analysis of the causes of self-care, including characteristics of the child, family, and community, policymakers will have the information they need to make policy decisions, formulate community objectives, implement educational programs, and enhance family resources.

Communities will have a solid basis for reviewing existing resources, establishing new options and increasing accessibility of services to those families with the highest-risk profiles. By identifying patterns of self-care, community planners will be able to target populations. For example, parents who say "My kids are never left alone," when, in fact, they *are* left alone while parents make the occasional run to the grocery store, will not be moved by public service campaigns that urge parents to choose supervised day care over self-care. These parents must be addressed in such a way that they are able to see that occasional risk is still risk. Different approaches must be made to parents who leave their children in self-care because they are uninformed, or have no transportation, or because children say the after-school care program is boring. Schools will have both a real picture of the need in their community and a blueprint for action. The findings would enable them to make their own recommendations for educational intervention and for public and private support to create alternatives to self-care, such as establishing after-school programs within the school.

The assessment of need and risk reported here offers new insights, but the short- and long-term consequences of unsupervised care are still not clear. Prevention programs and initiatives responsive to actual need can evolve once an accurate picture of what is actually happening in American homes is available. Only when we full understand how care patterns evolve can there be an effective national policy that enables families to reduce risk to children.

REFERENCES

Bronfenbrenner, Urie. The Ecology of Human Development: Experiences by Nature and Design. Cambridge, MA: Harvard University Press, 1979.

Fryer, George E.; Kraizer, Sherryll; and Miyoshi, Thomas. "Measuring Actual Reduction of Risk to Child Abuse: A New Approach." Child Abuse and Neglect 11, 2 (1987a): 173–180.

___. "Measuring Children's Retention of Skills to Resist Stranger Abduction: Use of the Simulation Technique." Child Abuse and Neglect 11, 2 (1987b): 181–186.

Galambos, Nancy, and Garbarino, James. "Identifying the Missing Links in the Study of Latchkey Children." Children Today 12, 4 (July–August 1983): 2–4.

___. "Adjustment of Unsupervised Children in a Rural Ecology." Journal of Genetic Psychology 146, 2 (June 1985): 227–231.

Garbarino, James. "Latchkey Children: How Much a Problem?" Education Digest 46, 6 (February 1981): 14–16.

Grollman, Earl, and Sweder, G. The Working Parent Dilemma: How to Balance the Responsibilities of Children and Careers. Boston, MA: Beacon Press, 1986.

Hofferth, Sandra, and Cain, Virginia. Study Findings Presented at the Population Association of America Meeting, National Institute of Child Health and Human Development, Bethesda, MD, 1987.

Jones, L. R. "Child Care: Who Knows? Who Cares?" Journal of the Institute for Socioeconomic Studies 5 (January 1980): 55–62.

Kraizer, Sherryll; Witte, Susan; and Fryer, George E. "Preventing Child Sexual Abuse: Measuring Actual Behavioral Change Attributable to a School-Based Program." Children Today 18, 5 (September–October 1989): 23–27.

Kraizer, Sherryll; Fryer, George E.; and Miller, Marilyn. "Programming for Preventing Sexual Abuse and Abduction: What Does It Mean When It Works?" CHILD WELFARE LXVII, 1 (January–February 1988): 69–78.

Long, Lynette, and Long, Thomas. "Latchkey Children: The Child's View of Self-Care." Washington, DC: Catholic University of America (ERIC Document Reproduction Service No. ED 211 229), 1982.

Robinson, Bryan E.; Rowland, Bobbie H.; and Coleman, Mick. Latchkey Kids/Unlocking Doors for Children and their Families. Lexington, MA: D. C. Heath and Co., 1986.

Rodman, Hyman; Pratto, David J.; and Nelson, Rosemary S. "Child Care Arrangements and Children's Functioning: A Comparison of Self-Care and Adult-Care Children." Developmental Psychology 21, 3 (May 1985): 413–418.

Steinberg, Laurence. "Latchkey Children and Susceptibility to Peer Pressure: An Ecological Analysis." Developmental Psychology 22, 4 (July 1986): 433–439.

U.S. Bureau of the Census. "After-School Care of the School-Age Child." Current Population Reports, Series p-23, No. 149 (January 1987).

Vandell, Deborah L., and Corasaniti, Mary Anne. After-School Care: Choices and Outcomes for Third Graders. Paper presented at the meeting of the American Association for Advancement of Science, Los Angeles, May 27, 1985.

Woods, M. B. "The Unsupervised Child of the Working Mother." Developmental Psychology 6, 1 (January 1972): 14–25.

NO

John L. Woodard and Mark A. Fine

LONG-TERM EFFECTS OF SELF-SUPERVISED AND ADULT-SUPERVISED CHILD CARE ARRANGEMENTS ON PERSONALITY TRAITS, EMOTIONAL ADJUSTMENT, AND COGNITIVE DEVELOPMENT

This study investigated long-term effects of being in a "latchkey" or self-supervised child care situation compared with being in an adult-supervised arrangement. Data on former child care arrangements and several measures of cognitive development, emotional adjustment, and the personality traits of dominance, responsibility, and achievement via independence were collected from 248 college students. Students who reported having been in adult care did not differ from students who regularly cared for themselves during out-of-school hours on any of the dependent measures, which concurs with previous findings on short-term effects of the self-care arrangement. Age at which the self-care situation was initiated, and gender, individually and collectively, failed to predict outcome on any dependent measure. These results suggest that children are resilient to short-term separation from their parents and may be able to structure their time constructively during out-of-school hours.

Among the various forms of child care available to American families, perhaps none is more controversial than the "latchkey" or self-supervised situation (Rodman & Pratto, 1980), that is, allowing a child to care for himself/herself during out-of-school hours. The potential effects of the latchkey situation may have considerable impact on a large number of children. According to the U.S. Bureau of the Census (1987), there were 28.9 million children aged 5 to 13 who were enrolled in school in December of 1984. Although all of these children may potentially enter into a latchkey situation

From John L. Woodard and Mark A. Fine, "Long-Term Effects of Self-Supervised and Adult-Supervised Child Care Arrangements on Personality Traits, Emotional Adjustment, and Cognitive Development," *Journal of Applied Developmental Psychology*, vol. 12, no. 1 (January–March 1991), pp. 73–85. Copyright © 1991 by Ablex Publishing Corporation. Reprinted by permission.

at some point, approximately 2.1 million children 13 years of age and under *regularly* care for themselves after school (U.S. Bureau of the Census, 1987).

Vandell and Corasaniti (1988) speculated about potential effects that a latchkey situation may have on a child's academic, emotional, social, and behavioral development. Within the academic domain, a latchkey child may have poorer grades and standardized test scores because of the absence of direct adult supervision relative to nonlatchkey children. With respect to the emotional sphere, a latchkey child may spend more time alone, resulting in augmented feelings of loneliness, sadness, fearfulness, and isolation. Diminished opportunities for social interaction, which may be present in a latchkey arrangement, may inhibit the ability of these children to develop adequate social skills. Finally, the lack of direct adult supervision may result in an increase in conduct difficulties and a decrease in the effectiveness of discipline. In contrast to this grim scenario, Vandell and Corasaniti pointed out that the latchkey situation may alternatively provide the child with a chance to engage in and rehearse mature, responsible behavior that may be subsequently reinforced by parents.

Despite the potential impact that self-care arrangements may have on psychological function, surprisingly little research has addressed this issue. The few studies which have investigated possible outcomes of the latchkey situation have yielded inconsistent findings. One possible reason for these problems may be difficulty in operationalizing the concept of the latchkey child. Not all self-care arrangements are alike, and there are a number of variables that should be taken into account when examining

the social and psychological development of the latchkey child. The age of the child at the time the self-care arrangement is initiated, the duration of the arrangement (both in terms of number of months or years and number of hours per week), the presence or absence of older siblings, the quality of parent–child relationships, parental attitude toward the arrangement, and whether the self-care arrangement was selected voluntarily (because of confidence in the child's competence) or involuntarily (due to financial constraints), have been proposed as important factors to consider in evaluating the overall effects of self-care on the child (Cole & Rodman, 1987; Etaugh, 1980; Rodman, Pratto, & Nelson, 1985). Because of the numerous variables which appear to be relevant in conceptualizing what is meant by a self-care arrangement, the exact nature of the impact of such an arrangement on children has been very difficult to evaluate.

Past research, which focused on immediate effects of the latchkey situation, occasionally suggested that adverse results are associated with allowing children to care for themselves. However, some of these studies have various methodological flaws. For instance, Woods (1972) assessed 108 fifth-grade black children from a low-income socioeconomic group on measures of personality and social adjustment, academic achievement, IQ, and rates for accidents, illnesses, and delinquency. Twelve out of 106 comparisons between self-care and adult-care children were significant beyond the $p < .05$ level, 11 of which were in the hypothesized direction. Woods concluded that children from a self-care arrangement (especially girls) had lower IQ scores, lower achievement scores, and were less socially adjusted than their adult-care counterparts.

However, Woods's conclusions must be questioned in light of the large number of comparisons that were made without adjustment for experimentwise Type 1 error rate and the potential for capitalization on chance.

Long and Long (1982) interviewed 85 first- through sixth-grade black children from an urban setting using a semistructured interview schedule. A number of areas were examined, including the degree of fear expressed by the children, the frequency of nightmares, and the adequacy of parental instructions for self-care for the children. Although their results were not based on the children's responses to standardized questions, and may have been subject to interviewer bias and/or inadequate precision in measuring the constructs of interest, the investigators concluded that latchkey children reported a greater degree of fear and a higher frequency of nightmares than children under continuous adult supervision.

In a more recent study, Diamond, Kataria, and Messer (1989) reported a pilot study that evaluated prevalence of the latchkey arrangement, as well as academic performance and behavior characteristics of latchkey children. Forty-four fifth and sixth graders from a rural setting served as subjects. The authors did not report socioeconomic status (SES) or race. Three groups were formed: (1) latchkey children who remained alone or with younger siblings for at least 2 hours per day after school for at least 1 year; (2) semilatchkey children who returned home to the presence of an older sibling under 17 years of age and/or were unsupervised fewer than 2 hours per day and/or were unsupervised fewer than 5 days per week; (3) nonlatchkey children who returned home

from school each day to an adult figure who was at least 17 years of age. Using the California Achievement Test, Youth Self-Report (Achenbach & Edelbrock, 1987), and Teacher's Report Form of the Child Behavior Checklist (Achenbach & Edelbrock, 1986), the authors generally found few differences between the groups. The most salient finding was that latchkey boys had the most parent-acknowledged and self-acknowledged behavior problems and a nonsignificant trend toward lower academic achievement. However, the authors interpreted these findings cautiously in light of the small sample size employed.

In contrast to the studies citing negative effects of self-care, the majority of studies in this area reveal no significant differences between children from self-care situations and those from adult-care arrangements. Gold and Andres (1978a) sampled low and middle SES, 10-year-old white children from suburbs of a large Canadian city and measured personality and social adjustment, academic achievement, and sex role concept. No significant differences between latchkey and nonlatchkey children were obtained. Similar findings were obtained in a separate study that sampled low and middle SES, 14- to 16-year-old white children from the same area, using the same dependent measures (Gold & Andres, 1978b).

Galambos and Garbarino (1983) examined 77 low and middle SES, fifth- and seventh-grade white children from a rural area of New York State. Again, no significant differences emerged between self-care and adult-care children on: (1) the AML Behavior Rating Scale (Cowen et al., 1973), a measure of school adjustment; (2) Stanford Achievement Test score, a measure of academic achievement; and (3) the Scale of Intrinsic versus Extrinsic Orientation in the Classroom (Harter, 1981). Rodman et al. (1985) studied 48 pairs of children, matched on the basis of age, sex, race, family composition (one parent vs. two parents), and SES. No significant differences between the self-care group and the adult-care group were detected on the Coopersmith Self-Esteem Inventory (Coopersmith, 1967), the Personal Reaction Survey (Nowicki & Strickland, 1973), or social adjustment and interpersonal relations as measured by the Behavior Rating Form (Coopersmith, 1967).

Finally, Vandell and Corasaniti (1988) sampled 150 white, middle-class, suburban third graders and examined the relation between types of after-school care and social, academic, and emotional functioning. When comparing latchkey and adult-care children, no differences were found with respect to peer evaluations, academic grades, standardized test score, teacher's evaluation of conduct, parent and teacher ratings of social, emotional, and academic functioning, or self-ratings. However, children who attended day-care centers had significantly lower peer evaluations, lower academic grades, and lower standardized test scores than either latchkey or nonlatchkey children. It should also be noted that a number of studies compared cognitive development and emotional adjustment of children of working and nonworking mothers (cf. Etaugh, 1980; Hoffman, 1979), and generally found numerous *positive* benefits of maternal employment for lower SES families, and mixed results for children from middle- and upper-income families. However, it is important to note that there is no indication of whether children in these stud-

ies are under self-supervision or adult supervision.

Steinberg (1986) proposed that the type of *behavior* in which the self-care child engages after school (e.g., going directly home, going to a friend's house in the absence of adult supervision, or "hanging out" with friends) is an important variable for identifying potentially adverse effects of a self-care situation. Steinberg tested this hypothesis on a sample of fifth, sixth, eighth, and ninth graders using susceptibility to peer pressure as the outcome construct of interest. No differences emerged between children from adult-care and self-care situation. However, within the self-care group, Steinberg found that the more removed the children were from adult supervision, the more susceptible they were to peer pressure to engage in antisocial activity. Steinberg concluded that the proximity of adult supervision is a particularly relevant variable.

In summary, most studies suggested that there are no differences between latchkey and nonlatchkey children on a variety of measures. However, it is important to note that each of these studies did not operationalize the latchkey situation in exactly the same way. This raises the question of whether these previous studies are directly comparable. The lack of consensually adopted criteria to define the latchkey situation, and conflicting findings regarding the effects of the self-care arrangement, have been particularly vexing at this early stage of research. In addition, few studies examined a sample from the middle to upper SES range; much of the past research in this area focused on subjects from the lower SOS range. Related to this point is the fact that studies involving white children have found few significant differences between latchkey and non-latchkey children, whereas studies of black latchkey children have found more negative effects. This trend suggests that racial/cultural differences may play an important role in the latchkey experience. Finally, to date, no studies have investigated potential long-term consequences of self-care arrangements.

The purpose of this study is to address some of the shortcomings in the literature from the perspective of potential long-term (adverse or positive) effects of being in a latchkey situation. First, individuals who formerly experienced a self-care situation were compared with individuals from adult-care arrangements to determine if differences would emerge on measures of cognitive development, academic achievement, emotional adjustment, self-esteem, and personality traits (responsibility, dominance, and achievement via independence). These three personality constructs were chosen because they are often cited in the literature as characteristics which may be influenced by the self-care situation.

A second focus of this study was to determine the extent to which gender, and age at which self-supervision was initiated, could predict outcome among individuals who experienced the latchkey arrangement. A significant relationship between the predictors and the outcome variables could further understanding of the impact of the latchkey child care arrangement. Given the lack of research in this area and conflicting research findings, it is premature to generate hypotheses regarding the nature of the expected relationships.

METHOD

Subjects

Subjects were 260 introductory psychology students at a large, private, midwestern university. In order to establish whether subjects had experienced a latchkey arrangement, the following question was asked on a demographic questionnaire, "During elementary school, junior high school, or high school, did you ever *regularly* come home from school to the absence of direct adult supervision?" If the subject answered "yes" to this question, he/she indicated the age at which this arrangement began. Following the recommendation of Rodman et al. (1985), subjects who indicated that they returned home from school to an empty house, or to younger siblings between the ages of 6 and 13, were classified as having experienced a latchkey arrangement. Next, for each of three periods (elementary school, Grades K–6; junior high school, Grades 7–9; high school, Grades 10–12), subjects were asked to indicate: (1) who was *usually* home when they got home from school; (2) the number of days per week not under direct adult supervision; (3) the number of hours per day not under direct adult supervision; and (4) whether one or both parents were employed during this period. There was a disproportionate number of white participants in the sample; therefore, all nonwhite participants were dropped from the study to render the sample more racially homogeneous. This manipulation yielded a sample size of 248.

Subjects were grouped according to whether their child care situation was self-care (21 males, 38 females) or adult-care (85 males, 104 females). The mean age of onset of the latchkey arrangement was 12.8 years of age ($SD = 2.6$). The mean age of all participants was 18.9 years ($SD = 0.8$ years). All groups were comparable in SES according to Hollingshead's (1977) four-factor index.

The majority of individuals came from intact families. Of the 27 subjects coming from nonintact families, 17 had experienced their parents' separation due to divorce, and 10 reported the death of one parent. There was a significant association between child care arrangement and parents' marital status (X^2 (2, $N = 248$) = 13.19, $p < .002$. Cramer's $V = 0.231$): Approximately half of the subjects from nonintact families reported having participated in self-care, compared to only 20% of the subjects from intact families. Subjects from intact families came predominantly from single-provider families during the elementary school years, although there was a substantial shift toward dual-provider families in the junior high and high school years. In addition, there was also a statistically significant association between being in a self-care situation and coming from a dual-provider family.

Instrumentation

All subjects completed the following five self-report instruments:

1. A short demographic questionnaire was used to identify gender, age, race, grade-point average (GPA), number and gender of siblings, community size, socioeconomic and occupational status of the subject's parents, and the latchkey status of the subject.

2. *The Quick Test* (Ammons & Ammons, 1962). The Quick Test is a brief test designed to provide an estimate of general intelligence. Traub & Spruill (1982) reported a Pearson

correlation of .64 between Quick Test scores and Wechsler Adult Intelligence Scale-Revised (WAIS–R) full-scale IQ scores. A number of other studies (Joesting & Joesting, 1972; Ogilvie, 1965; Pless, Snider, Eaton, & Kearsley, 1965; Violato, White, & Travis, 1984) supported its use as a valid measure of global intelligence.

3. *Coopersmith Self Esteem Inventory–Adult Form (SEI);* (Coopersmith, 1967). The 25-item adult form of the Coopersmith SEI was employed as a measure of self-esteem. Correlations of .59–.60 between the SEI short form and the Rosenberg (1965) scale for college students have been reported (*Manual for the Coopersmith Self-Esteem Inventory,* 1981). Bedeian, Geagud, & Zmud (1977) reported test–retest reliability coefficients of .80 for men and .82 for women.

4. *California Psychological Inventory (CPI)–Dominance (Do), Responsibility (Re) and Achievement via independence scales (Ai)* (Gough, 1975). These three scales were used to provide measures of the constructs of dominance, independence, and responsibility. Hase and Goldberg (1967) reported that short-term test–retest reliabilities of the CPI scales range between .71–.90 ($M = .83$). The individual scales of the CPI have also been subjected to extensive validation as measures of various personality traits (Groth-Marnat, 1984).

5. *Symptom Checklist 90–Revised (SCL-90–R;* Derogatis, 1983). This 90-item multidimensional self-report inventory measures an individual's perceived degree of psychological distress. Only the Global Severity Index (GSI) was used as a measure of emotional maladjustment in this study, as

Derogatis claimed that the GSI provides the most sensitive single measure of psychological distress on the SCL–90–R. Extensive evidence supporting the reliability and validity of the GSI and SCL–90–R is provided in Derogatis (1983).

Procedure

Testing was performed in groups of approximately 25. Subjects were initially asked to fill out the demographic questionnaire. Next, the Quick Test, SEI, and CPI scales were administered in a counterbalanced fashion for each group of subjects. The SCL–90–R was administered last, due to the emotional and symptomatic content of the items. When the material was collected, subjects received a description of the study and an invitation to ask further questions. Testing sessions ranged in length from 75 to 90 minutes.

RESULTS

Preliminary analyses of variance (ANOVAs) for each of the seven dependent measures revealed no significant interaction effects between the variables of interest (gender and group membership), and (a) marital status of the parents (intact, marital separation due to divorce, or marital separation due to death of one parent); (b) working status of the parents (single provider or dual-provider family); and (c) population of the community in which the subjects lived prior to college (large city, 1 million or more; suburb of large city; medium city, 100,000–999,999; suburb of medium city; small city, 25,000–99,999; suburb of small city; other urban area, 10,000–24,999; rural town, 5,000–10,000; rural village or farming community, 4,999 and below; or other rural area).

Therefore, the data were collapsed over these control variables.

Multivariate analyses of variance (MANOVAs) were performed in order to compare individuals from self-care arrangements with those from adult-care situations. The constructs of: (a) cognitive development (Quick Test score and college GPA); (b) emotional adjustment (SEI score and overall GSI); and (c) personality development (scores on the *Re*, *Do*, and *Ai* subscales from the CPI) were examined separately. Each analysis tested for the main effects of gender, group, and for their interaction. The regression approach to partitioning the sums of squares was selected. In this approach, each effect is adjusted for all other effects in the model and is appropriate when cell frequencies are unequal (Norusis, 1985). Table 1 depicts the means and standard deviations for each of the four groups. There were no significant ($p < .05$) effects for group, or for the group by gender interaction on any of the three sets of comparisons.

Relationship Between Mediating Variables and Outcome in Self-Care Children

It was also of interest to determine whether gender, age at which the latchkey situation was initiated, or an interaction between these variables could predict outcome on any of the seven dependent measures. To address this issue, a hierarchical multiple-linear regression analysis was then performed for each of the seven outcome measures.

Two sets of variables were entered sequentially into each of the regression equations. The first set contained two variables: gender, and age at which the latchkey situation was initiated. The second set of variables contained the

Table 1
Scores of Self-Care Individuals Versus Adult-Care Individuals on Dependent Measures Broken Down by Gender

| | Self-Care | | | | Adult-Care | | | |
| | Males N = 21 | | Females N = 38 | | Males N = 85 | | Females N = 104 | |
Test	M	SD	M	SD	M	SD	M	SD
CPI-*Do*	27.38	3.72	26.76	4.19	26.87	3.94	26.73	4.66
CPI-*Re*	24.76	4.55	24.41	5.44	25.05	4.64	27.08	4.82
CPI-*Ai*	18.14	3.35	18.03	4.21	18.37	3.71	18.64	3.99
Quick								
Test	130.01	16.59	123.16	16.97	119.72	17.73	123.01	16.82
GPA	2.82	0.43	2.89	0.49	2.72	0.57	2.76	0.57
GSI	0.89	0.47	1.12	0.60	1.08	0.52	0.96	0.50
SEI	76.57	16.16	68.63	21.42	74.45	16.16	75.65	19.32

interaction of the two variables described above. No significant interaction effects or main effects were obtained for any of the seven outcome measures. Therefore, none of the predictors was effective in predicting any of the outcome variables.

DISCUSSION

In summary, long-term differences in cognitive development, emotional adjustment, and personality development did not emerge between the self-care and adult-care individuals in this study. This finding concurs with previous studies which found no short-term differences between self-care and adult-care children on similar dependent measures (Galambos & Garbarino, 1983; Gold & Andres, 1978a, 1978b; Rodman et at., 1985; Steinberg, 1986). The absence of detectable long-term differences between self-care and adult-care individuals on global cognitive, affective, and personality indices suggests that self-care, in general, may not be as detrimental as previously imag-

ined, at least for those individuals who later go on to college. There are several possible explanations for this finding. First, it may be that children are generally resilient to short-term separations from their parent(s). As long as children are aware that parents will return home shortly and are available in the case of emergency, they may not experience the potential fear and sense of isolation that Vandell and Corasaniti (1988) discussed. The absence of group differences on the dependent measures based on the age at which the latchkey arrangement was initiated suggests that children between the ages of 6 to 13 years may be developmentally capable of structuring their own time for short periods. This possibility may partially explain racial and SES differences reported in the literature, as middle to upper SES and white children may have more "enriched" home environments than their lower SES counterparts (Bouchard & Segal, 1985). The enriched home environments, possibly including educational videotapes and/or computers, for example, may provide more opportunity for children to structure time for themselves.

A second explanation for the lack of clear group differences is that differences among various self-care arrangements may actually exist and could potentially be a worthwhile focus for future study. According to Steinberg (1986), such differences may include degree of parent-child telephone contact, proximity of adult neighbors, or formality and rehearsal of rules and procedures with which the child must be familiar in the absence of adult supervision. In addition, the operational definition used in this study was relatively broad. Future studies with more specific criteria for differentiating self-supervision from adult supervision may find differences between these two groups by reducing the heterogeneity of the sample. Although no differences were observed on general measures of emotional adjustment and cognitive and personality development, differences within the self-care group may emerge on more specific or behaviorally oriented measures.

An attempt was made to examine the effects of potential sources of variation within the self-care arrangement by looking for a relationship between outcome measures, and age at which the arrangement commenced, and gender. The absence of any significant relationships between predictor and outcome variables suggests that the effect of the self-care experience on the outcome measures is likely to be relatively heterogeneous in nature. Such a finding points toward the need to focus on other variables that could potentially account for this heterogeneity, enabling practitioners and parents to identify children for whom this form of child care may be particularly

detrimental. Previous research, and this study, have not yet been successful in identifying such relevant variables. Future research might fruitfully examine the potency of those (previously described) effects identified by Steinberg (1986).

One limitation to this study is that it relies on retrospective reports to determine latchkey status and duration of the latchkey arrangement. Halvorsen (1988) criticized the use of such information because it is difficult to trust peoples' memories without corroborating objective evidence. Ross and Conway (1986) also noted that adults tend to recall memories of complex events inaccurately. Thus, retrospective data tends to be biased and distorted, particularly with complex events. However, McCrae and Costa (1988) argued that memory for broad patterns of behavior is less susceptible to such distortions. Although this study is not immune to the potential flaws inherent in the use of retrospective data, it is directed toward recollection of general facts (i.e., who was usually home when the subject returned from school), which are likely to be recalled more accurately than more complex information (i.e., what did the subject usually do after school). Indeed, more detailed information requested in this study, such as number of hours per day and number of days per week of self-care, is more likely to be susceptible to retrospective bias: subjects were generally less able to provide this information consistently compared with the more general facts requested by the demographic questionnaire. In addition, it has been argued that an individual's perceptions of events may be as important as the objective accuracy of the actual incidents (McCrae & Costa, 1988) as reactions to situations are necessarily based upon subjective appraisals of their meaning.

Rodman, Pratto, and Nelson (1988) discussed the difficulties inherent in the operationalization of what is meant by "a latchkey child." A consensually adopted definition is necessary both to avoid confusion and to evaluate more reliably the effects of such arrangements. Moreover, a reliable definition will likely be used by parents, practitioners, and policymakers to make decisions regarding the best form of after-school care for a particular child. Although previous studies, and this study, have employed rather broad definitions of the latchkey situation (e.g., a child between the ages of 6 and 13 who comes home regularly to the absence of direct adult supervision), there is a trend in the literature toward using more narrow definitions (cf. Diamond et at., 1989; Rodman et at., 1985, 1988). There are advantages and disadvantages to each approach. Although it is usually easily and quickly applied, a broad definition may result in considerable heterogeneity within the sample, potentially resulting in erroneous conclusions that there are no negative effects of such arrangements. However, compared to a more narrow definition, a broad definition would be more likely to identify children who are potentially at risk of experiencing detrimental effects of self-care (should these effects exist). A more narrow definition of the latchkey construct would decrease heterogeneity, thereby enhancing the reliability of research findings. However, one may be more likely to miss identifying children who are potentially at risk, but who do not explicitly fit the narrow criteria when applied to the population as a whole. We suggest that the broad definition be used as a screening technique to identify children who may be at risk for

experiencing negative effects from self-care. Once these at-risk children have been identified, more specific definitions could pinpoint more sensitively those individuals for whom self-care might be particularly detrimental.

Clearly, the results of this study do not lay to rest the issue of whether or not the latchkey situation is detrimental to children and adolescents. Because the subjects in this study were all middle to upper SES college students, the results should not be generalized to all individuals who have experienced a self-care arrangement. College students are likely to be brighter than average, and perhaps more resourceful in adjusting to a self-care situation. Indeed, replication of this study using a sample who never attended college and/or a sample which possessed greater variability in SES would be an important contribution to this area of research. Moreover, the dependent measures used in this study do not exhaust the number of available constructs on which self-care and adult-care individuals may be expected to differ. In addition to the concepts of latchkey and nonlatchkey arrangements, the concept of the "semilatchkey" arrangement (Diamond et at., 1985) reserved for children who do not clearly fit the two former categories may be a useful category to examine in future research.

Finally, it would be worthwhile to refine further our understanding of the effects of a number of variables contributing to the heterogeneous latchkey experience. For example, detailed information on parental attitude toward the latchkey situation, whether the arrangement was chosen due to perceived necessity or because of confidence in the child, the quality of parent-child relationships, and related variables have not yet been examined in the context of the self-care arrangement.

REFERENCES

Achenbach, T. M., & Edelbrock, C. (1986). *Manual for the teacher's report form and teacher version of the child behavior profile*. Burlington: University of Vermont, Department of Psychiatry.

Achenbach, T. M., & Edelbrock, C. (1987). *Manual for the youth self-report*. Burlington: University of Vermont, Department of Psychiatry.

Ammons, R. B., & Ammons, C. H. (1962). *The Quick Test*. Missoula, MT: Psychological Test Specialists.

Bedeian, A. G., Geagud, R. J., & Zmud, R. W. (1977). Test–retest reliability and internal consistency of the short form of Coopersmith's self-esteem inventory. *Psychological Reports, 41*, 1041–1042.

Bouchard, T. J., Jr., & Segal, N. L. (1985). Environment and IQ. In B. B. Wolman (Ed.), *Handbook of intelligence: Theories, measurements, and applications* (pp. 391–464). New York: Wiley.

Cole, C., & Rodman, H. (1987). When school-age children care for themselves: Issues for family life educators and parents. *Family Relations, 36*, 92–96.

Coopersmith, S. (1976). *The antecedents of self-esteem*. Palo Alto, CA: Consulting Psychologists Press.

Cowen, E. L., Dorr, D., Clarfield, S., Kreling, B., McWilliams, S. A., Pokracki, F., Pratt, M., Terrell, D., & Wilson, A. (1973). The AML: A quick screening device for early identification of school maladaptation. *American Journal of Community Psychology, 1*, 12–35.

Derogatis, L. (1983). *SCL–90–R: Administration, scoring, and procedures manual for the revised version*. Baltimore, MD: Johns Hopkins University School of Medicine.

Diamond, J. M., Kataria, S., & Messer, S. C. (1989). Latchkey children: A pilot study investigating behavior and academic achievement. *Child & Youth Care Quarterly, 18*, 131–140.

Etaugh, C. (1980). Effects of nonmaternal care on children: Research evidence and popular views. *American Psychologist, 35*, 309–319.

Galambos, N. L., & Garbarino, J. (1983, July–August), Identifying the missing links in the study of latchkey children. *Children Today*, pp. 2–4, 40–41.

Gold, D., & Andres, D. (1978a). Developmental comparisons between 10-year-old children with employed and nonemployed mothers. *Child Development, 49*, 75–84.

Gold, D., & Andres, D. (1978b). Developmental Comparisons of adolescent children with employed and nonemployed mothers. *Merrill–Palmer Quarterly, 24*, 243–254.

Gough, H. G. (1975). *Manual for the California Psychological Inventory*. Palo Alto, CA: Consulting Psychologists Press.

Groth-Marnat, G. (1984). *Handbook of Psychological Assessment*. New York: Van Nostrand Reinhold.

Halverson, C. F. (1988). Remembering your parents: Reflections on the retrospective method. *Journal of Personality, 56*, 435–443.

Harter, S. (1981). A new self-report scale of intrinsic versus extrinsic orientation in the classroom: Motivational and informational components. *Developmental Psychology, 17*, 300–312.

Hase, H. D., & Goldberg, L. R. (1967). Comparative validity of different strategies of constructing personality inventory scales. *Psychological Bulletin, 67*, 231–248.

Hoffman, L. W. (1979). Maternal employment: 1979. *American Psychologist, 34*, 859–865.

Hollingshead, A. B. (1977). *Four-factor index of social status*. Unpublished manuscript, Yale University, New Haven, CT.

Joesting, J., & Joesting, R. (1972). Quick Test validation: Scores of adults in a welfare setting. *Psychological Reports, 30*, 537–538.

Long, T. J., & Long, L. (1982). *Latchkey children: The child's view of self-care*. Washington, DC: Catholic University of America. (ERIC Document Reproduction Service No. ED 211 229)

Manual for the Coopersmith Self-Esteem Inventory. (1981). Palo Alto, CA: Consulting Psychologists Press.

McCrae, R. R., & Costa, P. T. (1988). Do parental influences matter? A reply to Halverson. *Journal of Personality, 56*, 445–449.

Norusis, M. J. (1985). *SPSSX advanced statistics guide*. New York: McGraw-Hill.

Nowicki, S., Jr., & Strickland, B. R. (1973). A locus of control scale for children. *Journal of Consulting and Clinical Psychology, 40*, 148–154.

Ogilvie, R. D. (1965). Correlations between the Quick Test (QT) and the Wechsler Adult Intelligence Scale (WAIS) as used in a clinical setting. *Psychological Reports, 16*, 497–498.

Pless, I. B., Snider, M., Eaton, A. E., & Kearsley, R. B. (1965). A rapid screening test for intelligence in children. *American Journal of Diseases of Children, 109*, 533–537.

Rodman, H., & Pratto, D. J. (1980). *How children take care of themselves: Preliminary statement on magazine survey* (Report submitted to the Ford Foundation). Unpublished manuscript.

Rodman, H., Pratto, D. J., & Nelson, R. S. (1985). Child care arrangements and children's functioning: A comparison of self-care and adult-care children. *Developmental Psychology, 21*, 413–418.

Rodman, H., Pratto, D. J., & Nelson, R. S. (1988). Toward a definition of self-care children: A commentary on Steinberg (1986). *Developmental Psychology, 24,* 292–294.

Rosenberg, M. (1965). *Society and the adolescent self-image.* Princeton, NJ: Princeton University Press.

Ross, M., & Conway, M. (1986). Remembering one's own past: The construction of personal histories. In R. Sorrentino & E. T. Higgins (Eds.), *Handbook of motivation and cognition* (pp. 122–144). New York: Guilford.

Steinberg, L. (1986). Latchkey children and susceptibility to peer pressure: An ecological analysis. *Developmental Psychology, 22,* 433–439.

Traub, G. S., & Spruill, J. (1982). Correlations between the Quick Test and Wechsler Adult Intelligence Scale–Revised. *Psychological Reports, 51,* 309–310.

U.S. Bureau of the Census. (1987). *Current population reports, Series P-23, No. 149. After-school care of school-age children: December 1984.* Washington, DC: U.S. Government Printing Office.

Vandell, D. L., & Corasaniti, M. A. (1988). The relation between third graders' after-school care and social, academic, and emotional functioning. *Child Development, 59,* 858–875.

Violato, C., White, W. B., & Travis, L. D. (1984). Some concurrent, criterion-related data on validity for the Quick Test based on three Canadian samples. *Psychological Reports, 54,* 775–782.

Woods, M. B. (1972). The unsupervised child of the working mother. *Developmental Psychology, 6,* 14–25.

POSTSCRIPT

Are Children in Self-Care at a Disadvantage?

Kraizer et al. found that urban children were left alone more often than rural children and that, as children got older, they were more likely to be left without supervised care after school. These researchers also found that the responses of unsupervised children who were faced with threatening situations put those children at significant risk of being exploited or abused.

Woodard and Fine compared self-care children to children who had adult supervision. Students who had been in adult care showed no differences in cognitive development, emotional adjustment, achievement, or responsibility when compared to children who had cared for themselves after school. At least for children who later attended college, self-care did not have any lasting detrimental effects.

Experts agree that successful self-care requires some maturity on the part of the child; good parental monitoring, such as phone calls; a secure home environment with clear rules and procedures; and an understanding, by the child, of basic safety skills. Other factors that affect the consequences of self-care are the total amount of interaction the child has with adults, the amount of time the child is left alone, the number of siblings left in the self-care situation, food or entertainment left in the home, and how the child feels about the self-care option compared to other care options.

As long as there is a disparity between the number of hours that a parent works and the number of hours that a child is in school, after-school care will be an issue. This issue has not been satisfactorily answered by society since there are very few options open to parents.

SUGGESTED READINGS

Coleman, M., Robinson, B., & Rowland, B. (1993). A typology of families with children in self-care: Implications for school-age child care programming. *Child and Youth Care Forum, 22*, 43–53.

Galambos, N., & Maggs, J. (1991). Out-of-school care of young adolescents and self-reported behavior. *Developmental Psychology, 27*, 644–655.

Posner, J., & Vandell, F. (1994). Low-income children's after-school care: Are there beneficial effects of after-school programs? *Child Development, 65*, 440–456.

Seligson, M. (1993). Continuity of supervised child care for school-aged children. *Pediatrics, 91*, 206–208.

ISSUE 11

Is Home Schooling an Effective Method of Education?

YES: David Guterson, from "When Schools Fail Children: An English Teacher Educates His Kids at Home," *Harper's Magazine* (November 1990)

NO: Jennie F. Rakestraw and Donald A. Rakestraw, from "Home Schooling: A Question of Quality, an Issue of Rights," *The Educational Forum* (Fall 1990)

ISSUE SUMMARY

YES: David Guterson, a public school English teacher, argues that home schooling is more effective than public schooling. Home schooling teaches children that learning is life, not separate from life. Guterson maintains that in public schools, children are not focused; they are simply free to retain any incidental learning that they may be exposed to throughout the day.

NO: Jennie F. Rakestraw and Donald A. Rakestraw, both professors at Georgia Southern College, state that by schooling their children at home, parents are undermining a fundamental social institution, the public school. They argue that interaction with a school peer group, which is usually missing in home schools, is imperative for the healthy social development of children.

Although home schooling was the accepted method of education in the United States until the 1850s, its comeback, beginning in the 1970s, has raised quite a bit of controversy. According to Michael Farris, president of the Home School Legal Defense Association, responsible home schooling is now legal in every state of the union.

In a 1991 article in *Essence* magazine, Constance Garcia-Barrio discusses reasons for home schooling. Factors related to why a parent would choose home school over public school include a parent's disagreement with the values presented in both public and private schools, as well as a dislike for certain curricula and particular teaching approaches. In addition, some parents who favor home schooling believe that public schools do not promote self-discipline and self-motivation or provide an environment in which each child's particular talents may flourish.

However, some experts fear that home schooling may be harmful to a child's overall development. Children schooled at home may not have the opportunity to develop and interact with a same-age peer group, through which children learn social skills. Another common concern is that home-school teachers may not have the appropriate skills, training, education, and knowledge to teach children effectively.

In the following selections, David Guterson provides an array of examples and reasons as to why he, a public school teacher, chose to educate his children at home. Jennie F. Rakestraw and Donald A. Rakestraw then offer their reasons as to why such a course of action may not be optimal for children.

YES

David Guterson

WHEN SCHOOLS FAIL CHILDREN

Although it remains unarticulated among us, we Americans share an allegiance to schools, an assumption that schools are the foundation of our meritocracy and the prime prerequisite to a satisfying existence. In fact, to the oft-cited triumvirate of what is ineluctable in life—birth, death, and taxes—we are prone to add an unspoken fourth: education in classrooms.

In my classroom at a public high school in an upper-middle-class milieu where education is taken relatively seriously, we read with great purpose precisely those stories that tacitly reaffirm this loyalty to schools: In *Lord of the Flies* a pack of schoolboys degenerate into killers because no teachers are around to preserve the constraints of civilization. In *To Kill a Mockingbird* the venerable Atticus Finch insists that, for all of its shortcomings—and despite the fact that his daughter, Scout, is best educated by his own good example and by life in the larger web of Maycomb County—Maycomb Elementary is *mandatory*. *The Catcher in the Rye* is in large part the story of its protagonist's maladjustment to schools, and J. D. Salinger is highly critical of the hypocrisy behind a good education; still he ultimately offers up Mr. Antolini—an English teacher—as Holden Caulfield's last best hope.

The doctrine that school is necessary, which we early imbibe while within the very belly of the beast, is inevitably reinforced after we are disgorged. The daily implacability with which the media report the decline of schools, the constant knell of ominous statistics on the sorry state of American education, the curious popularity of such books as E. D. Hirsch's *Cultural Literacy* and Allan Bloom's *Closing of the American Mind*, are signs and portents, yes—but they also serve to bolster our shared assumption that school is required not merely because we attended it but also because our common life is in such a precarious state. Our national discussion about education is a desperate one, taking place, as it does, in an atmosphere of crisis, but it does not include in any serious way a challenge to the notion that *every child should attend school*. Why? Because, quite simply, there is no context for such a challenge: We live in a country where a challenge to the universal necessity of schools is not merely eccentric, not merely radical, but fundamentally un-American.

From David Guterson, "When Schools Fail Children: An English Teacher Educates His Kids at Home," *Harper's Magazine* (November 1990). Copyright © 1990 by David Guterson. Reprinted by permission of Georges Borchardt, Inc., for the author.

Yet there *are* those who have challenged not exactly the schools' raison d'être but the reason for their children's being *in* them. The children of such people have come to be called by a powerful misnomer, by a Newspeak conjoining: "homeschoolers." These children are not really *home*schoolers at all but rather young persons who do not go to school and are educated outside of institutions, persons best defined by what they don't do as opposed to what they do. There are currently about 300,000 homeschoolers in the United States —truants from one perspective, but, from another, following in the footsteps of Thomas Jefferson, Thomas Edison, Woodrow Wilson, Margaret Mead, and Andrew Wyeth.

A substantial majority of homeschooling parents in America are fervently religious and view schools as at odds with Christian doctrine. Overall, however, they are a diverse lot—the orthodox and the progressive, the Fundamentalist Christian and the libertarian, the urban, the rural, the social skeptic, the idealist, the self-sufficient, and the paranoid. And studies show little or no correlation between the degree of religious content in a homeschooling program or the level of its formal structure—ranging from orthodox "structuralists," with homes set up as miniature schools, to informal programs guided only by a child's ability to learn—or the education or affluence of homeschooling parents (or lack of affluence; the median annual income of homeschooling families is somewhere between $20,000 and $30,000) and the surprising academic success of homeschooled children, who tend to score well above average on standardized achievement tests.

But despite this—and despite the fact that teaching one's own was the norm in the United States until the 1850s— homeschooling today is little more than a fringe movement, an uprising perceived by many as a sort of insult and by others as a severe admonishment: *Take more interest in your children, like us!* (A Gallup poll revealed that 70 percent of the American population disapproved of homeschooling.) The movement inspires guilt in the hearts of too many parents— a lot of them baby boomers energetically seeking money and success yet worried that their children are growing up estranged from them—guilt and the sort of rage normally reserved for heretics and cultists.

Few people realize that the homeschooling movement is populated by a large number of educators or ex-educators—parents who teach or who have taught in the schools but keep their children out of them. Their paradoxical behavior makes them at first a curiosity and finally an affront to the schools that hired them; their students are confounded by their apparent hypocrisy; their colleagues are apt to tread delicately around the subject. So saying, I'll add my own confession: I am one of these walking contradictions. I teach my neighbors' children in my high school classroom, but my wife and I teach ours at home.

* * *

We came to this decision, I should admit from the outset, viscerally, with our understanding incomplete, pondering no more than a year's trial run. We were like most parents in the turmoil we felt far in advance of our oldest son's first step onto the school bus but unlike most in our response to it: We became existentially worried.

At first it seemed this anxiety signified that something was fundamentally wrong with us. Were we overzealous, overprotective, paranoid? It was our duty, we tried to tell ourselves, to override our parental instincts; school, after all, was ineluctable. And so my wife attempted to visit the local kindergarten (to no avail—its principal's policy forbade such visits) in order to assure herself that nothing dreadful might occur within its walls. Meanwhile I sought to convince myself that my own experience of student life as nightmarishly dreary and an incomparable waste of time was my own experience, only that, and that nothing legitimate could be deduced from it. And this was true: I could deduce nothing.

I wish I could write that my wife and I had excellent reasons for deciding to homeschool. We didn't. It was in the gut, and the gut, we knew, could be wrong either way. In May of 1986 we read books, in June we talked, July we wrung hands, August felt deep and hot and still, September came, and then one morning the big yellow bus arrived, waited a minute with its doors open, and our child did not get on it.

That fall we took to answering our inquisitors—friends, acquaintances, siblings, grandparents—with the all-purpose and ultimately evasive assertion that to hold a child out of kindergarten was not really so unusual, that many people do it.

Not schoolteachers, they replied.

But since then, each of our three sons has missed the bus, so to speak, and we find ourselves flung headlong into a life neither of us would have predicted.

* * *

As it turns out, it is a life our family likes, and this is our chief reason for continuing to homeschool. Our days and our children's days are various.

They pass with no sense that learning is separate from life, an activity that begins at a specific point in the morning and arbitrarily ends at another in the afternoon. Instead, learning proceeds *from* our children, spurred by their interests and questions. A winter day on which snow falls is the natural starting point for discussion and reading about meteorology, weather fronts, road salts, sloped roofs, Alaska, polar bears, the invention of touring skis. A spring evening spent on a blanket in the yard as the stars begin to show themselves is a proper time for talk of constellations, for bringing out a star chart, for setting up a telescope, for questions about satellites, eclipses, comets, meteors, navigation, Columbus, the Apollo space program. When the weather is poor for roaming out of doors, our boys—five, seven, and nine —might spend hours playing Scrabble or chess, or read to one another, or draw pictures, or comb through atlases and encyclopedias because the maps and pictures interest them. At dinner, if it is impending war in the Middle East that is in the news, the atlases and encyclopedias might end up on the table, and we might be there for two hours or more, eating, asking questions, looking up precise answers, discovering how oil is formed in the ground, why people fight over it, how Islam differs from other religions, why a person has to drink more water when it's hot, and why camels have humps.

There are hours in the morning—two at most—when my wife sits down with our nine-year-old and is systematic about writing and mathematics; later, they will practice violin together. Evenings are my time for nurturing our children's interest in geography, for discussing the day's news, and for reading poems to them before they go to bed. We try to be consistent about these matters, and yet no two days are ever much alike, and the curriculum is devised by us according to our children's needs and implemented by us according to our strengths and weaknesses as parents and teachers. Thus:

AUGUST 30: Reading: *The Wooden Horse*; violin: *Witches' Dance*; writing: letter to Adam, final draft; science: gas cannon, carbon dioxide.

SEPTEMBER 26: Visit to the chicken-butchering plant and Point Defiance Zoo; violin practice; journal and writing.

OCTOBER 16: Neighborhood recycling; banking; violin practice; Chess Club; finished letter to Aunt Mary.

NOVEMBER 7: *Mouse and the Motorcycle*, Chapters 3 and 4; math drill, multiplying by 4 and 5; violin practice; cursive writing; swimming with Nathan.

What else? An ant farm, a bug jar, a pair of field glasses, a rabbit cage, old appliances to take apart. An aquarium, a terrarium, a metronome, a collection of petrified wood, another of shells, a globe, a magnifying glass, a calculator, a microscope. Felt pens, watercolors, dry cell batteries, paper-airplane kits. Swimming teachers, lithographers, bakers, canoe builders, attorneys, inventors, flutists, fishermen. And time to ponder all of them. To read the information on the backs of baseball cards, dig butter clams, dye rice paper, weave on a homemade frame loom. To plant potatoes, tell tall tales, watch birds feed. To fashion a self in silence.

And people too, many of them, a large and shifting variety. Friends from Little League and music lessons, acquaintances made on the basketball court and in art

classes. The group of homeschoolers with whom our boys put on plays, beachcomb at low tide, play chess.

And salmon. Perhaps it began, one night, with merely eating one. Or with reading *Red Tag Comes Back*. Or with the man at the side of the road with the purse seine laid out in his yard. At any rate, the salmon life-cycle exhibit at the Seattle Aquarium and walking among the gill-netters at Fisherman's Terminal. And cleaning debris from a salmon stream, standing in it, one Saturday. Visiting the hatchery on the Elwha River, the fish ladders at the Rocky Reach Dam, the Pacific Science Center display on the Nootka people. Then seeing their grandfather's catch from the Hakai Peninsula, the bones and organs, the digestive tracts of fish—the blood and murder—and mulling over eating what was once living and the relative ethics of sportfishing. And then one day, abruptly —perhaps a plane has flown overhead or they have seen from the yard a crow fly—it is *flight* that interests them, the Wright Brothers, Charles Lindbergh, Amelia Earhart, draft and lift and thrust and wingspan, the Museum of Flight, the Boeing plant, pitch, yaw, and roll....

Their education is various, alive, participatory, whole—and, most of all, *theirs*. Quite frankly, no school can hope to match it. It is an education tuned to their harmonies, local and intimate as opposed to generic and imposed. They have not learned to be fearful of learning, to associate it with pain and dreariness, with competition, anxiety, dread. My wife and I hope that they will continue in this, that adolescence will find them earnestly seeking, that they will see enough of schools—by visiting them —to know what they are missing. We hope that colleges, if college is what they want, will recognize their strengths without school transcripts. (Admissions boards, incidentally, increasingly recognize homeschooled children as legitimate candidates.) And that their social lives will continue to be vigorous and sane, will continue to include people of all sorts and all ages. And finally that the life we have developed as a family will sustain itself on through *their* children, that our intimacy will not end when *they* are parents.

It is not always, of course, so idyllic, so wonderful, so easy to wax romantic over. Much of the time, though, it is satisfying and full, a fruitful existence for us all. We recognize that in the long run it may have drawbacks, but in the long run no life is perfect. We can't know, finally, if this is what is best for our children and, like all parents, we are playing it by ear to some extent, hoping to guess correctly what it is we should *do*. We do know that homeschooling has given us a life we wouldn't otherwise have, and we are thankful for that.

* * *

At the same time, I go on teaching English in a public high school. There my students might bemoan the dreary meaninglessness of classroom life and rail against its absurdities but also profess skepticism at the very mention of homeschooling. How are your kids going to make friends? they ask. Who's going to teach them algebra? How do you expect them to get into college? When do you find time to teach them anyway? What if you weren't a teacher—could you do it? Why are you *here*, Mr. Guterson?

Excellent questions, I say, sooner or later, in the approving voice of a high school English teacher. But answering them I feel the orbit of my reasoning widen—what high school students call "digression"—because in the end you can't discuss homeschooling as if it were divorced from other raging social issues. In fact, bring it up with your students' parents and you're soon fending off a touchy debate about such sacred matters as work, children, money, leisure time, and, above all, the self. Before long you are listening to hysterical pronouncements about democracy, capitalism, enculturation, the Japanese, and nearly everything else.

Let's take, for example, the assertion that children who don't go to school won't be "socialized." Most people believe school is the primary training ground for the social life we experience when we emerge from school: In its halls and classrooms, these skeptics recollect with mixed emotions, one sorts out the broad panoply of human types and then adjusts oneself to them, finds ways to modulate one's persona in the face of the great shifting tide of humanity. In this vision of things, the homeschooled child figures as an eternal outsider who, because he or she never attended school, will remain forever uninitiated in the tricky nuances of adult society. He will miss his cues at cocktail parties, he will not understand the subtleties of behaviors that come his way at the office or on the bus.

Furthermore, say homeschooling's detractors, homeschooling is *undemocratic*. They take at face value the portrait of schools as the irreplaceable agents of enculturation and, as E. D. Hirsch would have it, of cultural literacy. Jefferson's vision, after all, was that school would be democracy's proving ground, a place where all comers would take their best shot at the American Dream and where that dream would ultimately find its most basic and most enduring sustenance. Not to show up at all—at all!—is thus to give in to the forces of cultural decline, to withdraw at the moment of national crisis, and to suggest openly that if Rome is really burning, the best response is not to douse the flames or even to fiddle away beside the baths but to go home and lock the door.

Critics of homeschooling are likely to add that for America to work we must act in concert to repair our schools; that few parents are, in fact, well qualified to teach children the broad range of things they need to know; that homeschooling allows the bigoted and narrow-minded to perpetuate their types; that despite all the drawbacks to a peer-dominated world, such a world is required if children are to grapple with relationships more egalitarian than family ones. And more: Send your child to the school of hard knocks, they say, where some bigger boy will shove him from his place in line or steal his blocks or vandalize his fingerpaintings, where he will learn forbearance and self-reliance and meet in the form of his teacher an adult who is less than perfect and less than fully attentive to his every need—where, in short, life in all of its troubling glory will present itself daily to him. A dark inversion, perversely true, of Robert Fulghum's *All I Really Need to Know I Learned in Kindergarten.*

* * *

Let me address these criticisms in order. Evidence in support of homeschooling's academic virtues is both overwhelming and precisely what we would expect if we gave the matter some reflection. Public educators have complained, into a steady, implacable wind, that with much smaller classes and more one-to-one contact they might make better academic headway. Small wonder, then, that homeschoolers

score consistently well above the norm on standardized achievement tests: They're learning under the ideal conditions—alone or in groups small enough to make real learning possible—that schoolteachers persistently cry out for.

Recently, a strong case has been made that achievement tests don't tell us anything that matters, because they are culturally biased and because they are *tests*—and tests are attended by various levels of anxiety and a wide range of test-taking habits. Here some facts about homeschoolers are in order: They come predominantly from the very middle-class backgrounds that standardized achievement tests reportedly favor, and their parents are, for the most part, deeply interested in their education as well as themselves better educated than the average American adult. Thus, homeschoolers' test scores might best be compared with those of schoolchildren who come from similar test-favoring backgrounds and whose parents also are well educated and involved. Furthermore, it's true that some homeschooling parents teach "to" standardized tests—some classroom teachers do also—because states require that their children take them or because college entry is largely contingent on test scores in the absence of a school grade-point average. (Harvard, for example, admits homeschooled children and takes their SAT scores very seriously.)

Researchers have probed as well the more slippery question of whether homeschooled children are properly socialized. John Wesley Taylor V, using the Piers-Harris Self-Concept Scale—a measure of the "central core of personality"—concluded that "few homeschooling children are socially deprived." Mona Maarse Delahooke placed them in the "well-adjusted" range on a personality measure known as the Roberts Apperception Test for Children; Jon Wartes, in surveys of 219 Washington State homeschoolers, found that at least half spent more than twenty hours a month in organized community activities and that more than two thirds spent twenty to thirty plus hours a month with other children of varying ages. Linda Montgomery, after studying the leadership skills of homeschooled children, concluded that "homeschooling is not generally repressive of a student's potential leadership, and may in fact nurture leadership at least as well as does the conventional system." In my experience, homeschoolers are less peer-dependent than schoolchildren and less susceptible to peer pressure. In this regard, the research merely corroborates what seems to most observers obvious.

But although homeschooling may work, it is by no means easy. Most American adults are fully competent, of course, to learn whatever they have to learn—facts, skills, methods, strategies—in order to teach their children. But should they want to do it, they should strive to be good at it, and they should face the endeavor seriously. It should bring them satisfaction; it should feel like important work. *No one* should undertake to homeschool without coming to terms with this fundamental truth: It is the fabric of your own life you are deciding about, not just your child's education.

* * *

This matter—the fabric of a homeschooling life—is the concern of some critics who assert that in practice homeschooling is patently sexist, that its most obvious result is the isolation of women in the home, away from the fulfillments of the workplace. (That there may be fulfillments in the home, for both sexes, as educators of children, is another issue entirely.) Yet the question of who does what in a relationship is no more or less important with regard to homeschooling than with regard to anything else: who works outside the home, who works inside, who does the dishes, changes oil in the car, shops for food, flies to Miami on a business trip. The question of *who does what* remains: who takes responsibility for the child's introduction to long division, drives her to swimming lessons, teaches him to throw a baseball, shows her how to use a calculator. Homeschooling is, in fact, no more inherently sexist than anything else in a marriage (and is less so than schools), and if in many homeschooling families the mother is the prime mover and first cause of education and the father an addendum and auxiliary, this is a reflection on the culture at large and not on the phenomenon of homeschooling.

There are others who assert that although homeschooling might serve well for the American middle class, other groups—the poor, the disenfranchised, the immigrant—need schools to flourish. After all, the public schools have historically been a crucial conduit of upward mobility, they say, and point out the Vietnamese immigrants of the last twenty years, whose kids get full scholarships from places like the University of Texas and Columbia. Yet the mobility they describe is next to nonexistent; a permanent underclass is the reality in this country, and schools do as much as any other institution to reinforce this state of affairs. By systematizing unfairness, inequality, and privilege, schools prepare the children of the underclass to accept as inevitable the coming drudgery of their adult lives. At my school, for example, "basic" students are more likely to serve meals in Foods I while "honors" students join an organization called Future Business Leaders of America and enroll in courses like Leadership and Humanities. In both its social and academic structure, my school best instructs the disenfranchised in the cruel truth that disenfranchisement is permanent.

To say that homeschoolers, for the sake of American democracy, *must* be institutionalized is an undemocratic proposition. Both the courts and state governments recognize this, for homeschooling is legal in one form or another everywhere in the United States. The Supreme Court thus far has not ruled in any explicit way on homeschooling. The closest it came, in 1972, was to declare that Wisconsin's compulsory-education law could not, in fact, compel three Amish families to send their children to high school. Yet legal tension about homeschooling persists—mostly as First, Ninth, and Fourteenth Amendment issues: freedom of religion and the right to privacy—for the states have an interest in seeing children educated and are, rightly, concerned that in at least some cases "homeschool" ends up meaning no school. (When home-schooling parents in question are deemed incompetent, the courts have consistently—and properly—ruled against them.) Moreover, and more importantly, does anyone really believe that schools make students better democrats? Do they serve the individual and democratic society? I give them an A only for prompting peer-group relations of a sort conducive to the workings of our *economy:* Schools are in their social fabric nasty, competitive, mean-spirited, and status-conscious in the manner of the adult institutions they mimic.

Could there be something in the very nature of the school as an institution that prevents it from fully realizing its mandate to inform, educate, and develop both the individual and his or her society? Or, to put it another way, could there be something in its *manner* of being that prevents it from realizing its *reason* for being? At the high school where I teach, as at most, students come and go in sets of thirty or so at approximately one-hour intervals, an arrangement convenient to the daunting task of administering a crowd of more than 800 young people but not necessarily conducive to their education or in the best interests of society. The arrangement is instead both relatively expedient and indicative of the schools' custodial function—in essence, their primary one, since we have structured schools in such a manner as to allow this function to precede all others. Schools *keep* students first, and any education that happens along the way is incidental and achieved against the odds. It may be, finally, that schools temporarily *prevent* us from getting the education we persist in getting outside and beyond schools, where the conditions of life provide more natural motivations and learning is less abstract. *Never let your schooling get in the way of your education,* advised Mark Twain, who never attended school.

* * *

The school I teach in is fortunate to employ some excellent teachers, honorable and earnest men and women who are quietly heroic for the sake of their students and whose presence does much to salvage some good from an otherwise untenable institution. They bring humanity to an inhumane setting and pit it against the *design* of schools, which were envisioned as factories dedicated to the efficient production of predictable, formulaic human beings.

But I find myself, like many teachers, beating my head against the classroom wall on a daily, even hourly, basis. My students are compelled to herd themselves from room to room, to sit in daily confinement with other people of precisely their age and approximately their social class, to hear me out on "Sailing to Byzantium" whether or not they are ready. They are scrutinized, sorted, graded, disciplined, and their waking hours are consumed by this prison life: thirty hours a week, thirty-six weeks a year, seven to ten hours a week of "homework" twelve years running—the heart of their young lives consumed by it. What can we expect of them as adults, other than that they become, as New York City Teacher of the Year John Taylor Gatto says, "dependent human beings, unable to initiate lines of meaning to give substance and pleasure to their existence"? Penned up and locked away, shaped by television and school instead of by their community, they must struggle as adults for a satisfying life they can neither grasp nor envision.

* * *

Confining children to school is emblematic of the industrialized twentieth century, but it is also convenient for our current generation of young parents, which might best be characterized in general terms as terrifyingly selfish, persistently immature, and unable to efface its collective ego for the sake of the generation that will follow it and is *already* following it. While these people go about the business of saving the world—or of extracting everything they can from it—their children (they can hardly believe

they have children, can hardly grasp the privilege of nurturing them when they are so thoroughly occupied by their attentions to themselves) need *someplace* to go. The truth is that for too many contemporary parents the school system is little more than convenient day care—day care they can feel good about as long as they don't reflect on it too deeply.

Many parents I know put more hours into their golf games or their wardrobes or into accumulating enough capital for the purchase of unnecessary luxuries than into their child's education. Because they are still children themselves, it simply doesn't occur to them to take an active role in their child's learning—in part because they expect the schools to do it all, in part because there isn't room in their souls for anybody to loom as large as themselves. For many the solution is simply to buy an education as one buys a BMW—your child's school as yet another commodity to show off. So when I talk about homeschooling I am talking about choosing less affluence in the name of more education. I am talking about giving matters intense and vital thought before one ships one's child off to school.

And while it's easy—and understandable—for parents to protest that one hasn't the time or energy for homeschooling, there is much, short of pulling children out of school, that parents can undertake today. Homeschooling is only the extreme form of a life in which all of us can and should take part. The notion of parents as educators of their children is, in the broad sense, neither extreme nor outlandish, and we should consider how instinctively parents engage in the instruction of their children—at the dinner table, for example—and how vital a role an expanded homeschooling movement might play in repairing families. We should think clearly about the problems of schools, ask ourselves why every attempt to correct them seems doomed to fail, replace in our hearts the bankrupt notion of "quality time" with a reassessment of our role as parents. We should recognize that schools will never solve the bedrock problems of education because the problems are problems of *families*, of cultural pressures that the schools reflect and thus cannot really remedy.

Today it is considered natural for parents to leave their children's education entirely in the hands of institutions. In a better world we would see *ourselves* as responsible and our schools primarily as resources. Schools would cease to be *places* in the sense that prisons and hospitals are places; instead, education would be embedded in the life of the community, part of the mechanics of our democracy, and all would feel a devotion to its processes. Parents would measure their inclinations and abilities and immerse themselves, to varying degrees and in varying ways, in a larger educational system designed to *assist* them. Schools—educational resource centers—would provide materials, technology, and expertise instead of classrooms, babysitters, and bureaucrats.

Admittedly, I am a professional educator, part of this vast bureaucracy. Yet I see no contradiction in what I am doing: coming each day to where young people are, attempting within the constraints of the institution to see to their education. Each year I come to admire many of my students, to like them so well that I am sad to see them go; each year there are moments in which I am gratified, even moved, by a sentence a student has written in an essay, by a question somebody asks. Yet for all this, for all the quiet joys of the classroom, I am forever aware of some amorphous dissatisfaction, some inkling that things might be better. It seems to me that many of my students should simply be elsewhere, that they would be better served by a different sort of education, that their society would be better served by it, too. I believe this education is one their parents can best provide and that they should expect schools to assist them. These parents love their children with a depth that, finally, I can't match—and finally, teaching is an act of love before it is anything else.

NO
Jennie F. Rakestraw and Donald A. Rakestraw

HOME SCHOOLING: A QUESTION OF QUALITY, AN ISSUE OF RIGHTS

Home schooling is an educational practice that is spreading throughout grass-roots America. Fifteen years ago it was rare to find parents teaching their children at home rather than sending them to traditional schools. But in recent years, there has been a surprising increase of interest in, and commitment to, home schooling. In 1986, Lines, a policy analyst for the U.S. Department of Education, estimated that there were between 120,000 and 260,000 home-schooled children in the United States. Public school officials, state legislators, and professional educators have had to take notice of the presence of these home-schooling families and, at times, take action about them. When parents educate their children at home, they depart from the mass-schooling ethic that has been perceived as a cornerstone of the 20th-century American way of life. This departure has raised questions concerning who holds responsibility for providing education and who is accountable for insuring quality education. Not surprisingly, such questions have been fundamental issues of home schooling and keynotes of continuing debate.

Although states have had reasonable and obvious interest in education, advocates of home schooling have regarded their parental freedom to educate as a Constitutional right, a moral duty and, for some, a Biblical command. With their opinions concerning educational philosophy, curriculum, socialization, institutionalization of children, and teacher qualifications usually at variance with public school practices, home educators have felt their decisions to home-school a matter of conscience. Home schooling, meanwhile, has a foundation in American history and has developed a legal foundation in most states. Even so, home schools face skepticism. They have reappeared

From Jennie F. Rakestraw and Donald A. Rakestraw, "Home Schooling: A Question of Quality, an Issue of Rights," *The Educational Forum*, vol. 55, no. 1 (Fall 1990). Copyright © 1990 by Kappa Delta Pi, an international honor society in education. Reprinted by permission. References omitted.

out of the past with a new face, one that looks unfamiliar and maybe even unsafe. Are parents able to meet *all* the needs of their children in the home setting? Can we concede that parents are ultimately responsible and accountable for the education of their children?

THE HISTORICAL BACKGROUND

We believe that the historical perspective must be taken when deciding on the advisability of home schooling. And we would be wise to examine how the contemporary movement toward home schooling evolved, as well as how effective these schools are in meeting children's academic and social needs.

During America's colonial and early national periods, home schooling was commonplace and, as a matter of fact, a predominant form of education. The primary responsibility for education clearly rested with parents. Although the Constitution of the United States addressed a wide range of powers, limitations, and duties, it did not expressly mention education. It was only after the passing in 1791 of the Tenth Amendment in the Bill of Rights that education became a function of the states. At that point, the states were empowered to provide education, but schooling still was not universal, compulsory, or tax supported. Although state-sponsored "charity schools" were established to provide formal schooling locally to those in need, American education remained a private and religious effort until the late 1800s. Private schools, many of which were church supported, assumed a large role in providing academic as well as religious instruction. There was no division between religious and secular authority and the Bible was considered the moral guide for the nation

and, consequently, for the developing educational system.

During the 19th century, the state's interest in education grew. Universal public education was the means by which individual liberty and a democratic state would be guaranteed. The interests and goals of the state, in contrast with those of the church, were considered to be representative of the people. The purposes of the state, namely, to promote cultural, economic, and social equality, gradually superseded the purposes of the church in American education. After the Civil War, the majority of states passed legislation providing for free public education. Even though the concept of public education had been slow to gain acceptance, every state established public schools by the early 1900s. Nevertheless, the presumption of family responsibility and control remained, and parents could use the "right of excusal" to have their children excused from any objectionable course or programs of study. Parents believed schools should conform to their values and reinforce their authority, while preparing their children for success in American society. Public education was regarded as a service to families, "an opportunity to which children were entitled, not as a requirement to be imposed."

The free educational opportunities offered by public schools were not always accepted. Indifferent parents, inadequate school facilities, rejection of a regimented school setting by children, opportunities for child labor, and the generally low standard of living—all worked against the efforts of public education. In due time, the problems of child neglect and exploitation prompted the passage of compulsory school attendance laws and child labor laws. By 1918 every state had a compulsory attendance law in effect, and the relationship between families and schools changed. The locus of responsibility had shifted from the family to the institutionalized school operated by the state. Since schools were responsive to group, rather than individual, demands, various social groups began to battle over whose values, pedagogy, and world view should be adopted by public schools. This created a problem for parents who, while accepting the idea of public education itself, perhaps did not realize that public education, when mandated by compulsory attendance laws, would usurp their rights over their children's education. By yielding to state compulsory attendance laws, parents found themselves increasingly removed from the responsibility for their children's education.

The goals of public education, generally condoned, reflected a national concern over (a) advancing the ideals of, and preserving, a democracy, (b) economically strengthening the country, and (c) equalizing opportunity among races and classes of people. In addition, the socialization of children in the school was a major emphasis of compulsory education, as it provided a powerful means of political control. Indeed, some have claimed that the essence of the common school movement was "its rhetorical commitment to the deliberate use of education as a tool for social manipulation and social progress."

Naturally, many Americans questioned the appropriateness and effectiveness of school socialization and, from the beginning, public education has been challenged and pressured to reform. In the more recent past, when Sputnik was launched by the Soviet Union in 1957, the event shocked the American public and its educational system. The satellite undermined the American people's confidence in their educational and technological superiority, as well as their sense of national security. Fear and survival became the motive for change. The attitudes and emotions thus provoked during the late 1950s greatly affected American educational policies and created an era of self-inspection, criticism, and disequilibrium. Many of the educational innovations and practices of the present can be traced to this period. Not only were alternative public schools established to counteract the growth of private schools, but some parents withdrew their children from traditional schools and initiated the contemporary home education movement. Since the 1960s, skepticism has continued to increase over how acceptable and even necessary public education is to the education and socialization of children and to the maintenance of American democracy. The renewed interest in home schooling has been an outgrowth of this sentiment.

Present-day home schools have thus evolved from a dissatisfaction with organized public schooling, a dissatisfaction based on philosophical differences in educational thought. For instance, during the 1960s and early 1970s, educators and noneducators alike called for reforms. Many recognized the need for changes but felt they should be implemented within the framework of the existing educational system. For example, Silberman described the schools as "grim, joyless places" but argued that they need not be: "Public schools *can* be organized to facilitate joy in learning and esthetic expression and to develop character... This is no utopian hope." Yet, for some this unrealized hope is indeed utopian and has not been fulfilled.

NO Rakestraw and Rakestraw / 235

Others believed in a radicalization of the school, while still others contended that reform was impossible and that schools should simply be abolished. Holt, as an example, once felt that school reform was possible, but has since reconsidered his position. He now believes that the conditions for true education "do not exist and cannot be made to exist within compulsory, coercive, competitive schools." According to him:

> While the question "Can the schools be reformed?" kept turning up "No" for an answer, I found myself asking a much deeper question. Were schools, however organized, however run, necessary at all? Were they the best place for learning? Were they even a good place? Except for people learning a few specialized skills, I began to doubt that they were.

Holt has therefore encouraged concerned parents to withdraw their children from institutionalized schools and to teach them at home. Moore has also advocated home schooling on the basis of his research, through the Hewitt Research Foundation, on the effects of institutionalizing young children. He suggested that children should not be enrolled in formal school programs before ages 8 to 10 unless they are severely disadvantaged or handicapped. Instead, parents should be assured their rights by the state to teach their children "systematically" at home.

While the home schooling movement, under the leadership of Holt and Moore, has expanded and stabilized in every state, the fundamental issue still remains: Who holds responsibility for the education of American children? With this question unanswered, many local school officials faced difficult, multi-faceted decisions involving home-schooling families. These decisions sometimes led to the charging, prosecution, and imprisonment of parents for child neglect and/or violation of state compulsory school attendance laws. Nevertheless, every state has been allowing home schooling in some form or another, even while imposing some regulations to protect the right of the state to an educated citizenry.

The legal foundation of home schooling has involved numerous court rulings and individual state's compulsory education statutes. The acceptance of home schooling implies that, although states have assumed a prominent role in providing education over the years, ultimate responsibility stays with parents. Many public educators cringe at the notion, but President Reagan was voicing a widely-held opinion when he in 1984 stated that, "The primary right, duty and responsibility of educating children belongs to parents. Their wishes should be heeded."

THE QUESTION OF QUALITY

In heeding the parental wishes, however, we must be careful that the quality of education is preserved. Public educators have often contended that some parents do not have the ability or the patience to teach their children well. Observations have been made that home-schooled children tend to be students with better-than-average potential but that their achievement is uneven due to a "spottiness" in the parents' preparation. Some school officials have been concerned about the lack of documentation and objective evaluation of home-schooled children. Some state legislators and school officials have addressed these concerns, and, since 1980, 28 states have adopted home school statutes or regulations. Compulsory attendance laws in 31 states now explicitly recognize an exception for home schooling. In legally providing for home schooling, most of these statutes established varying sets of requirements for home schools, including such criteria as teacher qualifications, achievement testing, and record keeping....

In addition to academic concerns, the socialization of home-schooled children has been a primary consideration. Many educators insist that peer interaction in the school environment is necessary for normal development and speculate that home schooling will produce social isolates. Home schooling has also been criticized as elitist, appealing mainly to educated, middle-class families. Critics also fear that the domination of parents over their children would deny the protection of society to the neglected or indoctrinated child. Some have even questioned the motives of parents who home-school their children, suspecting that some mothers use home schooling as a rationalization to stay home while others home-school for status or ego reasons. These criticisms and concerns have mounted in parallel with the growth of home schooling....

THE EFFECTIVENESS OF HOME SCHOOLING

In spite of concerns over academic progress, several studies have found that home-schooled children achieve higher than national averages on standardized measures. For example, the Tennessee Education Department reported that home-schooled students in Grades 2, 3, 6, and 8 in that state scored higher in every major area of the Stanford Achievement Test than the statewide public school averages for the 1985–1986 school year. Similar results were reported in studies by the New York and Washington State Departments of Education. In Alabama, home-schooled children in Grades 2, 3, 5, and 6 scored in 1986 at or above the national norms in all areas of the Stanford Achievement Test. In Illinois, a study concluded that home-schooled children are not disadvantaged academically by their home-school setting.

A few studies have examined the achievement of home-schooled children working with differing home-school curricula. Two such studies were conducted by home-school curriculum publishers: the Hewitt Research Foundation found that the average standardized test score of children, who use the Hewitt-Moore Child Development Center home-school curriculum, was approximately at the 80th percentile, while researchers at the Christian Liberty Academy found that home-schooled children who use their curriculum performed two to three grade levels above the national norms. In addition, studies done since 1981 by the Alaska Department of Education have found that the home-schooled children in the first through eighth grades outperformed their classroom counterparts on the California Achievement Test and the Alaska Statewide Assessment Tests.

Now, the effects of home schooling on the socialization of children have been more difficult to examine, since there is apparently no convenient instrument available to measure the equivocal elements of socialization. However, Taylor, himself a proponent of home schooling, used a self-concept inventory with a sampling of home-schooled children and found that these children scored higher than conventionally-schooled children in all areas on the scale. His conclusion was that few home-schooled children are socially deprived. Other studies that have surveyed parents' reasons for home-schooling commonly report that parents see socialization as a negative aspect of school. They wish to help their children develop social skills without negative peer influences, learning socialization skills from parent models in the home rather than from peer models in the school. While those wary of home schooling worry about the children's socialization, the parents worry about the quality of socialization that takes place in traditional schools.

THE "THREAT" OF THE HOME SCHOOLING MOVEMENT

Home schooling has been regarded as a major educational movement in America even though the actual number of home-schooled children is still negligible, being less than 1 percent of the school-age children. Nevertheless, there is apprehension over possible negative effects that this movement could have on public schooling. Even as the function and effectiveness of public education in today's society have been questioned, schools seem to have maintained a certain level of general support. Thus, Jackson, for one, advanced an argument that previous challenges to public education simply reaffirmed how deep-rooted our society's allegiance to public education had become.

On their part, advocates of home schooling have maintained that granting the right to educate their children would not significantly deplete public school attendance or damage the system. For any family not to opt for the convenience of public schooling would be not only impractical but also inconsistent with the typical American lifestyle. Rather than rocking the foundations of American

schooling, the definition and concept of education would merely be revised and broadened. Toffler, for instance, visualized an increased role of families in the education of children and maintained that home schoolers should be aided by the schools and not regarded as "freaks or lawbreakers."

Of course, the prevalence of home schooling in the future of American education cannot be clearly foreseen now. Nevertheless, [it] is ironic to note that several current trends have encouraged the growth of home schooling. The increased emphasis on parent education, parental choice and participation in the educational process, and alternative educational options worked indirectly to promote the home-schooling movement. Widely-publicized issues concerning secular humanism in public education and the reassessment of teacher certification requirements have provided added incentives for home schoolers. In addition, recent national reports such as A *Nation at Risk*, offering many sweeping indictments and reform recommendations, have been seen as evidence that public education is moving farther away from the educational ideals of home-schooling parents. Any future dissatisfactions with public education will increase the possibility of more families turning to home schooling.

* * *

Compulsory public schooling in the United States originated from genuine societal needs and has grown strong as an American institution. However, future needs might create a more distinctive place for home schooling. Parental freedom to home school has been promoted as a right which a democratic society should allow. Before it can become a viable educational alternative, nevertheless, underlying issues regarding the balance of power between parents and society over the education of children must be settled. Only mutual interest in the welfare of the child, a cooperative spirit, and a genuine objectivity in discussing the sensitive issues surrounding home schooling will provide satisfactory solutions.

POSTSCRIPT

Is Home Schooling an Effective Method of Education?

Parents who do not want their children to be shaped by hours of rigid institutional learning may opt for the more flexible home-school setting. However, it should be noted that home schooling is challenging and difficult at best. Parents must be willing to take the time to learn so as to be able to teach their children effectively. Home schooling can be a full-time job and may therefore necessitate a separate income source for the parent-educator.

Another issue that must be considered is college recognition of high school credits earned through home schooling. Although increasing numbers of colleges and universities are accepting home-schooled students with adequate ACT or SAT scores, parent-teachers must be mindful of meeting state and local requirements for certification. Class meeting times and course content must be sanctioned by authorities so that home-school credits will be recognized by local boards of education.

There is also a possibility that home schooling will promote parental enmeshment with children in some families. Abuse and neglect could go unnoticed if children remain within the family for schooling, whereas abusive situations are more likely to be detected by school officials in public and private schools. Furthermore, home educators must provide their children with social outlets and activities. If not, children could become overly dependent upon their parents and unable to function effectively in social situations, especially among peers. On the other hand, in the public and private schools, children may model themselves after their peers and adopt behaviors and values that are unacceptable.

Parents can choose to educate their children at home or send them to a public or private school. While one type of setting may look more attractive than the other, it would seem prudent for parents to remember to look at their children individually and offer each the type of educational environment that considers the child's unique needs.

SUGGESTED READINGS

Gahr, E. (1991). Home and not alone. *Insight, 7,* 10–13.
Garcia-Barrio, C. (1991). Home is where the school is. *Essence, 22,* 104–106.
Pike, B. (1992). Why I teach my children at home. *Phi Delta Kappan, 73,* 564–565.
Smith, D.S. (1993). Home schooling. *Mother Earth News, 139,* 53–54.

ISSUE 12

Should Bilingual Education Programs Be Abandoned?

YES: Diane Ravitch, from "Politicization and the Schools: The Case of Bilingual Education," *Proceedings of the American Philosophical Society* (June 1985)

NO: Donaldo Macedo, from "English Only: The Tongue-Tying of America," *Journal of Education* (Spring 1991)

ISSUE SUMMARY

YES: Professor Diane Ravitch, who has written widely on educational issues, questions the effectiveness of bilingual programs. She suggests that they have become simply a means to attain certain political ends. Do these programs operate in the best interests of the children who are placed in them? she asks.

NO: Linguistics professor Donaldo Macedo believes that English should *not* be the only language used for educating children. He maintains that bilingual education programs are effective for educating children who cannot speak or read English and that they improve the academic performance of non-English-speaking children. In addition, these programs also contribute to furthering the cause of racial equality in our society.

There are several types of bilingual education programs in the United States, each with its own strengths and shortcomings. For example, in one type of billingual curriculum, a child who does not speak English is placed in a class taught by a teacher who speaks both English and the child's original language. The intent is to teach the child in English and in his or her native tongue, as well as to maintain the child's appreciation of the native culture of his or her parents. Problems can arise in such a program, however, when a language is common to many cultures. Consider the teacher who is from one Spanish-speaking country, Guatemala for example, and who teaches a class composed of Spanish-speaking students from diverse countries, such as Spain, Mexico, San Salvador, Bolivia, and so on. These children may enter high school with a thorough understanding of the Spanish language and Guatemalan culture, but they will likely have little idea of their own culture. To further exacerbate the problem, these children often lack sufficient immersion in the dominant, American culture. As a consequence, these children, who may be just as intelligent as their English-speaking counterparts, could do poorly on culturally relevant standardized tests and thus become discouraged.

Some bilingual education programs give the parents of non-English-speaking children the choice of enrolling their children in a completely native-speaking classroom or a completely English-speaking classroom, where they will receive no extra help or assistance. The problem here is that neither option may benefit the children. If children go to native-speaking classrooms, it can impede their acquisition of English. If they are put into English-only classrooms, they may become frustrated and discouraged.

Some bilingual programs, however, seem to be enjoying great success in recognizing a child's native culture and language and teaching them about American culture. In so-called English immersion programs, children are enrolled in classrooms where they are "immersed" in the English language, but only after they have been oriented to the language and the happenings of an American classroom. However, these immersion programs seem to work best in preschool curricula, since children acquire language more readily in early childhood.

In the following selections, the authors offer different arguments regarding bilingual education. As you read each selection, take note of the ways in which non-English-speaking children can be integrated most effectively into the educational system, according to Diane Ravitch and Donaldo Macedo. Which arguments seem to be most closely aligned with the best interests of the children?

YES
Diane Ravitch

POLITICIZATION AND THE SCHOOLS: THE CASE OF BILINGUAL EDUCATION

There has always been a politics of schools, and no doubt there always will be. Like any other organization populated by human beings, schools have their internal politics; for as long as there have been public schools, there have been political battles over their budget, their personnel policies, their curricula, and their purposes. Anyone who believes that there was once a time in which schools were untouched by political controversy is uninformed about the history of education. The decision-making processes that determine who will be chosen as principal or how the school board will be selected or whether to pass a school bond issue are simply political facts of life that are part and parcel of the administration, financing, and governance of schools. There is also a politics of the curriculum and of the profession, in which contending forces argue about programs and policies. It is hard to imagine a school, a school system, a university, a state board of education, or a national department of education in which these kinds of political conflicts do not exist. They are an intrinsic aspect of complex organizations in which people disagree about how to achieve their goals and about which goals to pursue; to the extent that we operate in a democratic manner, conflict over important and even unimportant issues is inevitable.

There is another kind of politics, however, in which educational institutions become entangled in crusades marked by passionate advocacy, intolerance of criticism, and unyielding dogmatism, and in which the education of children is a secondary rather than a primary consideration. Such crusades go beyond politics-as-usual; they represent the politicization of education. Schools and universities become targets for politicization for several reasons: First, they offer a large captive audience of presumably impressionable minds; second, they are expected to shape the opinions, knowledge, and values of the rising generation, which makes them attractive to those who want to influence the future; and third, since Americans have no strong educational philosophy or educational tradition, almost any claim—properly clothed in rhetorical appeals about the needs of children or of American society—can make its way into the course catalogue or the educational agenda

From Diane Ravitch, "Politicization and the Schools: The Case of Bilingual Education," *Proceedings of the American Philosophical Society*, vol. 129, no. 2 (June 1985). Copyright © 1985 by The American Philosophical Society. Reprinted by permission.

Ever since Americans created public schools, financed by tax dollars and controlled by boards of laymen, the schools have been at the center of intermittent struggles over the values that they represent. The founders of the common school, and in particular Horace Mann, believed that the schools could be kept aloof from the religious and political controversies beyond their door, but it has not been easy to keep the crusaders outside the schoolhouse. In the nineteenth century, heated battles were fought over such issues as which Bible would be read in the classroom and whether public dollars might be used to subsidize religious schools. After the onset of World War I, anti-German hostility caused the German language to be routed from American schools, even though nearly a quarter of the high school population studied the language in 1915. Some of this same fervor, strengthened by zeal to hasten the process of assimilation, caused several states to outlaw parochial and private schools and to prohibit the teaching of foreign language in the first eight years of school. Such laws, obviously products of nationalism and xenophobia, were struck down as unconstitutional by the United States Supreme Court in the 1920s. The legislative efforts to abolish nonpublic schools and to bar the teaching of foreign languages were examples of politicization; their purpose was not to improve the education of any child, but to achieve certain social and political goals that the sponsors of these laws believed were of overwhelming importance.

Another example of politicization in education was the crusade to cleanse the schools of teachers and other employees who were suspected of being disloyal, subversive, or controversial. This crusade

began in the years after World War I, gathered momentum during the 1930s, and came to full fruition during the loyalty investigations by state and national legislative committees in the 1950s. Fears for national security led to intrusive surveillance of the beliefs, friends, past associations, and political activities of teachers and professors. These inquiries did not improve anyone's education; they used the educational institutions as vehicles toward political goals that were extraneous to education.

A more recent example of politicization occurred on the campuses during the war in Vietnam. Those who had fought political intrusions into educational institutions during the McCarthy era did so on the ground of academic freedom. Academic freedom, they argued, protected the right of students and teachers to express their views, regardless of their content; because of academic freedom, the university served as a sanctuary for dissidents, heretics, and skeptics of all persuasions. During the war in Vietnam, those who tried to maintain the university as a privileged haven for conflicting views, an open marketplace of ideas, found themselves the object of attack by student radicals. Student (and sometimes faculty) radicals believed that opposition to the war was so important that those who did not agree with them should be harassed and even silenced.

Faced with a moral issue, the activist argued, the university could not stand above the battle, nor could it tolerate the expression of "immoral" views. In this spirit, young radicals tried to prevent those with whom they disagreed from speaking and teaching; towards this end, they heckled speakers, disrupted classes, and even planted bombs on campus. These actions were intended to politicize schools and campuses and, in some instances, they succeeded. They were advocated by sincere and zealous individuals who earnestly believed that education could not take place within a context of political neutrality. Their efforts at politicization stemmed not from any desire to improve education as such, but from the pursuit of political goals.

As significant as the student movement and the McCarthy era were as examples of the dangers of politicization, they were short-lived in comparison to the policy of racial segregation. Segregation of public school children by their race and ancestry was established by law in seventeen states and by custom in many communities beyond those states. The practice of assigning public school children and teachers on the basis of their race had no educational justification; it was not intended to improve anyone's education. It was premised on the belief in the innate inferiority of people whose skin was of dark color. Racial segregation as policy and practice politicized the schools; it used them to buttress a racist social and political order. It limited the educational opportunities available to blacks. Racial segregation was socially and politically so effective in isolating blacks from opportunity or economic advancement and educationally so devastating in retarding their learning that our society continues to pay a heavy price to redress the cumulative deficits of generations of poor education.

The United States Supreme Court's 1954 decision, *Brown v. Board of Education*, started the process of ending state-imposed racial segregation. In those southern states where segregation was the cornerstone of a way of life, white resistance to desegregation was prolonged and intense. The drive to disestablish racial segregation and to uproot every last vestige of its effects was unquestionably necessary. The practice of assigning children to school by their race and of segregating other public facilities by race was a national disgrace. However, the process through which desegregation came about dramatically altered the politics of schools; courts and regulatory agencies at the federal and state level became accustomed to intervening in the internal affairs of educational institutions, and the potential for politicization of the schools was significantly enlarged.

The slow pace of desegregation in the decade after the *Brown* decision, concurrent with a period of rising expectations, contributed to a dramatic buildup of frustration and rage among blacks, culminating in the protests, civil disorders, and riots of the mid-1960s. In response, Congress enacted major civil rights laws in 1964 and 1965, and the federal courts became aggressive in telling school boards what to do to remedy their constitutional violations. Initially, these orders consisted of commands to produce racially mixed schools. However, some courts went beyond questions of racial mix. In Washington, D.C., a federal district judge in 1967 directed the school administration to abandon ability grouping, which he believed discriminated against black children. This was the first time that a federal court found a common pedagogical practice to be unconstitutional.[1]

In the nearly two decades since that decision, the active intervention of the federal judiciary into school affairs has ceased to be unusual. In Ann Arbor, Michigan, a federal judge ordered the school board to train teachers in "black English," a program subsequently found to be ineffectual in improving the education of black students. In California, a federal judge barred the use of intelligence tests for placement of students in special education classes, even though reputable psychologists defend their validity. In Boston, where the school board was found guilty of intentionally segregating children by race, the federal judge assumed full control over the school system for more than a decade; even reform superintendents who were committed to carrying out the judge's program for desegregation complained of the hundreds of court orders regulating every aspect of schooling, hiring, promotion, curriculum, and financing. In 1982, in a case unrelated to desegregation, a state judge in West Virginia ordered the state education department to do "no less than completely reconstruct the entire system of education in West Virginia," and the judge started the process of reconstruction by setting down his own standards for facilities, administration, and curriculum, including what was to be taught and for how many minutes each week.[2]

Perhaps this is as good a way of bringing about school reform as any other. No doubt school officials are delighted when a judge orders the state legislature to raise taxes on behalf of the schools. But it does seem to be a repudiation of our democratic political structure when judges go beyond issues of constitutional rights, don the mantle of school superintendent, and use their authority to change promotional standards, to reconstruct the curriculum, or to impose their own pedagogical prescriptions.

Now, by the definition of politicization that I earlier offered—that is, when educational institutions become the focus of dogmatic crusaders whose purposes are primarily political and only incidentally related to children's education—these ex-amples may not qualify as politicization, although they do suggest how thin is the line between politics and politicization. After all, the judges were doing what they thought would produce better education. The court decisions in places like Ann Arbor, Boston, California, and West Virginia may be thought of as a shift in the politics of schools, a shift that has brought the judiciary into the decision-making process as a full-fledged partner in shaping educational disputes, even those involving questions of pedagogy and curriculum.

The long struggle to desegregate American schools put them at the center of political battles for more than a generation and virtually destroyed the belief that schools could remain above politics. Having lost their apolitical shield, the schools also lost their capacity to resist efforts to politicize them. In the absence of resistance, demands by interest groups of varying ideologies escalated, each trying to impose its own agenda on the curriculum, the textbooks, the school library, or the teachers. Based on the activities of single-issue groups, any number of contemporary educational policies would serve equally well as examples of politicization. The example that I have chosen as illustrative of politicization is bilingual education. The history of this program exemplifies a campaign on behalf of social and political goals that are only tangentially related to education. I would like to sketch briefly the bilingual controversy, which provides an overview of the new politics of education and demonstrates the tendency within this new politics to use educational programs for noneducational ends.

Demands for bilingual education arose as an outgrowth of the civil rights movement. As it evolved, that movement contained complex, and occasionally contradictory, elements. One facet of the movement appealed for racial integration and assimilation, which led to court orders for busing and racial balance; but the dynamics of the movement also inspired appeals to racial solidarity, which led to demands for black studies, black control of black schools, and other race-conscious policies. Whether the plea was for integration or for separatism, advocates could always point to a body of social science as evidence for their goals.

Race consciousness became a necessary part of the remedies that courts fashioned, but its presence legitimized ethnocentrism as a force in American politics. In the late 1960s, the courts, Congress, and policymakers—having been told for years by spokesmen for the civil rights movement that all children should be treated equally without regard to their race or ancestry—frequently heard compelling testimony by political activists and social scientists about the value of ethnic particularism in the curriculum.

Congress first endorsed funding for bilingual education in 1968, at a time when ethnocentrism had become a powerful political current. In hearings on this legislation, proponents of bilingual education argued that non-English-speaking children did poorly in school because they had low self-esteem, and that this low self-esteem was caused by the absence of their native language from the classroom. They claimed that if the children were taught in their native tongue and about their native culture, they would have higher self-esteem, better attitudes toward school, and higher educational achievement. Bilingual educators also insisted that children would learn English more readily if they already knew another language.

In the congressional hearings, both advocates and congressmen seemed to agree that the purpose of bilingual education was to help non-English speakers succeed in school and in society. But the differences between them were not then obvious. The congressmen believed that bilingual education would serve as a temporary transition into the regular English language program. But the bilingual educators saw the program as an opportunity to maintain the language and culture of the non-English-speaking student, while he was learning English.[3]

What was extraordinary about the Bilingual Education Act of 1968, which has since been renewed several times, is that it was the first time that the Congress had ever legislated a given pedagogical method. In practice, bilingual education means a program in which children study the major school subjects in a language other than English. Funding of the program, although small within the context of the federal education budget, created strong constituencies for its continuation, both within the federal government and among recipient agencies. No different from other interest groups, these constituencies pressed for expansion and strengthening of their program. Just as lifelong vocational educators are unlikely to ask whether their program works, so career bilingual educators are committed to their method as a philosophy, not as a technique for language instruction. The difference is this: techniques are subject to evaluation, which may cause them to be revised or discarded; philosophies are not.

In 1974, the Supreme Court's *Lau v. Nichols* decision reinforced demands for bilingual education. The Court ruled against the San Francisco public schools for their failure to provide English language instruction for 1,800 non-English-speaking Chinese students. The Court's decision was reasonable and appropriate. The Court said, "There is no equality of treatment merely by providing students with the same facilities, textbooks, teachers, and curriculum; for students who do not understand English are effectively foreclosed from any meaningful education." The decision did not endorse any particular remedy. It said "Teaching English to the students of Chinese ancestry who do not speak the language is one choice. Giving instruction to the group in Chinese is another. There may be others."[4]

Despite the Court's prudent refusal to endorse any particular method of instruction, the bilingual educators interpreted the *Lau* decision as a mandate for bilingual programs. In the year after the decision, the United States Office of Education established a task force to fashion guidelines for the implementation of the *Lau* decision; the task force was composed of bilingual educators and representatives of language minority groups. The task force fashioned regulations that prescribed in exhaustive detail how school districts should prepare and carry out bilingual programs for non-English-speaking students. The districts were directed to identify the student's primary language, not by his proficiency in English, but by determining which language was most often spoken in the student's home, which language he had learned first, and which language he used most often. Thus a student would be eligible for a bilingual program even if he was entirely fluent in English.[5]

Furthermore, while the Supreme Court refused to endorse any given method, the task force directed that non-English-speaking students should receive bilin-

gual education that emphasized instruction in their native language and culture. Districts were discouraged from using the "English as a Second Language" approach, which consists of intensive, supplemental English-only instruction, or immersion techniques, in which students are instructed in English within an English-only context.

Since the establishment of the bilingual education program, many millions of dollars have been spent to support bilingual programs in more than sixty different languages. Among those receiving funding to administer and staff such programs, bilingual education is obviously popular, but there are critics who think that it is educationally unsound. Proponents of desegregation have complained that bilingual education needlessly segregates non-English speakers from others of their age. At a congressional hearing in 1977, one desegregation specialist complained that bilingual programs had been funded "without any significant proof that they would work.... There is nothing in the research to suggest that children can effectively learn English without continuous interaction with other children who are native English speakers."[6]

The research on bilingual education has been contradictory, and studies that favor or criticize the bilingual approach have been attacked as biased. Researchers connected to bilingual institutes claim that their programs resulted in significant gains for non-English-speaking children. But a four-year study commissioned by the United States Office of Education concluded that students who learned bilingually did not achieve at a higher level than those in regular classes, nor were their attitudes toward school significantly different. What they seemed to learn best, the study found, was the language in which they were instructed.[7]

One of the few evidently unbiased, nonpolitical assessments of bilingual research was published in 1982 in the *Harvard Educational Review*. A survey of international findings, it concluded that "bilingual programs are neither better nor worse than other instructional methods." The author found that in the absence of compelling experimental support for this method, there was "no legal necessity or research basis for the federal government to advocate or require a specific educational approach."[8]

If the research is in fact inconclusive, then there is no justification for mandating the use of bilingual education or any other single pedagogy. The bilingual method may or may not be the best way to learn English. Language instruction programs that are generally regarded as outstanding, such as those provided for Foreign Service officers or by the nationally acclaimed center at Middlebury College, are immersion programs, in which students embark on a systematic program of intensive language learning without depending on their native tongue. Immersion programs may not be appropriate for all children, but then neither is any single pedagogical method. The method to be used should be determined by the school authorities and the professional staff, based on their resources and competence.

Despite the fact that the Supreme Court did not endorse bilingual education, the lower federal courts have tended to treat this pedagogy as a civil right, and more than a dozen states have mandated its use in their public schools. The path by which bilingual education came to be viewed as a civil right, rather than as one method of teaching language, demonstrates the politicization of the language issue in American education. The United States Commission on Civil Rights endorsed bilingual education as a civil right nearly a decade ago. Public interest lawyers and civil rights lawyers have also regarded bilingual education as a basic civil right. An article in 1983 in the *Columbia Journal of Law and Social Problems* contended that bilingual education "may be the most effective method of compensatory language instruction currently used to educate language-minority students."[9] It based this conclusion not on a review of educational research but on statements made by various political agencies.

The article states, for example, as a matter of fact rather than opinion: " ... by offering subject matter instruction in a language understood by language-minority students, the bilingual-bicultural method maximizes achievement, and thus minimizes feelings of inferiority that might accompany a poor academic performance. By ridding the school environment of those features which may damage a language-minority child's self-image and thereby interfere with the educative process, bilingual-bicultural education creates the atmosphere most conducive to successful learning."[10]

If there were indeed conclusive evidence for these statements, then bilingual-bicultural education *should* be imposed on school districts throughout the country. However, the picture is complicated; there are good bilingual programs, and there are ineffective bilingual programs. In and of itself, bilingualism is one pedagogical method, as subject to variation and misuse as any other single method. To date, no school district has claimed that the bilingual method succeeded in sharply decreasing the dropout rate of Hispanic children or markedly raising their achievement scores in English and other subjects. The bilingual method is not necessarily inferior to other methods; its use should not be barred. There simply is no conclusive evidence that bilingualism should be preferred to all other ways of instructing non-English-speaking students. This being the case, there are no valid reasons for courts or federal agencies to impose this method on school districts for all non-English speakers, to the exclusion of other methods of language instruction.

Bilingual education exemplifies politicization because its advocates press its adoption regardless of its educational effectiveness, and they insist that it must be made mandatory regardless of the wishes of the parents and children who are its presumed beneficiaries. It is a political program whose goals are implicit in the term "biculturalism." The aim is to use the public schools to promote the maintenance of distinct ethnic communities, each with its own cultural heritage and language. This in itself is a valid goal for a democratic nation as diverse and pluralistic as ours, but it is questionable whether this goal is appropriately pursued by the public schools, rather than by the freely chosen activities of individuals and groups.

Then there is the larger question of whether bilingual education actually promotes equality of educational opportunity. Unless it enables non-English-speaking children to learn English and to enter into the mainstream of American society, it may hinder equality of educational opportunity. The child who spends most of his instructional time learning in Croatian or Greek or Spanish is likely to learn Croatian, Greek, or Spanish. Fluency in these languages will be of little help to those who want to apply to American colleges, universities, graduate schools, or employers, unless they are also fluent in English.

Of course, our nation needs much more foreign language instruction. But we should not confuse our desire to promote foreign languages in general with the special educational needs of children who do not know how to speak and read English in an English-language society.

Will our educational institutions ever be insulated from the extremes of politicization? It seems highly unlikely, in view of the fact that our schools and colleges are deeply embedded in the social and political mainstream. What is notably different today is the vastly increased power of the federal government and the courts to intervene in educational institutions, because of the expansion of the laws and the dependence of almost all educational institutions on public funding. To avoid unwise and dangerous politicization, government agencies should strive to distinguish between their proper role as protectors of fundamental constitutional rights and inappropriate intrusion into complex issues of curriculum and pedagogy.

This kind of institutional restraint would be strongly abetted if judges and policymakers exercised caution and skepticism in their use of social science testimony. Before making social research the basis for constitutional edicts, judges and policymakers should understand that social science findings are usually divergent, limited, tentative, and partial.

We need the courts as vigilant guardians of our rights; we need federal agencies that respond promptly to any violations of those rights. But we also need educational institutions that are free to exercise their responsibilities without fear of pressure groups and political lobbies. Decisions about which textbooks to use, which theories to teach, which books to place in the school library, how to teach, and what to teach are educational issues. They should be made by appropriate lay and professional authorities on educational grounds. In a democratic society, all of us share the responsibility to protect schools, colleges, and universities against unwarranted political intrusion into educational affairs.

REFERENCES

1. *Hobson v. Hansen*, 269 F. Supp. 401 (D.D.C., 1967); Alexander Bickel, "Skelly Wright's Sweeping Decision," *New Republic*, July 8, 1967, pp. 11–12.
2. Nathan Glazer, "Black English and Reluctant Judges," *Public Interest*, vol. 62, Winter 1980, pp. 40–54; *Larry P. v. Wilson Riles*, 495 F. Supp. 1926 (N.D. Calif., 1979); Nathan Glazer, "IQ on Trial," *Commentary*, June 1981, pp. 51–59; *Morgan v. Hennigan*, 379 F. Supp. 410 (D. Mass., 1974); Robert Wood, "The Disassembling of American Education," *Daedalus*, vol. 109, no. 3, Summer 1980, pp. 99–113; *Education Week*, May 12, 1982, p. 5.
3. U.S. Congress, Senate, Committee on Labor and Public Welfare, Special Subcommittee on Bilingual Education, 90th Cong., 1st sess., 1967.
4. *Lau v. Nichols*, 414 U.S. 563 (1974).
5. U.S. Department of Health, Education, and Welfare, "Task Force Findings Specifying Remedies Available for Eliminating Past Educational Practices Ruled Unlawful under *Lau v. Nichols*" (Washington, D.C., Summer 1975).
6. U.S. Congress, House, Subcommittee on Elementary, Secondary, and Vocational Education of the Committee on Education and Labor, Bilingual Education, 95th Cong., 1st sess., 1977, pp. 335–336. The speaker was Gary Orfield.
7. Malcolm N. Danoff, "Evaluation of the Impact of ESEA Title VII Spanish/English Bilingual Education Programs" (Palo Alto, Calif.: American Institutes for Research, 1978).
8. Iris Rotberg, "Some Legal and Research Considerations in Establishing Federal Policy in Bilingual Education," *Harvard Educational Review*, vol. 52, May 1982, pp. 148–168.
9. Jonathan D. Haft, "Assuring Equal Educational Opportunity for Language-Minority Students: Bilingual Education and the Equal Educational Opportunity Act of 1974." *Columbia Journal of Law and Social Problems*, vol. 18, no. 2, 1983, pp. 209–293.
10. Ibid., p. 253.

NO

Donaldo Macedo

ENGLISH ONLY: THE TONGUE-TYING OF AMERICA

During the past decade conservative educators such as ex-secretary of education William Bennett and Diane Ravitch have mounted an unrelenting attack on bilingual and multicultural education. These conservative educators tend to recycle old assumptions about the "melting pot theory" and our "common culture," assumptions designed primarily to maintain the status quo. Maintained is a status quo that functions as a cultural reproduction mechanism which systematically does not allow other cultural subjects, who are considered outside of the mainstream, to be present in history. These cultural subjects who are profiled as the "other" are but palely represented in history within our purportedly democratic society in the form of Black History Month, Puerto Rican Day, and so forth. This historical constriction was elegantly captured by an 11th-grade Vietnamese student in California:

> I was so excited when my history teacher talked about the Vietnam War. Now at last, I thought, now we will study about my country. We didn't really study it. Just for one day, though, my country was real again. (Olsen, 1988, p. 68)

The incessant attack on bilingual education which claims that it serves to tongue-tie students in their native language not only negates the multilingual and multicultural nature of U.S. society, but blindly ignores the empirical evidence that has been amply documented in support of bilingual education.... [T]he present overdose of monolingualism and Anglocentrism that dominates the current educational debate not only contributes to a type of mind-tied America, but also is incapable of producing educators and leaders who can rethink what it means to prepare students to enter the ever-changing, multilingual, and multicultural world of the 21st century.

It is both academically dishonest and misleading to simply point to some failures of bilingual education without examining the lack of success of linguistic minority students within a larger context of a general failure of public education in major urban centers. Furthermore, the English Only position points to a pedagogy of exclusion that views the learning of English as education itself. English Only advocates fail to question under what conditions

From Donaldo Macedo, "English Only: The Tongue-Tying of America," *Journal of Education*, vol. 173, no. 2 (Spring 1991). Copyright © 1991 by the Trustees of Boston University. Reprinted by permission.

English will be taught and by whom. For example, immersing non-English-speaking students in English as a Second Language [ESL] programs taught by untrained music, art and social science teachers (as is the case in Massachusetts with the grandfather clause in ESL Certification) will hardly accomplish the avowed goals of the English Only Movement. The proponents of English Only also fail to raise two other fundamental questions. First, if English is the most effective educational language, how can we explain that over 60 million Americans are illiterate or functionally illiterate (Kozol, 1985, p. 4)? Second, if education solely in English can guarantee linguistic minorities a better future, as educators like William Bennett promise, why do the majority of Black Americans, whose ancestors have been speaking English for over 200 years, find themselves still relegated to ghettos?

I want to argue in this paper that the answer lies not in technical questions of whether English is a more viable language of instruction or the repetitive promise that it offers non-English-speaking students "full participation first in their school and later in American society" (Silber, 1991, p. 7). This position assumes that English is in fact a superior language and that we live in a classless, race-blind society. I want to propose that decisions about how to educate non-English-speaking students cannot be reduced to issues of language, but rest in a full understanding of the ideological elements that generate and sustain linguistic, racial, and sex discrimination. That is, educators need to develop, as Henry Giroux has suggested, "a politics and pedagogy around a new language capable of acknowledging the multiple, contradictory, and complex subject posi-tions people occupy within different social, cultural, and economic locations" (1992, p. 27). By shifting the linguistic issue to an ideological terrain we will challenge conservative educators to confront the Berlin Wall of racism, classism, and economic deprivation which characterizes the lived experiences of minorities in U.S. public schools. For example, J. Anthony Lukas succinctly captures the ideological elements that promote racism and segregation in schools in his analysis of desegregation in the Boston Public Schools. Lukas cites a trip to Charlestown High School, where a group of Black parents experienced firsthand the stark reality their children were destined to endure. Although the headmaster assured them that "violence, intimidation, or racial slurs would not be tolerated," they could not avoid the racial epithets on the walls: "Welcome Niggers," "Niggers Suck," "White Power," "KKK," "Bus is for Zulu," and "Be illiterate, fight busing." As those parents were boarding the bus, "they were met with jeers and catcalls 'go home niggers. Keep going all the way to Africa!'" This racial intolerance led one parent to reflect, "My god, what kind of hell am I sending my children into?" (Lukas, 1985, p. 282). What could her children learn at a school like that except to hate? Even though forced integration of schools in Boston exacerbated the racial tensions in the Boston Public Schools, one should not overlook the deep-seated racism that permeates all levels of the school structure....

Against this landscape of violent racism perpetrated against racial minorities, and also against linguistic minorities, one can understand the reasons for the high dropout rate in the Boston public schools (approximately 50%). Perhaps racism and other ideological elements are part of a school reality which forces a high percentage of students to leave school, only later to be profiled by the very system as dropouts or "poor and unmotivated students." One could argue that the above incidents occurred during a tumultuous time of racial division in Boston's history, but I do not believe that we have learned a great deal from historically dangerous memories to the degree that our leaders continue to invite racial tensions as evidenced in the Willie Horton presidential campaign issue and the present quota for jobs as an invitation once again to racial divisiveness.

It is very curious that this new-found concern of English Only advocates for limited English proficiency students does not interrogate those very ideological elements that psychologically and emotionally harm these students far more than the mere fact that English may present itself as a temporary barrier to an effective education. It would be more socially constructive and beneficial if the zeal that propels the English Only movement were diverted toward social struggles designed to end violent racism and structures of poverty, homelessness, and family breakdown, among other social ills that characterize the lived experiences of minorities in the United States. If these social issues are not dealt with appropriately, it is naive to think that the acquisition of the English language alone will, somehow, magically eclipse the raw and cruel injustices and oppression perpetrated against the dispossessed class of minorities in the United States. According to Peter McLaren, these dispossessed minority students who

> populate urban settings in places such as Howard Beach, Ozone Park, El Barrio, are more likely to be forced to learn about Eastern Europe in ways set forth by neo-conservative multiculturists than they are to learn about the Harlem Renaissance, Mexico, Africa, the Caribbean, or Aztec or Zulu culture. (McLaren, 1991, p. 7)

While arguing for the use of the students' native language in their educational development, I would like to make it very clear that the bilingual education goal should never be to restrict students to their own vernacular. This linguistic constriction inevitably leads to a linguistic ghetto. Educators must understand fully the broader meaning of the use of students' language as a requisite for their empowerment. That is, empowerment should never be limited to what Stanley Aronowitz describes as "the process of appreciating and loving oneself" (1985). In addition to this process, empowerment should also be a means that enables students "to interrogate and selectively appropriate those aspects of the dominant culture that will provide them with the basis for defining and transforming, rather than merely serving, the wider social order" (Giroux & McLaren, 1986, p. 17). This means that educators should understand the value of mastering the standard English language of the wider society. It is through the full appropriation of the standard English language that linguistic minority students find themselves linguistically empowered to engage in dialogue with various sectors of the wider society. What I must reiterate is that educators should never allow the limited proficient students' native language to be silenced by a distorted legitimation of the standard English language. Linguistic minority students' language should never be sacrificed, since it is the only means through which they make sense of their own experience in the world.

Given the importance of the standard English language in the education of linguistic minority students, I must agree with the members of the Institute for Research in English Acquisition and Development when they quote Antonio Gramsci in their brochure:

> Without the mastery of the common standard version of the national language, one is inevitably destined to function only at the periphery of national life and, especially, outside the national and political mainstream. (READ, 1990)

But these English Only advocates fail to tell the other side of Antonio Gramsci's argument, which warns us:

> Each time that in one way or another, the question of language comes to the fore, that signifies that a series of other problems is about to emerge, the formation and enlarging of the ruling class, the necessity to establish more "intimate" and sure relations between the ruling groups and the popular masses, that is, the reorganization of cultural hegemony. (Gramsci, 1971, p. 16)

This selective selection of Gramsci's position on language points to the hidden curriculum with which the English Only movement seeks to promote a monolithic ideology. It is also part and parcel of an ongoing attempt at "reorganization of cultural hegemony" as evidenced by the unrelenting attack by conservative educators on multicultural education and curriculum diversity....

In contrast to the zeal for a common culture and English only, these conservative educators have remained ominously silent about forms of racism, inequality, subjugation, and exploitation that daily serve to wage symbolic and real violence against those children who by virtue of their language, race, ethnicity, class, or gender are not treated in schools with the dignity and respect all children warrant in a democracy. Instead of reconstituting education around an urban and cultural studies approach which takes the social, cultural, political, and economic divisions of education and everyday life as the primary categories for understanding contemporary schooling, conservative educators have recoiled in an attempt to salvage the status quo. That is, they try to keep the present unchanged even though, as Renato Constantino points out:

> Within the living present there are imperceptible changes which make the status quo a moving reality.... Thus a new policy based on the present as past and not on the present as future is backward for it is premised not on evolving conditions but on conditions that are already dying away. (1978, p. 201)

One such not so imperceptible change is the rapid growth of minority representation in the labor force. As such, the conservative leaders and educators are digging this country's economic grave by their continued failure to educate minorities. As Lew Ferlerger and Jay Mandle convincingly argue, "Unless the educational attainment of minority populations in the United States improves, the country's hopes for resuming high rates of growth and an increasing standard of living look increasingly dubious" (1991, p. 12).

In addition to the real threat to the economic fabric of the United States, the persistent call for English language only in education smacks of backwardness in the present conjuncture of our ever-changing multicultural and multi-ingual society. Furthermore, these conservative educators base their language policy argument on the premise that English education in this country is highly effective. On the contrary. As Patrick Courts clearly argues in his book *Literacy for Empowerment* (1991), English education is failing even middle-class and upper-class students. He argues that English reading and writing classes are mostly based on workbooks and grammar lessons, lessons which force students to "bark at print" or fill in the blanks. Students engage in grudgingly banal exercises such as practicing correct punctuation and writing sample business letters. Books used in their classes are, Courts points out, too often in the service of commercially prepared ditto sheets and workbooks. Courts's account suggests that most school programs do not take advantage of the language experiences that the majority of students have had before they reach school. These teachers become the victims of their own professional ideology when they delegitimize the language experiences that students bring with them into the classroom.

Courts's study is basically concerned with middle-class and upper-middle-class students unburdened by racial discrimination and poverty, students who have done well in elementary and high school settings and are now populating the university lecture halls and seminar rooms. If schools are failing these students, the situation does not bode well for those students less economically, socially, and politically advantaged. It is toward the linguistic minority students that would like to turn my discussion now.

THE ROLE OF LANGUAGE IN THE EDUCATION OF LINGUISTIC MINORITY STUDENTS

Within the last two decades, the issue of bilingual education has taken on a heated importance among educators. Unfortunately, the debate that has emerged tends to recycle old assumptions and values regarding the meaning and usefulness of the students' native language in education. The notion that education of linguistic minority students is a matter of learning the standard English language still informs the vast majority of bilingual programs and manifests its logic in the renewed emphasis on technical reading and writing skills.

I want to reiterate in this paper that the education of linguistic minority students cannot be viewed as simply the development of skills aimed at acquiring the standard English language. English Only proponents seldom discuss the pedagogical structures that will enable these students to access other bodies of knowledge. Nor do they interrogate the quality of ESL instruction provided to the linguistic minority students and the adverse material conditions under which these students learn English. The view that teaching English constitutes education sustains a notion of ideology that systematically negates rather than makes meaningful the cultural experiences of the subordinate linguistic groups who are, by and large, the objects of its policies. For the education of linguistic minority students to become meaningful it has to be situated within a theory of cultural production and viewed as an integral part of the way in which people produce, transform, and reproduce meaning. Bilingual education, in this sense, must be seen as a medium that constitutes and affirms the historical and existential moments of lived culture. Hence, it is an eminently political phenomenon, and it must be analyzed within the context of a theory of power relations and an understanding of social and cultural reproduction and production. By "cultural reproduction" I refer to collective experiences that function in the interest of the dominant groups rather than in the interest of the oppressed groups that are objects of its policies. Bilingual education programs in the United States have been developed and implemented under the cultural reproduction model leading to a de facto neocolonial educational model. I use "cultural production" to refer to specific groups of people producing, mediating, and confirming the mutual ideological elements that merge from and reaffirm their daily lived experiences. In this case, such experiences are rooted in the interest of individual and collective self-determination. It is only through a cultural production model that we can achieve a truly democratic and liberatory educational experience. I will return to this issue later.

While the various debates in the past two decades may differ in their basic assumptions about the education of linguistic minority students, they all share one common feature: they all ignore the role of language as a major force in the construction of human subjectivities. That is, they ignore the way language may either confirm or deny the life histories and experiences of the people who use it.

The pedagogical and political implications in education programs for linguistic minority students are far-reaching and yet largely ignored. These programs, for example, often contradict a fundamental principle of reading, namely that stu-dents learn to read faster and with better comprehension when taught in their native tongue. The immediate recognition of familiar words and experiences enhances the development of a positive self-concept in children who are somewhat insecure about the status of their language and culture. For this reason, and to be consistent with the plan to construct a democratic society free from vestiges of oppression, a minority literacy program must be rooted in the cultural capital of subordinate groups and have as its point of departure their own language.

Educators must develop radical pedagogical structures which provide students with the opportunity to use their own reality as a basis of literacy. This includes, obviously, the language they bring to the classroom. To do otherwise is to deny minority students the rights that lie at the core of a democratic education. The failure to base a literacy program on the minority students' language means that oppositional forces can neutralize the efforts of educators and political leaders to achieve decolonization of schooling. It is of tantamount importance that the incorporation of the minority language as the primary language of instruction in education of linguistic minority students be given top priority. It is through their own language that linguistic minority students will be able to reconstruct their history and their culture.

I want to argue that the minority language has to be understood within the theoretical framework that generates it. Put another way, the ultimate meaning and value of the minority language is not to be found by determining how systematic and rule-governed it is. We know that already. Its real meaning has to be understood through the assumptions that govern it, and it has to be understood via the social, political, and ideological relations to which it points. Generally speaking, this issue of effectiveness and validity often hides the true role of language in the maintenance of the values and interests of the dominant class. In other words, the issue of effectiveness and validity becomes a mask that obfuscates questions about the social, political, and ideological order within which the minority language exists.

If an emancipatory and critical education program is to be developed in the United States for linguistic minority students in which they become "subjects" rather than "objects," educators must understand the productive quality of language. James Donald puts it this way:

> I take language to be productive rather than reflective of social reality. This means calling into question the assumption that we, as speaking subjects, simply use language to organize and express our ideas and experiences. On the contrary, language is one of the most important social practices through which we come to experience ourselves as subjects.... My point here is that once we get beyond the idea of language as no more than a medium of communication, as a tool equally and neutrally available to all parties in cultural exchanges, then we can begin to examine language both as a practice of signification and also as a site for culture struggle and as a mechanism which produces antagonistic relations between different social groups. (Donald, 1982, p. 44)

It is to the antagonistic relationship between the minority and dominant speakers that I want to turn now. The antagonistic nature of the minority language has never been fully explored. In order to more clearly discuss this issue of antago-

nism, I will use Donald's distinction between oppressed language and repressed language. Using Donald's categories, the "negative" way of posing the minority language question is to view it in terms of oppression—that is, seeing the minority language as "lacking" the dominant standard features which usually serve as a point of reference for the minority language. By far the most common questions concerning the minority language in the United States are posed from the oppression perspective. The alternative view of the minority language is that it is repressed in the standard dominant language. In this view, minority language as a repressed language could, if spoken, challenge the privileged standard linguistic dominance. Educators have failed to recognize the "positive" promise and antagonistic nature of the minority language. It is precisely on these dimensions that educators must demystify the standard dominant language and the old assumptions about its inherent superiority. Educators must develop liberatory and critical bilingual programs informed by a radical pedagogy so that the minority language will cease to provide its speakers the experience of subordination and, moreover, may be brandished as a weapon of resistance to the dominance of the dominant standard language of the curriculum.

In this sense, the students' language is the only means by which they can develop their own voice, a prerequisite to the development of a positive sense of self-worth. As Giroux elegantly states, the students' voice "is the discursive means to make themselves 'heard' and to define themselves as active authors of their worlds" (Giroux & McLaren, 1986, p. 235). The authorship of one's own world also implies the use of one's own language, and relates to what Mikhail Bakhtin describes as "retelling a story in one's own words" (Giroux & McLaren, 1986, p. 235).

A DEMOCRATIC AND LIBERATORY EDUCATION FOR LINGUISTIC MINORITY STUDENTS

In maintaining a certain coherence with the educational plan to reconstruct new and more democratic educational programs for linguistic minority students, educators and political leaders need to create a new school grounded in a new educational praxis, expressing different concepts of education consonant with the principles of a democratic, multicultural, and multilingual society. In order for this to happen, the first step is to identify the objectives of the inherent colonial education that informs the majority of bilingual programs in the United States. Next, it is necessary to analyze how colonialist methods used by the dominant schools function, legitimize the Anglocentric values and meaning, and at the same time negate the history, culture, and language practices of the majority of linguistic minority students. The new school, so it is argued, must also be informed by a radical bilingual pedagogy, which would make concrete such values as solidarity, social responsibility, and creativity. In the democratic development of bilingual programs rooted in a liberatory ideology, linguistic minority students become "subjects" rather than mere "objects" to be assimilated blindly into an often hostile dominant "common" culture. A democratic and liberatory education needs to move away from traditional approaches, which emphasize the acquisition of mechanical basic skills while divorcing education from its ideological

and historical contexts. In attempting to meet this goal, it purposely must reject the conservative principles embedded in the English Only movement I have discussed earlier. Unfortunately, many bilingual programs sometimes unknowingly reproduce one common feature of the traditional approaches to education by ignoring the important relationship between language and the cultural capital of the students at whom bilingual education is aimed. The result is the development of bilingual programs whose basic assumptions are at odds with the democratic spirit that launched them.

Bilingual program development must be largely based on the notion of a democratic and liberatory education, in which education is viewed "as one of the major vehicles by which 'oppressed' people are able to participate in the sociohistorical transformation of their society" (Walmsley, 1981, p. 74). Bilingual education, in this sense, is grounded in a critical reflection of the cultural capital of the oppressed. It becomes a vehicle by which linguistic minority students are equipped with the necessary tools to reappropriate their history, culture, and language practices. It is, thus, a way to enable the linguistic minority students to reclaim "those historical and existential experiences that are devalued in everyday life by the dominant culture in order to be both validated and critically understood" (Giroux, 1983, p. 226). To do otherwise is to deny these students their very democratic rights. In fact, the criticism that bilingual and multicultural education unwisely question the traditions and values of our so-called "common culture" as suggested by Kenneth T. Jackson (1991) is both antidemocratic and academically dishonest. Multicultural education and curriculum diversity did not create the

S & L scandal, the Iran-Contra debacle, or the extortion of minority properties by banks, the stewards of the "common culture," who charged minorities exorbitant loan-sharking interest rates. Multicultural education and curriculum diversity did not force Joachim Maitre, dean of the College of Communication at Boston University, to choose the hypocritical moral high ground to excoriate the popular culture's "bleak moral content," all the while plagiarizing 15 paragraphs of a conservative comrade's text.

The learning of English language skills alone will not enable linguistic minority students to acquire the critical tools "to awaken and liberate them from their mystified and distorted views of themselves and their world" (Giroux, 1983, p. 226). For example, speaking English has not enabled African-Americans to change this society's practice of jailing more Blacks than even South Africa, and this society spending over 7 billion dollars to keep African-American men in jail while spending only 1 billion dollars educating Black males (Black, 1991).

Educators must understand the all-encompassing role the dominant ideology has played in this mystification and distortion of our so-called "common culture" and our "common language." They must also recognize the antagonistic relationship between the "common culture" and those who, by virtue of their race, language, ethnicity, and gender, have been relegated to the margins. Finally, educators must develop bilingual programs based on the theory of cultural production. In other words, linguistic minority students must be provided the opportunity to become actors in the reconstruction of a more democratic and just society. In short, education conducted in English only is alienating to lin-

guistic minority students, since it denies them the fundamental tools for reflection, critical thinking, and social interaction. Without the cultivation of their native language, and robbed of the opportunity for reflection and critical thinking, linguistic minority students find themselves unable to re-create their culture and history. Without the reappropriation of their culture, the valorization of their lived experiences, English Only supporters' vacuous promise that the English language will guarantee students "full participation first in their school and later in American society" (Silber, 1991, p. 7) can hardly be a reality.

REFERENCES

Aronowitz, S. (1985, May). "Why should Johnny read." *Village Voice Literary Supplement*, p. 13.

Black, C. (1991, January 13). Paying the high price for being the world's no. 1 jailor. *Boston Sunday Globe*, p. 67.

Constantino, R. (1928). *Neocolonial identity and counter consciousness*. London: Merlin Press.

Courts, P. (1991). *Literacy for empowerment*. South Hadley, MA: Bergin & Garvey.

Donald, J. (1982). Language, literacy, and schooling. In *The state and popular culture*. Milton Keynes: Open University Culture Unit.

Ferlerger, L., & Mandle, J. (1991). *African-Americans and the future of the U.S. economy*. Unpublished manuscript.

Giroux, H. A. (1983). *Theory and resistance: A pedagogy for the opposition*. South Hadley, MA: Bergin & Garvey.

Giroux, H. (1991). *Border crossings: Cultural workers and the politics of education*. New York: Routledge.

Giroux, H. A., & McLaren, P. (1986). Teacher education and the politics of engagement: The case for democratic schooling. *Harvard Educational Review, 56*(3), 213–238.

Gramsci, A. (1971). *Selections from Prison Notebooks*, (Ed. and Trans. Quinten Hoare & Geoffrey Smith). New York: International Publishers.

Jackson, D. (1991, December 8). The end of the second Reconstruction. *Boston Globe*, p. 27.

Jackson, K. T. (1991, July 7). Cited in a *Boston Sunday Globe* editorial.

Kozol, J. (1985). *Illiterate America*. New York: Doubleday Anchor.

Lukas, J. A. (1985). *Common ground*. New York: Alfred A. Knopf.

McLaren, P. (1991). Critical pedagogy: Constructing an arch of social dreaming and a doorway to hope. *Journal of Education, 173*(1), 9–34.

Olsen, L. (1988). *Crossing the schoolhouse border: Immigrant students and the California public schools*. San Francisco: California Tomorrow.

Silber, J. (1991, May). *Boston University Commencement Catalogue*.

Walmsley, S. (1981). On the purpose and content of secondary reading programs: Educational and ideological perspectives. *Curriculum Inquiry, 11*, 73–79.

POSTSCRIPT

Should Bilingual Education Programs Be Abandoned?

Macedo blames an ineffective bilingual education program for the fact that the vast majority of the country's high school dropouts are minorities. He maintains that learning English alone will not assist minority students in becoming equal members of society. Bilingual programs must do more to acculturate students.

Is bilingual education effective? Although Macedo thinks it can be, some studies suggest that bilingual programs may be ineffective. What can society do? Can we, in good conscience, take a "sink or swim" attitude and do nothing while some children become so frustrated and discouraged that they no longer want to go to school? Is society willing to continue to support those people who cannot earn a living because they cannot read and write in English? Is it possible that current bilingual programs are not very effective because they are designed in such a way that children are actually taught little English and instead spend their time in special "transitional" classes?

A. M. Thernstrom, in his article "Bilingual Miseducation," *Commentary* (vol. 88, 1990), encourages bilingual educators to teach the English language while emphasizing the culture of the students' new country. This could prevent the children from feeling like strangers in a foreign land.

The debate on the utility of bilingual education rages on in courtrooms, school boards, and families. However, as we engage in these arguments, we must not lose sight of the true focus of our discussion—the children. What approach will provide the most expedient way to give non-English-speaking children the best possible education?

SUGGESTED READINGS

Citrin, J. (1990). Language, politics, and American identity. *Public Interest, 99,* 96–109.

Hokuta, K. (1992). At issue: Do bilingual education programs help Hispanic children learn English and assimilate into American culture? *CQ Researcher, 2,* 945.

Imhoff, G. (1990). The position of the U.S. English on bilingual education. *Annals of the American Academy of Political and Social Science, 508,* 48–51.

Miller, J. A. (1990). Native-language instruction found to aid L.E.P.'s. *Education Week, 10,* 1, 23.

Porter, R. P. (1991). Language choice for Latino students. *The Public Interest, 105,* 48–60.

ISSUE 13

Will Stricter Dress Codes Improve the Educational Environment?

YES: Jessica Portner, from "Dressing for Success," *Education Week* (February 14, 1997)

NO: Karon L. Jahn, from "School Dress Codes v. The First Amendment: Ganging Up on School Attire," Paper Presented at the 78th Annual Convention of the Speech Communication Association (October 30, 1992)

ISSUE SUMMARY

YES: Jessica Portner, who writes for *Education Week*, reports that uniforms are good for schools. After a policy on uniforms was adopted by schools in Long Beach, California, teachers and administrators saw a decrease in violence and an increase in academic achievement.

NO: Karon L. Jahn, dean of students at Chaminade University, Honolulu, Hawaii, contends that strict dress code policies interfere with students' First Amendment right of freedom of speech. Dressing alike teaches children to follow the crowd and not think for themselves, she states, and strict dress codes do more harm than good.

Dress codes have always been a part of school policy in public and private schools, but the issue of school dress took a political turn in 1996 when the president of the United States, Bill Clinton, took a stand in favor of school uniforms for all children, by mentioning the Long Beach school uniform policy in his State of the Union address. The president signed an executive order to send all school districts in the country a manual on school uniforms. Schools were not mandated to implement the policy of uniforms but were encouraged to consider the advantages of school uniforms and were asked to use the *School Uniform Manual* to guide them in the process.

In 1994 Long Beach, California, became the first city in the United States to require a uniform dress policy in the public elementary and middle schools. The Long Beach School District found that after students started wearing similar outfits there was a decrease in student drug cases, sex offenses, assault and battery, and fights. It was felt that the reason for the change was that uniform dress created a positive environment and that this new environment allowed teachers to focus on education instead of spending all their time on discipline issues. Many states have since followed this trend by instituting mandatory or suggested forms of school dress.

School districts are under pressure from community groups and parents to adopt stricter dress codes, and this pressure is usually translated into requiring some type of school uniform. Caruso (1996) summarized the arguments for and against school uniforms. Reasons for uniforms: attendance increases because students claim it is easier to come to school when a "fashionable wardrobe" is not required; students' concentration on school work increases; students' self-esteem increases because students all look the same and differences are not so apparent; school spirit increases in the same way that team uniforms promote unity; clothing costs for families decrease; classroom behavior improves; gang member clothing and gang activity is eliminated; academic performance increases.

Reasons against school uniforms: First Amendment rights of personal expression are denied; students feel controlled and prevented from expressing themselves; economic hardship for families; gang violence is not deterred; social class differences are not eliminated; there is no empirical data that uniforms have a positive impact on school and children.

As you think about how you dressed in school and how students dress now, are there real differences? Do students want to look very different from their peers? Do you believe that simply wearing the same thing to school makes it a better and safer place to be? Are there other factors that accompany a school uniform policy that could be affecting the school environment?

In the following selection, Jessica Portner details the dressing rules for the districtwide K–8 uniform policy in Long Beach, California. She supplies statistical evidence that the wearing of uniforms does indeed provide a solution to school disorganization and violence. Conversely, Karon L. Jahn questions the legality of setting dress codes and requiring uniform dress of children. She wonders if it sends the wrong message about individual freedom. She provides significant information about gang dress, its relationship to gang violence, and how it fits into questions about universal school dress codes.

YES
Jessica Portner

DRESSING FOR SUCCESS

Linda Moore has been feeling especially proud lately.

And she has President Clinton to thank.

In his State of the Union Address last month, Mr. Clinton praised student uniforms as a way to promote safety and discipline in public schools. Ms. Moore, the principal of Will Rogers Middle School here, felt a particular satisfaction in the endorsement.

"Everybody is looking for answers, and here is a district that is doing something that is working," she said. For more than a year, the 83,000-student Long Beach system has required its elementary and middle school students to dress in uniform fashion. It was the first public school district in the nation to do so.

Mr. Clinton may have had this Southern California school system in mind when, in his speech, he challenged public schools to mandate uniforms "if it meant that teenagers [would] stop killing each other over designer jackets."

Dramatic Results

Since the mandatory-uniform policy was launched in 56 elementary and 14 middle schools here in fall 1994, violence and discipline problems have decreased dramatically, a recent survey by the district shows.

From the year before uniforms were required, 1993–94, to last year, assault and battery cases in grades K–8 have dropped 34 percent. Physical fights between students have dropped by 51 percent, and there were 32 percent fewer suspensions.

Though each school in the district can choose its own uniform, most Long Beach students are required to wear black or blue pants, skirts, or shorts with white shirts. Nearly 60,000 K–8 students are affected by the policy.

Parents have the option of excusing their children from the requirements. But, so far, only 500 parents have filled out petitions to exempt their children, according to Dick Van DerLaan, a spokesman for the district.

In addition to Long Beach, a few other districts in California and across the country are testing the benefits of requiring students to come to school in color-specific, and sometimes style-specific, clothing.

From Jessica Portner, "Dressing For Success," *Education Week*, vol. 15, no. 21 (February 14, 1997). Copyright © 1997 by Editorial Projects in Education, Inc. Reprinted by permission of *Education Week*.

The Oakland, Calif., schools began a similar uniform policy last September. And a small number of other districts —including Dade County, Fla.; Seattle; and Charleston, S.C.—allow schools to decide for themselves whether to require uniforms.

But Long Beach appears to be the first school system to have documented measurable success in improving student behavior.

Since students at Rogers Middle School started wearing black bottoms, white tops, and red jackets or sweaters, fights have declined by 40 percent, and academic performance has improved, school official said.

Uniforms are an effective method of reducing unwanted behavior, she said, because the more formal clothing puts students in the right mind-set to learn.

"It's about dressing for success," said Ms. Moore, who said she wears the school uniform as a gesture of solidarity with her students. She has a selection of bright red blazers in her home closet.

Not one parent at Rogers Middle School has opted out of the plan this year, and a quick look around campus at the unbroken stream of red, white, and black shows that students are largely compliant. But there are some exceptions.

Last week, as Ms. Moore darted down the hall between classes, the former basketball coach was scanning the crowds.

"Tuck in that shirt," she called out to one disheveled teenager who was slouching against a locker. She looked disparagingly at another whose sweatshirt was clearly purple, not red.

In addition to choosing uniform colors, each of the district's schools is allowed to choose the fabric and style of dress. One elementary school requires its pupils to wear ties, and a few others prefer plaid, but most stick with blue or black and white.

"This isn't a private, prep school, with a coat-of-arms and saddle shoes look," Mr. Van DerLaan said. "It's a little more California casual."

Generation Gap

A catalyst for adopting uniforms in Long Beach was parents' fears over students being attacked for inadvertently wearing a wrong color scarf or hat that might provoke rivalry among local gangs.

The district adopted a dress code more than a decade ago that prohibits gang-related attire, as well as caps, bandanas, baggy pants, and electronic pagers. But many felt the district had to take a more drastic approach.

When Judy Jacobs had two children attending Rogers Middle School, she was among the organizers of the effort to bring uniforms to that school. She now has a child in a district elementary school and has remained enthusiastic about uniforms. "There are so few boundaries for kids these days, with the drug use and violence, so if we can give them some limits, that's good," she said.

The uniformity tends to bolster safety because it makes it easier to spot people who may not belong on campus, school leaders say.

Many who teach in areas where gangs are prevalent argue that students are safer walking to school when dressed in uniform.

"If gang members see one of our students in uniform, they'll leave them alone," as if they belong to a different clique, said William Ferguson, who has been a gym teacher at Franklin Middle School here for 14 years.

But a large portion of the district's students aren't as upbeat as parents and teachers appear to be. And the older they get, the less they seem to like it—which may not bode well for talk in the district of expanding the uniform requirement to high schools.

"It's like we're all in jail," said Hector Gonzalez, a 7th grader at Rogers.

"It's totally bogus," said Gan Luong, an 8th grader at Franklin. "If you wear decent clothes, you shouldn't have to wear uniforms."

Alicia Nunez, also an 8th grader at Franklin, complained that the regimented attire stifles her creativity. "You come to school to get your education, not for them to tell you how to dress," the 14-year-old said as she strode across campus wearing a chocolate-brown T-shirt and jeans.

Legal Challenge

The U.S. Supreme Court hasn't directly addressed the question of whether public schools can impose dress requirements on their students. Lower courts, however, have generally upheld school dress codes.

Last fall, in one of the first legal tests of a mandatory-uniform policy, an Arizona state judge upheld a Phoenix middle school's policy, even though it does not give students the right to opt out of the requirement.

Most public schools and districts offer a parent or guardian the opportunity to excuse a child from wearing a uniform. And most do not impose harsh penalties on students who are supposed to wear uniforms but don't.

"Schools generally feel they need to exercise latitude when they put their foot down," said Gary Marx, a spokesman for the American Association of School Administrators in Arlington, Va.

The American Civil Liberties Union of Southern California, on behalf of a group of low-income families, filed a lawsuit in state court last October against the Long Beach Unified School District claiming that the district's uniform policy is a financial burden on poor families. The ACLU also claimed that the district has violated state law by neglecting to adequately inform parents about their right to exempt their children from the program.

The lawsuit signed in 1994 by California Gov. Pete Wilson to allow state public schools to require uniforms also says that parents must have a way to opt out of such requirements.

The ACLU lawyers say many parents can't afford the cost of school uniforms. About 66 percent of the district's elementary and middle school students qualify for free or reduced-price lunches. The case is currently in mediation.

Hope Carradine, who dresses three of her five children in uniforms, said she had to ask other family members to help pay for them. "I shop thrift and buy in bulk and you can't do that with uniforms," she said.

Other Strategies

But district officials say that parents can buy the essential items—a white shirt and a pair of pants—for $25 from several area stores. In addition, many schools sell sweatshirts or shorts for $6 each. Many local charities also provide free uniforms, backpacks, and shoes to needy students.

And if parents find the costs too burdensome, Mr. Van DerLaan, the district spokesman, said, they can always opt out. A flier explaining this right was sent to parents nine months before any uniform policies became effective, he said.

Despite their commitment to the school-uniform policy, Long Beach officials don't view it as a panacea for discipline problems.

Other efforts, such as stepped-up parent involvement and additional conflict-resolution classes also have contributed to the more peaceful climate on campuses, school leaders here say.

The district is continuing to evaluate the benefits of uniforms to determine whether last year's improved numbers for behavior were more than a blip on the screen.

And while some Long Beach students complain that the regulation dress is monotonous and dampens their personal style, many also see a positive side.

"The good thing is people judge you on your inner characteristics rather than what you wear," said Nick Duran, an 8th grader and the student-body president at Rogers Middle School. Plus, he said, it's easier to choose what to put on in the morning.

NO

Karon L. Jahn

SCHOOL DRESS CODES V.
THE FIRST AMENDMENT

Teenagers, clothes and gang behavior—what can school administrators do, or not do, with this volatile combination? Nation-wide educators and parents are watching their schools become increasingly an arena of serious and constant violence. No longer a concern limited to the inner city emotional and physical safety of students has become an issue on all campuses. While violence stems from many causes—racial tensions, use of illegal drugs, lack of security at home—school administrators consistently point to student dress as an important element in propagating violence at school.

Few things are more personal than an individual's body and its appearance. Throughout a lifetime, individuals may create their own realities by managing their appearance—which includes developing ideas and actions —and acting toward other people on the basis of the meanings their appearance offers. Communication scholars argue that all behavior, both verbal and nonverbal, communicates. The U.S. Supreme Court (Court) has agreed, protecting speech that contains elements of nonverbal behavior such as leafleting, picketing, flag burning, and contribution of money. At one end of the spectrum is behavior that is entirely symbolic, that which functions only to create meanings inside of people. Such behavior is usually easy to identify because it employs traditional symbols of words, gestures, pictures, flags, and emblems. Wearing green, for example, on St. Patrick's day because one is Irish—or would like to be. On the other end of the spectrum is conduct that is not communicated as merely symbolic, but is made symbolic because of the manner in which it is communicated. A student's dress or hair length, for example, can be chosen for personal pleasure or style or to advertise an attitude or culture.

If schoolchildren truly are not required to "shed their constitutional rights at the schoolhouse gate?" then why have school administrators nation-wide, and in particular Anchorage School District in Anchorage, Alaska, taken one giant step backward by writing and enforcing stricter dress codes whose goal is to provide a safe environment for education by banning clothing or items associated with gangs or ganglike behavior? They are, as C. Edwin Baker

From Karon L. Jahn, "School Dress Codes v. The First Amendment: Ganging Up on School Attire," Paper Presented at the 78th Annual Convention of the Speech Communication Association (October 30, 1992). Copyright © 1992 by Karon L. Jahn. Reprinted by permission. Notes omitted.

would argue, "imagining the worst case scenarios and then proceeding to base analyses on the need to prevent it."

The worst case scenarios of gang behavior and the violence associated with such, implies that without dress codes students will be inundated with offensive behavior. The assumption is that students will not be inclined to exhibit, engage, or be harmed by violent behavior if they do not see or wear clothing that glorifies gangs. Wearing an unapproved Raiders jacket or ball cap, therefore, sends a message that the student is a member of a gang (which may be the intent of the message) rather than a message that the student needs to stay warm, likes the team spirit of the Raiders, or was given the clothing by his grandmother and is obligated to wear it.

The basic question this essay attempts to answer is whether school dress codes written with the specific purpose of limiting individual dress preferences, including dress associated with gangs, infringe on speech freedoms granted to individuals by the First Amendment. Can school officials reconcile their responsibility to provide a safe environment to educate all with the First Amendment mandate that government has "no power to restrict expression because of its message, its ideas, its subject matter, or its content"? Does a student have the right to select clothing for his or her body if others fear that selection of certain articles of clothing may suggest that the individual is a member of a gang, or lead to gang behavior and/or violence? Does a student have the right not to see what he or she considers an offensive article of clothing? If so, does the unwillingness of any student to receive a message outweigh another's right to offer such? Do school administrators have the power to write and enforce dress codes

that permit certain types of clothing and deny other types? Are these codes to be uniform across the district, or left up to each individual school principal to decide based on the unique circumstances —and preferences—of the principal and his or her school? The answer to these questions requires examination of the literature on gang behavior, school dress codes, and First Amendment doctrine of specifically that of the captive audience.

School officials have a responsibility, often spelled out in their respective state constitutions, to provide an education for students in a safe environment. Suspension of students from school for violent action, including fighting, must be administered by school authorities. But administrative action, which often includes suspension for nonverbal speech acts which include, for example the wearing of red suspenders, ball caps, buttons, or "gang" colors, which have *not* led to violent conduct skids across the line of school safety concerns and crashes on the doorstep of the First Amendment.

Although the Court has extended its protection of political speech to nonverbal acts of communication, it has refused to decide for the nation as a whole whether there are elements of freedom of expression in the way public school students wear their hair or clothing. The Court has addressed other issues for students including protest, and right to organize, cautioning that authorities could interfere with the exercise of basic free-speech rights of elementary and secondary school students for good reason, such as to prevent disruption of the educational enterprise, but emphasizing that students in school are "persons" under the Constitution.

The Court's choice to let the issue lie with individual states has meant for students that their choice of dress and expression can be regulated by the current attitude of the officials in charge of their school. This attitude often reflects the perceived mind-set of the state and nation at large, giving preference to the majority viewpoint at the expense of minority expression. Changes may occur, as they did in a limited fashion during the late 1960s and early 1970s when schools eventually allowed boys to wear long hair and became more tolerant of dress. At least one court stated that students rights "will not be denied in deference to governmental benevolence or popular social theories." During the Reagan years of the 1980s, hair styles for boys became more conservative and boys who chose to let their hair grow were barred from attending school, or forced to sit in a booth or other sequestered area facing a wall, in order to complete their studies.

Over the last two decades, dozens of federal judges have carefully considered whether the guarantees of privacy and free speech apply to a teenager's choice of dress. They have divided roughly evenly on the question, with those courts who have struck down arbitrary rules insisting on a balance of the rights of the student against the need of the school to make reasonable health and safety regulations. Thomas Tedford writes that the "result is a continuing division among the twelve circuits of the federal courts of appeal, for some circuits have discovered constitutional issues whereas others have not."

Theorists George Herbert Mead and Herbert Blumer suggest that individuals come to social contexts with a storehouse of meanings, and this storehouse is developed and refined over time based on social interactions. Individuals use the cues provided by the appearance of others, interpret these cues, and attempt to organize their actions toward others accordingly. Meanings derived from appearance, therefore, are not passively received, on the contrary, each individual must learn, discover, or develop a meaning on his or her own. If every action that an individual takes, or fails to take, is behavior capable of being understood as communication, the question begging to be answered is: what happens when individuals attempt to offer their ideas and actions by choosing dress which falls out of mainstream acceptance?

There is no argument that adolescents are stealing the clothes off of other's backs, or in extreme instances, killing their peers for Nike shoes and Triple F.A.T Goose parkas. "Dressing for success has never been so risky. The combination of crack-quickened tempers, availability of guns and the flashy clothes of the drug culture has taken fashion awareness to a wicked level," wrote one author in a popular news magazine. While very little of this violence is taking place in the schoolyard, school officials are not taking any chances. They are reacting swiftly to the media's coverage and police information which details an increase in armed robbery and shootings over clothing and other gang dress by establishing dress codes. Many schools, like Crenshaw High School in Los Angeles have banned gang dress which includes bandannas and dangling earrings for boys. Other schools have banned excessive jewelry, shearling coats and decorative gold caps for teeth. In January 1990, the Detroit Board of Education required all of its 259 schools to design and enforce their own mandatory dress codes. During the summer of 1991, the Anchorage school district changed its dress code to include a senence declaring "students may not wear clothing or items that are associated with gangs or gang-like groups."

Characteristics of gangs are certainly not limited to dress. Scholars and police investigators have recorded everything from the fact that white gangs (known as "stoners" or "heavy metalers") perform Satanic rituals, to the importance of the neighborhood (known as "the 'hood" to Hispanics). Certainly a gang's name Miami's Mazda Boys who steal Mazda cars) is important, as is its graffiti, gang dress and colors. Today's gang member may wear baggy khaki pants riding low on the hips (known as "busting a sag"), patterns shaved into their heads, bandannas or colored rags hanging from their back pockets, or untucked flannel shirts. Their dress sends a message to others of who they are or who they want to be. They persist in using dress as a message even though it assists police in keeping track of them.

Despite the fact that there is obviously more to gang behavior than dress, school officials are targeting dress as the focal point in determining gang behavior. They are using the goals of their dress codes as a platform to support specific ban of gang, and other "inappropriate" attire. A review of school dress codes nationwide reveals three distinct goals. First is the goal of individual preference. Most school districts have recognized that a student's dress and grooming is a "manifestation of personal style and individual preference." Administrators, apparently, will not interfere with the right of the students and their parents to make decisions regarding their appearance *except when their choices affect the educational program of the school or the health and safety of others.* Most codes include a discussion of "tight fitting, sheer, brief, low cut, or re-

vealing attire that can cause embarrassment or indecency," and "graphics that are suggestively obscene or offensive on any garments," as examples of unacceptable dress that would violate the health or safety of others.

A second goal which emerges is that of personal hygiene, which again hinges on whether the student will disrupt the educational process by his personal grooming and cleanliness, or lack thereof. Again, most codes include language such as "Good grooming promotes pride and good behavior" or "Each student shall attend school clothed in a manner which is clean." School officials interviewed state that students are rarely sent home for poor grooming, most are given clean clothes available at school, or an opportunity to take a shower or wash their clothes.

A third, and perhaps the most important, goal is whether the student's dress and grooming "are within the limits of generally accepted community standards." School Boards are supporting School District Administrator's decisions to allow individual school officials to set the community standards for their schools. Some school officials, therefore, within a district may require uniforms for its students while others may allow shorts or more casual clothes—and both may claim to support existing community standards. The dress code of the Oakland Unified School District, for example, relies on the mandate provided by Article 1, section 28(c) of the California Constitution which states: "All students and staff of public primary, elementary, junior high and senior high schools have the inalienable right to attend campuses which are safe, secure and peaceful." The Board of Education, therefore, has an obligation, legally and morally, to establish a policy which "insures that schools are a safe and secure learning environment free from violence or the threats of violence and intimidation by gangs, gang regalia, gang gestures, weapons, the sale of dangerous and illegal drugs, drug or alcohol use, profanity, and bigotry and/or intolerance against people on the basis of race, ethnicity, religion, sex, or sexual preference." The code also states that students who dress in an "appropriate manner" (without defining what appropriate means) "make a statement by their appearance that they are in school to learn and that their behavior will be consistent with the serious goals of an academic environment." The code lays out specific articles of dress which may not be worn— T-shirts with designs or wording that demeans people on the basis of race or sex or jewelry which incorporates swastikas; smooth fabric jogging suits, "which are a leading symbol worn by gang members and drug dealers." In addition, students are not allowed to wear clothing designating membership in non-school organizations but official school sweaters jackets, athletic suits, ROTC uniforms, etc. are permitted.

Of these three goals, the desire for a well-groomed student seems to run the least risk of interfering with a student's free speech protection. Poor grooming habits (assuming long hair and/or braids for boys is not considered poor grooming) is probably not speech—symbolic or otherwise. The student's individual preference, however, when it comes in conflict with the school's community standards and safety responsibility would appear to create problems for speech rights. An examination of Anchorage's dress code can shed some light on the difficulties administrators face when balancing the rights of students speech

with the responsibility of a safe place for education.

The Anchorage dress code does not list, as the Oakland school district and others have, what specific articles of dress are banned. The code is broadly written to allow each principal to determine what dress is acceptable for his or her school as long as the district's ban of gang clothing and items are prohibited. In-service training provided information on the procedure for reporting dress code violations to secondary education administrators, who would notify the school board, who would handle the final decision of whether the behavior was gang related or not. Few other characteristics of gangs were discussed, but principals were able to discuss among themselves at district meetings some of the particular problems that arose within their schools with the enforcement of the new code. In general, most of the principals agreed that it was difficult last year to determine what is "gang-like behavior" or "gang-like groups." After a one year effort, the district dropped the phrase "gang-like groups" from the code. The phrase "gangs," however, remains and with it the difficult challenge of supporting speech choice from inappropriate action.

Anchorage's secondary schools are a mixed bag of choices. Students who have had a difficult time meeting the attendance and education requirement of the district's six more traditional high schools scattered throughout the city and outlying area may choose to attend SAVE I or SAVE II, schools that give students a second chance—with very strict requirements. Students who choose to get a head start on the work world may attend King Career Center. Students who have had problems with law enforcement authorities may attend McLaughlin high school or REACH. Like most schools across the nation, each school boasts of its own distinct student population which reflects both the geographic and economic location as well as the school's curriculum choices.

Principals of each of the schools have the freedom to decide what is appropriate dress for his or her students. The code allows them to reinforce their requirements of good grooming and dress. Many stated that the behavior of students is "better" when the dress is appropriate—clean, no torn clothing, and "all body parts covered." All principals had no difficulty prohibiting clothing worn in a suggestive manner or clothing offering suggestive, or pornographic phrases. Each had different ways of handling the issue, some would provide a new t-shirt, others would allow the student to cover the message or turn the shirt inside out, and still others would call the parent to come to the school and take the child home to change. Principals in charge of a smaller number of students have an advantage because they are able to work-one-on-one with a student to arrange a clothing "compromise." Some principals may decide to institute total bans, for example, on baseball caps because the students grab them from the heads of others or throw them in the hallways, thereby creating a safety issue. Another principal, however, might not ban all ball caps, only those with an X or other racial or gang symbol.

Many of the principals were adamant about banning specific items that are symbols of racial hatred—swastikas, red suspenders—or gang dress—colored bandannas, black clothing. While they may be tolerant up to a point with students' "testing" behavior, they are quick to enforce the code if they suspect school safety problems. One Junior High principal suspended a student for wearing a button that displayed a racist message. He stated that the "button caused the suspension—not the behavior" because the student "refused to give up racist ideas." Despite his attempts to educate the student and her friends through counselors, special programs, support groups and leadership workshops, she continued to wear the button. He stated that any symbols or dress that sends a message "hateful to minorities" will not be tolerated in his school.

While some expressed discomfort in deciding what was a "gang" most focused on the actual behavior of the student, irrespective of the dress. Some principals have suspended students, for example, who attend school wearing red suspenders, leather boots and a shaved head, citing protection for the safety of the "skinhead" and other students. Most principals stated that they would speak with the student wearing skinhead attire, and his or her peers and teachers prior to taking discipline procedures. At least one principal during the 1991–92 school year had a difficult decision to make regarding a student who had improved his school track record during his high school years, but had taken to dressing in the attire of skinheads his Senior year. While his peers and teachers were convinced he just wanted to "dress that way," had not made any statements that offended anyone, and had kept his grades and job responsibilities up to school standards, the principal took seriously the school dress code mandate that "students may not wear clothing or items that are associated with gangs." After meeting with the principal, the student changed his dress choice and was allowed to stay in school and graduate.

Currently a principal at another high school has used the dress code and other school policies to suspend students dressed as skinheads. Several of these students have chosen to go beyond merely wearing the dress to blocking hallways and engaging in fights which has resulted in disciplinary actions. Physically prohibiting other students from attending class or fighting with other students is behavior which warrants discipline. Students who "show up" on campus dressed as skinheads are immediately sent home.

Most of the principals interviewed see their roles as a "firefighter" for angry students. They watch for behavior that takes the dress out of passive, nonverbal speech and moves it into action before enforcing disciplinary actions. All indicated that it is the behavior—and they generally do not associate dress with behavior—which they discipline. They are willing to tolerate students individual preferences for dress as long as it meets the grooming standards of the school (which shows that students take pride in themselves and their school) and that their preferences do not interfere with school safety goals. A few state that the code is "a very good deterrent" in preventing gang behavior, others say they have no reason to use the code, and yet others feel the code leaves too much choice up to the principals for deciding a student's fate.

The actions of Anchorage principals mirror those of the rest of the nation. Tolerance for student dress varies with the school and individual in charge of administering the code. When questioned about certain First Amendment issues that may arise when enforcing dress codes, most school officials are insistent that there is a "time, place and manner" for everything —and school may not be the place. They suggest that students are held "captive" at the location and look to administrators for education and safety. Despite numerous Court cases invoking the captive audience doctrine, a clear definition of this doctrine has not been articulated. One conclusion which can be drawn, however, is that the captive audience doctrine is more likely to be invoked to restrict speech when the individual is viewed as captive in a home rather than on the street, and if the speech is spoken, rather than written.

Individuals encounter daily unwanted messages. Because of the inevitability of undesired speech outside the protection of our home, the burden is placed on the recipient of information to avoid "further bombardment of his sensibilities." In some instances the Court has ruled that the viewer, when outside the home, has responsibility to turn away or avert his or her eyes to the message. This is almost always the case if the message is written. Marcy Strauss cautions that regulators and courts must not confuse "captivity in a *place* with being captive to *speech*." Students, for example, could solve the problem of unwanted dress messages by requesting different seat assignments in classrooms, selecting lockers in a different hallway, or turning their head at the first glance of an offensive message. While some students will certainly find some dress messages offensive, others may be more willing viewers and would presumably not want their right to view messages denied because the sender has been suspended from school. The question becomes: what is a reasonable burden in the context of school classrooms, cafeterias, libraries or hallways? Is it too much for students to glance at an offensive mural or poster and to turn away? Is it too difficult for those who don't want to read an offensive button to not get close enough to the student to do so? Should the burden of turning one's head when passing someone in the hallway wearing red suspenders and a shaved head outweigh the right of the individual to use dress as a message?

Strauss argues that the captive audience doctrine is "an elastic theory that could expand to curtail most free expression rights." The audience, all too often, acquires "veto power," and the doctrine could be used to prohibit freedom of speech, particularly with "respect to unorthodox views." School officials who regulate dress messages, i.e. deny gang colors, accessories, allow "clean-cut" clothing, violate content-neutral requirements. They are deciding that some messages are more worthy than others. In banning gang dress, school officials have not demonstrated that there is no less restrictive means available to achieve their objective of a safe educational environment.

The Court has ruled that schools may restrict the speech of students who urge the use of drugs to others—and could presumably ban the wearing of dress advocating such. But clothing that does not identify an illegal or pornographic message, should not be banned. Banning dress—or verbal speech—of students who advocate unpopular ideas in a place meant for educational purposes strikes at the very heart of learning and the First Amendment.

Those students who ask to be "left alone" and not be forced to view messages that may cause them discomfort are failing to participate in the democratic process. The right to make choices is essential if students are going to be free thinking, independent, autonomous individuals. Forced listening or viewing of a prescribed, sanitized message removes decision-making choices for the student. Students who do not see the student wearing red suspenders, because the student, if he or she chooses to wear that dress, has been banned from campus, cannot make a decision for themselves to speak, or not to speak, to the student about the meaning of his or her red suspenders. Is the student's right to choose to see or not to see certain messages one worth protecting? If we believe that speech is powerful, and that dress is a manifestation of speech, than this form of communication has the opportunity to inform, convince, persuade and possibly hurt everyone.

To provide for greater freedom we should permit the predictably occasional offensive uses of that freedom. When students send a message of dress or hairstyle they are telling others that their values and preferences have changed, or that their values and preferences have been suppressed. Regulations are created to maintain the status quo—and to prevent people from creating a new status quo. "When people feel compelled to engage in disruptive activity, the greatest need is for the government to respond appropriately to this dissatisfaction, not to suppress the dissidents," writes Baker. Public schools have legitimate interests in the free and open communication of ideas; they are in the learning business. School administrators are charged with the responsibility to provide an atmosphere of education for all. This responsibility includes allowing students to speak freely on issues of the day, to question ideas and concepts they are unsure—or too sure —about, and to wear clothing that may represent statements that are designed to shock or offend. School administrators do not have the right to decide for others which speakers are dressed appropriately and therefore fit to be heard and deserve to take place; they should exhibit greater, not less, freedom of expression than prevails in society at large.

Learning is not a spectator sport. Students have an obligation to attend classes and attend to discussions that will increase their knowledge—no matter how painful that may be. To limit the communication of some, because others find the dress message disgusting or the context unacceptable, dead-ends an avenue for debate. Dress codes may keep unwelcome attire out of the schools, and ultimately suppress what students think. Such a prescribed standard for speech ignores the uniqueness of speech and each person's interest in his or her personal selection of dress. Prohibiting dress will not solve the problems of cultural, economic, or educational differences. To force students to dress in lock-step fashion—as is evidenced by those schools advocating wearing of uniforms and those who determine from month to month what is acceptable "because clothing that is neutral one month may suddenly cause trouble the next"—because of the effect dress may have on their peers is to deny an opportunity for exploring the meaning of equality and understanding. More speech, rich in the vibrant colors, textures, and meanings, dress can provide, is the answer, not less.

POSTSCRIPT

Will Stricter Dress Codes Improve the Educational Environment?

Jessica Portner reports that significant changes in the school environment were documented after elementary and middle school students started dressing uniformly. Karon Jahn addresses several problems that school systems are beginning to face as they adopt a stricter dress code policy. Controlling the way students dress will not solve the problems of envy, hatred, or intolerance for differences. Only education, discussion, and critical thinking can change students' views. Jahn believes that uniform dress suppresses the one instrument that can combat violence and tolerance—individual thought and freedom of expression.

One wonders why conservatives like the idea of school uniforms when it represents such an intrusion into personal lives by the government. As the introduction pointed out, the reasons espoused in favor of school uniforms are very similar to the reasons stated against them. There appear to be many opinions surrounding this issue but very little concrete data to support either view. The issue needs to be studied empirically.

SUGGESTED READINGS

Behling, D. (1994, October). School uniforms and person perception. *Perceptual and Motor Skills, 79,* 723–729.

Caruso, P. (1996, September). Individuality vs. conformity: The issue behind school uniforms. *NASSP Bulletin, 80,* 83–88.

Evans, Dennis. (1996, October). School Uniforms: An unfashionable dissent. *Phi Delta Kappan, 78,* 139.

Grantham, K. (1994, October). Restricting student dress in public schools. *School Law Bulletin, 25,* 1–10.

Holloman, L. (1995, Winter). Violence and other antisocial behaviors in public schools: Can dress codes help solve the problem? *Journal of Family and Consumer Sciences, 87,* 33–38.

McCarthy, C. (1996, March). Uniforms not a cure for school's ills. *National Catholic Reporter, 32,* 22.

McDaniel, J. (1996, September). Can uniforms save our schools? *Readers Digest, 149,* 79–82.

Should you have to wear a school uniform? (1996, March). *Current Events, 95,* 3.

Will school uniforms help curb student violence? (1996, April). *Jet, 89,* 12–16.

On the Internet . . .

http://www.dushkin.com

Positive Parenting On-Line
This site contains information and articles related to how parents and educators can communicate more effectively with children and adolescents. Most of the linked information is specific to adolescence.
http://www.positiveparenting.com/features.html

CYFERNet
The Children, Youth, and Families Education Research Network is sponsored by the Cooperative Extension Service, U.S. Department of Agriculture, and provides practical, research-based information in areas including health, child care, family strengths, science, and technology.
http://www.cyfernet.mes.umn.edu:2400/

The American Academy of Child and Adolescent Psychiatry Home Page
Provides information as a public service to assist families and educators in socializing children and adolescents.
http://www.aacap.org/

COHIS: Teen Pregnancy and Maternal/Neonatal Health
This site contains facts and summaries related to adolescent pregnancy and drug abuse.
http://web.bu.edu:80/COHIS.teenpreg.htm#aboutteenpreg

AMA Adolescent Health On-Line
This Web site links to numerous other sites related to adolescent health issues.
http://www.ama-assn.org/adolhlth/adolhlth.htm

PART 4

Adolescence

Many people use the term teenage years *to describe adolescence. This is the period of time from ages 13 through 19. During this period of development the child experiences puberty, and there are dramatic physical changes that occur as the child becomes a young adult. Much less obvious than the physical changes are the cognitive and emotional changes in children at this stage of development. In early adolescence the child is increasingly able to think on an abstract level. Adolescents also undertake the process of identity development, defining who they are. This final section considers some of the key issues related to decision making about values and sexuality that teens make as they move through adolescence.*

◼ Should Children Who Are at Risk for Abuse Remain With Their Families?

◼ Should Parents Be Doing More to Impart Values to Children?

◼ Is Abstinence Education the Best Sex Education?

◼ Can Memories of Childhood Sexual Abuse Be Recovered?

ISSUE 14

Should Children Who Are at Risk for Abuse Remain With Their Families?

YES: Lisa Kolb, from "Family Preservation in Missouri," *Public Welfare* (Spring 1993)

NO: Mary-Lou Weisman, from "When Parents Are Not in the Best Interests of the Child," *Atlantic Monthly* (July 1994)

ISSUE SUMMARY

YES: Lisa Kolb, a public information specialist, believes that the family preservation model is the best way to help families in crisis. Family preservation keeps all the family members together in the home while helping the family solve its problems. Kolb contends that this approach is more successful than taking the children to foster homes or other out-of-home placements because parents and children are more receptive to treatment in their own homes.

NO: Mary-Lou Weisman, an author, argues that orphanages and out-of-home placements are necessary for children whose parents abuse or neglect them. Society has an obligation to take children away from parents who are doing serious harm to them. Some children have their only real family experience when living in an institutional setting.

Newspaper headlines and television accounts of parents who neglect, abuse, or even kill their children show that the unthinkable does happen. Parents, the very people who are obligated to nurture and protect their children, do not always meet their children's needs. Parents may forfeit their responsibility to nurture and provide for their children because of drug addiction, mental illness, an abusive childhood, or poor parenting skills.

In the past, children who did not have parents or family members to care for them were sent to orphanages, but presently these children are placed in foster homes, residential treatment centers, or small group care homes. In addition to these types of placements, another alternative, family preservation, has emerged. In the 1980s the large numbers of children who needed foster care exceeded the number of foster homes available. Thus, the idea of family preservation became a popular alternative to out-of-home placement for needy children.

Family preservation is a model of intervention that is family centered and available 24 hours a day, seven days a week. Social workers spend a lot of time with families in their caseload and try to build on the strengths of the family to help create a more functional family unit. At first family preservation was seen to be a cost-effective answer to helping battered children. Now it has come under fire from some critics, who contend that it does more harm than good, because the characteristics and standards of the programs have become so varied.

Can all families be served by the family preservation model, and are children protected from abuse during the treatment period? Are children in out-of-home placements or foster care protected from abuse? Studies provide conflicting answers to these questions. Proponents from each side point to cases of abuse and poor care in foster care as well as in family preservation situations.

How can society best care for children who are at risk for abuse or worse? Should we keep the whole family (including children) together and work with them in that context? Should we place children in foster care until the family's problems are solved? Should we remove children from parents entirely and send them to an institution for the rest of their childhood?

What do the children think about these choices? We suspect that when most children are faced with being removed from their home, no matter what the reason, they want to stay at home. Often children will defend their parents before authorities even if their home situation is not safe. In these cases, who intervenes for children when parents cannot meet their responsibilities and when the children themselves want what may be harmful to them? How can society keep its children safe?

In the following selections, Lisa Kolb states that children are further damaged when they are removed from their homes as their family deals with a crisis. She sees family preservation as a successful way to solve families' problems while keeping children at home and believes it works because parents value the family unit. On the other hand, Mary-Lou Weisman presents evidence that some children are not safe with parents who physically and emotionally scar their children. She states that we as a society must bite the bullet, take children out of their abusive homes, and put them where they will survive and thrive.

YES

Lisa Kolb

FAMILY PRESERVATION IN MISSOURI

It's 3:00 A.M. in a small, rural town in southwest Missouri. Vanessa Johnston, a family preservation services (FPS) worker, is combing the streets looking for Heidi, one of her clients. Earlier that night, Vanessa learned that Heidi, a 19-year-old single mother, had been accosted by "Stacey," a "friend." Stacey had heard a rumor that Heidi was involved with Stacey's boyfriend, so she had set out to even the score: she surprised Heidi in the dark stairwell leading to her apartment and beat her up.

Heidi has a habit of running when things get rough. Finding no trace of her client, and knowing Heidi's penchant for hitching rides with truckers, Vanessa heads for the local truck stop. She has to talk with only a few drivers to find out that Heidi, with her infant son in tow, has hitched a ride to Oklahoma City.

Vanessa goes back to her office and waits. She knows the rumor about Heidi and Stacey's boyfriend is unfounded, and she wonders how Heidi has been affected by Stacey's assault. She knows that Heidi has felt that Stacey was her only friend, the one person she could trust.

After several hours, the telephone rings: it's Heidi, asking for help to get back home. Vanessa arranges for the bus ride back to Missouri, goes home, and gets ready for work.

Welcome to the world of an FPS worker. The work is harried, and time is a precious commodity. The job is frustrating: one step forward can be followed by two steps backward. And it is emotionally draining—six weeks of being on 24-hour call can take its toll. But it is encouraging: to see a family learn from its mistakes is what this job is all about. Frustrated and eager for a change, many social workers, caseworkers, and others are willing to accept the challenge and take on the daunting job description that comes with FPS.

...[F]amily preservation services are designed to protect children who are at immediate risk of out-of-home placement, by providing immediate, intensive, comprehensive, 24-hour, in-home services to these children and their families. FPS is guided by these premises:

- Children have a right to their families.
- The family is the fundamental resource for nurturing children.

From Lisa Kolb, "Family Preservation in Missouri," *Public Welfare*, vol. 51 (Spring 1993), pp. 8–19. Copyright © 1993 by The American Public Welfare Association. Reprinted by permission. Notes omitted.

- Parents should be supported in their efforts to care for their children.
- Families are diverse and have a right to be respected for the special cultural, racial, ethnic, and religious traditions that make them distinct.
- Children can be reared well in different kinds of families, and one family form should not be discriminated against in favor of another.

Operating statewide since October 1992, FPS is working for a large number of Missouri families. The state measures success by the number of children who remain safely in their homes rather than being removed and placed in foster care. From October 1991 to September 1992—roughly the year before FPS was operating statewide—the program reported serving 656 families. According to the Department of Social Services, Division of Family Services (DFS), which administers the program, 128 of those families ended up having children placed outside the home.

Since it began operating statewide, the program has succeeded in diverting about one-third of the children who otherwise would have entered foster care. Statewide preliminary data show that in the six months to a year following completion of FPS, 81.93 percent of FPS families are intact. A year or more following FPS, 77.89 percent of FPS families are intact.

Vanessa started with the program in November 1991 and had worked with only eight other families before Heidi and her baby. Vanessa identifies the benefits of a program like FPS, which is designed to deal with long-term issues by meeting immediate needs: "We know families will still cycle [in and out of various services] after they've gone through the program, but we hope that what they learned through FPS will help them to pull themselves up and not sink so low the next time."

For Vanessa, one of the most attractive qualities of FPS is the program's flexibility. FPS allows her the latitude to tailor her services to meet the specific needs of her client families. Typically, FPS workers

- teach problem-solving skills to family members;
- teach families how to cope with future crises without relying on harmful behavior;
- provide information to families regarding other sources of assistance;
- teach family members life skills, such as finding an apartment, bargain hunting, nutrition, and money and management;
- focus all services on empowering families to solve their own problems and avert crises.

Statewide, FPS has 114 full-time workers: 36 are employees of DFS, and 78 are working under contract. FPS also has four part-time workers, three in-house and one contractual.

FPS workers must meet a number of requirements:

- They must have a master's degree in social work, counseling, psychology, or a related field. Or, with the approval of DFS, they can have a bachelor's degree and extensive experience in treatment of families in crisis. Vanessa has a bachelor of arts degree in psychology and five and a half years' experience with DFS in investigations, foster care, and casework.
- They must have experience working with children and their families.

- They must demonstrate knowledge of crisis intervention, communications skills, and family education methods.
- They must demonstrate a willingness to work a nonstructured, flexible schedule, routinely including evenings and weekends.
- Contracted workers must meet applicable state licensing criteria.

FPS workers are assigned two families at a time and work with those families for six weeks. The two assignments rarely begin and end at the same time, so there is frequent overlap of cases. Though she could use as much as two weeks between cases to complete the required paperwork—since she has little time to work on anything but the family's needs while the case is in progress—the demand for FPS is so great that Vanessa usually gets no more than two to five days between family assignments.

Vanessa's personality is ideally suited for FPS's nondirective approach. Her ability to act as mother, confidant, and counselor, coupled with her innate sense of when to advise, when to pull back, and when to listen, are key to her rapport with families in crisis. Vanessa admits she works best when encouraging family members to identify their problems and arrive at their own solutions. Although each FPS worker has his or her own style, Vanessa emphasizes that the priority in each FPS case is the same—to make all families safe. If she accomplishes nothing else in her six weeks with a family, Vanessa strives to instill one vitally important attitude: "respect for the kids and their view of the world."

The six-week time frame forces FPS workers to prioritize the elements that are critical to keeping a family together. Vanessa's work with Heidi on parenting and other life skills had to wait until mother and son had a roof over their heads. Kima and Jerry, Vanessa's other FPS family, were not searching for food and shelter, but rather salvation for their marriage.

HEIDI AND ZACH

Like many clients, Heidi chose FPS as the less of two evils. Faced with the removal of her son, Heidi reluctantly allowed FPS into her life for one simple reason: "Zach is all I have." Many of Vanessa's clients have a history of physical or sexual abuse, and Heidi's background is no different. Her childhood in Alabama was little more than a series of new addresses and new guardians, and she did not develop relationships with any of them. Her parents divorced when she was very young. The few times she lived with them were brief, unpleasant interruptions in her travels from one foster home to another. When she turned 18, Heidi aged out of the Alabama foster care system and finally escaped the instability of foster care; but she found that life in an Alabama group home was not much better. She soon ran away to Arkansas, then to Mt. Vernon, Missouri, where she met Micky.

Within a year, Heidi found herself homeless and pregnant with Micky's child. She delivered Zach while living in an area home for unwed mothers. But, restless and longing for her old lifestyle, Heidi soon left to run with her baby's 15-year-old father and his friends. The drugs, alcohol, and delinquency of the group led to the intervention of DFS and Vanessa.

Immediately, Vanessa learned that, with Heidi, she would have to shelve her counselor's hat. Heidi's past had left her stubborn and independent, with a deep mistrust of adults and no tolerance for advice. Heidi likes the fact that FPS allows her to retain control over her own life: "Vanessa doesn't tell me what to do —the decisions are mine to make. I'm learning to trust in myself. I'm a good person."

With Vanessa's help, Heidi was able to begin pursuing her lifelong dream of becoming a nurse. Daycare, provided by FPS, allowed Heidi to work on her general equivalency diploma (GED); and she scored well in preliminary testing. For the first time in her life, she not only is setting goals but also is working to meet them. "I'll do it," she says, "if it takes me till I'm 80."

Vanessa's teaching methods allowed Heidi to learn by example. "My families learn much more from what I do," she says, "than from what I say." For Heidi, many of life's most mundane tasks —including looking for an apartment —were a mystery; and, as Vanessa explained, "You can't ask about something you know nothing about." Armed with a newspaper, a telephone book, and a map, Vanessa talked Heidi through the procedure—looking in the classified section, calling apartment managers for details, and filling out applications.

The scarcity of rental housing in the area limited Heidi's options, and her monthly income—$234 from Aid to Families with Dependent Children and $200 in food stamps—prevented her from qualifying for federal housing. Finding nothing more suitable, Vanessa and Heidi were forced to make do with a small, windowless basement apartment for $100 a month. With money from the Crisis Intervention Fund, an FPS emergency fund earmarked for high-priority needs, Vanessa took Heidi to garage sales, teaching her to bargain-shop for kitchen items, other household goods, and baby clothes for Zach. One of Vanessa's FPS coworkers obtained a used sleeper sofa, chairs, and a lamp to complete the apartment's furnishings.

Although the apartment soon looked livable, Vanessa worried about the steep, dark stairwell leading to the apartment and the lack of heating or air conditioning. Heidi objected to turning on the gas stove for fear of an explosion, but Vanessa explained that utilities are a good way to establish credit. Meanwhile, Vanessa would look for a used microwave oven.

Vanessa also subtly tried to change Heidi's nutritional habits and attitudes about medical care. Heidi, a frail 80 pounds, frequently skipped meals; and this sometimes would carry over to $4^{1}/_{2}$-month-old Zach, who needed regular feedings of formula. Vanessa was concerned that Heidi would not prepare balanced meals for Zach as his nutritional needs changed. She learned that Heidi occasionally would fix instant soup or other one-step preparation foods if she had access to a microwave. Vanessa knew that Heidi was concerned about Zach staying on target with his weight gain, and she hoped this would entice Heidi to do more cooking.

Whereas Heidi did not seem very concerned about her own health, Vanessa did begin to see improvements in her concern for Zach's health. Heidi would become defensive at the suggestion of seeking medical care for herself, and she ignored her doctor's diagnosis of strep throat and recommendation for a tonsillectomy. With Vanessa's encouragement, however, Heidi began to understand the importance of regular checkups for Zach, who had developed a chronic cough soon after he was born. Heidi was afraid of the "hurt" that doctors cause and the bad-tasting medicine they prescribe, but Vanessa helped her to see that these were the only ways to make Zach better. Watching Heidi follow Zach's medication schedule gave Vanessa a renewed sense that mother and son would make it —together.

As determined as she was to become a better mother, Heidi experienced an equally strong pull to return to her old lifestyle on the streets, running with Micky and his friends. Vanessa had to suppress her own maternal instincts. As a mother of three, she knew that if Heidi were her own child, she likely would have reacted to Heidi's involvement with Micky and his friends by criticizing their behavior and prohibiting Heidi from seeing them. But Vanessa knew that reaction not only would be a waste of time, but also would damage her relationship with Heidi.

As an FPS worker, Vanessa strongly believes that it is neither her position nor beneficial to her clients for her to judge them. She realizes that Micky's role as Zach's father is important to Heidi and that it is unlikely that his influence and that of his friends will diminish.

During a scheduled visit, Vanessa found Micky and his friends at Heidi's apartment. Vanessa's theory is that every moment spent with a family is "teachable," so she turned what could have been a wasted afternoon into a group counseling session by including the entire group in her discussion with Heidi. By opening a discourse about their influence on Zach's well-being, Vanessa believes Micky, and perhaps some of his friends, came away with a sense of the consequences of their actions. Heidi says Micky likes her involvement with FPS and that he admits he has gained a new perspective through Vanessa.

Vanessa's presence gradually began to have a calming effect on Heidi's life. Heidi describes her past experiences with the Department of Social Services (DSS) as having had a "bad thing" with the agency. But she says her relationship with Vanessa is "okay"—a glowing endorsement from the reserved teenager. "DDS has always been rude," Heidi says. "They make me feel like they don't have the time. FPS is making me think some of them do care. Maybe they do."

KIMA AND JERRY

Vanessa met Kima and Jerry as their two-year marriage was showing signs of breaking up. Jerry, a 25-year-old unemployed welder, was starting to drink; and drinking made him mean. Kima had plenty of experience with abusive men, and she wasn't going to risk Jerry's angry words turning to violence. Fed up, she had filed for divorce; and, as a would-be single mother of three with no job, she saw FPS as the only way to keep her family together.

Kima's nightmare had begun in her early teens. After months of sexually abusing her, Kima's stepfather one day had escalated his assault to a violent rape, after which he had left her tied in an abandoned barn. She escaped by breaking a window and sawing herself free with a shard of glass. The stepfather, serving an eight-year sentence for the crime, was threatening Kima from prison. Family members who were in contact with him warned her about his plans to find her when he was released. In fact, shortly after his release early in 1993, he was rearrested for attempting to poison the water supply of Sarcoxie, Missouri, a town close to where Kima lived.

Although her stepfather's incarceration gave Kima a sense of release from the pain he had caused, she had had other equally devastating relationships in the years since—sadly, a common occurrence for sexual abuse victims. Kima's oldest son, Travis, 7, was born out of a later rape. Then a boyfriend killed his and Kima's 6 1/2-month-old son. Kima has two other children, Megan, 5, and Miles, 11 months; only Miles is Jerry's child.

Kima and Jerry's first contact with DFS came after Jerry jerked a crying Miles out of his crib, breaking his arm. Although the doctor who treated Miles's injury originally suspected abuse, his final report called the incident "accidental." Jerry now feels DFS is suspicious of him, and his disdain for what he believes was an unfair investigation has left both Kima and Jerry with a blatant distrust of DFS.

Despite this mistrust, Kima saw FPS as the only way to save her marriage, something she very much wanted to preserve. Middle-class values are important to Kima. Her father, killed when she was 11, was a positive influence on her life; and she wants the same for her children. Referred to the program by a DFS worker, the couple was willing to work with FPS because they saw it as an answer to their marital troubles, not acknowledging that the children were at issue.

"I just wanted Jerry to realize he is an equal partner," Kima said. "You can't take 90 percent and give 10. I realize he had a lot of problems growing up. I guess I just wanted us both to start fresh. It's easier for Jerry to talk with someone else present —he's not as apt to walk out."

Jerry says he and Kima immediately accepted Vanessa by "detaching" her from DFS. "I kind of had feelings... I didn't know Vanessa or anything about her. I wasn't sure if I was ready to talk to an outsider. But she's strong on offering suggestions. She's even told us several times she'd leave if we wanted her to. I thought we'd have to sit in a circle and play a game. Everything was to our advantage, because it helped."

Kima and Jerry's problems escalated after Kima lost her job with a local trucking company. Until then, it had not been important to Kima that Jerry work—she was willing to do almost anything to keep the peace: "When Jerry is unhappy, the whole house suffers." But when the loss of Kima's paycheck forced Jerry to look for employment, the tension began to mount. Although Jerry eventually landed a job at an area factory, one with good wages and benefits as well as safe working conditions, he found many excuses to skip work. After three weeks, Jerry had clocked in for only seven shifts.

Now that Kima was unemployed, she had time to begin work on her GED, and FPS enabled her to do that. Since Travis was in the first grade and Megan was enrolled in Head Start, Miles was the only child needing daycare. Unfortunately, Mt. Vernon happens to have the highest teen pregnancy rate in Missouri, which makes state-funded daycare scarce. After Kima completes her GED, she plans to attend college full-time. Through Vanessa, Kima learned that many area colleges have daycare facilities on campus. "FPS points out opportunities," Kima says. "I always knew I had college potential, but until I met Vanessa, I wasn't aware what was available in this area."

Kima and Jerry seemed to be getting past the communication barriers that had caused so many of their problems. "Overall, I feel Jerry has more consideration and respect for me," Kima said. "He has learned to voice his anger rather than just letting it build up. He has been harsh with the kids in the past; but he has learned that if we are to respect his feelings, he has to respect ours. You can't solve your problems when you're angry."

Vanessa points out that FPS's nondirective approach doesn't always work for her. Sometimes, she explains, the atmosphere is just right for physical violence to erupt: "After all, FPS strives to build a rapport while family members are learning to vent their frustrations. Some families become so comfortable with my presence that they forget I'm there and start swinging. That's the time to become very directive."

During counseling, Jerry admitted that he often became frustrated with the children when they would not help Kima around the house. Vanessa helped turn a major point of conflict between Kima and Jerry into a workable solution by developing a chore chart with a reward system for the children. "They learned that there are certain things that have to be done," Kima said. "Now they know that Mom isn't going to do everything for them."

Jerry admitted he had been self-centered and that his moods had made life hard for Kima and the children, but he seemed unwilling to share the decision-making with his wife. Money management had been a problem, and Jerry's new role as the breadwinner gave him a sense of ownership over his paycheck. For instance, the rent was due and the family needed a second car; but Jerry went out and bought a motorcycle. Vanessa worried that Kima and Jerry would be evicted since they were already behind on their rent. Their finances for the coming month looked no better. Because Jerry had missed so much work, his paycheck was going to be short; and, though they had applied, the family was not yet receiving food stamps.

Vanessa's first inclination was to dip into the program's Crisis Intervention Fund. FPS workers have discretion over how and when to use the money, and they do not usually make clients aware that the money is available, so that families do not become dependent on it. FPS workers spend an average of $350 from this fund per family, and Vanessa already had nearly depleted Kima and Jerry's share. Vanessa thought better of bailing Kima and Jerry out of their financial troubles. "Jerry lost his safety net when Kima lost her job," Vanessa said. "These are hard lessons for Jerry, and it's too bad the whole family has to suffer. He needs to learn." The family did manage to scrape by, but later had to move when the landlord raised the rent.

Most FPS workers are women, but Jerry's respect for male authority made Vanessa wonder if he would be more inclined to open up with a male counselor. Jerry dispelled those fears, however: "To me it doesn't matter whether it's a male or female counselor as long as they are helping. Vanessa taught me to stop and think before I say anything—but there are still times I wish I would do more thinking."

"I can't speak for all families, but it's been very beneficial for us," Kima said. "Jerry and I talk more than we ever would have before. Jerry's focus used to be on the bad side of things. He would always focus on the bad things the kids did. I guess something from his childhood made him feel like he didn't measure up. Vanessa has helped him see the good things."

FPS workers and their families often develop a closeness that makes it difficult to let go at the end of six weeks. This was the case between Vanessa and Kima and Jerry. When asked if he felt that the progress he and Kima had made with Vanessa would continue, Jerry said, "She's not going to leave our lives—we know where she lives." Vanessa's first FPS family still calls her on occasion, she says, just for reassurance that what they are doing is okay.

After leaving the FPS program, families are assigned aftercare (AC) workers from their home counties. AC workers continue the case plan that the FPS worker has started with the family. To make the transition easier for families, Vanessa is in constant communication with the AC workers to prepare them for the next phase of a family's treatment. "From the very first day I'm with a family, I begin pulling in other services that they can rely on when I'm gone," Vanessa says. "Actually, I guess you could say aftercare begins with that very first session."

* * *

Vanessa winds up a whirlwind week with Heidi, Kima, and Jerry with a trip to McDonald County, Missouri, where she will attend a "staffing"—a periodic screening of clients to determine progress and alternative services. The two-hour drive will account for part of the 2,000 miles she puts on her family van each month. Accompanying Vanessa are Angela, a private provider of outpatient therapy from a nearby county, and Keith, an FPS coworker.

The room is filled with social workers, FPS workers, and private providers such as Angela, all of whom offer additional insight to the cases they hear. Amid the often horrifying stories of the plight of area families are the occasional lighthearted jokes and repeated trips to the coffeepot—both necessary for the long meetings. Vanessa relates Heidi's progress, and all are impressed. Vanessa appreciates the recognition from her colleagues, but she warns that Heidi has much work ahead of her. Then Vanessa says she is not taking any more FPS families until she returns from a much-needed vacation. Everyone in the room nods in enthusiastic agreement.

Having already had its final staffing, Kima and Jerry's case is closed for Vanessa. She speaks hopefully of their chances for success, knowing they are better prepared for the inevitable rough turns their lives will continue to take. The AC worker has taken over and will continue to guide them toward services should they need assistance.

Families receive a follow-up survey up to one year after they have completed FPS, and this is an FPS worker's final barometer of the program's impact on each family. Vanessa is not ready to say that FPS has succeeded in Kima and Jerry's case. If the survey shows that the children still are living with their family, and if Kima and Jerry are talking and not yelling, then she can say that FPS was successful for this family.

Meanwhile, Vanessa steals a few minutes each day for her own family's needs. Her private life is sandwiched between FPS families, but she has no complaints; and the sparkle in her eye reveals her firm belief that she is doing the right thing. She smiles as she relates how her clients' gratitude is rewarding, but misguided. "It's great that some families say they are doing it for me," says Vanessa. "But if I'm the motivation, then I'm out of there, and where do they go? Believe me, they are doing all the work, and they are doing it for their family."

NO

Mary-Lou Weisman

WHEN PARENTS ARE NOT IN THE BEST INTERESTS OF THE CHILD

Orphanages are not what they used to be. They aren't even called orphanages anymore. The residents no longer sleep in metal beds, twenty to a dormitory room. At the Boys Town campus, just outside Omaha, Nebraska, children live eight to a suburban-style home, two to a bedroom. Bureaus have replaced lockers. Uniforms and standardized haircuts are gone. So are the long wooden tables where, in the orphanages of legend, children sat awaiting their portions of cornmeal mush for breakfast, or bread and gravy for dinner. For instance, at the former St. James Orphanage, in Duluth, Minnesota, known since 1971 as Woodland Hills, young people wearing clothes from places like The Gap and Kmart push plastic trays through a cafeteria line, choosing baked chicken or shrimp and rice. The weight-conscious detour to the salad bar.

In 1910 some 110,000 orphans lived in 1,200 orphan asylums throughout the United States. At the end of 1990, according to data from the American Public Welfare Association, there were approximately 406,000 children in out-of-home placements. About three-quarters of these children were in adoptive and foster homes. About 16 percent, or 65,000, were emotionally disturbed children in need of therapy, most of whom lived in the group homes and residential treatment centers that are the institutional descendants of the orphanage. (The remainder, less than 10 percent, were cared for by a variety of temporary and emergency services.) What little research is available indicates that most of this smaller subset of "homeless" children have been physically or sexually abused, often by the adults charged with their care. At Boys Town, now a residential treatment center—and no longer just for boys—virtually all the girls and nearly half the boys have been sexually abused. The director, Father Val J. Peter, tells of a teenager who asked him on the day she arrived, "Who do I have to sleep with to get along here?"

Child-care workers agree that children in residential treatment today are likely to be far more disturbed than the children who were in need of protective services twenty years ago and who, in turn, were probably more disturbed than the good-hearted orphans with chips on their shoulders who preceded them. These kids have had it with parents—biological, adoptive,

From Mary-Lou Weisman, "When Parents Are Not in the Best Interests of the Child," *Atlantic Monthly*, vol. 274, (July 1994), pp. 43–63. Copyright © 1994 by Mary-Lou Weisman. Reprinted by permission.

or foster—and the feeling is usually mutual. These kids do not trust adults, especially parents. They cannot tolerate the intensity of family life, nor do they behave well enough to attend public school. During a first screening at a residential treatment center a psychiatrist often asks a child, "If you had three wishes, what would they be?" Twenty years ago a typical answer was "I want a basketball," or "I wish my father didn't drink." Today, according to Nan Dale, the executive director of The Children's Village, a residential treatment center for boys in Dobbs Ferry, New York, one is likely to hear "I wish I had a gun so I could blow my father's head off." Child-care professionals call these young people "children of rage." Some of them take antidepressants and drugs to control hyperactivity. In addition to the behavior and attachment disorders common to children who have been abused and moved around a lot, some suffer from having been exposed *in utero* to crack and some from other neurological problems.

Most of the children who live in institutions are between the ages of five and eighteen. According to a 1988 study 64 percent of children in residential treatment centers were adolescents thirteen to seventeen years old. Approximately 31 percent were younger than thirteen, a percentage that has been increasing. According to the same study, the majority, about 70 percent, were male, a factor attributed to the more aggressive nature of the sex. Approximately 25 percent of the children were black, and eight percent were Hispanic.

A group home may house as few as four children, whereas a residential treatment center may be home to a hundred or more, although in either facility usually no more than eight to twelve are housed together, supervised by house parents or by child-care personnel working eight-hour shifts. At Woodland Hills an old three-story red-brick orphanage building has been renovated so that the first floor can be used for administration, classrooms, and the cafeteria. The second- and third-floor dormitory rooms have been divided into meeting rooms, staff offices, and apartments with bedrooms that sleep two.

Unlike the orphanages from which they are descended, most group homes and residential treatment centers are not meant to be long-term abodes. A typical stay at such a center lasts from several months to two years, after which most children return to their birth, foster, or adoptive families. A significant minority, those who either have no homes to return to or do not wish to go home, move on to less restrictive group homes or to independent living arrangements, also under the aegis of the child-welfare system.

HISTORY

The first orphan asylum in the United States was established in 1729 by Ursuline nuns, to care for children orphaned by an Indian massacre at Natchez, Mississippi. Thereafter the number of orphanages increased in response to wars, especially the Civil War, and to epidemics of tuberculosis, cholera, yellow fever, and influenza. (Contemporary epidemics such as AIDS, the resurgence of tuberculosis, and the rampant use of crack cocaine have the potential to create another orphan crisis in the twenty-first century. By the year 2000, it is estimated, 100,000 children, most of them from female-headed households, will lose their mother to AIDS. Senator Daniel Patrick Moynihan, among others, foresees the return of the orphanage as inevitable.)

In spite of the Dickensian reputation that outlives them, orphanages, which began to proliferate in this country in the mid-1800s, represented a significant social reform for their time, just as the group homes and residential treatment centers that took their place are now seen as reforms. Before orphan asylums were common, orphaned, homeless, and neglected children, if they were not living, stealing, and begging on the streets, were housed, along with adults, primarily in almshouses, but also in workhouses and jails. The Victorian conviction that childhood was a time of innocence influenced attitudes toward destitute children. People came to believe that even street urchins could be rescued —removed to a better environment and turned into productive citizens.

Most orphanages were private institutions, the result of the combined efforts of passionately committed "child savers," children's-aid societies, and a variety of mostly religious but also ethnic organizations that raised the money to build and maintain them. But even as the orphanage was becoming the nation's dominant mode of substitute child care, an anti-institutional effort called "placing out" was under way, setting the stage for a debate that continues to this day. By the mid-1800s children were being transported on "orphan trains" from crowded eastern slums and institutions to the West, where they were adopted by farm families in need of extra hands. By the late nineteenth century, in a further move away from institutionalization, cottage-style "homes," which more closely mimicked family life and each of which housed about twenty-five children, began to take the place of large orphanages.

In the twentieth century, psychology —first psychoanalytic theories and then behaviorism—has dominated the field of child welfare. Unlike psychoanalytic theories, which focus on the child's inner personality, behaviorism emphasizes the way the child interacts with his world. In this view a child is not "bad"; his unacceptable behavior is. By changing the behavior, so the thinking goes, one changes the child. Behavioral theories replaced psychoanalytic theories, which were used only to limited effect by Bruno Bettelheim and others in the "homes" and "schools" for emotionally disturbed children which appeared mid-century. The therapeutic hour remains important, but what goes on in the child's life during the other twenty-three hours of the day is seen as potentially even more valuable. (A book by that name, *The Other 23 Hours*, by Albert E. Trieschman, James K. Whittaker, and Larry K. Brendtro, is the classic text of residential treatment.) The goal of residential treatment is to create a "therapeutic milieu," an environment in which everyday events are turned to therapeutic use. Any activity in a child's day—from refusing to get dressed in the morning to answering a question correctly at school to picking a fight—offers the child-care worker an opportunity to teach, change, or reinforce behavior through therapeutic intervention. Residential treatment aims to seize the moment while it is happening and the child's feelings are still fresh.

POLICY VERSUS REALITY

Orphanages as such had virtually disappeared by the late 1970s as a result of a decrease in the number of orphans and a growing conviction that children belong in families. That every child needs parents and a home has become an article of faith and a guiding principle for social-policy makers and a matter of federal law as well. The philosophy of "permanency planning," as set forth in the Adoption Assistance and Child Welfare Act of 1980, considers the goal of the foster-care system to be keeping children in families. The law allows for but discourages "out-of-home placement"—institutionalization in group homes or residential treatment centers—and calls for the return of the children to a family, biological or otherwise, whenever possible and as quickly as possible. But for many practitioners in residential treatment the law has become increasingly irrelevant.

Richard Small is the director of The Walker Home and School, in Needham, Massachusetts, a residential and day treatment center for severely disturbed pre-adolescent boys. Writing recently in a professional journal with Kevin Kennedy and Barbara Bender, Small expressed a concern shared by many of his colleagues.

> For at least the past decade, we in the field have been reporting, usually to each other, a worsening struggle to work with a much more damaged group of children and families, and a scramble to adjust our practice methods to meet both client needs and policy directives that may or may not have anything to do with client needs.... Those of us immersed in everyday residential treatment practice see these same guidelines as less and less applicable to the real children and families with whom we work. Many of our child clients and their families suffer from profound disruptions of development that we believe are likely to require long-term, multiple helping services, including (but not limited to) one or more time-limited stays in residential treatment. Despite a policy that seems to see clear boundaries between being "in care" (and therefore sick and vulnerable) and "reunified" (and therefore fixed and safe) our experience tells us that many of our clients are likely to live out their lives somewhere between these poles.

In keeping with the goal of permanency planning, institutions are supposed to maintain close communication with the parents of the children they treat. Many centers offer counseling for parents and for the entire family. The Children's Village runs evening and weekend programs especially for parents who have abused their children. At institutions that adhere most closely to the goal of reuniting parent and child, parents are encouraged to visit, and good behavior on the part of children is rewarded with weekend visits home. Green Chimneys, a residential treatment center that serves primarily inner-city kids, regularly transports parents and children in vans between New York City and its campus in Brewster, New York. Nationally, nobody really knows how many families are reunited, for how long or how successfully. Those who work with children in institutions complain that the pressure from departments of social service to reunite parent and child is so intense that the workers sometimes yield to it despite their better judgment.

The objective of residential care is to discharge healthier children into the care of healthier parents—an outcome that authorities agree is desirable in theory but not always likely in fact. In their recent casebook for child-care workers, *When Home Is No Haven*, Albert J. Solit, Barbara

Nordhaus, and Ruth Lord write that "one of the hardest tasks for a new worker is becoming reconciled to the inherent contradictions in the Protective Services worker's role. The worker is expected to aim for two goals, which in some instances may be mutually exclusive: reunification of the family, and protection of the child and the child's best interests." ...

INSTITUTIONAL FAMILY VALUES

In the paradoxical world of "child protective services," an institution may be the first home some children have ever known, providing their first chance to sit down to meals with other people at regular times, blow out birthday candles, and be taken care of by adults who do not hit or even yell. All but one of the staple ingredients of a happy home life are replicated in the best group homes and treatment centers. Intimacy is purposely missing. Love and family bonding may be what these children will need and be capable of having eventually, but for the moment the emotional thermostat must be set at neutral. These children are believed to be too disturbed to handle the intensity of real family life; that is precisely why they have been institutionalized.

The best institutions offer emotionally disturbed children a chance at a second childhood. They are given the opportunity to shed cynicism, develop self-esteem, and grow back into innocence and vulnerability. Candy will become a treat. This time they will be protected from harm. This time they will come to think of adults as kind and dependable. They will learn to play. They will learn to care about others.

Treatment communities teach Judeo-Christian values—the work ethic and the golden rule. Institutions offer vocational training and courses in computer literacy. At The Children's Village the best computer students teach their newfound skills to other children and adults in the surrounding communities, and The Children's Village has its own Boy Scout troop. The kids at Woodland Hills collect and pack supplies for national and international relief efforts. In addition, they split wood and deliver logs to the elderly in the Duluth community. Boys Town children host Special Olympics games.

A highly controlled environment is required to create a second childhood for severely disturbed children. Safety is the key issue. Keeping these children from harm involves more than keeping them safe from sexual abuse, physical abuse, drugs, and crossfire; they must be kept safe from themselves and their peers. Newly institutionalized children often try to run away. When a young person at Woodland Hills forgets to bring the appropriate book to class, two peers accompany the student back to the dormitory to retrieve it, thereby minimizing the possibility of an escape attempt. At The Children's Village burly guards equipped with walkie-talkies and trained in firm but gentle techniques of physical restraint stand ready to intervene should fights or tantrums develop beyond the regular staff's ability to control them. Children are never left unattended, not even when they sleep. In every one of the twenty-one cottages at The Children's Village one staff member remains awake throughout the night. The children in these cottages are sometimes suicidal. The bedroom doors in all the cottages open into the corridor, so that youngsters cannot barricade themselves in their rooms. Sexually abused children sometimes become sexual predators. At

The Villages in Kansas some young girls will not allow anyone to comb their hair; for girls who have been sexually abused, even grooming can be too threatening.

This antidotal second childhood must be highly structured and predictable as well as safe. Treatment communities impose rules, chores, and schedules, and emphasize neatness, cleanliness, and order. "Everybody wakes up at 7:30 in the morning," writes eleven-year-old Robert, describing his day at The Children's Village, where hairbrushes, combs, toothbrushes, and toothpaste tubes are lined up with military precision on bureau tops. "The first thing we do is make our bed, wash our face, brush our teeth, last but not least put on some clothes. We eat our breakfast by 8:15 and do our chores. At 8:45 we go to school. In school the first thing we do is math, then reading and spelling. We go to lunch at 12:00 noon...." Homer, the orphan hero of John Irving's *The Cider House Rules*, thrives on the routine of orphanage life. He enjoys "the *tramp*, *tramp* of it, the utter predictability of it." "An orphan," Irving writes, "is simply more of a child than other children in that essential appreciation of the things that happen daily, on schedule." A well-structured day serves the child as a kind of armature within which to build a new, less chaotic, inner self. "How to succeed and how to fail is very clear here," says Daniel Daly, the director of research at Boys Town. "These children are looking for consistency and for an environment they can understand." ...

PARADIGMS AND POLITICS

[Five] years ago legislation called the Family Preservation Act was vetoed by President George Bush. The bill asked for about $2 billion to strengthen families. About half of that amount was earmarked for "family preservation"— programs to preserve troubled families *before* they broke up, so that fewer children would enter the foster-care system in the first place. Families in crisis would be assigned a licensed social worker, who would be available to them around the clock for a period of about three months, for help with problems ranging from substance abuse to landlord-tenant relations. Parents in imminent danger of abusing their children could find relief in a "respite program." Last year's [1993] budget legislation provided $1 billion for similar purposes, with a substantial portion also to be spent on family preservation. It had the backing of leading child-advocacy groups, including the Child Welfare League of America, the Children's Defense Fund, and The National Association of Homes and Services for Children. The Edna McConnell Clark Foundation has produced media kits claiming that family-preservation programs cost less per family ($3,000 for one family for a year) than family foster care, which it says costs $10,000 per *child*, or institutional care, which costs $40,000 per child.

Directors of some children's institutions are convinced that "family preservation" will take money directly out of institutional pockets. Sam Ross, [founder and executive director of Green Chimneys,] likes to point out that the family, theoretically the best way to rear children, also happens to be the least expensive. He calls this coincidence good news for advocates of family preservation, whom he calls "the liberal-conservative conspiracy." The way Ross sees it, liberal family preservationists believe that residential treatment centers are warehouses for children who could best be served in homes in their own communities. Conservative preservationists are horrified by the cost of residential treatment and are looking for a cheaper alternative. "For once in their lives," Ross says, "they agree on something: let's get rid of residential treatment."

"It makes about as much sense as closing down emergency rooms and intensive-care units in order to lower hospital costs," says Brenda Nordlinger, the executive director of the National Association of Homes and Services for Children.

"Family preservation? Who can be opposed to that?" says David Coughlin, of Boys Town. "But," he warns, "some kids are going to be in trouble all their lives. These kids are always going to need help. You can't just blow across the top of a family for three months and expect their woes to go away."

As of this year [1994] The Villages in Kansas will be responding to pressure from the state, which provides 78 percent of its operating expenses, to institute a family-preservation program in addition to its group-foster-care program. One of the eight Kansas residences will be rededicated as a ninety-day "home away from home" for abused children. Meanwhile, therapists trained by The Villages will work with the abusing parents and the abused children in an effort to reunite the family. "We want to provide the services that the state wants to purchase. We'd be foolish not to," says Mark Brewer, who has been the executive director since last June [1993].

Nan Dale, of The Children's Village, thinks that the fervor to reduce the numbers of children in residential treatment is reminiscent of what is now generally considered the disastrous policy of de-institutionalizing adult mental patients in the 1970s. Program directors are very skeptical about whether preventive-intervention programs are really as successful as their advocates claim. Those who believe that family preservation is being oversold see an ally in John Schuerman, a professor of social work at the University of Chicago. Schuerman has studied preventive-intervention programs and believes that many of the families that were treated and did not split up were not likely to split up in the first place.

Nan Dale is feeling the anti-institutional heat and resenting it. "We're as pro-family a place as you can find. The fact that we serve a child who has been removed from a family does not make us anti-family. We involve parents." Nevertheless, she says, "the lines have been drawn. When the words 'preventive service' got applied to everything up to the doorstep of residential care, some of us had apoplectic fits. We all would have told you that what we did here *was* preventive. We prevent lifetimes in mental hospitals, lifetimes in prisons. All of a sudden some bureaucrat in Washington defines preventive service as preventing placement outside the home, and we become the thing to be prevented." For the first time in anyone's memory The Children's Village, one of the largest and considered one of the best residential treatment centers in the country, has no waiting list. Dale says that children who might once have been sent there are being diverted to less restrictive, less expensive, and less appropriate options, such as foster-home care, on the presumption that a family setting is always better.

"What's in vogue right now is family preservation," says Father Val, of Boys

Town. "Just follow the trend. Watch the little lemmings dashing toward the sea. They will tire of family preservation the way they tired of de-institutionalization. It's as if they just discovered that it's a good idea to try to keep kids in families. It's an exegesis of the obvious." Father Val thinks that the need to frame the debate as either anti-family or anti-institution is inevitable, given the longing that human beings feel for simple answers to complex questions. Certainly the people who make child-welfare policy, as well as those who carry it out, believe that the either-or approach is self-defeating. Nevertheless, it persists. Earl Stuck, who was one of the supporters of the Family Preservation Act, acknowledges the problem. "When you try to sell something politically, you have to oversell your case."

David Fanshel was until retirement a professor at the Columbia University School of Social Work. A leader in the field of social work, and foster care in particular, Fanshel was the principal investigator in two major longitudinal studies on foster children in homes and institutions. At a time when many experts are questioning the value of residential treatment and promoting family preservation, Fanshel is going against the tide. He foresees a greater need for residential care in the near future. In fact, Fanshel, for decades one of the leading proponents of permanency planning, has modified his views. He now believes that permanent placement with a family is not an appropriate goal for about a quarter of the older, more seriously damaged and criminally inclined children in the system. He would like to see foster care reorganized into a two-tiered system in which permanent placement would remain the goal for the larger group, and the forestalling of criminal behavior through treatment would be the goal for the other group, which he calls "Subsystem B." He sees institutions playing a significant role in treating such dangerous children. The creation of two subsystems, Fanshel argues, "might help to avoid the inappropriate underfunding of Subsystem B now taking place in the interest of permanency planning."

The debate between family preservationists and those who advocate the wider use of institutions has been going on for decades. Until as late as the 1920s pro-family reformers used the "orphan trains" to place children with farm families. Today their anti-institutional counterparts, in their determination to provide a home for every child, sometimes resort to "adoption fairs," where difficult-to-adopt children are viewed by prospective parents. The social worker who organized one such event told a reporter from *Vogue* that although these fairs can result in the adoption of as many as half the children, "it felt like a slave auction."

Richard Small tells prospective adoptive parents, "If you're going to adopt a child from The Walker School, you're going out of your way to ask for trouble." Small is uncertain about whether it will be possible to find parents for six of the eight children at the school who were recently freed for adoption. One is a very disturbed twelve-year-old boy who has already suffered two failed adoptions. Small is faced with the opposite of King Solomon's conundrum: this time no mothers want the child. How hard should he try to find another adoptive family?

"Another adoption with this boy would be likely to fail," says Small, who also knows that another rejection might harm the boy more than a lifetime without parents. On the other hand, can he consign the child to such permanent and profound loneliness? "He has no one," Small says, "absolutely no one."

Small talked at length with the boy about the pros and cons of risking another adoption. Together, they had just about made up their minds in favor of life without parents when the boy wondered out loud, "Then who will take me for my driver's license?"

"I wish," Small says, "that there were a place, a group home, where kids could live at those times when they couldn't live at home. We've got a number of youngsters in this society—who knows how many?—who are capable of being connected to people, who wish to be connected, who should be connected, but who can't live full-time with the people they're connected to. When they do, terrible things happen to both sides, the kids and the caretakers. These kids get placed in families repeatedly and they repeatedly fail. What are we going to do with these children? Right now we either put them in an institution or we put them in a family."

GOING HOME

A good children's institution is a hard place to leave. In the institutional world the child has the advantage; in the real world the child does not. The experts consult. Parents and children consult. Is the family ready? Is the child ready?

Twenty-five years ago 80 percent of the children who "graduated" from The Children's Village went home to some family member, most likely the mother. But starting about five years ago the percentage began to drop. Today only 55 percent go home to family. Nan Dale, citing her own subjective standard

of measurement, the "GFF" (gut-feeling factor), estimates that half of that narrow majority are returning to a home situation that is fragile. At Woodland Hills, where most of the kids are released to the care of their families, David Kern says he feels uneasy about the prospects for success almost half the time. He calls sending vulnerable children home the worst part of the job. While he was at The Villages, Don Harris felt uneasy about returning kids to their parents about 80 percent of the time. "The reality is we can help these kids build some bridges to their families, but they probably will never be able to live with them."

Not sending vulnerable children home can also be the worst part of the job. People who work with institutionalized children continually face a quandary to which they have no satisfactory solution: What should they do when, in spite of everyone's best efforts, family seems not to be in the best interests of the child? What the system has to offer is life in a group home followed by independent apartment living, and then nothing.

Life without parents is a difficult sentence to pronounce upon a child, but it's happening more and more often. "Sometimes children have gone beyond the opportunity to go back and capture what needed to be done between the ages of three and eight," says Gene Baker, the chief psychologist at The Children's Village. "Sometimes the thrust of intimacy that comes with family living is more than they can handle. Sometimes the requirement of bonding is more than they have the emotional equipment to give. As long as we keep pushing them back into what is our idealized fantasy of family, they'll keep blowing it out of the water for us."

POSTSCRIPT

Should Children Who Are at Risk for Abuse Remain With Their Families?

Kolb summarizes the family preservation model and documents its success in Missouri. Family preservation workers teach family members problem-solving skills and ways to cope with family crises while keeping family members, including children, together as a unit. Family preservation workers in Missouri meet certain educational and experiential requirements and work with two families at a time for six weeks.

Parents choose the family preservation treatment to avoid removal of their children from the home and, according to Kolb, want to preserve the family unit because they value it and want to make it work. Whereas traditional social service focuses on the individual for an indefinite amount of time, Kolb reports that family preservation is more successful because it focuses on the family system for a specific amount of time—four to six weeks.

Policymakers have been instrumental in child welfare by diverting funds from one treatment program to another. When family preservation became a lower-cost alternative to foster care in the 1980s, money was diverted into the family preservation model in lieu of other child protection programs. Was this action in the best interests of the children? Who should decide? Parents? Policymakers? Protective service workers?

SUGGESTED READINGS

Berliner, L. (1993, December). Is family preservation in the best interest of children? *Journal of Interpersonal Violence, 8,* 556–557.

Carp, E. W. (1996, June). Two cheers for orphanages. *Reviews in American History, 24,* 277–284.

Craig, C. (1995, Summer). What I need is a mom. *Policy Review, 73,* 41–49.

Ingrassia, M. (1994, April). Why leave children with bad parents? *Newsweek, 123,* 52–58.

McKenzie, R. (1996, May). Revive the orphanage (but don't expect help from child care professionals). *American Enterprise, 7,* 59–62.

Neuman, E. (1992, July). Caring for kids when parents don't. *Insight, 8,* 6–11

Shealy, C. (1995, August). From Boys Town to Oliver Twist: Separating fact from fiction in welfare reform and out-of-home placement of children and youth. *American Psychologist, 50,* 565–580.

Van Biema, D. (1994, December). The storm over orphanages. *Time, 144,* 58–62.

ISSUE 15

Should Parents Be Doing More to Impart Values to Children?

YES: William J. O'Malley, from "Don't Upset the Kids," *America* (September 28, 1991)

NO: Kathleen Kennedy Townsend, from "Why Johnny Can't Tell Right from Wrong," *The Washington Monthly* (December 1992)

ISSUE SUMMARY

YES: William J. O'Malley, a professor of theology and English, posits that as children move into adolescence, they lack the ability to understand the implications of adulthood and its responsibilities. He contends that parents are largely to blame for this because they do not want their children to encounter any discomfort. As a result, parents unknowingly undermine the purpose of adolescence, which is the development of a personally validated adult self, arrived at through decision making and encounters with adversity.

NO: Kathleen Kennedy Townsend, who was a key administrator for the Maryland Department of Education at the time she wrote this selection, agrees that many children lack socially constructive values. However, she contends that expecting parents to instill values is not realistic. She states that in many homes parents simply are not around or motivated to teach children. In others, family role models can include close relatives who are criminals, making it less likely that children will develop positive values. She concludes that teaching values in the schools can yield excellent results for children and for society.

Few would argue that a solid moral foundation can empower children as they move into adolescence, providing them with the ability to resist cheating, abusing drugs and alcohol, sexual exploitation, and the multitude of other temptations that will confront them. It would be impossible for parents or educators to provide children with prescriptions for what to do and what not to do in every questionable situation that will confront them in life. However, in addition to the issues and suggestions stated in the selections that you will read in this debate, you need to realize one important fact: morality and appropriate values are not easily verbalized. This is one reason why it may be difficult to teach good values.

Children and adolescents learn most readily from observing how people around them conduct their lives. Children model behavior, and the role models in children's lives can include parents, other family members, teachers, peers, politicians, and television, sports, and movie stars. The fact is, the more a child identifies with a role model, the more apt the child is to imitate the behavior of that person. What message does the high school basketball player get when a professional basketball superstar inexcusably cuts practice or flagrantly fouls an opponent? Or what message does pop singer Madonna send when she intimates that she enjoys numerous, casual, sexual liaisons? The message becomes even more significant when it is a family member who acts in questionable ways.

It is incumbent upon society for children and adults to embrace the responsibility of acting morally, and role models should discuss moral decisions with the children in their lives. Certainly, these discussions should be offered at a developmentally appropriate level for the intended child, and they should be to the point (children tend to tune out long sermons). People sometimes fail to be clear when talking with children. While adolescents can certainly think and understand abstract concepts and analogies, younger children need more concrete examples of the values one is trying to impart.

In the selections that follow, William J. O'Malley and Kathleen Kennedy Townsend both maintain that the level of value impartation today is cause for concern, but they disagree as to who is at fault and who could best improve the situation.

YES

William J. O'Malley

DON'T UPSET THE KIDS

A few years ago, a father came to me and said, "I'd like to talk to you about marketing my sons to colleges." Gasp! In the first place, he didn't even realize he was trying to solve his sons' first genuine adult challenge *for* them. In the second place, he didn't realize that his question tacitly admitted that his sons were inferior academic goods that needed a little belated parental razzmatazz to mesmerize—and dupe—college admission officers into accepting them.

I had taught both boys, and they hadn't bestirred their (quite modest) talents in any way, but they were "nice kids": well-mannered, sharp-looking, savvy, "popular," which apparently had been enough—up to the crunch point —for their parents. Actually, they should have been working twice as hard as their classmates, and I shouldn't have been the only one who consistently failed them. Of course, they graduated and were accepted into colleges. But they got high school diplomas without getting the education the diplomas fraudulently testified to. Their number is legion.

In *Iron John: About Men*, Robert Bly makes a strong case for the deleterious effect, on any society, neutering adolescent initiation rituals to meaningless "gestures." In "less enlightened" societies, after the onset of puberty, young people are stranded in the wilderness away from their families, starved for days, subjected to ritual scarring and terrifying midnight tableaux that, almost literally, scare them into "growing up." After such an ordeal, the youngster willingly—and most often placidly—takes his or her place in the adult-world, accepting both its privileges and its responsibilities.

Not so with us, either as a church or as a nation. In Christian churches, caring adults prepare the candidate *cognitively* for Confirmation, but amid symbols more meaningful to experts than to ordinary children. As with Christmas, most weddings and even many liturgies, the surface trappings have all but smothered any genuine conviction that something truly important is going on beneath them. There is little *affective* content to the confirmation/initiation ritual other than a bit of dress-up and fuss and presents, and very little internalized sense of a personal shift in the recipient's relationship to the community.

From William J. O'Malley, "Don't Upset the Kids," *America*, vol. 165, no. 8 (September 28, 1991). Copyright © 1991 by William J. O'Malley. Reprinted by permission.

What's more, it occurs usually before the child has any genuine understanding of what the church and he or she are mutually "confirming." (Most often, as with all religious rituals, it is not a mutual acceptance; rather, the church takes over any assertions of the will, other than submission.) Metaphors like "Now you are soldiers of Christ" might have appealed to children in a simpler age, when we felt beleaguered by all those predatory Masons, Protestants and Jews. Now, however, the metaphor seems more than slightly corny to youngsters. especially since most of the people in the parish don't appear very aggressively apostolic. Worst of all, Confirmation frequently occurs *before* puberty and certainly with no overt connection whatever with that life-shaking sexual event and (judging from the results) with no felt realization of a new, more demanding role in the community.

* * *

Outside the churches, other than the few fortunates who remain in the Scouts or young people who enter military service, there aren't even any mediocre rituals to body forth a realization, not only of a new physical status in society, but also (and in large part *because* of that physical change) of a new *moral* relationship to the self, to the family, to lovers, to those under whom they work, to the community at large. In the prosperous First World, puberty is merely an opportunity to remain a child while enjoying the advantages of an adult body.

* * *

Not that a new Confirmation ritual, rigorously revamped by poets and dramatists rather than academics, would automatically usher in the brave new world. But the near total lack of such means to internalize a new-found adulthood and its responsibilities, coupled with a more laid-back—or even absent—style of parenting and with an even more indulgent school system, have left us with a world that is to a great extent spiritless and spineless. It is a world of children in adult bodies, wherein men and women in their forties—and even later—dump spouses and families to go off to "finally find myself," a task most psychologists believe should have been at least tentatively wrapped up at the end of chronological adolescence.

The radical cause, I believe, is overly pliant parents and an embarrassingly untaxing school system, public and private.

In an article called "A Bedtime Story That's Different" (The New York Times, 4/8/91), Carol Lawson details interviews she conducted with parents who, however reluctantly, had learned to live with their teen-age children and their dates having sex upstairs while the parents watched television downstairs. (Understandably, they were even more reluctant to be identified.) The justification the parents offered were painfully mealy-mouthed: at least the young people don't have to have sex in unsafe places and with people the parents don't know; better to have sex and be honest than to lie about it; "You can't tell people not to do things they are going to do anyway." Teen-agers, the parents say, feel uncomfortable if they are fooling their parents. The bottom line seems to be that we don't want young people to be uncomfortable about anything—despite the fact that that is precisely the purpose of adolescence: to surmount the uncomfortable, to achieve a personally validated adult self by conquering unnerving challenges.

The evidence that teen-agers are avoiding those challenges—with the connivance of parents and the educational system—is both overwhelming and disheartening.

According to an Alan Guttmacher Institute survey in 1988, 53 percent of girls 15–19 had had intercourse, contrasted to 36 percent in 1973. That's a quantum leap in a mere 15 years. In that age group in 1988, 60 percent of boys had had intercourse. (All of which makes the chaste minority feel left out and nerdy, but no one seems concerned about *their* discomfort.) Proposals to distribute condoms in senior high schools not only throw in the sponge on any attempt to encourage abstinence or to treat human sexual intercourse as anything but merely a *practical* problem, but they also fortify youngsters' convictions that more efficient birth control devices have severed any link whatever between sex and commitment.

According to the National Center for Health Statistics, at least 19 million unmarried young women between 15 and 24 use birth control—which says nothing of how many young men do, and makes one wonder if (and why) the only reason is that a woman needs a doctor's prescription for birth control devices and a man doesn't. Despite that fact, however, there were in one year 828,124 unwanted births and 1,368,987 abortions, and most of them to very young women—which, in the long run, is a great deal more upsetting than being told that sex is not just another indoor sport, that it has *inescapable* human consequences.

Morality cannot be taught explicitly in public schools because of the mind-withering belief—among otherwise educated people—that to teach morality is somehow to teach religion. On the contrary, one must be moral to be a good human being; immorality is a rending of the objective web of human relationships we have with everybody and everything on this planet, whether there is a God or not. Religion adds a completely different, trans-terrestrial dimension to those relationships. But because norms for human behavior can't be taught in public schools and because parents are incapable or unwilling to do it themselves or even to discomfit their young, we are faced with a generation who are to a terrifying extent what John McLaughlin, S.J., used to call "moral morons."

But even in the religious schools and colleges where I have taught, the vast majority of students routinely say sex with one's steady or with a willing stranger is at worst a venial sin. Class after class estimate that 60–70 percent of their classmates routinely cheat on homework and exams. The majority consistently (and unblushingly) say they do not give their parents an honest day's work for an honest day's pay. There seems to be no guilt about that. Guilt, in fact, is something too upsetting to be allowed. Ditto, responsibility. Ditto, gratitude. One begins to long for an aboriginal Australian subincision ritual.

Moral behavior is not the only area in which one can discern that we dare not upset the kids. According to a 1990 survey conducted by the Institute for Social Research at the University of Michigan, U.S. senior high school students spend 30 hours weekly on school work (26.2 hours in class, 3.8 hours a week at homework) whereas Japanese senior high school students spend 60.4 hours (41.5 hours in class, 19 hours a week at homework). U.S. students spend 1.6 hours a week reading, while Japanese students spend 3.3 hours a week, and yet Japanese students watch three hours more television a week. One major difference is that Japanese students spend less than one hour a week at sports, contrasted to the U.S. seven hours, and the Japanese sleep seven hours less a week than American senior high students. The cult of the body may be more subtly in control of our values than we suspected.

* * *

Out of 13 countries, U.S. students rank 13th in biology, 11th in chemistry, ninth in physics; in all three subjects, only Italy is lower in scientific performance than the United States and Canada. One would have a far greater chance of a strong scientific education in Hungary. There seems to be a difference in national priorities, not to mention a difference in attitudes about who calls the shots in the requirements for a young person's *gradual* growth as an adult.

According to the National Assessment of Educational Progress, only 44 percent of high school *graduates* could read at the 11th-grade level. They had difficulty in finding solutions for everyday problems: Four out of five had difficulty deciphering a bus schedule; two out of three could not follow map directions; three out of four could not understand a long newspaper feature. Nearly one-third of our citizens are functionally illiterate. They can decipher street signs, but they cannot read a recipe or the helpful guidelines the government publishes for making the most out of a meager food budget. They cannot even make and adhere to a budget because they cannot add numbers.

In 1987, 26.9 percent of America's high school students dropped out. In the District of Columbia, the figure was 40.5 percent; in New York, 33.3; in California, 31.5. The effects on the job market, welfare and street crime are both obvious and incalculable. Average SAT scores across the nation out of a possible 800/800 in 1967 were: Verbal—466, Math—492; 20 years later in 1988, they were: Verbal—428; Math—476. One must remember that a candidate gets 200 simply for signing his or her name. Our schools are not improving. The *average* high school senior in the U.S., with a combined score of 904, is not likely to run for public office or win a Nobel Peace Prize or even vote, and roughly half of our students are *below* average. The only way to raise at least verbal scores is by reading books, beginning in kindergarten if not before, not by memorizing lists of words or taking a crash course, which is the academic equivalent of steroids. But kids don't *want* to read books; they'd rather watch a film. So give them a film.

Our purpose as parents and teachers *is* to upset the kids. As Dr. Lawrence Aber, an associate professor of psychology at Barnard College, says: "Parents need to set limits, and it is the children's job to push them. But when parents don't set limits, it can be scary and disruptive for children." Every parent and teacher knows what an abrasive hassle it is to face down kids with their chins set, snarling over not getting their own way. But if we don't want that job, we should have remained childless or become hermits. To allow students to graduate without facing the inescapable *fact* of failure—or at least less than satisfying success—is to send them out into a minefield with no other skills than the ability to play volleyball. Too many young people have a false sense of security that leads them to believe that, at least until age 22, life is going to be pretty much spring break. Or it ought to be, and anybody who tries to disrupt that is a mean-spirited Puritan.

Most parents I know believe their job is to *reassure* their young: to shield them from harm and to provide "the best" they can for them. But to shield them from harm is to shield them from risk, from loss, from the galvanizing and soul-searing experience of surmounting suffering. If the only major setback a boy has is failure to move an inflated pig bladder through eleven other boys on a field with white stripes, if the only major challenge a girl faces is being cut from the musical, our socializing mechanisms —parents and school—not only do no long-range service to our young, but we hamstring them with a perniciously false sense of security.

If a game is worth playing, it is worth losing—and that is true both of the interpersonal family game and of the academic game as well. As Francis T. (Fay) Vincent Jr. said recently in these pages, "We learn that failure often teaches us more than success. We never forget that test or paper we failed and why. A perfect grade or paper gets forgotten much more quickly. Failure is searing... it burns. Success is a liquid... it evaporates." The operative two words in that wise statement are: "and *why*" ("Education and Baseball," 4/6/91).

But children *can't* fail if their overly protective parents continue to make their decisions for them, type out the envelopes for their college applications, yield to their whims (sexual and otherwise) lest the kids be upset—or worse, dislike the parents. Our children *can't* fail —and learn by failing—if kindly (and overworked) teachers let the 10-minute swamp-gas essay slide by, if a child has gotten to senior year without the verbal and mathematical skills that Hun-garian children take for granted, if they *know* they can get a diploma while finess-ing an education. How can we hold the self-deceptive hope that our children will have spine when we refuse to display it ourselves?

* * *

Any truly caring parent should find out, with as close to conviction as possible, just what the child's capabilities are. If the counseling department offers a picture more bleak than the parent is willing to accept, there are agencies more than willing to test the child out for a fee. But after two or three reliable opinions, the parent—and the child—have to accept serenely that this is not the child of one's dreams but the child of one's love, then work with what they have. Settle for what the child is capable of *now*—but absolutely no *less* than that. And demand performance on that level, not only of the child, but of the *teachers* as well—to say nothing of the administration, which is, especially in schools depending on financial support, loath to upset parents and, *ipso facto*, to upset kids.

A youngster needs time to unwind, but many of the young I've taught in the last 30 years find it essential to keep taking breaks—to play handball, to shoot the breeze, to play the guitar, to watch television, to talk on the phone, to go to the movies—and many of their breaks are breaks from their breaks. And when I say that, they almost inevitably grin, with a "knowing" though tolerable guilt. Get a job.

If our knowledge of young people over the past 3,000 years has not become somehow obsolete overnight, there is no youngster who is lazy—just unmotivated. There has to be a *reason*—apprehended as valid *by* the adolescent

—to do this "stuff." And yet many parents and teachers are incapable of demonstrating why any sane person would submit to ingesting this "stuff." The data one may not remember, but the difference is what working on ever more complex data does to the thinking machine.

For a high school senior, five or six years down the road is a nearly limitless (and subsidized) length of time. As a result, many of the college students I deal with evenings in the dorm still can't believe, in March of their senior year, that Oz time is over; even at that late date, they do not know what they want to do with their lives. Unless students begin to internalize, at least as early as junior high, that welfare is going to come to an end in a few years, we will continue to have a nation of children in grown-up bodies. Let them begin to pay their own tuition, to put money in the bank —not for college spending money, but for tuition. Let them begin to contribute to family vacations—not just for their own pleasures, or the family's. "If we go to Florida, you'll have to contribute 200 bucks." After puberty, they are— objective fact—no longer babies.

Most high school students are subsidized to the tune of at least $15,000: tuition, food, heat, insurance, clothes, car. At that cost, taking an honest day's pay without giving an honest day's work is *grand* larceny. Yet many parents blithely collude in their own children's larcenous habits.

* * *

Psychiatrist Erik Erikson shows that life is a natural series of upsets, stages of disequilibrium that have a *purpose:* to crack open the individual's comfortable security and lead him or her out into a wider, richer humanity. Birth itself is an upset: forced from the warm serenity of the womb out into the cold and noise, and the first present is a whack on the rear end. But without that pain, the child would die. A child resents the upset of weaning and potty training, but without them the child remains a mewlying baby for a lifetime. A child resents being hauled from the television and shoved outside to play with the other children, but without that the child is impoverished. There is no bigger upset in a small child's life than being stranded at the kindergarten door by a woman who has suddenly changed from Fairy Godmother into Wicked Stepmother, but without that upset the child would lack the skills he or she needs to survive as a breadwinner working with other people. And none of us would want to face the upset of adolescence again. But its natural purpose is to force a child to cope with life as an adult, to achieve and understand a personally validated identity, which—as anyone blessed with the upset of therapy knows—is a painful process many choose to avoid.

It is much more comfy in the womb, being pampered by Mommy and Daddy, sprawled in front of the television, dumping school, living off the family. But comfy is the Freudian death wish, like giving candy to a diabetic or booze to an alcoholic because they whine and pout for them. With painful irony, our very attempts to shield our young and give them the best is depriving them of precisely what their puberty invites them to.

NO

Kathleen Kennedy Townsend

WHY JOHNNY CAN'T TELL
RIGHT FROM WRONG

"What would you like to be when you graduate?" asked a grade school teacher of her students in a Baltimore County classroom I visited recently. A young man raised his hand: "A pimp. You can make good money." The teacher then turned to a female student and asked, "Would you work for him?" "I guess so," the young woman replied lethargically.

In my five years in the Maryland Department of Education, I've heard hundreds of similar stories—rueful teachers' lounge chronicles of abject moral collapse by children barely old enough to make grilled cheese sandwiches by themselves. But these days you don't need to work in education to hear such mind-numbing tales. Turn on the TV news and there you have it: Our schools are hotbeds of violence, vandalism, and unethical behavior. Recently we've heard of a student-run LSD ring in one Virginia school and the bartering of stolen college entrance exams in one of New York City's most selective high schools. Sixty-one percent of high school students say they cheated on an exam during the past year. Nationwide, assaults on teachers are up 700 percent since 1978. Each month 282,000 students are attacked. And for the first time ever, the risk of violence to teenagers is greater in school than on the streets.

Obviously, we've got a problem here—a problem not just of violence, but of values. Plain and simple, many of our kids don't seem to have any, or at least any of a socially constructive kind. But what to do about 12-year-old aspiring pimps and cheaters? You might think the solution lies with that "family values" constituency, the Republicans. Yet a year of podium-thumping in favor of "values" by the Bush administration was not backed by a single concrete plan of action. In his four years as president, George Bush offered nothing more substantial than a PR stunt—his Thousand Points' of Light Foundation. Still, at least the Republicans have been willing to *talk* about values. For all of Bill Clinton's 12-point plans, he has yet to come up with a specific agenda for restoring values.

To explain away that omission, Democrats argue that the ultimate responsibility for inspiring values lies not with the government, but with the family.

From Kathleen Kennedy Townsend, "Why Johnny Can't Tell Right from Wrong," *The Washington Monthly*, vol. 24, no. 12 (December 1992). Copyright © 1992 by The Washington Monthly Company, 1611 Connecticut Avenue, NW, Washington, DC, 20009, (202) 462-0128. Reprinted by permission of *The Washington Monthly*.

A day in one of the nation's public schools might well convince the average citizen that those Democrats need a reality check. Face it: In some homes, parents simply aren't paragons of civic or ethical virtue. If we rely on the family alone to instill values, we will fail. As one 21-year-old ex-con said, "Kids grow up with a father or an uncle who is robbing stores. They figure, 'If my father can do it, so can I.'" In other homes, parents simply aren't around. In a series of recent workshops sponsored by the Maryland state government, high school students suggested a number of solutions they thought would help them better withstand the antisocial pressures that buffet them. While much of what they said was expected—more information about drugs, greater student participation in school and county decisions—one was a real eye-opener: They asked that their parents have dinner with them more often.

Ultimately, the goal should be to help parents raise kind and law-abiding children. But how do we get there? Why not turn to the one institution that sees the problem more closely than any, and that touches children on a regular and sustained basis: the public school. Why not teach values in school?

Before you dismiss this suggestion as a William Bennettesque ploy to end calls for more school resources, additional jobs programs, or parental-leave legislation—all worthy goals—hear me out. Teaching values does *not* mean using the classroom to push a particular point of view on any political issue—say, abortion or the death penalty—that has worked its way to the core of the values debate. We're not even talking about school prayer or requiring the Pledge of Allegiance. It's much simpler than that: Teaching values means quietly helping kids to learn honesty, responsibility, respect for others, the importance of serving one's community and nation— ideals which have sufficiently universal appeal to serve as the founding and guiding principles of this country. In the schools, values education means lessons about friendship and anger, stealing and responsibility, simply being polite, respecting others, serving the needs of those who may be less fortunate— all lessons sadly absent from today's curriculum.

Teaching these sorts of values does more than yield heart-warming anecdotes of students helping old ladies across the street. It brings results— tangible improvement to the lives of children and their families. A survey of 176 schools that have adopted a values curriculum found that 77 percent reported a decrease in discipline problems, 68 percent boasted an increase in attendance, and 64 percent showed a decrease in vandalism. Three years after the Jackie Robinson Middle School in New Haven, Connecticut, initiated a values curriculum, the number of student pregnancies went from 16 to zero. After the Merwin Elementary School in Irwindale, California, instituted a character education program, damage due to vandalism was reduced from $25,000 to $500; disciplinary action decreased by 80 percent; and—could it be?—academic test scores went up.

Teaching values is clearly worth the trouble. So why is "values education" still one of education's neglected stepchildren? Why is it that schools that now teach values are rare—most often independent efforts by one or two inspired educators? Because, despite the family values chitchat, there's been no political or popular consensus that values should be as much a part of the curriculum as reading and writing. We need a more organized approach. If we are ready to instill a sense of values in America's youth, it will take a concerted effort by both political leaders and educators to make it happen.

SELECTIVE SERVICE

So where to begin? How about with a notion relegated to the back burner in the get-it-while-you-can eighties: community service. Serving others is held in such low regard among our youth that 60 percent of high school students said in a recent survey they simply would not be willing to "volunteer to serve their community for a year." That's a remarkable figure not only because so many aren't willing to serve, but because so many of those who responded negatively have never served to begin with. The students' distaste for service could largely be a distaste for the unknown. But when students are exposed to this unknown—through activities such as tutoring, visiting the elderly, rehabilitating homeless shelters, lobbying for new laws—their reaction is appreciably different.

Alethea Kalandros, as a ninth-grade student in Baltimore County, missed more than 70 days of school and was tempted to drop out. The next year she missed two days of school. What happened? She enrolled in a program that allows her to volunteer at the Maryland School for the Blind. "It gives me a reason to come to school," she says. Alethea is part of Maryland's pioneering effort in promoting community service. While the program is now voluntarily offered by only a couple of schools, Maryland, after years of heated debate, recently became the first state to require all high school

students to perform community service in order to graduate. Starting next year, all students entering the ninth grade must complete 75 hours of service or classes which incorporate service into the lesson, such as stream testing in an environmental course or writing about visits to the elderly in an English class. As part of the program, students are required to "prepare and reflect." This means, for instance, complementing working in a soup kitchen with learning about the most common cause of homelessness.

Any of a wide variety of activities fulfill the requirement, from repairing a local playground to tutoring fellow students. The impact, however, goes beyond helping the needy. Community service, as the limited experience in schools has shown, teaches students values and citizenship. For instance, while fourth, fifth, and sixth graders at Jackson Elementary School in Salt Lake City, Utah, were studying ground water pollution, they discovered that barrels of toxic waste were buried just four blocks from their school. They waged a vigorous public relations and fundraising campaign to clean up the site, eventually winning the support of the city's mayor. When this effort was stymied—Utah state law does not allow for private donations to clean up such sites—they lobbied the legislature and changed the statute. And while service programs can help students make a difference outside the school, they also have an impact inside the classroom: They make learning more interesting by simply helping students to understand how to apply textbook lessons in the real world.

Despite successes in experimental programs, stubborn resistance to community service from educators is still the norm, even in Maryland where the Superintendents Association, the PTA, and the local boards of education all fought against the new service requirement. One of the most common knee-jerk reactions is cost. But ask educators in Atlanta, Georgia, who have been operating a regional service program for eight years, and they'll tell you it doesn't cost a dime. Of course, that doesn't mean all service programs can be run as efficiently, but it does show that costs can be kept low.

Beyond that, the arguments against service become more strained. The president of the Maryland Teachers Association, for example, called the proposal "enforced servitude" and claimed that it violated the Thirteenth Amendment. What's really bothering the educators? Probably the fact that they would be required to change their teaching methods. As Pat McCarthy, vice-president of the Thomas Jefferson Center, a non-profit foundation specializing in values education, says, "The biggest impediment to values education is teacher education." You can't teach community service out of a textbook; it takes time and thought, which, of course, takes effort. And that, for some educators, is a tough concept to accept.

While community service teaches values through hands-on experience, that's but one piece of the puzzle. If we want to instill values, why not take an even more straightforward approach: Teach them directly. It may sound radical, especially when we are talking about methods like memorizing passages from the Bible, "bribing" kids with discounts at the school store to behave decently, permitting students in class discussions to describe problems they face at home, and allowing teachers to make it clear that they might not approve of some parents' values. But while students are

sometimes taught that what happens at home is not always a good thing, teaching values does not mean separating the parents from the lessons. Quite the contrary, a smart values program includes parents, too. Before a values program at Gauger's Junior High in Newmark, Delaware, was implemented, 100 people —parents, teachers, students and community representatives—attended a two-day conference in which they learned about the purpose and goals of the program and the ways they could help implement it. Parents provided input and teachers knew they had community support. And in the end, nobody had to worry that little Petey would bounce home from values class clutching the collected works of Lyndon LaRouche.

Is it really possible to teach values that we all agree upon? Of course. In fact, schools in an indirect way already present students with a set of values that is universally respected: What are our efforts to integrate our schools and prohibitions against stealing or drinking in school if not an education in values? It's not difficult to take this type of thinking one step further, creating a curriculum that teaches other values that are universally accepted but are almost never actually taught directly to our youth. In districts such as Sweet Home, New York, and in Howard and Baltimore counties, Maryland, superintendents formed representative groups of community leaders that included people as ideologically diverse as fundamentalist ministers and ACLU attorneys. They held public forums and listened to community opinion and after months of extensive discussion, the groups produced a list of values with which everyone was comfortable. Now, when people in these communities ask,

"Whose values?" they can proudly say "Ours."

At places like Hebbville Elementary in a low-income section of Baltimore County, the results are impressive. There, teachers hold out the promise of tutoring the mentally retarded as a reward for children who have finished their assignments, done well on a test, shown improvement, or been helpful in class. The students actually vie for the privilege. Tiesha was picked to help out in a class of 15 seven- and eight-year-olds whose IQs are in the 30–45 range. "I like being a helper," she says. "I tried to teach my cousin that 100 percent and 100 percent equal 200 percent. When I saw her write two, I was so happy."

At the Waverly Elementary school in Baltimore City, values lessons are taught through discussions about peer pressure. The teacher chooses 15 students, divides them into four groups, and asks them to perform skits about peer pressure. One skit involves Daniel, whose three hip classmates mock him because he wears non-brand-name tennis shoes. Daniel persuades his parents to buy Nikes and when he returns to school, the gang accepts him. In reflecting upon the skit, Daniel says, "All the friends were making the decision rather than me making my own decision." Another student said, "Daniel could have decided to be different." It is significant that the students made up this fact pattern. In the kids-and-sneakers stories you usually hear, children are assaulting each other for Air Jordans. Here, they are girding themselves to accept an alternative.

That's well and good, but we're still missing one crucial element: accountability. For values education to succeed and prosper, schools need to show that it's paying off in tangible ways. That means, for instance, keeping track of indicators such as rates of crime and vandalism in schools or the number of students involved in community service where values are being taught.

CLASS WAR

Many may resent this call for values as a way for parents to shirk their own responsibility onto someone else, or may see it as another passing fad. As for parents, they may cling to concerns about which values their children should learn. But our collective trepidations pale next to the alternative: another generation of children growing up without a moral compass.

Changing will take courage, but we can take heart from one fifth-grade class I watched where the topic was "the right to be an individual." The purpose was to help the children decide when their own actions are inappropriate and to develop strategies for improving their classmates' behavior. The discussion began with a very simple story about a boy named Bobby who never washed himself and had no friends. Eventually he realized that he'd have to take a bath if he wanted his classmates to ask him to play. The immediate lesson was about cleanliness —about as innocuous a value as you can find. But the moral had pertinence even for frequent bathers: Sometimes change is not only good, but necessary. That's a lesson that should resonate, not just with fifth-graders, but with the next administration. Clearly, the old ways of inculcating values in our kids are no longer working. We grownups have got to change our thinking, too.

POSTSCRIPT

Should Parents Be Doing More to Impart Values to Children?

According to a 1992 article in *Education Week*, there seems to be a movement to include values education in school curricula across the country. Educators are promoting efforts to develop good character in young people. A network called the Character Education Partnership has been formed by leaders from education, business, religion, and youth groups across the country.

The issue of values or character education was a central mission of most school districts through the 1960s. It had little attention in the ensuing 30 years. Now, in the 1990s, it is enjoying a renewed prominence among school policymakers.

Educational institutions in our society have distanced themselves from teaching values in their curricula for fear of being controversial and because they are vulnerable to litigation from any of a number of oppositional groups. Also, many teachers educated in the 1960s and 1970s were taught not to impose their values on students. This renewed interest in teaching values in the schools is a direct result of some of the youth-related problems that currently plague society at large. Consider, for example, that among leading industrial nations, the United States has the highest murder rate for 15–24-year-olds; in excess of 1 million adolescent girls become pregnant each year; 76 percent of college freshmen admit to having cheated in high school; and 25 percent of college women have been victims of rape or attempted rape by dates or acquaintances (Viadero, 1992). These types of statistics lend a sense of urgency to the feeling many people have that things must change, and perhaps the time is ripe for a frank, constructive discussion of values, morality, and the role parents play in developing these in their children.

SUGGESTED READINGS

Buchholz, T. G. (1992, April 15). Teaching virtue. *Vital Speeches of the Day, 58,* 396–397.

Edelman, M. W. (1992, April). The challenges of the 90s: Saving our children. *Social Education, 56,* 240–243.

Roberts, Y. (1993, December 3). Teaching children to be bad. *New Statesman and Society, 6,* 14–15.

Ryan, K. (1993, November). Mining the values in the curriculum. *Educational Leadership, 51,* 16–18.

Sommers, C. H. (1993, December 13). How to teach right and wrong. *Christianity Today, 37,* 33–37

ISSUE 16

Is Abstinence Education the Best Sex Education?

YES: Thomas Lickona, from "Where Sex Education Went Wrong," *Educational Leadership* (November 1993)

NO: Peggy Brick and Deborah M. Roffman, from " 'Abstinence, No Buts' Is Simplistic," *Educational Leadership* (November 1993)

ISSUE SUMMARY

YES: Thomas Lickona, a developmental psychologist, states that Americans need to promote a higher standard of sexual morality in our society through "directive" sex education, which promotes abstinence before marriage. He argues that traditional sex education programs, such as "comprehensive" sex education and "abstinence but" sex education, have not only failed to reduce teen pregnancy but may also, inadvertently, be promoting it.

NO: Peggy Brick, director of education at Planned Parenthood of Northern New Jersey, and Deborah M. Roffman, a sexuality educator and consultant, refute the directive approach to sex education by suggesting that a comprehensive approach to sex education is more effective. They suggest that the reason sex education programs have not been as effective as they could be is because truly comprehensive programs exist in only about 10 percent of the schools across America.

The number of adolescent females in our society who bear out-of-wedlock children continues to rise. Most people understand that teenage pregnancy is a serious and epidemic problem. Unwed adolescent mothers lack sufficient skills and education to support themselves and their children. They are unlikely to receive emotional or financial support from the fathers of their children, for the fathers are too young and unprepared for the financial and emotional responsibilities of parenthood as well. The adolescent mother's needs are often met by her parents or, more often, through publicly supported programs. It is no surprise that the cost of providing such services, not only during pregnancy and at the time of birth but often throughout the life of the mother and child, is very high. Teen mothers and their children are at a distinct disadvantage in their ability to function successfully in society. As a consequence, they often turn to welfare programs, such as Aid to Families with Dependent Children, and other social programs for help.

The obvious solution is to lessen the number of out-of-wedlock births that are occurring. Sexuality education is the current method through which U.S. society has confronted the problem. However, what constitutes effective sexuality education? Professionals continue to debate which sex education approach to this emotionally and financially costly societal problem will yield the intended results. The sexuality programs considered acceptable by some researchers, teachers, clinicians, clergy, and parents are seen by others as contributing to the problem. As a result, the arguments about what is appropriate sex education continue, even as the century comes to a close. These arguments might be conceptualized into two extremes: (1) We have been much too liberal in our approach to teaching our children about sexuality. In our zeal to be nonjudgmental and open-minded, we have forgotten our responsibility to teach our children the morality and safety of abstinence in this world of unwanted infants and sexually transmitted diseases. (2) Comprehensive sex education in the schools, which begins in kindergarten and continues through grade 12, has not been given a chance in America. Virtually no school district has integrated teaching about the social and psychological aspects of human sexuality, along with its physical dimensions, into their curricula from the beginning of a child's school years until they end. If this were to occur, we could make significant progress in solving the problem of adolescent pregnancy.

Currently, in the United States, Congress has appropriated $250 million in abstinence education grants to the states. The program is controversial because many sex educators and policymakers at the state level are concerned about the efficacy of abstinence-only programs. Under federal guidelines, these abstinence-only programs must teach that sex outside of marriage is likely to have harmful psychological and physical effects. Other topics include how to reject sexual advances, avoiding drugs and alcohol, and being able to support oneself financially before engaging in sex. This funding is controversial because many sex educators advocate abstinence-plus programs, which discourage premarital sex but also discuss birth control and disease prevention for adolescents who may decide to engage in sex.

Thomas Lickona's selection elaborates the typical rationale for the morality and safety of a program similar to the one currently being adopted in the United States. Peggy Brick and Deborah M. Roffman contradict Lickona and argue for a more comprehensive approach to sex education that is even broader than the abstinence-plus programs.

YES

Thomas Lickona

WHERE SEX EDUCATION WENT WRONG

Most of us are familiar with the alarming statistics about teen sexual activity in the United States. Among high school students, 54 percent (including 61 percent of boys and 48 percent of girls) say they have had sexual intercourse, according to a 1992 Centers for Disease Control study. The number of 9th graders who say they have already had sex is 40 percent.[1]

In the past two decades, there has been an explosion in the number of sexually transmitted diseases. Twelve million people are infected each year; 63 percent of them are under 25.

Each year, 1 of every 10 teenage girls becomes pregnant, and more than 400,000 teenagers have abortions. One in 4 children is born out of wedlock, compared to 1 in 20 in 1960.

But statistics like these do not tell the whole story. The other side—one that should concern us deeply as moral educators—is the debasement of sexuality and the corruption of young people's character.

A LEGACY OF THE SEXUAL REVOLUTION

A 1993 study by the American Association of University Women found that four out of five high school students say they have experienced sexual harassment ("unwanted sexual behavior that interferes with your life") in school. Commented one 14-year-old girl: "All guys want is sex. They just come up to you and grab you."

In suburban Minneapolis, a mother filed state and federal complaints because 3rd and 4th grade boys on the school bus had tormented her 1st grade daughter daily with obscene comments and repeated demands for sexual acts. A 6th grade teacher taking my graduate course in moral education said, "The boys bring in *Playboy,* the girls wear make-up and jewelry, and the kids write heavy sexual notes to each other."

At an Indiana high school, a teacher said, "Kids in the halls will call out—boy to girl, girl to boy—'I want to f— you.'" At Lakewood High School in an affluent Los Angeles suburb, a group of boys formed the "Spur Posse," a

From Thomas Lickona, "Where Sex Education Went Wrong," *Educational Leadership,* vol. 51, no. 3 (November 1993), pp. 84–89. Copyright © 1993 by the Association for Supervision and Curriculum Development. All rights reserved. Reprinted by permission.

club in which participants competed to see how many girls they could sleep with.

Growing up in a highly eroticized sexual environment—a legacy of the sexual revolution—American children are preoccupied with sex in developmentally distorted ways and increasingly likely to act out their sexual impulses. The widespread sexual harassment in schools and the rising rates of teen sexual activity are not isolated phenomena but an outgrowth of the abnormal preoccupation with sex that children are manifesting from the earliest grades.

The sexual corruption of children reflects an adult sexual culture in which the evidence continues to mount that sex is out of control. In 1990, 29 states set records for the sex-and-violence crime of rape. By age 18, more than a quarter of girls and one-sixth of boys suffer sexual abuse. One in four female students who say they have been sexually harassed at school were victimized by a teacher, coach, bus driver, teacher's aide, security guard, principal, or counselor.[2] By various estimates, sexual infidelity now occurs in a third to one-half of U.S. marriages.

Sex is powerful. It was Freud who said that sexual self-control is essential for civilization. And, we should add, for character.

Any character education worthy of the name must help students develop sexual self-control and the ability to apply core ethical values such as respect and responsibility to the sexual domain. Against that standard, how do various contemporary models of sex education measure up?

The history of modern sex education offers three models. The first two are variations of the nondirective approach:

the third, by contrast, is a directive approach.

COMPREHENSIVE SEX EDUCATION

"Comprehensive sex education," which originated in Sweden in the 1950s and quickly became the prototype for the Western world,[3] was based on four premises:

1. Teenage sexual activity is inevitable.
2. Educators should be value-neutral regarding sex.
3. Schools should openly discuss sexual matters.
4. Sex education should teach students about contraception.

The value-neutral approach to sex soon showed up in American sex education philosophy, as in this statement by the author of the *Curriculum Guide for Sex Education in California*: " 'Right' or 'wrong' in so intimate a matter as sexual behavior is as personal as one's own name and address. No textbook or classroom teacher can teach it."[4]

What was the impact of nondirective, value-neutral, comprehensive sex education on teenage sexual behavior?

- From 1971 to 1981, government funding at all levels for contraceptive education increased by 4,000 percent. During that time teen pregnancies increased by 20 percent and teen abortions nearly doubled.[5]
- A 1986 Johns Hopkins University study concluded that comprehensive sex education did not reduce teen pregnancies,[6] a finding replicated by other studies.
- A 1986 Lou Harris Poll, commissioned by Planned Parenthood (a leading sponsor of comprehensive sex educa-

tion), found that teens who took a comprehensive sex education course (including contraceptive education) were significantly *more likely* to initiate sexual intercourse than teens whose sex education courses did not discuss contraceptives.[7]

THE "ABSTINENCE, BUT" MODEL

Negative results like those cited did not lead comprehensive sex educators to alter their approach—but AIDS did. AIDS led to two modifications: (1) teaching students to practice "safe [or "safer"] sex" through the use of barrier contraception (condoms); and (2) grafting an abstinence message onto the old comprehensive model. These changes resulted in what can be called the "Abstinence, But" approach, which says two things to students:

- Abstinence is the only 100 percent effective way to avoid pregnancy, AIDS, and other sexually transmitted diseases.
- But if you are sexually active, you can reduce these risks through the consistent, correct use of condoms.

This hybrid model, still found in many public and private schools, seems to many like a "realistic" compromise. But closer examination revels fundamental problems in the "Abstinence, But" model.

1. It sends a mixed message.

"Don't have sex, but here's a way to do it fairly safely" amounts to a green light for sexual activity. The problem is that "Abstinence, But" is still nondirective sex education. Abstinence is presented as the safest contraceptive option,[8] but "protected sex" is offered as a "responsible" second option. The emphasis is on "making your own decision" rather than on making the right decision.

As a rule, if educators believe that a given activity is ethically wrong—harmful to self and others (as teen sexual activity clearly is)—we help students understand why that is so and guide them toward the right decision. We don't say, for example, "Drug abuse is wrong, but make your own decision, and here's how to reduce the risks if you decide to become drug active."

2. An abstinence message is further weakened when schools provide how-to condom instructions and/or distribute condoms.

Teachers providing condom instruction will commonly demonstrate how to fit a condom to a model (or students may be asked to put a condom on a banana). In the same nonjudgmental atmosphere, discussion often includes the pros and cons of different lubricants, special precautions for oral and anal sex, and so on. Some schools also take what seems like the next logical step of actually distributing condoms to students. Both actions signal approval of "protected sex" and further undermine an abstinence message.

3. Condoms do not make sex physically safe.

For all age groups, condoms have a 10 percent annual failure rate in preventing pregnancy; for teens (notoriously poor users), the figure can go as high as 36 percent.[9] By one estimate, a 14-year-old girl who relies on condoms has more than a 50 percent chance of becoming pregnant before she graduates from high school.[10]

Contraceptive sex educators often cite AIDS as the main justification for "safe sex" education, but research shows that condoms do *not* provide adequate protection against AIDS (and, especially among teens, may generate a false sense of security). In a 1993 University of Texas study, the average condom failure rate for preventing AIDS was 31 percent.[11]

While AIDS is still relatively infrequent among teens, other sexually transmitted diseases are epidemic. Many of these diseases—and 80 percent of the time there are no visible symptoms—can be transmitted by areas of the body that are not covered by contraceptive barriers. Human Papilloma Virus, once very rare, is perhaps the most common STD among teens, infecting 38 percent of sexually active females ages 13 to 21. Victims may suffer from venereal warts, painful intercourse, or genital cancer. The virus can also cause cancer of the penis. Condoms provide no protection against this virus.[12]

Chlamydia infects 20 to 40 percent of sexually active singles; teenage girls are most susceptible. In men, chlamydia can cause infertile sperm; in women, pelvic inflammatory disease and infection of the fallopian tubes. A single infection in a woman produces a 25 percent chance of infertility; a second infection, a 50 percent chance. Medical research has found that condoms do not significantly reduce the frequency of tubal infection and infertility stemming from this disease.[13]

Given teenagers' vulnerability to pregnancy despite the use of condoms and the fact that condoms provide inadequate protection against AIDS and no protection against many STDs, it is irresponsible to promote the myth that condoms make sex physically safe.

4. Condoms do not make sex emotionally safe.

The emotional and spiritual dimensions of sex are what make it distinctively human. If we care about young people, we will help them understand the destructive emotional and spiritual effects that can come from temporary, uncommitted sexual relationships.

These psychological consequences vary among individuals but include: lowered self-esteem (sometimes linked to sexually transmitted diseases), a sense of having been "used," self-contempt for being a "user," the pain of loss of reputation, compulsive sexual behavior to try to shore up one's damaged self-image, regret and self-recrimination, rage over rejection or betrayal, difficulty trusting in future relationships, and spiritual guilt if one has a faith tradition that prohibits sex outside marriage (as world religions typically do).[14] Condoms provide zero protection against these emotional consequences.

5. Nondirective sex education undermines character.

From the standpoint of character education, the nondirective "Abstinence, But" model fails on several counts:

- It doesn't give unmarried young people compelling ethical reasons to abstain from sexual intercourse until they are ready to commit themselves to another person. Instead, students learn that they are being "responsible" if they use contraception.

- It doesn't help students develop the crucial character quality of self-control —the capacity to curb one's desires and delay gratification. To the extent that sex education is in any way permissive toward teenage sexual activity, it fosters poor character and feeds into the societal problem of sex-out-of-control.

- It doesn't develop an ethical understanding of the relationship between sex and love.
- It doesn't cultivate what young people desperately need if they are to postpone sex: a vision of the solemn, binding commitment between two people in which sex is potentially most meaningful, responsible, and safe (physically and emotionally)—namely, marriage.

DIRECTIVE SEX EDUCATION

By any ethical, educational, or public health measure, nondirective sex education has been a failure. As a result, schools are turning increasingly toward directive sex education—just as the national character education movement is embracing a more directive approach to promoting core ethical values as the basis of good character.

A directive approach means helping young persons—for the sake of their safety, happiness, and character—to see the logic of an "Abstinence, No Buts" standard, often called "chastity education." This standard says three things:

1. Sexual abstinence is the *only* medically safe and morally responsible choice for unmarried teenagers.
2. Condoms do not make premarital sex responsible because they don't make it physically safe, emotionally safe, or ethically loving.
3. The only truly safe sex is having sex *only* with a marriage partner who is having sex *only* with you. If you avoid intercourse until marriage, you will have a much greater chance of remaining healthy and being able to have children.

There are now many carefully crafted curriculums, books, and videos that foster the attitudes that lead teens to choose chastity—a moral choice and a lifestyle that is truly respectful of self and others. Here are some examples:

1. Decision-Making: Keys to Total Success. Facing a serious teen pregnancy problem (147 high school girls known to be pregnant in 1984–85), the San Marcos, California, school system implemented a multifaceted program, which included six-week courses for junior high students on developing study skills, self-esteem, and positive moral values;[15] daily 10-minute lessons on "how to be successful"; a six-week course for 8th graders using Teen Aid's curriculum on the advantages of premarital abstinence and how to regain them (for example, self-respect and protection against pregnancy and disease) after having been sexually active; *Window to the Womb*, a video providing ultrasound footage of early fetal development to show students the power of their sexuality to create human life; and summaries of all lessons for parents plus a parent workshop on teaching sexual morality to teens.[16]

After San Marcos implemented this program, known pregnancies at the high school dropped from 20 percent in 1984 to 2.5 percent in 1986 to 1.5 percent in 1988. Meanwhile, scores on tests of basic skills went up, and in 1988 San Marcos won an award for the lowest drop-out rate in California.

2. Teen S.T.A.R. (Sexuality Teaching in the context of Adult Responsibility) is currently used with more than 5,000 teens in various regions of the United States and in other countries. The program teaches that fertility is a gift and a power to be respected. Its premise is that "decisions about sexual responsibility will arise from inner conviction and knowledge of the self." More than half of the teens who enter the program sexually active stop sexual activity; very few initiate it.[17]

3. *The Loving Well Curriculum,* a literature-based program, uses selections from the classics, folktales, and contemporary adolescent literature to examine relationships from family love to infatuation and early romance to marriage. An evaluation finds that of those students who were not sexually active when they started the curriculum, 92 percent are still abstinent two years later, compared to 72 percent abstinent in a control group not exposed to the curriculum.[18]

4. *Postponing Sexual Involvement* was developed by Emory University's Marion Howard specifically for low-income, inner-city 8th graders at risk for early sexual activity. Of students in the program, 70 percent said it taught them that they "can postpone sexual activity without losing their friends' respect." Participants were *five times less likely* to initiate sexual activity than students who did not take the program.[19] . . .

ANSWERS TO COMMON QUESTIONS

Educators committing to directive sex education must be prepared to answer some common questions. Among them:

What about all the teens who will remain sexually active despite abstinence education? Shouldn't they be counseled to use condoms? Obviously, if a person is going to have sex, using a condom will reduce the chance of pregnancy and AIDS, but not to an acceptable level. Condoms offer no protection against many other STDs and their long-term consequences, such as infertility. Schools have the mission of teaching the truth and developing right values—which means helping students understand why the various forms of contraception do not make premarital sex physically or emotionally safe and how premature sexual activity will hurt them now and in the future.

Isn't premarital sexual abstinence a religious or cultural value, as opposed to universal ethical values like love, respect, and honesty? Although religion supports premarital abstinence, it can be demonstrated, through ethical reasoning alone, that reserving sex for marriage is a logical application of ethical values. If we love and respect another, we want what is in that person's best interest. Does sex without commitment meet that criterion? Can we say that we really love someone if we gamble with that person's physical health, emotional happiness, and future life? Given the current epidemic of sexually transmitted diseases, it's possible to argue on medical grounds alone that premarital sexual abstinence is the only ethical choice that truly respects self and other.

Isn't the recommendation to save sex for marriage prejudicial against homosexual persons, since the law does not permit them to marry? All students can be encouraged to follow the recommendation of the U.S. Department of Education's guidebook, *AIDS and the Education of Our Children:*

Regardless of sexual orientation, the best way for young people to avoid AIDS and other STDs is to refrain from sexual activity until as adults they are ready to establish a mutually faithful monogamous relationship.[20]

Is abstinence education feasible in places, such as the inner city, where poverty and family breakdown are harsh realities? Programs like Atlanta's Postponing Sexual Involvement have a track record of making abstinence education work amid urban poverty. Virginia Governor Douglas Wilder has argued that "the black family is teetering near the abyss of self-destruction" and that "our young, male and female alike, must embrace the self-discipline of abstinence."[21] Sylvia Peters, who won national acclaim for her work as principal of the Alexander Dumas School (K-8) in inner-city Chicago, made the decision to tell her students (6th graders were getting pregnant before she arrived), "Do not have sex until you are married—you will wreck your life."[22] These two black leaders know that the problem of black illegitimate births—up from 35 to 65 percent in little more than two decades— won't be solved until there is a new ethic of sexual responsibility.

Sexual behavior is determined by value, not mere knowledge. Studies show that students who have value orientations (for example, get good grades in school, have high self-regard, consider their religious faith important, have strong moral codes), are significantly less likely to be sexually active than peers who lack these values. These internally held values are more powerful than peer pressure.[23]

Our challenge as educators is this: Will we help to develop these values and educate for character in sex, as in all other areas? If we do not move decisively—in our schools, families, churches, government, and media—to promote a higher standard of sexual morality in our society, we will surely see a continued worsening of the plague of sex-related problems

—promiscuity, sexual exploitation and rape, unwed pregnancy, abortions, sexually transmitted diseases, the emotional consequences of uncommitted sex, sexual harassment in schools, children of all ages focused on sex in unwholesome ways, sexual infidelity in marriages, pornography, the sexual abuse of children, and the damage to families caused by many of these problems.

Non directive sex education obviously didn't cause all of these problems, and directive sex education won't solve all of them. But at the very least, sex education in our schools must be part of the solution, not part of the problem.

NOTES

1. Centers for Disease Control and Prevention, (1992), "Sexual Behavior Among High School Student, U. S.," in *Morbidity and Mortality Weekly Report 40*, 51–52.

2. American Association of University Women "Report on Sexual Harassment," (June 1993).

3. D. Richard, (1990), *Has Sex Education Failed Our Teenagers?*, (Colorado Springs: Focus on the Family Publishing).

4. S. Cronenwett, (1982), "Response to Symposium on Sex and Children," in *Character Policy*, edited by E. A. Wynne, (Lanham, Md.: University Press of America), p. 101.

5. R. Glasow, (1988), *School-Based Clinics* (Washington, D.C.: NRL Educational Trust Fund).

6. D. A. Dawson, (1986), "The Effects of Sex Education on Adolescent Behavior," *Family Planning Perspectives* 18, 4: 162–170.

7. L. Harris, (1986), "American Teens Speak: Sex, Myth, TV, and Birth Control," poll commissioned by the Planned Parenthood Federation of America.

8. Thanks to Onalee McGraw for this point.

9. E. Jones and J. Forrest, (May/June 1989), "Contraceptive Failure in the United States." *Family Planning Perspectives*.

10. W. Kilpatrick, (1992), *Why Johnny Can't Tell Right From Wrong*, (New York: Simon & Schuster).

11. Reported by CBS Evening News, 1993.

12. Source: Dr. Joe McIlhaney, Medical Institute for Sexual Health, Austin, Texas. For an in-depth treatment of sexually transmitted diseases, see McIlhaney's 1991 book *Safe Sex: A Doctor Explains the Realities of AIDS and Other STDs* (Grand Rapids: Baker Book House).

13. *Safe Sex: Slide Program Lecture Notes*, (1993), (Austin: Medical Institute for Sexual Health).

14. Thanks to Carson Daly for her contribution to this list.

15. These lessons are available from the Jefferson Center for Character Education, Suite 240, 202 S. Lake Ave., Pasadena, CA 91101.

16. Teen Aid, N. 1330 Calispel, Spokane, WA 99201-2320. For information on a similar program with comparable positive outcomes, contact: SEX RESPECT, P.O. Box 349, Bradley, IL 60915-0349

17. C. Balsam, (October 1992), "Letter to the Editor," *New Oxford Review*. For information about Teen S.T.A.R., contact Hanna Klaus, P.O. Box 30239, Bethesda, MD 20824-0239.

18. Based on an article by S. Ellenwood in *Character* (April, 1993), the newsletter of Boston University's Center for the Advancement of Ethics and Character. For information about the Loving Well Curriculum, contact Nancy McLaren, Project Coordinator, College of Communication, Boston University, 460 Commonwealth Ave., Boston, MA 02215

19. M. Howard and J. McCabe, (1990), "Helping Teenagers Postpone Sexual Involvement," *Family Planning Perspectives* 22: 1.

20. *AIDS and the Education of Our Children*, (1988), (Washington, D.C.: U.S. Department of Education).

21. L. D. Wilder, (March 28, 1991), "To Save the Black Family, the Young Must Abstain," *The Wall Street Journal*.

22. S. Peters, (February 1993), comments as a panel member at the annual conference of the Character Education Partnership, Washington, D.C.

23. I am indebted to William Bennett for this point.

NO

**Peggy Brick and
Deborah M. Roffman**

"ABSTINENCE, NO BUTS" IS SIMPLISTIC

There are no easy answers to the sexual health crisis afflicting our society, including those advocated by Thomas Lickona. The "Abstinence, No Buts" approach does not adequately address the developmental needs of children and adolescents, the reality of their lives, or the societal forces that condition their view of the world.

First, Lickona undermines rational dialogue by dividing educators into artificial, polar camps: "values-free-intercourse promoters," who push for contraception-based "comprehensive" sex education (the bad guys), and "values-based-intercourse preventers," who espouse chastity-based "character" education (the good guys). It is neither accurate nor helpful for him to imply that one particular interest group has a corner on instilling character, core values, and ethical thought; on wanting young people to grow up emotionally, socially, physically, and spiritually healthy; on working toward a day when developmental and social problems—such as premature sexual activity, teenage pregnancy, abortion, STD, HIV, sexism, and sexual harassment/abuse/exploitation—no longer threaten our children.

Second, Lickona's definition of "comprehensive" sex education bears little resemblance to the actual approach. Comprehensive sexuality education encompasses not only the complexities of sex and reproduction, but the enormously complicated subjects of human growth and development, gender roles, intimacy, and social and cultural forces that influence our development as males and females (Roffman 1992). Such an approach seeks to help young people understand sexuality as integral to their identity and enables them to make responsible lifelong decisions (SIECUS 1991).

More than 60 mainstream organizations support this approach through membership in the National Coalition to Support Sexuality Education. These include the American Medical Association, American School Health Association, American Association of School Administrators, National School Boards Association, and the Society for Adolescent Medicine. The majority of American adults support such a strategy as well. For example, recent surveys in New Jersey and North Carolina found that at least 85 percent of those sur-

From Peggy Brick and Deborah Roffman, "'Abstinence, No Buts' Is Simplistic," *Educational Leadership*, vol. 51 (November 1993), pp. 90–92. Copyright © 1993 by The Association for Supervision and Curriculum Development. All rights reserved. Reprinted by permission.

veyed approved of comprehensive sexuality education (Firestone 1993, North Carolina Coalition on Adolescent Pregnancy 1993).

A truly comprehensive approach is ongoing and begins during the preschool and elementary years (Montfort 1993). Curriculums of this type educate, rather than propagandize, children about sexuality. Youngsters learn to ask questions, predict consequences, examine values, and plan for the future. They confront real-life dilemmas: What would happen if? What would you do if? By the middle grades, students learn to take action on issues such as: What can we do to reduce teen pregnancies in this school? To educate students about HIV/AIDS? (See Reis 1989, Kirby et al. 1991, Center for Population Options 1992, O'Neill and Roffman 1992, SIECUS 1993). Ideally, this approach to sexuality education will be integrated throughout the entire curriculum (Brick 1991).

WHY DIRECTIVE APPROACHES FAIL

Those of us committed to comprehensive sex education and to public education in a pluralistic society are not persuaded by the arguments for "directive," ideological sex education for several reasons.

1. It is hypocritical and futile to expect efforts directed at adolescents to solve the nation's myriad sexual problems. Powerful social forces contribute to the early development of unhealthy sexual scripts—about who we are as males or females, how we should act, and issues of right and wrong.

For example, the early learning of male gender roles, often linked with violence and the need to dominate, is fundamentally related to problems of rape and ha-rassment (Miedzian 1991). The manipulation of the sexuality of both males and females from an early age, and the stimulation of sexual desires by advertising and other media, are fundamental to the operation of our economic system (D'Emilio and Freedman 1988). Adolescent child-bearing, sexually transmitted diseases, and the spread of HIV are highly correlated with poverty and lack of hope for the future (National Research Council 1987). Further, many problems attributed to teens are not just teen problems: the majority of *all* pregnancies in this country are unplanned (Heller 1993). Seventy percent of adolescent pregnancies are fathered by adult men (Males 1993).

2. Directive approaches require a delay of intercourse 10 or more years beyond biological maturity, which is contrary to practice in virtually all societies—unless there is a strict tradition segregating unmarried males and females and chaperoning women (Francoeur 1991).

3. The success of these proposals requires an immediate, fundamental change in the sexual attitudes and behaviors of a society through mere educational intervention. Such a radical change has never been accomplished. Traditionally, the majority of American males have accepted premarital intercourse, and as early as 1973, a study showed 95 percent of males and 85 percent of females approved of it (DeLamater and MacCorquodale 1979).

4. Advocates of the directive approach do not prepare youth to make decisions in a highly complex world. They permit no choice but *their* choice and deliberately deny potentially life-saving information to those who do no conform to their viewpoint.

5. The curriculums espoused are fear-based, characterized by devastating de-

scriptions of the dangers of all nonmarital intercourse and medical misinformation about abortion, sexually transmitted disease, HIV/AIDS, and the effectiveness of condoms. For example, the major cause of condom failure is incorrect usage. Knowledge of proper condom use, of the variations in quality among brands, and of the substantial increase in effectiveness when condoms are used in combination with spermicides greatly reduces the risk for those who choose to have sexual intercourse (Kestelman and Trussell 1991). These sex-negative, emotionally overwhelming, and potentially guilt-producing strategies may well induce problems rather than ameliorate them by leading to unhealthy sexual attitudes, irrational decision making, denial, or rebellion (Fisher 1989).

Moreover, these curriculums are promoted by groups such as Concerned Women for America, the Eagle Forum, Focus on the Family, and the American Life League, which are lobbying heavily to impose Fundamentalist Christian doctrine on public schools (Kantor 1993, Hart 1993).

DISTORTED AND MISREPRESENTED DATA

Given these concerns, claims about the success of abstinence-only programs must be examined with extreme caution. Take, for example, the claim that a program in San Marcos, California, greatly reduced teen pregnancies in the mid-80s. In fact, this claim was not based on a scientific study but on the observation of the high school principal reporting the number of students who *told* the school counselor they were pregnant. After a much-publicized program condemning premarital intercourse, far fewer students reported their pregnancies to school staff; actual census figures for San Marcos indicated that from 1980–1990, the birth rate for mothers aged 14–17 more than doubled (Reynolds 1991). Many other evaluators have challenged the integrity of research documenting these extraordinary claims in support of abstinence-only curriculums (Trudell and Whatley 1991, Kirby et al. 1991, Alan Guttmacher Institute 1993). Such programs may change attitudes temporarily (at least as reported to a teacher), but they do not change behavior in any significant way.

Similar statistical distortions have been used to discredit programs that are not abstinence-only in approach. Seriously flawed is the conclusion, based on data collected in a 1986 Lou Harris Poll, that "teens who took a comprehensive sex education course (defined as one including contraceptive education) were subsequently 53 percent more likely to initiate intercourse than teens whose sex education courses did not discuss contraceptives."

First, the survey did not ask when intercourse was initiated in relation to the timing of the program; therefore, the word "subsequently" (implying causation) is patently misleading. Second, the analysis ignored the crucial variable of chronological age. Sexual intercourse among teenagers increases with age, as does the experience of having had a "comprehensive" program. Therefore, causation was implied, when in reality, correlation was the appropriate interpretation.

Besides the use of distorted data, groups demanding an abstinence-only approach dismiss people whose values regarding sexual behaviors differ from their own, asserting that these people are "without values." In fact, comprehensive ex education is based upon core human values that form the foundation of all ethical behavior, such as personal responsibility, integrity, caring for others, and mutual respect in relationships.

Moreover, comprehensive sex education is based on values appropriate to our democratic and pluralistic society —including respect for people's diverse viewpoints about controversial issues.

A WAKE-UP CALL FOR SOCIETY

Our entire society, not just sex education, has failed to provide children and youth with the educational, social, and economic conditions necessary to grow toward sexual health. In fact, truly comprehensive K–12 sexuality education, which at most exists in only 10 percent of schools nationwide, has hardly been tried (Donovan 1989). Sexuality education—of whatever kind—is neither the cause, nor the cure, for our nation's sexual malaise.

In a society where children's consciousness is permeated by virulent images of sex—where their sexuality is manipulated by advertising and the media, where few adults provide helpful role models—we cannot expect sex education to perform a miracle. Curriculums that provide as their primary or sole strategy admonitions against nonmarital intercourse are destined to be ineffective and, in fact, insult the real-life needs of children and youth. In a society that conveys complex, confusing messages about sexuality, only comprehensive sexuality education can begin to address the diverse needs of youth and promote healthy sexual development.

REFERENCES

Alan Guttmacher Institute. (1993). *Washington Memo*, p. 4.

Brick, P. (1991). "Fostering Positive Sexuality." *Educational Leadership* 45, 1: 51–53.

Center for Population Options. (1992). *When I'm Grown: Vol. II. Grades 3 and 4; Vol. III, Grades 5 and 6*. Washington, D.C.: CPO.

DeLamater, J. D., and P. MacCorquodale. (1979). *Premarital Sexuality: Attitudes, Relationships, Behavior*. Madison: University of Wisconsin Press.

D'Emilio, J., and E. B. Freedman. (1988). *Intimate Matters: A History of Sexuality in America*. New York: Harper & Row.

Donovan, P. (1989). *Risk and Responsibility: Teach Sex Education in America's Schools Today*. New York: Alan Guttmacher Institute.

Firestone, W. A. (1993). "Support of Sex Education Grows." *Family Life Matters* 18: 1.

Fisher, W. A. (1989). "Understanding and Preventing Adolescent Pregnancy and Sexually Transmissible Disease/AIDS." In *Applying Social Influence Processes in Preventing Social Problems* edited by J. Edwards et al. New York: Plenum Press.

Francoeur, R. T. (1991). *Becoming a Sexual Person*. New York: Macmillan.

Harris, L. 91986). *American Teens Speak: Sex, Myths, TV, and Birth Control*. New York: Planned Parenthood Federation of America.

Hart, J. (August 28, 1993). "Battle Lines Drawn on Classroom Sex Education," *The Boston Globe*.

Heller, K. (February 21, 1993). "Out of Control." *Philadelphia Inquirer Magazine*: 18, 20–22.

Kantor, L. M. (1993). "Scared Chaste? Fear-Based Educational Curricula." *SIECUS Report* 21, 2: 1–15.

Kestelman, P., and J. Trussell. (1991). "Efficacy of the Simultaneous Use of Condoms and Spermicides." *Family Planning Perspectives* 23: 226–232.

Kirby, D., R. P. Barth, N. Leland, and J. V. Fetro. (991). "Reducing the Risk: Impact of a New Curriculum on Sexual Risk-Taking," *Family Planning Perspectives* 23: 253–263.

Males, M. (August 9, 1993). "Infantile Arguments." *In These Times*: 18–20.

Miedzian, M. (1991). *Boys Will Be Boys: Breaking the Link Between Masculinity and Violence*. New York: Doubleday.

Montfort, S., P. Brick, and N. Blume. (1993). *Healthy Foundations: Developing Positive Policies and Programs Regarding Children's Learning about Sexuality*. Hackensack: Planned Parenthood of Greater Northern New Jersey.

North Carolina Coalition on Adolescent Pregnancy. (Spring 1993). "New Stateside Poll Shows Overwhelming Support for Sex Education in Schools, for Adolescent Health Care Centers, and

Access to Contraceptive Services for Teens." *The Network:* 1.

National Research Council. (1987). *Risking the Future: Adolescent Sexuality, Pregnancy, and Childbearing.* Washington, D.C.: National Academy Press.

O'Neill, C., and D. Roffman, eds. (1992). "Sexuality Education in an Age of AIDS." *Independent School* 51, 3: 11–42.

Reis, B. 91989). *F.L.A.S.H.: Family Life and Sexual Health, 9/10.* (1986). *F.L.A.S.H. 7/8.* (1985). *F.L.A.S.H. 5/6.* Seattle: Seattle-King County Department of Public Health.

Reynolds, N. (December 19, 1991). "So-Called San Marcos Miracle Actually May Be Just a Myth." *San Diego Union.*

Roffman, D. (1992). "Teaching About Sexuality in Independent Schools." *Independent School* 51, 3: 11–18.

SIECUS. (1991). Guidelines for Comprehensive Sexuality Education. New York: Sex Information and Education Council of the U.S.

SIECUS. (1993). "Comprehensive Sexuality Education: A SIECUS Resource Guide of Recommended Curricula and Text Books." *SIECUS Report* 21, 6: 20–23.

Trudell, B., and M. Whatley. (1991). "Sex Respect: A Problematic Public School Sexuality Curriculum." *Journal of Sex Education and Therapy* 17, 2: 125–140.

POSTSCRIPT

Is Abstinence Education the Best Sex Education?

Out-of-wedlock births to adolescent mothers has become problematic in our society for several reasons. The onset of the menarche (first ovulation and subsequent menstruation) is coming at increasingly earlier ages for young females. This combined with the tendency for delaying marriage means that the adolescent female faces longer periods of singlehood during her fertile years than did her great-grandmother. Consider, for example, that it was not uncommon for a women born at the turn of the century to be married at age 17 or 18. Consider, too, that this woman's menarche was a year or more later than that of a contemporary adolescent female. The result is fewer years of singlehood and fewer opportunities for premarital sexual endeavors.

Current notions regarding adolescent sexuality suggest that teens will inevitably express themselves sexually as part of the developmental process of adolescence. Therefore, unless they are taught to exercise restraint and sexual abstinence, they should be apprised of the risks of early sexual activity and empowered with information about how to express themselves sexually while avoiding pregnancy and sexually transmitted diseases. But on the basis of current rates of teen pregnancy, the information teens are now receiving is not encouraging more responsible behaviors, be those behaviors abstinence or the use of contraceptives.

SUGGESTED READINGS

American Academy of Pediatrics, Committee on Adolescence (1995). Condom availability for youth. *Pediatrics, 95*(2), 281–185.

Jacobs, C. D. (1995). School sexuality education and adolescent risk-taking behavior. *Journal of School Health, 65*(3), 91–95.

Kasun, J. (1994, Spring). Condom nation. *Policy Review,* 79–82.

Post, S. (1992, October 17). Adolescents in a time of AIDS: Preventive Education. *America,* 278–282.

Sellers, D. E. (1994). Does the promotion and distribution of condoms increase teen sexual activity? Evidence from an HIV prevention program for Latino youth. *American Journal of Public Health, 84*(12), 952–959.

Whitehead, B. D. (1994, October). The failure of sex education. *Atlantic Monthly,* 55–80.

Wright, B. (1992, October). Condom availability in a small town. *SIECUS Report,* 13–17.

ISSUE 17

Can Memories of Childhood Sexual Abuse Be Recovered?

YES: May Benatar, from "Running Away from Sexual Abuse: Denial Revisited," *Families in Society: The Journal of Contemporary Human Services* (May 1995)

NO: Susan P. Robbins, from "Wading Through the Muddy Waters of Recovered Memory," *Families in Society: The Journal of Contemporary Human Services* (October 1995)

ISSUE SUMMARY

YES: May Benatar, a clinical social worker and a lecturer at the School of Social Work, New York University, argues that the mass media and contemporary culture question the accuracy and truthfulness of survivors of sexual abuse. By doing this the long-term effects of these abuses tend to be minimized. She traces some of the origins of contemporary thought regarding recovered memories of sexual abuse and suggests that people have a tendency to deny that such terrible things actually happen to children. This is why some question the veracity of these recovered memories.

NO: Susan P. Robbins, an associate professor of social work at the University of Houston, contends that the reason some professionals are skeptical of recovered memories is that there is no research that supports the accuracy of recovered memory. She cautions that the indiscriminate acceptance of recovered memories can lead to a serious backlash of disbelief when legitimate cases of abuse are reported.

There has been a definite shift in societal thinking about child abuse during the past 20 years. Historically, when an adult would come forth with an account of sexual abuse that was purported to have occurred decades earlier, these accounts were likely to have been considered by mental health professionals as fantasies. In the past decade or so, both the mass media and the helping professions have been much more likely to accept these allegations, which have come to be known as recovered memories of past sexual abuse, as true. It is easy to imagine not only the problems for the person recalling such difficult memories, but also the problems that families have had to endure as a result of these disclosures. One controversial question is how valid are allegations that are based upon repressed memories from years ago?

Few people would argue with the notion that human memory is not always accurate; our memories do indeed fail us at times. It has been documented in the literature, however, that traumatic memory is physiologically encoded differently than normal memory in one's brain. If so, should we assume that traumatic experiences are more indelibly etched and can be retrieved with greater accuracy than normal memory? Or is it possible that memories of abuse are not as easily recalled due to the trauma involved? Some mental health professionals believe that therapists can suggest memories to clients and these memories can become integrated into the client's memory as if they actually happened when they, in fact, did not.

In the first selection, May Benatar claims that we, as a society, do not pay enough attention to these heinous past traumas. Susan P. Robbins suggests that perhaps we accept these allegations as fact too readily.

YES

May Benatar

RUNNING AWAY FROM SEXUAL ABUSE: DENIAL REVISITED

After a period of increased professional and public awareness of how pervasive the sexual maltreatment of children is in our society, we appear to be in danger of vaulting away from hard-won insights into this major public health issue. Both propounding and expressing the prejudices of the culture, the press and other media have taken to indicting the veracity of traumatic memories of survivors of sexual abuse, minimizing the toxic long-term effects of the sexual maltreatment of children, and casting doubt on both the skill and good intentions of clinicians treating both child victims and adult survivors. We have seen front-page articles on the purported "false" memories of adult survivors of abuse; examples of "false" accusations of innocent parents, grandparents, or teachers; or speculations that therapists, many of whom are survivors themselves, intentionally or unintentionally suggest events to their patients that never took place.

A 1993 *Newsweek* cover photograph showed a middle-age couple convicted of molesting their grandchildren. The caption asks: "When does the fight to protect our kids go too far?" Does this strange juxtaposition of material imply that convicting child molesters is "going too far?" The article inside (Shapiro, 1993) reviews a few recent court cases and one reversal and addresses the issue of child testimony; the author asks whether we are panicking over child abuse. Is criminal prosecution tantamount to panic? And if it is, is the abuse of children not worthy of such a response?

In the *New Yorker*, Wright (1993a, 1993b) wrote a two-part article on the case of a Washington state deputy sheriff, who, after being accused of child abuse by his two daughters, confessed to sexually abusing them, prostituting them to family friends, and being part of a satanic cult. The case unraveled when it was discovered that at least some of the accusations and confessions by both parents resulted from overzealous questioning and suggestions by police interrogators on what were alleged to be highly suggestible subjects. The article clearly implies that this case represents one of many instances of modern-day witch hunts—the innocent "witches" in this case being

From May Benatar, "Running Away From Sexual Abuse: Denial Revisited," *Families in Society: The Journal of Contemporary Human Services* (May 1995). Copyright © 1995 by Families International, Inc. Reprinted by permission.

those accused of perpetrating unthinkable crimes such as ritual sexual abuse, torture, and murder.

In *Mother Jones*, a well-regarded if somewhat off-beat publication, Watters (1993) also expressed concern about false memories and false accusations in a report of a young woman's delayed discovery of childhood abuse. The woman entered therapy following a severe depressive episode and while in therapy recovered memories of sexual abuse. Although the facts of the case neither exculpate the accused nor affirm the victim's accusations, the author uses this case to propose that "a substantial segment of the therapy community has charged ahead, creating a *growth* industry around the concept of recovered memories."

Even Carol Tavris (1993), a noted feminist author, cast a skeptical eye on what she termed the "incest-survivor machine," an umbrella term for therapists working with adult survivors, writers of self-help books for survivors, and the grass-roots recovery movement of adult survivors.

For clinicians working with patients to address the post-traumatic effects of childhood sexual abuse and for adult survivors struggling to take their own stories seriously and understand the difficulties of their adult lives as sequelae of and adaptation to violations that occurred during childhood, this emphasis on the "hype" of sexual abuse is deeply troubling.

CHILD ABUSE: PAST AND PRESENT FINDINGS

The reality of child abuse is well established. Why then is it currently acceptable, even fashionable, to doubt the victims, those who prosecute for them, and those who treat their post-traumatic illnesses? This backlash against sexual-abuse survivors has social, cultural, political, and psychological roots. One reading is that this backlash is a response to the evolution in law regarding the issue of incest—an evolution that now allows some adult survivors to seek legal redress many years, even decades, after the commission of crimes. Another reason for this backlash may be related to the cultural mysogyny that Faludi (1991) documents in her book *Backlash*, which refers to the social forces that thwart the gains that women have achieved in society. On another level of analysis, we may understand this phenomenon of denial of social realities as "cultural dissociation." As a society we are unable to accept the reality of the cruelty, sadism, neglect, and narcissism that adults inflict upon children. In a world where some people still debate the reality of Nazi death camps, it is not surprising that we have difficulties acknowledging that 1 of every 3 girls and 1 of 7 to 10 boys are "used" by an adult in a manner that brings great harm to them for the rest of their lives.

The epidemiology of child sexual abuse has been carefully documented. Kinsey found in the early 1950s that 24% of his female sample of 4,000 women reported sexual abuse in childhood (before the age of puberty) (Brownmiller, 1975). Dozens of studies have confirmed this finding. Thirty years later, Russell (1986) carefully surveyed a nonclinical population of nearly 1,000 women. She reported that 38% of the sample reported being molested before the age of 18 and 28% before puberty. In addition, she found that most abusers are known to the child as trusted individuals who occupy a position of authority over the child.

In another significant study, Herman and Schatzow (1987) discussed recall of traumatic memories from childhood often dissociated by the child in an effort to maintain secrecy and safety. Fifty-three female patients in group psychotherapy reported delayed recall of traumatic memory; 74% of the women confirmed their memories of abuse by obtaining independent corroborating evidence—physical evidence, diaries, pictures, confirmation by perpetrators and/or corroboration by other family members who had also been victimized. This study appears to strengthen Russell's and Kinsey's data. Even those with delayed recall, when seeking confirmation of the reality of their memories many years after the fact, are able to confirm the memory. To my knowledge, no comparable study demonstrates *false* recall of childhood-abuse memories.

Interestingly, the conflict between the reality of child abuse and the voices of disbelief and disavowal is not unique to the 1990s; a century ago western psychiatry experienced a similar struggle and process. Masson (1984), in *The Assault on Truth*, presented important work done in 19th-century France regarding the criminal brutalization and sexual abuse of children. In setting the stage for his explanation of why Freud first adopted and later abandoned the "seduction theory" to explain the origins of hysterical neurosis, Masson discusses child abuse in Europe during that period. Forensic psychiatrists uncovered shocking facts about child abuse. Ambrose Tardieu, a professor and dean of forensic medicine at the University of Paris and president of the Academy of Medicine in Paris in 1860, published "A Medico-Legal Study of Cruelty and Brutal Treatment Inflicted on Children." He presented case after case of detailed medical evidence indicating severe child abuse, including the sexual abuse of children. He indicated that the phenomenon was not rare and that perpetrators were often parents and that victims were often very young and primarily girls.

Paul Brouardel, Tardieu's successor to the chair of legal medicine in Paris and also a contemporary of Freud, described perpetrators as "excellent family men" who were often the fathers of the victims. Brouardel was a collaborator of Jean-Martin Charcot, a neurologist who demonstrated the efficacy of hypnosis in the treatment of psychiatric patients, particularly female hysterics. Freud was fascinated by Charcot's work and came to Paris to study with him. Masson argues that Freud and his contemporaries were more than likely aware of the work of Tardieu, Brouardel, and other forensic psychiatrists in France through their studies with Charcot. Freud's early struggles to understand the underpinnings of neurosis suggest his awareness of the traumatic origins of psychic disturbance as well as the influence that the French pioneers had on his clinical awareness. In the late 1890s Freud (1984) wrote movingly and persuasively in *The Aetiology of Hysteria* about 18 cases of hysterical neurosis in which an early experience of sexual abuse had led to hysterical symptoms in adult life—symptoms similar to what we categorize today as post-traumatic stress disorder or dissociative disorder.

However, it was Pierre Janet, another visitor to Charcot's seminars, who developed both a complex theoretical understanding and efficacious treatment model for hysteria. Janet published many of his findings the year before Freud's *Aetiology of Hysteria* appeared, but unlike Freud he held fast to the trauma model that Freud renounced. Janet described many cases of what we have come to understand as dissociative disorders and multiple personality disorder. Janet understood his patients' symptoms, much as trained clinicians do today, as ingenious and creative adaptations to overwhelming childhood stress such as physical and/or sexual abuse. He saw hysterical symptoms, not as compromise formations of drive derivatives or expressions of drive conflicts, but rather as fossils from the past, derivatives of traumatic memory, communications of early betrayals and overwhelming affects (van der Kolk & van der Hart, 1989).

Yet for most of the 20th century, Janet was *not* studied and *not* employed in our attempts to understand mental life. Freud's development of psychoanalysis obliterated Janet's work. To read Janet today, 100 years later, is to be struck with how little modern trauma psychology and our understandings of traumatic memory can add to his understandings, how clearly he explicated what we have come to rediscover in the past decade and a half, and how brilliantly he anticipated modern findings on the psychophysiology of memory.

Herman (1992) and others have proposed that Freud and his students moved away from trauma theory or the "seduction theory," because the zeitgeist of the time and place could not support such conclusions. Earlier in the century, in Tardieu's and Charcot's France, the political atmosphere was one of reform: challenges to the monarchy and the church enabled a movement toward understanding mental illness as a rational, not magical, pursuit. They viewed mental illness as a sequela of early experience that could be understood and addressed by science. These sociopolitical forces ushered in an era of more humane treatment of the mentally ill that approached mental illness as trauma based. Freud's science grew in different soil—Viennese soil—where trauma-based theory was unable to take root.

For a brief period in the 1800s, clinicians and students of forensic psychiatry knew that many children were severely abused by their families and that such abuse led to dramatic effects in the mental health of adults. They also understood effective treatment of these symptoms involved revisiting early memory and processing these memories in the context of a solid therapeutic alliance. By the beginning of the 20th century, after Freud had published *The Aetiology of Hysteria*, the political winds had shifted, as had the politics of psychiatry. Traumatic etiology was relegated to the background and endogenous intrapsychic conflicts moved to the foreground. We stopped looking at the environmental surround—the maltreatment of children—and turned our scientific gaze inward toward fantasy formation and the intricate topography of the mind.

WHERE DO WE GO TODAY?

It has taken us nearly a century to get back to where we started—the work of Janet. Two concurrent social movements helped to reawaken our awareness of childhood trauma. In the 1970s, the returning Vietnam War veterans became quite active in seeking validation for their catastrophic experiences during the war. They organized themselves to obtain services from veterans hospitals and recognition for their suffering from their communities. Their illnesses became the focus for legal activity and psychiatric attention. Psychiatrists rediscovered "war neurosis" and learned from their patients about the aftereffects of severe, intense, and acute traumatic experience. Posttraumatic stress disorder became a diagnostic entity and was entered into the *Diagnostic and Statistical Manual of Mental Disorders* in 1980.

The other major social change that contributed to the reemergence of our awareness of childhood sexual abuse was the women's movement in the 1970s. Women meeting in consciousness-raising groups, helping one another to name their fears, their frustrations, and their hopes, began telling stories of sexual manipulation, sexual violence, and early experiences of sexual violation at the hands of family members. Women Against Rape centers sprang up across the country; from these centers rape-crisis-counseling centers were developed. Today, a strong grass-roots recovery movement exists, carrying the message about child abuse and dissociative disorders to the public. Individuals help one another in 12-step-type recovery groups, generating art, newsletters, books, workshops, and conferences to help heal themselves as well as educate clinicians and lay individuals.

As a result of these two powerful movements for social change, survivors of childhood sexual abuse found a voice and clinicians began to listen. By the 1980s we began to see new journals devoted to exploring the effects and the treatment of individuals so affected. A whole new subspecialty in psychiatry, psychology, and social work emerged: working with dissociative disorders. Today, however, troubling signs indicate that public and political retrenchment from various interconnecting and interactive factors are contributing to renewed denial and disavowal of the prevalence of child sexual abuse. Moreover, social, legal, political, and psychological pressures are undermining all that we have learned about the etiology and sequelae of this devastating societal problem.

Factor One

In many ways, the mass media have focused more attention on survivors than has the mental health establishment. Oprah, Phil, and Sally Jesse have featured shows alerting the public to the painful experiences of adult survivors, which has led to a "Geraldoizing" effect. Despite the fact that Geraldo Rivera has actually done a couple of interesting shows on multiple personality disorder and has devoted more time and attention to the consequences of severe childhood trauma than have many mental health professionals, his and other popular talk shows tend to be associated with sensationalism and exploitation. As a result, real problems are trivialized in the public mind. If Geraldo thinks it is interesting, it must be hype. The overall effect is chilling. Clients wonder whether their memories and intense psychic, even physical, pain associated with their abuse histories are merely childish bids for attention. A client who kept her childhood rape secret for 40 years spoke of her dread of being perceived as having the "designer" affliction of our time.

Factor Two

The effect on memory is one sequela of childhood trauma that muddies the water for both the layperson and professional. How reliable is memory?

Police and prosecutors of violent crime understand that survivors of psychological trauma make very poor witnesses. Janet brilliantly described the differences between what he termed "narrative memory" and "traumatic memory" (van der Kolk & van der Hart, 1989). Narrative memory is what we generally mean when we speak of memory. It involves a complex process whereby new experiences are integrated into preexisting schema or mental categories, along with the slow evolution and expansion of those schema. Traumatic memory is different. Trauma is an event or series of events that lies outside the ordinary, expectable events of life. It is overwhelming in its affective impact on the individual. It does not easily fit into preexisting schema, nor does it evolve easily with other memories. Traumatic memories are "dissociated." To use a computer analogy, narrative memory is stored on drive C, the drive that is generally available to consciousness and voluntary control processes. Although drive C may have subdirectories of unconsciousness as well, that is, memories that are repressed but can be brought into consciousness through psychoanalysis, dream work, free association, and the like, drive B, or dissociated, memories arise unexpectedly when someone or something triggers them into actualization: therapy, a child reaching a developmental milestone, a movie, a book, a television show, a death. Dissociated memories are fragmentary, illusive, uncertain, even terrifying.

If the trauma is not verifiable and if it occurred early in life and was severe, these dissociated states act as containers for memories and pain and assume the coherence of alternative selves, that is, separate personality or ego states that hold particular memories together. During the therapeutic process, the therapist and patient attempt to understand the nature of these drive B materials, retrieve them, and integrate them into drive C consciousness. In so

doing, traumatic memory is integrated and assimilated into narrative memory.

For example, a 36-year-old woman who has been in therapy for three years struggling with depression and periodic panic attacks glances at her four-year-old daughter playing at the beach and suddenly remembers being raped by her father when she was four years old. In the following days, she questions her sanity and is unable to understand what is happening to her. Her therapist may also wonder about this bewildering experience. She will likely try to forget or trivialize it.

The impulse to both know the secrets of early trauma, and to tell it most typically fight with the impulse to keep the secret: what emerges is often jumbled and contradictory. That is the nature of traumatic memory! This is why victims are poor witnesses. The most common scenarios for survivors is to want to discredit their dissociated memories, not particularly to elevate them to heroic status. False memories, or memories that are iatrogenically induced during therapy, are not that common. Although some types of memories can be distorted or implanted in the minds of individuals under certain circumstances, evidence does not indicate that this occurs frequently, or even occasionally, in psychotherapeutic work with survivors of trauma.

Factor Three
Faludi (1991) states that approximately every 30 years a cultural backlash arises against nascent feminism. Even modest status gains by women are quickly followed by a cultural response indicating that these changes and gains are not good for society or women.

Sexual abuse and sexual violence are cast as women's issues, despite the fact that children of both sexes are affected by abuse. Attacks on feminism focus energy on maintaining the *status quo* in power relationships. As a result, child victims and adult survivors may be discredited under the rubric of women's issues. Faludi points to the 1980s as a decade of government retrenchment on womens issues, disproportionate cuts in funding for women's programs, and decreased commitment in government funding for battered women's programs, despite increases in domestic violence. A dramatic rise in sexual violence against women, an increase that outstrips other types of violent crimes, has been met with indifference at all levels of government.

The retreat from renewed awareness of child-abuse problems in general and sexual abuse in particular reflects this backlash. Interestingly, patients' veracity in therapy was never an issue until we began discussing issues of sexual abuse.

Factor Four

The changing legal climate regarding prosecution in civil incest suits has also affected adult-survivor issues. In the early 1980s, legal scholars began to reconsider the problem of seeking legal redress for crimes involving sexual abuse years after the commission of these crimes and after the statute of limitations had expired. In the *Harvard Women's Law Review*, Salten (1984) persuasively argued, "Given the latent nature and belated detection of many incest related injuries, the parent's special duty of care to his [sic] child, the youth of the incest victim, and the likelihood of psychological disabilities which preclude timely action, a tort suit for latent incestuous injuries is perhaps the paradigmatic example of

special circumstances requiring equitable preservation of a potential remedy" (p. 220). As a result of this and other legal arguments, several U.S. state and Canadian provincial legislatures are considering changes in the law that toll the statute of limitations for both criminal prosecution of incest (incest *is* a crime) and civil incest suits from age 21 and/or from the time the facts of the crime are discovered. These changes in the law would acknowledge both the powerlessness of children to bring suit or initiate prosecution and the problem of associative memory, whereby memories of child sexual abuse may not be available to the victim until many years after the victimization.

This "delayed discovery" approach to civil litigation has precedent in cases involving injuries from asbestos and other harmful substances. Perpetrators are now within reach of the law years, even decades, after the commission of their crimes. This evolution in the law, however, has invigorated attacks against delayed memory in adult survivors. The False Memory Syndrome Foundation is dedicated to disseminating information on what its spokepersons describe as the growing threat of false accusations of incest and sexual abuse. Part of its mission is to provide financial assistance to families in need of legal services or legal counseling.

CONCLUSION

Freud anticipated the skepticism and criticism that would greet his views on sexual trauma as a cause of hysteria. Nevertheless, his views are as relevant today as they were 100 years ago. Freud discussed three aspects of work with traumatized patients:

- Patients reexperiencing an early life experience in a dissociative manner clearly demonstrate suffering, pain, shame, terror, and extreme helplessness. Suggested memories do not have this quality.
- Patients resist these memories both consciously and unconsciously and often disavow the memories immediately after the experience. People do not want to believe that they were betrayed by the adults whom they trusted for protection. Typically, such a belief requires a reorientation of one's frame of reference.
- Freud mentions that when he successfully suggested a scene to a patient, even the most compliant patients are unable to reproduce such scenes with the intensely appropriate affect and detail characteristic of dissociated memory. Although Freud did not speak of "dissociated memory" as such, he described it very sympathetically in *The Aetiology of Hysteria.*

Freud's critics had the final say, and Freud changed his mind about traumatic memories. The legacy of this intellectual struggle in psychiatry has affected tens of thousands of people whose early-life trauma has been ignored. For the past 15 years, we have struggled to reverse this legacy. We have made great strides in our understanding of female psychology, trauma, memory, and self-formation. Countervailing reactionary forces that are not grounded in scientific skepticism or informed by a spirit of inquiry would erase these gains. Both professionals and the lay public must meet this challenge by refusing to dishonor the struggles of those who refuse to forget.

REFERENCES

Brownmiller, S. (1975). *Against our will: Men, women and rape.* New York: Simon and Schuster.

Faludi, S. (1991). *Backlash: The undeclared war against American women.* New York: Crown Publishers.

Freud, S. (1984). The aetiology of hysteria. In J. M. Masson (Ed.), *Freud: The assault on truth* (pp. 251–282). London: Faber and Faber.

Herman, J. L. (1992). *Trauma and recovery: The aftermath of violence from domestic abuse to political terror.* New York: Basic Books.

Herman, J. L., & Schatzow, E. (1987). Recovery and verification of memories of childhood sexual trauma. *Psychoanalytic Psychology, 4,* 1–14.

Masson, J. (1984). *Freud: The assault on truth.* London: Faber and Faber.

Russell, D. (1986). *The secret trauma: Incest in the lives of girls and women.* New York: Basic Books.

Salten, M. (1984). Statutes of limitations in civil incest suits: Preserving the victim's remedy. *Harvard Women's Law Journal, 7,* 189–220.

Shapiro, L. (1993, April 19). Rush to judgment. *Newsweek,* 54–60.

Tavris, C. (1993, January 3). Beware the incest-survivor machine. *New York Times,* Sect. 7, p. 1.

van der Kolk, B., & van der Hart, O. (1989). Pierre Janet and the breakdown of adaptation. *American Journal of Psychiatry, 146,* 1530–1540.

Watters, E. (1993, January–February). Doors of memory. *Mother Jones,* p. 24.

Wright, L. (1993a, May 17). Remembering Satan, part I. *New Yorker,* pp. 60–81.

Wright, L. (1993b, May 24). Remembering Satan, part II. *New Yorker,* pp. 54–76.

NO

Susan P. Robbins

WADING THROUGH THE MUDDY WATERS OF RECOVERED MEMORY

In her essay "Running Away from Sexual Abuse: Denial Revisited" Benatar (1995) addresses a timely and important topic—recovered memories of childhood sexual abuse. Delayed recovery of memories of traumatic events and the nature, validity, and accuracy of these memories have been at the center of a controversial and bitter debate among mental health professionals and researchers (see Berliner & Williams, 1994; Butler, 1995; Byrd, 1994; Ewen, 1994; Gleaves, 1994; Gold, Hughes, & Hohnecker, 1994; Gutheil, 1993; Lindsay & Read 1994; Loftus & Ketcham, 1994; Peterson, 1994; Pezdek 1994; Pope & Hudson, 1995; Slovenko, 1993; Wylie, 1993; Yapko, 1994a, 1994b).

Proponents of recovered memory believe that many victims of repeated childhood sexual abuse repress or dissociate all memory of their trauma as a mechanism for coping. Although conscious memory of the trauma is not available to the victim, it nonetheless is believed to affect one's social and psychological functioning in adulthood. Seeking therapy for various problems such as substance abuse, eating disorders, depression, or marital difficulties, unhappy adults (primarily white, middle- and upper-class women in their thirties and forties) report memories of abuse that usually surface during the course of therapy. Such memories may also surface while participating in recovery groups, attending self-help conferences, reading incest-recovery books, or as the result of a specific trigger event. These memories typically appear as terrifying images or flashbacks that proponents believe are genuine, if not precise, memories of earlier abuse. Professional knowledge about recovered memory is derived primarily from clinical case reports, and most proponents accept these case studies as confirming evidence.

Critics are skeptical of recovered memories because no reproducible scientific evidence supports these claims. They contend that the growing body of research on memory has consistently shown memory to be subject to inaccuracy, distortion, and fabrication. They have also raised serious questions about the therapeutic methods used to help clients "recover" memories, and some claim that the real feminist issue is the victimization of clients by their therapists who, either knowingly or unconsciously, are suggesting,

From Susan P. Robbins, "Wading Through the Muddy Waters of Recovered Memory," *Families in Society: The Journal of Contemporary Human Services* (October 1995). Copyright © 1995 by Families International, Inc. Reprinted by permission. References omitted.

implanting, and reinforcing memories of abuse that never happened. Many critics have expressed concern that indiscriminate acceptance of recovered memories will lead to a serious backlash of disbelief in authentic cases of abuse.

In the past five years, a rapidly growing body of literature has supported both sides of this contentious debate. Although social workers are often cited as central figures in this debate, leading social work journals have not previously addressed this controversy. Benatar's essay, although timely, adds little to this debate and is a prime example of practice prescriptions based on ideology and theoretical conjecture. In addition to a woefully inadequate review of the current literature in this area, the essay suffers from a lack of conceptual clarity, unwarranted assumptions, and factual inaccuracy.

At the outset, the issue of child sexual abuse is confused with that of "recovered memories" of abuse. These are, in fact, two different issues that have recently come to be associated with each other. The former deals with a well-documented phenomenon—the sexual abuse of children by parents, relatives, other adult caretakers, friends, acquaintances, and strangers. The latter involves the debate about traumatic memory, including the repression of traumatic events and delayed recovery of these memories. According to Loftus and Ketcham (1994), this is a debate about memory and not a debate about childhood sexual abuse.

Benatar expresses disdain for the popular media's skeptical stance about delayed memory, the techniques used to uncover such memories, and the growing incest-survivor industry. Casting this skepticism as an antifeminist backlash

against sexual-abuse survivors, she discounts the crucial issue of "false memories" and asserts that those who even question the veracity of traumatic memories are eroding the important gains made in our recognition of childhood abuse. Throughout, she improperly equates skepticism about recovered memories with denial of child sexual abuse.

Adding to this conceptual confusion, Benatar fails to draw distinctions among children who are current victims of abuse, adults who have always remembered traumatic incidents of childhood abuse, and those who have only recently recovered previously amnesic memories. Because this important point is neither addressed nor explored, all client reports of childhood abuse (which she refers to as "their own stories") are inferentially cast as being equally valid descriptions of historical events.

CHILD ABUSE: PAST AND PRESENT FINDINGS

Benatar correctly notes that "the reality of child abuse is well established." Given the increasing empirical evidence substantiating the reality of child abuse, it is most unfortunate that her ensuing discussion is based on specious analogies, incomplete data, and the use of unverified historical theories.

For example, labeled as "cultural dissociation," she equates the denial of the reality of Nazi death camps to what she believes is a prevalent societal denial of child abuse. In comparing the widely discredited beliefs of a relative few to a broader cultural misogyny that disavows child abuse, she engages in fallacious and distorted logic based on improper generalization and false analogy (see Fischer, 1970).

More problematic is the narrow sample of studies Benatar cites to support her discussion on the epidemiology of child sexual abuse, a problem further compounded by the lack of any critical analysis or discussion of the methodological limitations of these studies. A more thorough review of the literature reveals a broad range in the estimated prevalence of childhood sexual abuse. Although studies on child sexual abuse date back to 1929, few systematic studies utilizing careful statistical analyses were done before the late 1970s and early 1980s (see Demause, 1991). Retrospective surveys have reported base rates ranging from 6% to 62% for women (Burnam, cited in Peters, Wyatt, & Finkelhor, 1986; Wyatt, 1985) and between 3% and 31% for men (Landis, 1956; National Committee for the Prevention of Child Abuse, cited in Goldstein & Farmer, 1994). Researchers attribute the wide disparity in prevalence rates to the varying methodologies and definitions of sexual abuse used in each study. Studies that broadly define sexual abuse to include verbal propositions, for example, yield much higher estimates than do those using narrower definitions that only include forced sexual contact. Other definitions have included exposure, peeping, masturbation, unwanted kissing, and fondling (see Baker & Duncan, 1985; Finkelhor, Hotaling, Lewis, & Smith, 1990; Lindsay & Read, 1994; Russell, 1986, 1988; Williams & Finkelhor, 1992). Further complicating this problem, some studies fail to clarify the definition of sexual abuse being used (see Wassil-Grimm, 1995).

Because the primary focus of Benatar's essay is on recovered memories of abuse, the data she cites are also shaded by her failure to distinguish between incestuous and nonincestuous abuse. This is a critical point because the pathogenic and traumagenic nature of child sexual abuse has been linked in numerous studies to incest by a biological parent in general and, more specifically, to repeated molestation by fathers involving contact abuse and the use of force specifically (see Conte & Berliner, 1988; Elliott & Briere, 1992; Herman, 1981; Russell, 1986). Significantly, recovered memories typically involve repeated incest (see Bass & Davis, 1994).

It is difficult to obtain reliable data on incest because most studies do not make sufficient distinctions in their categorization of abusers. Based on a small number of retrospective studies, estimates indicate that approximately 4% to 5% of girls have reported being abused by a father, adoptive father, or stepfather before the age of 18 (Wassil-Grimm, 1995). Data from Williams and Finkelhor (1992) and Russell (1986) indicate that between 1% to 2.8% of girls are abused by a biological father. The rates are higher, of course, when abuse by other family members is included. Further, most cases of sexual abuse involve exhibition, masturbation, and both nongenital and genital touching rather than forced penetration (Lindsay & Read, 1994; Wakefield & Underwager, 1992). Russell's (1986) data showed a marked trend toward stepfathers abusing more frequently, using verbal threats, and being more severely abusive.

Two separate reviews of retrospective studies of childhood sexual abuse (Lindsay & Read, 1994; Wassil-Grimm, 1995) concluded that the preponderance of surveys indicate that the prevalence of intrafamilial incest is lower than the rates reported in the memory-recovery literature. In contrast, Demause (1991) contended that the known rates should be increased by 50% in order to correct for factors that lead to underreporting, including repression. Although the factors he cited are valid, his figures are based on pure speculation. Likewise, Bradshaw (1992) claimed that approximately 60% of all incest is repressed. To date, no replicable scientific evidence supports these claims. In a critique of what she sees as a 'cycle of misinformation, faulty statistics, and unvalidated assertions" by incest-recovery authors, Tavris (1993) noted that inaccurate and sometimes concocted statistics are "traded like baseball cards, reprinted in every book and eventually enshrined as fact."

Another issue that is rarely discussed in the recovery literature is that not all children who are sexually abused experience the abuse as traumatic or develop psychological problems as an adult (Browne & Finkelhor, 1986; Kendall-Tacket, Williams, & Finkelhor, 1993; Russell, 1986). A review of recent empirical studies by Kendall-Tacket et al. (1993) found that many women are totally asymptomatic. Contradictory evidence also surrounds the relationship of sexual abuse to high levels of dissociation and multiple personality disorder (see Beitchman, Zucker, Heed, deCosta, & Cassavia, 1992; Brier & Elliott, 1993; Hacking, 1995; Kluft, 1985; Lindsay & Read, 1994; Nash, Hulsey, Sexton, Herralson, & Lambert, 1993a, 1993b). These findings should not minimize the severe trauma and psychological distress that some abuse victims experience; rather, they should alert us to the fact that the sequelae of childhood sexual abuse is not the same for all victims. Not surprisingly, those who demonstrate higher levels of traumatization and psychopathology are more often found in clinical samples than in the population in general (Russell, 1986).

It should be clear from the above discussion that *all* statistics on child sexual abuse should be interpreted very cautiously. Because of its hidden nature, child sexual abuse is seriously under-reported. However, data from clinical samples, especially those samples undergoing therapy for childhood sexual abuse, are likely to overestimate its prevalence. Conversely, underestimates are likely if the data are based on retrospective surveys of adults in the general population, because some may choose not to report their abuse and some may not remember it. Despite discrepancies in the data, it is painfully clear that sexual abuse of children is a serious and pervasive problem that occurs more often than previously believed. As Pope and Hudson (1995) have astutely pointed out, even when conservative estimates of 10% for women and 5% for men are used, this means that 14,000,000 adults in the United States are former victims.

REVISITING FREUD AND JANET

Benatar gives a brief description of Freud and Janet's theories of repressed or dissociated trauma, supported only by historical case studies. Although case studies are an important source of information, they should not be confused with scientific findings. Despite a widespread belief in the validity of case reports that show repression or dissociation to be a common response to sexual abuse (see Blume, 1990; Chu & Dill, 1990; Courtois, 1988, 1992; Ellenson, 1989; Erdelyi & Goldberg, 1979; Fredrickson, 1992; Kluft, 1985; Mennen & Pearlmutter, 1993), little support for this belief can be found in empirical studies. In a review of 60 years of research, Holmes (1990) could not find any controlled studies that supported the concept of repression.

The few studies that were initially thought to provide possible evidence of repression (Briere & Conte, 1993; Herman & Schatzow, 1987; Loftus, Polonsky, & Fullilove, 1994; Williams, 1994) have yielded divergent results, with rates ranging from 18% to 59%. Methodological limitations, however, restrict the ability of any of these studies to support fully the mechanism of repression or dissociation (see Lindsay & Read, 1994; Loftus, 1993; Pope & Hudson, 1995). Despite Benatar's assertion that the Herman and Schatzow study supports the claim of delayed traumatic recall, this study has received widespread criticism because of its nonrepresentative sample, lack of specification of methodology (including criteria for confirmation of abuse), the use of composites of cases, little or no amnesia in the majority of cases, and the possibility of suggestion during therapy (see Lindsay & Read, 1994; Pope & Hudson, 1995; Wassil-Grimm, 1995). In short, Herman and Schatzow's study is far from conclusive.

Studies have shown to the contrary that people typically remember their past abuse. Loftus, Polonsky, and Fullilove (1994) found that in their sample of 105 women involved in outpatient treatment for substance abuse, the majority (54%) reported a history of childhood sexual abuse; the vast majority (81%) had always remembered their abuse. In Williams's (1994) study of 100 women with documented histories of sexual abuse, the majority (62%) acknowledged their abuse when asked by the researcher. Because no follow-up interview was conducted in either of these studies, it is impossible to know whether those failing to report their past abuse did so due to repression, ordinary forgetting, normal childhood amnesia, or the desire not to disclose a painful event. Femina, Yeager, and Lewis's (1990) longitudinal study of 69 adults with documented histories of child abuse (primarily physical) found no evidence of total amnesia. The majority (62%) readily reported their abuse to the interviewer. Those who initially denied or minimized their abuse acknowledged in a follow-up "clarification" interview that they did, in fact, remember their abuse but chose to withhold the information for various reasons.

In order for us to validate the clinical impressions gained from current and historical case histories, we need carefully designed studies to test the repression/dissociation hypothesis. Pope and Hudson (1995) suggested that the design of the Williams study is a useful starting point. Strict criteria for inclusion and the use of clarification interviews, similar to those used by Femina et al. (1990) would be a necessary addition to the study design. Pope and Hudson proposed that a series of case reports could be used to present preliminary evidence if they strictly adhered to the research criteria. They noted that given the high prevalence of repression suggested by many authors, this area "begs further carefully designed studies to resolve one of its most critical questions." In sum, both the existence and prevalence of repression have yet to be scientifically validated; the same is true for the type of dissociative amnesia hypothesized in the recovery literature.

TRAUMATIC MEMORY

In her discussion of traumatic memory, Benatar exhibits a serious misunderstanding of memory, in general, and memory organization, storage, and retrieval, in particular. Based on a narrow and inaccurate reading of van der Kolk and van der Hart's (1989) article, she presents an oversimplified typology of memory and compounds it with a misleading computer analogy.

Memory researchers widely accept that memory is *constructive* and *reconstructive*, not reproductive (Loftus, 1993; Loftus & Ketcham, 1994; Rose, 1992; Squire, 1987). Neuroscientist Steven Rose (1992) cautioned against the use of a flawed brain/computer metaphor:

> Brains do not work with information in the computer sense, but with *meaning* [which] is a historically and developmentally shaped process...because each time we remember, we in some senses do work on and transform our memories; they are not simply being called up from store.... Our memories are recreated each time we remember [emphasis added].

In their review of current research on memory processing, encoding, and state-dependent learning, van der Kolk and van der Hart (1989) reappraise Janet's early theory of psychopathological dissociation in an attempt to link it with recent findings. However, in contrast with Benatar's firm assertion that "traumatic memory is different," this is not what the authors conclude. They state that

> [Janet's notion] that traumatic memories are stored in memory in ways different from ordinary events is as challenging today as it was... almost 100 years ago. One century later, much remains to be learned about how memories are stored and keep on affecting emotions and behavior.

Likewise, in her ensuing discussion of trauma, dissociation, and memory, Benatar confuses theory with fact, stating that "if the trauma is verifiable and if it occurred early in life and was severe,

these dissociated states act as containers for memories and pain and assume the coherence of alternate selves." Numerous studies on verifiable traumas (Leopold & Dillon, 1963; Malmquist, 1986; Pynoos & Nader, 1989; Strom et al., 1962; Terr, 1979, 1983) have shown to the contrary that vivid (although not necessarily accurate) recall of traumatic events is common. No subjects in these studies repressed the event or developed dissociative amnesia. Post-traumatic symptomatology most commonly involves intrusive images, flashbacks, nightmares, and anxiety attacks, such as those seen in Vietnam veterans.

It is also well established that adults rarely have recall of any events prior to the age of two or three and only sketchy memories up until age five (Fivush & Hudson, 1990; Loftus & Ketcham, 1994; Pendergast, 1995; Usher & Neisser, 1993). This normal "infantile amnesia" is developmentally based and is not due to trauma. Traumatic amnesia in adults is a well-documented phenomenon and involves either large portions of the memory (one's name, address, and other personal information) or circumscribed traumatic events, with good recall of everything prior to and subsequent to the event. In both cases, people are *aware* of the fact that they have amnesia (see Loftus & Ketcham, 1994).

In the last decade, with the revival of Freud's seduction theory and Janet's theory of dissociation, some clinicians and researchers have begun *theorizing* that traumatic memories of *repeated* childhood sexual abuse are encoded differently from other traumas and result in a total loss of awareness of not only the events but of the amnesia itself (see Herman, 1992; Terr, 1991, 1994). The idea that these painful memories are somehow "split off" or dissociated into compartmentalized areas of the mind remains an untested hypothesis. To date, attempts to establish a link between dissociated or repressed trauma and current findings in the neurobiology of memory have been speculative at best. Despite her personal conviction that traumatic memories and ordinary memories are qualitatively different, Herman (1992) acknowledged that "the biological factors underlying ... traumatic dissociation remain an enigma." To paraphrase Klein (1977), we must avoid confusing what a theorist has merely claimed or believed with what she or he has actually proved or demonstrated. Even van der Kolk and van der Hart (1989) conceded that "we can neither confirm or [sic] contradict most of Janet's observations on memory disturbances following traumatization."

VERACITY OF CLIENT REPORTS

Benatar is partly correct in her assertion that "veracity in therapy was never an issue until we began discussing issues of sexual abuse." However, this conclusion is based on the faulty premise that acceptance of a client's narrative truth is presumed to be an accurate historical account of events, which is not necessarily the case. In most cases, the veracity of a client's narrative report of life events is not an issue unless the therapist becomes aware of contradictions. It is important to note that allegations of sexual abuse, when made by children or adolescents, are now routinely subjected to extensive collateral verification by an independent investigator (Faller, 1988).

Although psychoanalysts since Freud have been trained to believe that memories of seduction and sexual abuse are incestuous wishes (Masson, 1990),

the response on the part of most mental health professionals has been to ignore, minimize, or avoid the topic of sexual abuse (Craine, Henson, Colliver, & MacLean 1988; Jacobson, Koehler & Jones-Brown, 1987; Post, Willett, Franks, House, & Weissberg, 1980; Rose, Peabody, & Stratigeas, 1991). Whether this is a result of disbelief is, according to Rose et al. (1991), a topic of endless debate. The fact that clinicians have routinely failed to inquire about or respond to reports of sexual abuse represents a serious omission, especially given the prevalence of abuse found in clinical populations.

Contrary to Masson's (1984) and Miller's (1984) assertions that Freud abandoned his theory about the primacy of incest in the etiology of hysteria, Demause (1991) argued that an unbiased reading of Freud shows that he continued to believe in his patients' spontaneous reports of *conscious* memories of abuse. Freud concluded that only *unconscious* memories of early infantile scenes of seduction were "phantasies which my patients had made up or which myself had perhaps forced on them" (cited in Demause, 1991). If Demause is correct, it would appear that even Freud came to question the veracity of *recovered* memories of sexual abuse but did not doubt those memories that were always remembered. In a similar vein, Hacking (1995) noted that Janet revised his early formulations and dropped the concept of dissociation in his later writings. He eventually came to believe that double (or multiple) personality was a special and rare case of bipolar disorder, which he termed "les circulaires." It is interesting that the proponents of recovered memory extensively cite his earlier work while ignoring his later ideas.

It is widely acknowledged that it is impossible to verify charges of sexual abuse in the absence of external corroboration. Because of its hidden nature and the tendency for perpetrators to deny their guilt, it is sometimes difficult to find the necessary corroboration, especially decades after the alleged abuse occurred. But we must be clear that clinical judgment alone is not a sufficient predictor of veracity. In his discussion of the child sexual abuse accommodation syndrome, Summit (1983, 1992) acknowledged that "there is no clinical method available to distinguish valid claims from those that should be treated as fantasy or deception." He further cautioned that "the capacity to listen and the willingness to believe ... is not an admonition to interrogate or assume that every disclosure is real" (Summit, 1992). Clearly, we must be open to listening to our clients and willing to help them explore issues of past abuse. However, we must be cautious about accepting a client's narrative truth as historical fact in the absence of corroboration. This is especially true in the case of recovered memories; some memories may be fully accurate, some may be partly accurate, and some may be totally false. This does not imply that we should disbelieve our clients but rather that we maintain a neutral stance about historical accuracy. Historical accuracy becomes mandatory, however, when this debate is moved from the therapist's office into the courtroom (see Gutheil, 1993; Slovenko, 1993).

A more controversial but intricately related issue that Benatar fails to address is that of recovered memories of satanic ritual abuse, alien abductions, past lives, preverbal body memories, in *utero* trauma, and cellular memory (see Goldstein & Farmer, 1993, 1994; Mack,

1994; Mulhern, 1991; Pendergrast, 1995; Richardson, Best, & Bromley, 1991; Robbins, 1995; Smith, 1995; Victor, 1993). These memories raise interesting questions regarding both the veracity of client reports and the therapeutic methods used to retrieve or recover them: Are all such memories possible? If not, which ones are? Where do we draw the line? Based on what criteria? How can we determine their accuracy? These questions are significant because a growing number of therapists involved in memory-recovery therapy believe in the validity and accuracy of all recovered memories (Loftus, Garry, Brown, & Rader, 1994; Smith, 1995; Yapko, 1994a, 1994b). Not surprisingly, their clients come to believe in them as well.

FALSE MEMORIES: FACT OR FICTION?

Skepticism about "false memories" is often voiced by proponents of recovered memory because it is seen as a backlash to the discovery of childhood sexual abuse and an attempt to silence the victims; as such, false memories are equated with "denial" of abuse (Bloom, 1995; Rockwell, 1995). In the past several years this has become the subject of debate in scholarly journals and professional conferences. Because these issues become tangled and confused, it is important once again to make the distinction between the debate about memory and the documented reality of abuse; the false-memory debate is not about the latter.

A growing body of research has shown that partially and wholly inaccurate memories are not an unusual phenomenon. Because memory is extremely malleable, it is influenced by various factors, and false memories can be created through exposure to misinformation (Loftus, 1993; Terr, 1994). According to Terr, a false memory can be "a strongly imagined memory, a totally distorted memory, a lie, or a misconstructed impression." Numerous studies have shown that people can be led to construct not only inaccurate and confabulated details of past events, but detailed memories of entire events that never happened (see Haugaard, Reppucci, Laurd, & Nauful, 1991; Loftus, 1993; Loftus & Ketcham, 1994; Neisser & Harsch, 1992; Pynoos & Nader, 1989; Spanos, Menary, Gabora, DuBreuil, & Dewhirst, 1991).

Evidence about erroneous memory has sparked concern that memories of abuse are being created by therapists who, through well-intentioned but misguided therapeutic methods, may directly or indirectly evoke specious memories with the use of hypnosis, guided visualization, "truth" drugs, abreactive therapy, dream and body memory interpretation, or suggestive questioning (Byrd, 1994; Gangelhoff, 1995; Gutheil, 1993; Lindsay & Read, 1994; Loftus, 1993; Ofshe & Watters, 1994; Pendergast, 1995; Yapko, 1994a). Although proponents of recovered memory therapy incorrectly believe that false or suggested memories cannot be experienced with the same emotional intensity as can recovered memories of real trauma, evidence suggests otherwise (see Loftus & Ketcham, 1994; Yapko, 1994a). As Loftus and Ketcham noted, reconstructed memories, once adopted, come to be believed in as strongly as genuine memories. Concern about false memory is bolstered by detailed accounts of coercive therapy and lawsuits filed by "retractors"—hundreds of women who have left therapy and recanted their allegations of abuse (see Goldstein & Farmer, 1993, 1994; Pendergrast, 1995).

Studies documenting distorted and confabulated memory in children and adults have been discounted by some proponents of memory recovery because they do not speak directly to the issue of false memories of childhood sexual abuse. Benatar echoes this position along with reservations similar to those noted by Berliner and Williams (1994) and Pezdek (1994) that little scientific evidence supports the claim that false memories of abuse are common or that memory-recovery therapy is widespread. Because little research has been done in this area, this is an accurate appraisal of our lack of scientific knowledge about false memories induced in therapy. However, it is noteworthy that many who accept the "truth" of recovered memories of childhood victimization are not willing to extend the same credibility to those who claim they were victimized by their therapists. Nonetheless, methodologically sound studies are necessary to validate the phenomena of false memory as well as recovered memory; we must rely on the same standard of proof for both.

WHERE DO WE GO FROM HERE?

Clearly, the reluctance of clinicians to address the reality of child sexual abuse poses a serious barrier to accurate and effective assessment and treatment. Rose et al. (1991) noted that "short- and long-term sequelae result not only from sexual and physical abuse, but from inappropriate treatment and nonrecognition of the abuse." Given social work's commitment to multidimensional assessment and holistic, nondichotomous thinking (see Compton & Galaway, 1989; Haynes

& Holmes, 1994; Hepworth & Larsen, 1993; Morales & Sheafor, 1995), it is critical that clinical practitioners gather accurate information about their client's past and present biopsychosocial functioning, strengths and resources, developmental history, significant life events, and reactions to and feelings about these events. In this holistic context, it would be unconscionable to fail to inquire about physical and sexual abuse—past or present. We must be sensitive to the fact that clients may choose initially not to disclose their abuse until a level of trust is developed in the therapeutic relationship. Failure to disclose should not *automatically* be assumed to be due to repression or dissociation.

We must also be cautious about hastily attributing a laundry list of nonspecific symptoms to prior abuse, as this defeats the purpose of a multidimensional assessment. When a previously repressed history of sexual abuse is revealed, it is especially important to consider the use of collateral sources of information because clients may themselves be confused about these memories. However, collateral sources should never be used without the client's express permission. The use of collateral sources does not imply that the social workers should take on the dual roles of investigator and therapist, because doing so represents a serious conflict of interest (Mason, 1991). Instead, collateral information should be used to help both the practitioner and the client gain a well-rounded picture of the situation. Hepworth and Larsen (1993) noted that important factors that may otherwise be overlooked can often be identified by persons close to the client. According to van der Kolk and van der Hart (1989), Janet frequently interviewed his patients' family members and acquaintances in order to get as complete a picture as possible.

CONCLUSION

Social workers who work with victims of childhood sexual abuse, especially those whose claim is based solely on recovered memories, should become acquainted with the full range of clinical and social scientific literature on the topic. Clinical case studies must be balanced with scientific findings; both are crucial sources of knowledge. Many clinicians receive only training or information that supports a narrow ideology and practice methodology. As I have suggested elsewhere (Robbins, 1995), social workers must be fully informed in order to "evaluate critically these disparate ideological positions and the adequacy of the research that supports them." This is especially important because a recent study by Feld (1995) found that few social workers are provided with any content about memory or memory retrieval in their academic programs.

In addition, social workers need to be fully aware of their own personal biases in order to prevent them from interfering with assessment and treatment. Preconceived beliefs about repression, dissociation, and recovered memories may lead to an ideological stance that inhibits thorough and accurate assessment. It is imperative that we recognize the serious consequences for our clients and their families when our personal biases lead us to either underdiagnose or overdiagnose childhood sexual abuse. Further, we must remember that the imposition of our personal values and beliefs is antithetical to our deeply held value of client self-determination (Hepworth & Larsen, 1993).

As a result of the lack of scientific verification and the polemical debate shaping research and practice, we must wade cautiously through the muddy waters of recovered memory. Social workers may feel caught between two conflicting sets of claims that demand allegiance to one side or the other. It is doubtful, however, that positioning ourselves at the extremes of this debate will lead to a stance that is in the best interests of our clients. Amid the black and white positions of what Loftus and Ketcham (1994) call the "true believers" and "skeptics," a middle-ground stance is often hard to find, despite the grey areas of uncertainty and ambiguity that exist. Acknowledgment of these grey areas does not mean, however, that one is in "denial" or is uncaring or negligent as a practitioner. We must be open to new findings in this area but we must also be cautious in distinguishing between conjecture and fact.

Finally, when skepticism about the ideology of the recovery movement is based on a thorough review of valid, scientific findings, it must not be cast as antifeminist backlash. As Klein (1977) aptly noted, "Scientific questions are to be settled by appeals to evidence rather than by appeals to authority—even the authority of a Freud."

POSTSCRIPT

Can Memories of Childhood Sexual Abuse Be Recovered?

The controversy surrounding the accuracy of recollections of abuse (sometimes called false memories) tends to obscure the issue regarding the susceptibility of human beings to adopt false beliefs at the suggestion of someone else. In typical cases a person establishes a belief that abuse has occurred before any memory of it has surfaced and then looks for evidence to confirm the belief. Robbins uses this explanation to reject the accuracy of these memories, whereas Benatar argues that we should accept them more readily.

Making a revelation about child abuse may leave an individual deeply depressed and even suicidal. Equally problematic is the impact on the family, who is often torn apart psychologically and forced to endure a nightmarish court battle when the alleged perpetrator of the abuse is summoned to court. The challenge is to ascertain the difference between what a person feels and believes versus the literal, physical reality upon which the memories are based. Should we, as a society, turn our backs in disbelief on all those coming forth with repressed memories? Do we continue our present trend of predominant belief and acceptance of these allegations? What about a person who cannot prove such allegations but experiences the pain of the abuses and believes they occurred? Do we merely turn our backs or do we try to help even though the allegations may not be true? Finally, if we do choose to help, how do we go about providing such assistance?

SUGGESTED READINGS

Berliner, L., & Loftus, E. (1992). Sexual abuse accusations: Desperately seeking reconciliation. *Journal of Interpersonal Violence, 7* (4), 570–578.

Gardner, R. A. (1994). Differentiating between true and false sex abuse accusations in child custody disputes. *Journal of Divorce and Remarriage, 21* (3), 1–20.

Gellert, G. A. (1995). Sensitivity and specificity in child abuse detection. *Journal of Child Sexual Abuse, 4,* 99–104.

Ney, T. (Ed.). (1995). *True and false allegations of child sexual abuse: Assessment and case management.* New York: Brunner/Mazel.

Scotford, R. (1995). Myths, memories and reality. *Contemporary Hypnosis, 12* (2), 137–142.

Yapko, M. (1993, September/October). The seductions of memory. *The Family Therapy Networker,* 30–37.

CONTRIBUTORS
TO THIS VOLUME

EDITORS

DIANA S. DelCAMPO is the child development and family life specialist with the New Mexico Cooperative Extension Service at New Mexico State University in Las Cruces, New Mexico, and holds the rank of professor. She is a member of the National Council on Family Relations and the National Extension Family Life Specialists' Association. She received a B.S. from Concord College (West Virginia); an M.S. from Virginia Polytechnic Institute and State University, and a Ph.D. in curriculum and instruction from the University of Michigan. She presently develops educational programs in child and family development, supervises grant projects, and coordinates projects with other state agencies in New Mexico. She has published educational guides, chapters in several books, symposium proceedings, and articles in various journals.

ROBERT L. DelCAMPO is a professor of family science at New Mexico State University in Las Cruces, New Mexico. He is a licensed marriage and family therapist, clinical member, and approved supervisor of the American Association for Marriage and Family Therapy. He also holds memberships in the International Family Therapy Association, the National Council on Family Relations, and the New Mexico Association for Marriage and Family Therapy. He received a B.S. from the State University of New York, an M.S. from Virginia Polytechnic Institute and State University, and a Ph.D. in family relations and child development from Florida State University. His work has appeared in such journals as *Family Relations* and *Contemporary Family Therapy*.

STAFF

David Dean   List Manager
David Brackley   Developmental Editor
Ava Suntoke   Developmental Editor
Tammy Ward   Administrative Assistant
Brenda S. Filley   Production Manager
Juliana Arbo   Typesetting Supervisor
Diane Barker   Proofreader
Lara Johnson   Graphics
Richard Tietjen   Publishing Systems Manager

AUTHORS

KAREN E. ABLARD is a professor in the Center for Talented Youth Research at Johns Hopkins University in Baltimore, Maryland.

SUSAN A. BEEBE is in the Department of Pediatrics at the University of Utah Medical Center in Salt Lake City, Utah.

JAY BELSKY is a professor in the College of Health and Human Development at Pennsylvania State University. He is the author of numerous articles on maternal employment, child care, and family issues.

MAY BENATAR is a clinical social worker in private practice in Montclair, New Jersey. She currently teaches and lectures to professional groups on the subjects of sexual abuse and the treatment of dissociative disorders. Her publications include "Marrying Off Children as a Developmental Stage," *Clinical Social Work*, Fall 1989.

WILLIAM J. BENNETT is the codirector of Empower America. He served as secretary of education under President Reagan and as director of the White House Office of National Drug Control Policy under President Bush.

PEGGY BRICK is director of education at Planned Parenthood of Greater Northern New Jersey, located at Hackensack. She is the president of SIECUS (Sex Information and Education Council of the United States).

HELEN L. BRITTON is an associate professor in the Department of Pediatrics at the University of Utah Medical Center in Salt Lake City.

JOHN R. BRITTON is an associate professor in the Department of Pediatrics at the University of Utah Medical Center in Salt Lake City.

BARBARA BYRD is an associate of the Department of Professional Psychology at Seton Hall University in South Orange, New Jersey.

BRANDON S. CENTERWALL is an assistant professor of epidemiology in the School of Public Health and Community Medicine at the University of Washington in Seattle, Washington.

K. ALISON CLARKE-STEWART is a professor of social ecology at the University of California–Irvine. She is the author of several articles and coauthor, with C. P. Gruber and L. M. Fitzgerald, of *Children at Home and in Daycare* (Lawrence Erlbaum, 1994).

STEPHEN S. CRAIG is a professor in the Department of Professional Psychology at Seton Hall University in South Orange, New Jersey.

ARNOLD P. DeROSA is a professor in the Department of Counseling Psychology at Seton Hall University in South Orange, New Jersey.

DAVID EGGEBEEN is a professor in the College of Health and Human Development at Pennsylvania State University.

MARK A. FINE is a professor in the Department of Psychology at the University of Dayton in Dayton, Ohio.

DAVID GATELY was a graduate student of psychology at the Ohio State University in Columbus, Ohio, when he was coauthor of "Favorable Outcomes in Children After Divorce" for the *Journal of Divorce and Remarriage*.

DAVID GUTERSON is an English teacher at Bainbridge High School in Bainbridge Island, Washington. His publications include *Family Matters: Why Home Schooling Makes Sense* (Harcourt Brace Jovanovich, 1992).

KARON L. JAHN is dean of students at Chaminade University in Honolulu, Hawaii.

DOREEN KIMURA is a neuropsychologist and a professor in the Department of Psychology at the University of Western Ontario in London, Ontario, Canada. She is a fellow of the Royal Society of Canada and the author of *Neuromotor Mechanisms in Human Communication* (Oxford University Press, 1993).

LISA KOLB is a public information specialist for the Missouri Department of Social Services in Jefferson City.

SHERRYLL KRAIZER is the executive director of the Coalition for Children, Inc. in Denver, Colorado. She has written several books, including *The Safe Child Book* (Fireside, 1996).

THOMAS LICKONA, a developmental psychologist, is a professor of education at the State University of New York College at Cortland and director of the Center for the Fourth and Fifth Rs (Respect and Responsibility). He is a frequent consultant to schools across the United States, and he has also lectured abroad.

DONALDO MACEDO is a professor of English and program director for Bilingual English as a Second Language Studies at the University of Massachusetts–Boston. He is the author of *Literacies of Power: What Americans Are Not Allowed to Know* (Westview Press, 1994).

STEVEN MELLOR is a professor in the Department of Psychology at the University of Connecticut in Storrs, Connecticut.

CAROL J. MILLS is the director of research in the Center for Talented Youth Research at Johns Hopkins University in Baltimore, Maryland.

WILLIAM J. O'MALLEY teaches theology and English at Fordham Preparatory School in Bronx, New York.

JESSICA PORTNER is a freelance writer in Long Beach, California.

DONALD A. RAKESTRAW is an assistant professor in the Department of History at Georgia Southern College in Statesboro, Georgia.

JENNIE F. RAKESTRAW is an associate dean of the College of Education at Georgia Southern College in Statesboro, Georgia.

DIANE RAVITCH is senior research scholar at New York University in New York City and a fellow of the Brookings Institution. She served as assistant secretary of education during the Bush administration. She is the author of *National Standards in American Education: A Citizen's Guide* (Brookings Institution, 1995) and coeditor, with Joseph Viteritti, of *New Schools for a New Century: The Redesign of Urban Education* (Yale University Press, 1997).

SUSAN P. ROBBINS is an associate professor in the Graduate School of Social Work at the University of Houston in Texas.

DEBORAH ROFFMAN is a sexuality educator, trainer, and consultant. Since 1975 she has taught human sexuality education.

JOHN K. ROSEMOND is head of the Center for Affirmative Parenting in Gastonia, North Carolina, as well as a family psychologist and syndicated columnist. He is the author of several books, including *Because I Said So!* (Andrews & McMeel, 1996).

LISBETH B. SCHORR is the director of the Harvard University Project on Effective Services in Boston. She is the author of *Within Our Reach: Breaking the Cycle of Disadvantage* (Doubleday, 1988).

ANDREW I. SCHWEBEL is a professor in the Department of Psychology at the Ohio State University in Columbus, Ohio.

BRIAN SIANO is a writer and researcher based in Philadelphia, Pennsylvania. His column "The Skeptical Eye" appears regularly in the *Humanist*.

MURRAY A. STRAUS is a professor of sociology and codirector of the Family Research Laboratory at the University of New Hampshire in Durham, New Hampshire. He has held academic appointments within the United States as well as at universities overseas. He is the author or coauthor of over 150 articles and 15 books on the family, research methods, and South Asia.

HEINRICH STUMPF is a professor in the Center for Talented Youth Research at Johns Hopkins University in Baltimore, Maryland.

CAROL TAVRIS is a social psychologist and author based in Los Angeles, California. Her publications include *The Longest War: Sex Differences in Perspective*, 2d ed. (Harcourt Brace, 1984) with coauthor Carole Wade, and *Anger: The Misunderstood Emotion* (Simon & Schuster, 1989).

ELIZABETH H. THILO is an associate professor of pediatrics at the University of Colorado School of Medicine and the Children's Hospital in Denver, Colorado. She is also the medical director at Provenant St. Anthony Central Hospital Nursery and Aurora Regional Medical Center Nursery in Denver, Colorado.

SUSAN F. TOWNSEND is an assistant professor of pediatrics at the University of Colorado School of Medicine and the Children's Hospital in Denver. She is also the medical director at the University Hospital Newborn Nursery in Denver, Colorado.

KATHLEEN KENNEDY TOWNSEND is lieutenant governor of Maryland. She is the chair of the Cabinet Council on Criminal and Juvenile Justice, the Governor's Task Force on Children, Youth, and Families Systems Reform, and cochair of the Maryland Family Violence Council.

MARY-LOU WEISMAN is a freelance writer who has written about children, ethics, and social issues for the *New York Times* and the *New Republic*.

AMERICAN ASSOCIATION OF UNIVERSITY WOMEN is an organization of college and university graduates that was founded in 1881 to work for the advancement of women.

JOHN L. WOODARD is a professor at Wayne State University in Detroit, Michigan.

KARL ZINSMEISTER is editor in chief of the *American Enterprise* and the author of a book on the American family to be published soon.

INDEX

4898

392.3 T136 1998

Taking sides: clashing
views on controversial
c1998.

DATE DUE

OCT 2 6 1999			
JE 16 05			
GAYLORD			PRINTED IN U.S.A